The Death, Burial, and Resurrection of Jesus, and the Death, Burial, and Translation of Moses in Judaic Tradition

Roger David Aus

Studies in Judaism

University Press of America,® Inc.

Lanham · Boulder · New York · Toronto · Plymouth, UK

Copyright © 2008 by
University Press of America,® Inc.
4501 Forbes Boulevard
Suite 200
Lanham, Maryland 20706
UPA Acquisitions Department (301) 459-3366

Estover Road
Plymouth PL6 7PY
United Kingdom

Library of Congress Control Number: 2008925819
ISBN-13: 978-0-7618-4087-9 (paperback : alk. paper)
ISBN-10: 0-7618-4087-7 (paperback : alk. paper)
eISBN-13: 978-0-7618-4216-3
eISBN-10: 0-7618-4216-0

⊖™ The paper used in this publication meets the minimum
requirements of American National Standard for Information
Sciences—Permanence of Paper for Printed Library Materials,
ANSI Z39.48—1984

Studies in Judaism

Dedicated

to

All those who, like myself,
firmly believe in the resurrection of the dead,
and who are willing to openly explore
its historical origins in their own religious traditions.

"With joy you will draw water from the wells of salvation."
(Isa 12:3)

"The well of knowledge has neither limit nor ending."
(Philo of Alexandria, *Somn.* 1.11)

"La vérité est au fonds du puits."
(French proverb)

Table of Contents

x   *Table of Contents*

Preface

My thanks go to Peter von der Osten-Sacken, professor emeritus of New Testament and former director of the Institut Kirche und Judentum at Berlin's Humboldt University, for his willingness to comment on the chapters in this volume. Dr. Niko Oswald, now retired from the Free University's Institut für Judaistik, also kindly read the manuscript, especially in regard to the Semitic expressions. Professor Tal Ilan of the same institute graciously helped me track down an obscure rabbinic source. The Rev. Dr. Thomas Day not only proofread the manuscript; he also offered numerous helpful suggestions in regard to style and content. Finally, my son Jonathan Aus of Oslo again generously formatted the volume.

The staff at the theological library of the Humboldt University has, as always, been very helpful. This is especially true because the financial situation has limited its resources more and more. I also thank the library staff of Luther Seminary in St. Paul, Minnesota, from which I graduated over forty years ago, for supplying me with a number of items not available here in Berlin. I also made good use of the bookstore there by having them send me new volumes, especially related to the Resurrection, yet the size of my wallet is also limited. Professors Christopher Tuckett of Oxford and Michael Wolter of Bonn also kindly provided me with copies of essays in volumes edited by them, and Professors James Crossley of Sheffield and Birger Olsson of Lund also generously procured several pieces of secondary literature for me.

In the following I have attempted to dialogue with the most important secondary literature as it has been available to me, without over-burdening the footnotes. My emphasis, however, has been on letting the primary sources speak for themselves. Therefore they are extensively quoted. This is especially true for the rabbinic sources, to which many New Testament scholars intentionally or non-intentionally have little or no access in spite of the numerous modern translations by Jacob Neusner, his students, and others. It is often quite strenuous when working with the various parallel traditions, and the perplexing problem of dating an individual saying or narrative will always remain. Yet there is still much gold to be found in such creek beds, and the great effort involved in panning for it is indeed worthwhile. The section on the relevance of Judaic Moses traditions to the Gethsemane narrative is a revised and expanded version of a previous study, also edited by Jacob Neusner: *The Wicked Tenants and Gethsemane*. Isaiah in the Wicked Tenants' Vineyard, and Moses and the High Priest in Gethsemane: Judaic Traditions in Mark 12:1-9 and 14:32-42 (USFISFCJ; Atlanta: Scholars Press, 1996) 73-99. An index of modern authors will help the reader to see where and how I differ from the opinions of contemporary New Testament scholars.

My sincere thanks go to Professor Jacob Neusner for accepting this volume, my fourth, in his series "Studies in Judaism." It is a tribute to his ecumenical openness that he as an ordained Jewish rabbi continues to welcome studies dealing with the earliest Jewish Christians from an ordained Protestant pastor.

For those not steeped in rabbinic sources, the following list explaining some of the most frequently used abbreviations in this volume should be helpful. Others such as *Midr. Pss.* are clear by themselves. The editions employed by me are noted in the "Sources and Reference Works" at the end of the volume.

m.	Mishnah
t.	Tosefta
b.	Babylonian Talmud
y.	Yerushalmi or Jerusalem Talmud
Mek. R. Ish.	Mekilta de Rabbi Ishmael, on Exodus
Mek. R. Šim. b. Yoḥ.	Mekilta de Rabbi Šim'on b. Yoḥai, also on Exodus
Sifra	Halakhic (primarily legal) midrash on Leviticus
Sifre	Halakhic midrashim on Numbers and Deuteronomy
Midr.	Midrash
'Avot R. Nat.	'Avot de Rabbi Nathan (versions A and B)
Pesiq. R.	Pesiqta Rabbati
Pesiq. Rav Kah.	Pesiqta de Rav Kahana
Pirq. R. El.	Pirqe de Rabbi Eliezer
Tanḥ.	Tanḥuma
Tanḥ. B	Tanḥuma, ed. Buber
Tanna	An authority ranging from Hillel and Shammai to the early third century CE, the time of Judah the Prince
Amora	An authority ranging from after the Tannaim to ca. 500 CE

bar.   Baraitha, a Tannaitic tradition not found in the
                             Mishnah

The death, burial and Resurrection of Jesus, including the narrative of
the empty tomb, are extremely important as a foundation of the
Christian faith. It is my hope that contemporary Christians, as well as
Jews, through the following studies will better appreciate how the first
Palestinian Christians, all Jews, very creatively applied traditions
regarding the first redeemer of Israel, Moses, to him whom they now
regarded as the final redeemer of Israel, their Messiah Jesus.

Roger David Aus
Advent 2007
Berlin, Germany

Introduction

In my short volume *Matthew 1-2 and the Virginal Conception in Light of Palestinian and Hellenistic Judaic Traditions on the Birth of Israel's First Redeemer, Moses*,[1] I analyzed the very beginning of Jesus' life, his birth story in Matthew, with the aid of Judaic traditions on the birth of Moses. In this study I do the same in regard to the very end of Jesus' life: his death, burial and Resurrection. The jump, so to speak, is from Exodus 1-2 to the very end of the Pentateuch, Deuteronomy 34, which describes the death and burial of Moses.[2]

A well-known rabbinic saying is: "As [it was with] the first redeemer, so [it will be with] the final redeemer."[3] Here Moses as the redeemer of the Israelites from slavery in Egypt is meant, as well as the final or great redeemer, the Messiah, who will redeem his people from subjugation to the last of the four kingdoms, Rome.[4] This "typological" thinking[5]

---

[1] Studies in Judaism; Lanham, MD: University Press of America, 2004.

[2] The importance of the "life of Moses," contained in the Hebrew Bible from Exodus to Deuteronomy, has not yet been properly appreciated as a *partial* background for the genre of "gospel," first found in Mark (even though it still lacked a birth story, added on later by Matthew and Luke). In the revised edition of his *What are the Gospels? A Comparison with Greco-Roman Biography* (Grand Rapids, MI, Cambridge, U.K.: Eerdmans, 2004[2]), Richard Burridge mentions Moses only briefly in passing (p. 19), as well as Philo's double tractate on "Moses" (p. 128). Dependent on Philip Alexander and Jacob Neusner, he nevertheless strangely concentrates on the issue of why there are no real biographies in rabbinic sources (pp. 331-37). The "biography" of Moses, however, was *already present* in Scripture, and Judaic haggadah continued to embellish it for centuries from the LXX to the Amoraim. This is shown, for example, in the tremendous amount of material on the life of Moses noted by Louis Ginzberg in his *Legends of the Jews*, in Vol. II., section IV., and all of Vol. III., together with the relevant notes. More research is necessary in this area. The informed reader will note how indebted I frequently am to Ginzberg's magisterial study, which should be compared wherever relevant.

[3] Cf. the examples in Str-B 1.69-70, which could easily be supplemented.

[4] On Babylonia, Media, Greece and Rome as the four kingdoms, cf. the sources cited in Str-B 1.9 and 4.1004-06.

[5] Cf. the title of the study by Dale Allison, Jr., *The New Moses. A Matthean Typology* (Minneapolis: Augsburg Fortress, 1993).

enabled early Jewish Christians to apply haggadic materials[6] from Judaic tradition on Moses' birth to the birth of their Messiah Jesus, but also similar materials on Moses' death, burial and "translation" in Judaic tradition to Jesus' death, burial and Resurrection.[7]

Wayne Meeks' 1967 study, *The Prophet King. Moses Traditions and the Johannine Christology*,[8] called attention to many new areas of possible research in the Fourth Gospel, including aspects towards the end of Moses' life, and his death, of relevance to the present study.[9] Yet as the recent survey of Moses in the New Testament by John Lierman shows, especially concerning the latter themes, very little has been done in this regard since Meeks.[10] Lierman's statement that "there might be more to Jesus as a Mosaic Messiah than readily meets the eye"[11] certainly also applies to a comparison of the death and burial of Moses, and to what was thought to have happened at that point. Samuel Loewenstamm could also state in regard to Moses: "The death of Moses occupied the mind of apocryphal and midrashic writers unceasingly. They never tired of seeking new and innovative ways to understand it."[12] This also was

---

[6] "Haggadah" or "aggadah" is non-legal material, often simply the embellishment of something already present, just as the biblical books of Chronicles already supplemented 1-2 Samuel and 1-2 Kings. Cf. an extensive definition and discussion at the beginning of chapter IV. below.

[7] Cf. also the influence of Eccl 1:9, "What has been is what will be," in regard to Moses and the Messiah, the first and last redeemers, in *Eccl. Rab.* 1:9 § 1 (Vilna 8; Soncino 8.33). By "translation" I mean being taken up, rapture (German "Entrückung"), without dying. See chapter III. B. below.

[8] SuppNovT 14; Leiden: Brill. I have also been indebted to him in many respects ever since he was the advisor of my 1971 Yale dissertation, "Comfort in Judgment: The Use of Day of the Lord and Theophany Traditions in Second Thessalonians 1."

[9] Cf. 141-42, as well as 209-14.

[10] Cf. his *The New Testament Moses. Christian Perceptions of Moses and Israel in the Setting of Jewish Religion* (WUNT 2.173; Tübingen: Mohr Siebeck, 2004), esp. 258-70, which includes a survey of recent writers, yet nothing on the death of Moses and that of Jesus. Following Martin Hengel, Lierman maintains: "in the description of the actual ends of their lives there could hardly be a greater disparity between Jesus and Moses" (p. 284). The essay volume edited by him, *Challenging Perspectives on the Gospel of John* (WUNT II/219; Tübingen: Mohr Siebeck, 2006), also does not address the topic of this study. This is also true for his own contribution, "The Mosaic Pattern of John's Christology," on pp. 210-34.

[11] *The New Testament Moses*, 286.

[12] Cf. his "The Death of Moses" in *Studies on the Testament of Abraham*, ed. George Nickelsburg, Jr. (Septuagint and Cognate Studies 6; Missoula, MT: Scholars

true for the first Palestinian Jewish Christians, who in part cast their descriptions of Jesus' death, burial and Resurrection in light of Moses' death, burial and translation, as I will show in the following chapters. Before examining two aspects of the Crucifixion itself in sections I. 8 and 9, however, it will be helpful to analyze seven other aspects of biblical and Judaic traditions on Moses' final days which influenced how the earliest Jewish Christians described Jesus in other pericopes in the Gospels.

Most NT scholars have had at least some biblical Hebrew, yet they lack the expertise to deal with rabbinic Hebrew, not to speak of Aramaic. This often makes them dependent on secondary sources such as Paul Billerbeck's commentary (Str-B),[13] and they employ the very difficult

---

Press, 1976) 185-217 and 219-25, quotation p. 185. Several other relevant studies, in addition to Ginzberg's *Legends*, are the following: "Moses," "In Rabbinical Literature," by Jacob Lauterbach in *JE* (1905/25) 9.46-54; art. "Moses" in *EJ* (1971) 12.388-98 by David Winston, Louis Jacobs and Aaron Rothkoff; Aaron Rosmarin, *Moses im Lichte der Agada* (New York: The Goldblatt Publishing Co., 1932), esp. 133-49; art. Μωυσῆς by Joachim Jeremias in *TDNT* 4.848-73, esp. 853-55; Renée Bloch, "Die Gestalt des Moses in der rabbinischen Tradition," in *Moses in Schrift und Überlieferung*, ed. Fridolin Stier and Eleonore Beck (Düsseldorf: Patmos-Verlag, 1963; translation of *Moïse, l'homme de l'Alliance*, 1955) 95-171, esp. 127-38; Michael Stone, "Three Armenian Accounts of the Death of Moses" in *Studies on the Testament of Moses*, ed. George Nickelsburg, Jr. (Septuagint and Cognate Studies 4; Cambridge, MA: Society of Biblical Literature, 1973) 118-21, as well as the other studies in the volume; Klaus Haacker and Peter Schäfer, "Nachbiblische Traditionen vom Tode Moses," in *Josephus-Studien*, Festschrift for Otto Michel, ed. Otto Betz and Martin Hengel (Göttingen: Vandenhoeck & Ruprecht, 1974) 147-74; Judah Goldin, "The Death of Moses: An Exercise in Midrashic Transposition," in *Love & Death in the Ancient Near East. Essays in Honor of Marvin H. Pope*, ed. John Marks and Robert Good (Guilford, CT: Four Quarters Publishing Company, 1987) 219-25, who states on p. 224 regarding Moses: "no other biblical personality so succeeded in shortening the distance between God and man as he did"; Ephraim Urbach, *The Sages* (Cambridge, MA: Harvard University Press, 1987) 172-75; Louis Feldman, "Josephus' Portrait of Moses," in *JQR* 82 (1992) 285-328; Rella Kushelevsky, *Moses and the Angel of Death* (Studies on Themes and Motifs in Literature 4; New York, etc.: Peter Lang, 1995); and *Moses in Biblical and Extra-Biblical Tradition*, ed. Axel Graupner and Michael Wolter (BZNW 372; Berlin: de Gruyter, 2007). I call attention to other secondary literature at the relevant points below.
[13] As a Lutheran pastor myself, I may point to the pious Lutheran pastor Billerbeck's slightly anti-Jewish bent in terms of what he (and other Lutherans of the Law-Gospel dichotomy) falsely perceived as Jewish "works-righteousness." His collection of background materials is nevertheless still very helpful if used

issue of dating the rabbinic sources as a cheap excuse for not even considering them.[14] Many gladly cite the Church Fathers up to the fifth century CE, who with only few exceptions such as Origen, Jerome and the Syrians Aphrahat and Ephraem knew no Hebrew and had no access to rabbinic traditions. Yet they strangely characterize the rabbinic Amoraim from the same era as too late to be of any relevance to the Gospels, even though these often stood in a tradition of biblical interpretation which was similar to that of the first Palestinian Jewish Christians who composed incidents and compiled sayings which later entered the Gospels.

Philip Alexander correctly issued a list of seven caveats the NT scholar of today should observe in dealing with rabbinic texts, yet he could also note: "only good can come from New Testament students studying Rabbinic literature...."[15] Geza Vermes also maintains that

---

judiciously. See also Samuel Lachs, *A Rabbinic Commentary on the New Testament. The Gospels of Matthew, Mark and Luke* (Hoboken: KTAV Publishing House, 1987), and Frank Stern, *A Rabbi Looks at Jesus' Parables* (Lanham, MD: Rowman & Littlefield Publishers, 2006).

[14] Raymond Brown, for example, was extremely wary of citing rabbinic sources. Although a specialist in Semitic languages, Joseph Fitzmyer concurred with him in this respect (see William Horbury's remark's below). The same is true for the otherwise excellent commentary on Mark by Adela Yarbro Collins, *Mark. A Commentary* (Hermeneia; Minneapolis: Fortress Press, 2007), in which she succeeds admirably in exploring "the affinities of the Markan Jesus with Hellenistic philosophers and heroes" (p. 1), but apparently considers the final dating of haggadic midrashic collections too late for such sources to be of direct relevance to the Gospels (e. g., pp. 353 and 727; see also her citations of them as found in Str-B and modern authors, as well as the garbled references to rabbinic materials on pp. 858-59, uncorrected even if someone else did the index). Yarbro Collins believes in regard to Mark that "the author and at least some members of his audience knew Aramaic as well as Greek" (p. 8); he could have been acquainted with the Hebrew version of a prophetic text (p. 727); and that "Antioch is especially interesting as a possible setting for the composition of Mark," particularly because of the Aramaic language and its Jewish community (p. 101). Yet then the author Mark would certainly also have been acquainted with Jewish haggadic traditions, to which Yarbro Collins almost never refers. Interestingly, many scholars today locate the bilingual author of the Gospel of Matthew also in Antioch, and it is clear that he knows such traditions.

[15] Cf. his "Rabbinic Judaism and the New Testament" in *ZNW* 74 (1983) 237-46, quotation p. 238. See also his statement that "Rabbinic models may be particularly relevant to elucidating how the early Christian groups elaborated and passed on their traditions," in "Orality in Pharisaic-Rabbinic Judaism at the Turn of the Eras" in *Jesus and the Oral Tradition*, ed. Henry Wansbrough (London

"rabbinic literature, judiciously and sensitively handled, can throw valuable and sometimes unique light on the study of the Gospels."[16] Finally, in his essay "Rabbinic Literature in New Testament Interpretation," William Horbury quotes Vermes in this regard, adding a similar statement by David Flusser. He also notes that while the relevance to the NT of the Dead Sea Scrolls and Jewish sources in Greek is generally acknowledged today, one should also consider "not only the presence of early material in rabbinic sources, but also their extent and richness, and the light which they shed on Jewish texts of the Herodian and even the Hasmonaean age - and the benefit of combining this with light from other sources."[17]

In the following chapters I employ as sources wherever possible the MT, the LXX, the Apocrypha and the Pseudepigrapha, Qumran, Philo and Josephus. Yet the reader will also encounter a large number of rabbinic sources, not only Tannaitic, in part in my own translation.[18] One reason for my citing them so extensively is that often the texts are not easily accessible to the non-specialist. At times a tradition relevant to a Gospel pericope has only survived in what is now a very late source, such as the midrash "Petirat Mosheh," the "Departure / Death of Moses." In such a case it is helpful when a "cluster" of analogous expressions, motifs and narrative flow can be ascertained. This is usually a sign that an earlier tradition has survived in this text, although perhaps in a

---

and New York: T & T Clark International, 2004; original 1991) 159-84, quotation p. 184. See also his helpful studies "Midrash and the Gospels" and "Rabbinic Biography and the Biography of Jesus: A Survey of the Evidence," in *Synoptic Studies. The Ampleforth Conferences of 1982 and 1983*, ed. Christopher Tuckett (JSNT Suppl. Series 7; Sheffield: JSOT Press, 1984), 1-18 and 19-50.

[16] Cf. his *The Religion of Jesus the Jew* (London: SCM Press, 1993) 7. On p. 8 he chides some Qumran enthusiasts for ignoring the rabbinic texts.

[17] Cf. his *Herodian Judaism and New Testament Study* (WUNT 193; Tübingen: Mohr Siebeck, 2006) 221-35, quotations on pp. 226 and 228. On pp. 224-25, agreeing with Vermes in this regard, he points out how rabbinic sources which Joseph Fitzmyer does not (want to) cite could strengthen specific arguments at Qumran. Horbury correctly emphasizes the continuity in Judaic sources in spite of the events of 70 (and I would add 132-35) CE (see p. 234).

[18] Thus when, for example, I cite something from "Midrash Rabbah," and in a footnote have "Soncino 7.135," this means the tradition is definitely found there and in English, yet I may modify the Soncino translation. In unfortunate contrast to many other writers who cite rabbinic materials, I note the edition with its page number so that the interested reader can conveniently find the passage and evaluate it himself / herself. The reader should not be alarmed at the amount of Greek, Hebrew and Aramaic in the text; it is all translated.

modified form. The argument is thus often cumulative. Each case, however, must be judged individually.[19]

When a Judaic or NT text quotes a certain verse from Scripture, the latter passage is usually easily identifiable.[20] The same is true for an "allusion," which can be defined as "an implied or indirect reference esp. when used in literature."[21] Yet many Judaic and Gospel texts only "echo" a particular passage of Scripture. In his volume *Echoes of Scripture in the Letters of Paul*, Richard Hays speaks of "The poetic freedom with which Paul echoes Scripture...," which I find true of the Gospels too. I also appreciate his differentiation between an "allusion" as "used of obvious intertextual references, *echo* of subtler ones."[22] I would maintain, for example, that while no Scriptural passage is quoted or clearly alluded to in Mark 16:1-8, there are nevertheless echoes or subtle allusions there to the unit Gen 28:10 and 29:1-14 *in Judaic tradition*: the "inability" of the (three) shepherds of three flocks to "roll away" a "large stone." In Judaic tradition Jacob's ability to do so was considered a "miracle," which produced "amazement / astonishment" (see chapter III. below). The first Palestinian Jewish Christian hearers of this narrative in their own language (Aramaic, perhaps Hebrew then translated into Aramaic) in the pre-Markan tradition would have caught this cluster of echoes or subtle

---

[19] A good example of this is the haggadic narrative of the child Moses' taking Pharaoh's crown and placing it on his own head. When Pharaoh's counselors learn of this, they want to slay Moses, but first test him. Through Gabriel's intervention the child is rescued. Cf. *Exod. Rab.* Shemoth 1/26 on Exod 2:10 (Mirkin 5.41; Soncino 3.33-34; a partial parallel is found in *Tanḥuma* Shemoth 8 on Exod 2:6 [Eshkol 1.213; Berman 325]). If we did not have a variant of this episode in Josephus, *Ant.* 2.232-36, we would probably consider the rabbinic tradition quite late, which it obviously is not. Nevertheless, I would be the first to concede that many of the Amoraic traditions are indeed late.

[20] The rabbis knew the Hebrew Bible by heart, and often they quoted from memory. This means slight variations do occur. When only the beginning of a verse is cited, as was usual because everyone knew its continuation, that at times also led to later misinterpretation of which text was meant.

[21] Cf. *Webster's Ninth Collegiate Dictionary* (Springfield, MA: Merriam-Webster, 1987) 73.

[22] New Haven / London: Yale University Press, 1989, quotations on pp. xiii and 29. I myself avoid the broad designation "intertextuality" because, as Steve Moyise says, it is an "umbrella term" and needs to be divided into subcategories in order to be meaningful. Cf. his art. "Intertextuality and the Study of the Old Testament in the New" in *The Old Testament in the New Testament: Essays in Honour of J. L. North*, ed. Steve Moyise (JSNTSup 189; Sheffield: Sheffield Academic Press, 2000) 17 and 41.

allusions to the above biblical text *as it was already interpreted in Judaic tradition.* They would have deeply appreciated the "author's" artistic ability to create a new narrative partly on the basis of a biblical model, just as many other Jewish narrators did at the time. It was a common procedure. Unfortunately, most of these echoes or subtle allusions are lost on us modern-day Gentile Christians, and even on Jews who have not grown up in, or studied, early Judaic sources. It is my hope that in the following chapters my arguments for echoes or subtle allusions to specific biblical texts will be convincing to the reader.

"Orality" is a key buzz-word in NT circles today, and I greatly appreciate its aims, especially in regard to Jesus' sayings. Nevertheless, it has not been very helpful in analyzing the Gospel texts I examine in this volume. I have the impression from such presentations at the annual meetings of the Society of New Testament Studies (SNTS) and from relevant publications that many scholars in this area reach a certain stage and then say: "We can't get back any further than this, so we can only deal with the text at this level." This is exemplified in James Dunn's statement regarding his "methodological principle, that our only visible subject matter for historical investigation is the impact made by Jesus as it has impressed itself into the tradition."[23] It is my contention, however, that in many cases, especially in narrative material, we can indeed get back to the Judaic traditions which inform them. By the echoes or subtle allusions being pointed out in the texts treated in the following chapters, which were indeed caught, understood and deeply appreciated by the first Palestinian Jewish Christians, we today can also better appreciate a text's original intention(s).

No one should feel threatened in his or her Christian faith because of the results of the following studies, although often the result has been for me to acknowledge that a given account is not "historical" in the modern sense of the word. A particular narrative, however, always has its own "religious truth(s)," which I then describe. One of the major aims of this volume is to try to overcome the widespread false dichotomy in NT studies between "historical" and "non-historical," between "true" and "false." My contention is that a proper understanding of Palestinian Judaic haggadah at the time of Jesus - which Christian theology has basically ignored for at least nineteen centuries - will aid us in resolving the above conflict. Therefore the final chapter, IV., is so important not

---

[23] Cf. his *Jesus Remembered* (Grand Rapids, MI and Cambridge, U.K.: Eerdmans, 2003) 876. Dunn means not only the sayings of Jesus, but also the narratives concerning him.

only in order to properly appreciate the results of the preceding chapters, but also in order to indicate what insights can still be gained in regard to the contents of many other Gospel texts by a deeper appreciation of Palestinian Jewish and Jewish Christian haggadah.

The following studies thus invite others to interact with them, and even possibly to continue and further develop the basic approach employed here. As indicated in the Preface, it is my hope that they may not only deepen present-day Christians' understanding of the death, burial and Resurrection of Jesus, but also invite Jewish readers to appreciate how biblical and Judaic traditions on the death, burial and translation of Moses influenced the Gospel accounts in major ways.[24]

Rabbi Tarfon, a second generation Tanna,[25] appropriately stated in regard to the above suggestion: "You don't have to finish the task, but you are not free to desist from it either."[26]

---

[24] Since several of the individual sections are of necessity somewhat detailed, the reader may first wish to read the Summary at the end of the volume in order to gain an overview, and then return to the text itself.

[25] Strack and Stemberger, *Introduction to the Talmud and Midrash* 80, from now on cited simply as *Introduction*. On the issue of sayings attributed to specific authorities, see the recent discussion by Martin Jaffee, "Rabbinic Authorship as a Collective Enterprise," in *The Cambridge Companion to the Talmud and Rabbinic Literature*, ed. by him and Charlotte Fonrobert (Cambridge: Cambridge University Press, 2007) 17-37.

[26] Cf. *m. 'Avot* 2:16 in Albeck 4.362.

I. The Death of Jesus, and the Death of Moses in Judaic Tradition

Before Jesus' Crucifixion and actual death are analyzed in sections I. 8-9, seven other aspects in the Gospels leading directly up to them will be discussed in I. 1-7. These too are significantly informed by Judaic tradition on the impending death of Moses.

I. 1 The Passion Predictions of Jesus' Death, and Divine Predictions of Moses' Death

A.   In the Gospel of Mark there are three predictions on the part of Jesus that he will suffer and be put to death (in Jerusalem).[1] The first is found in 8:31 par., where Jesus says that "The Son of Man [I] must undergo great suffering, and be rejected by the elders, the chief priests, and the scribes, and be killed...." Mark 9:31 par. relates the second: "The Son of Man is to be betrayed into human hands, and they will kill him...." The third prediction is the most detailed, related by Jesus on the road leading to Jerusalem. Mark 10:33-34 par. states: "See, we are going up to Jerusalem, and the Son of Man will be handed over to the chief priests and the scribes, and they will condemn him to death; then they will hand him over to the Gentiles; 34) they will mock him, and spit upon him, and flog him, and kill him...."

In all three predictions Jesus' dying / being killed (in Jerusalem) is a major element. The divine necessity of this event is emphasized by the verb "must" (δεῖ) in Mark 8:31. This motif also appears in Matt 26:54; Luke 13:33, 17:25 and 24:7,26;[2] and John 3:14 and 12:34.[3]

---

[1] The third section of each prediction, that he would then rise after three days, is a post-Resurrection addition by the earliest Christians. See chapter III. C below on "the third day." It is quite plausible that Jesus purposely went up to Jerusalem, expecting to suffer and perhaps even to die there. Cf., e.g., Luke 13:33. However, the passion predictions already betray heavily stereotyped language (almost creedal) in the earliest Gospel, that of Mark.

[2] Cf. also Luke 22:22, "as it has been determined."

I suggest that the threefold prediction of Jesus' death in Mark, and its divine necessity, were crafted by the earliest Palestinian Jewish Christians on the basis of Moses' death as described in Scripture. In this form they later reached the Evangelist Mark. This means that he himself already found three predictions in the tradition, which he then expanded and placed in their present positions.

B.   Deuteronomy 33 consists of the blessing of Moses upon each of the twelve tribes, in the form of a testament,[4] and chapter 34 describes Moses' actual death. Just before this, in chapters 31-32 the Lord states three times the necessity of his death.

Deut 31:2 has Moses first inform Israel that the Lord has told him, "You shall not cross over this Jordan," [but die].[5] In v 14 the Lord tells Moses a second time, "Your time to die is near," to which the adjacent v 16 belongs: "Soon you will lie with your ancestors."[6] Finally, in 32:49 the Lord addresses Moses for the third time. He should "ascend this mountain of the Abarim, Mount Nebo." Verse 50 continues by stating: "you shall die there on the mountain that you ascend and shall be gathered to your kin...."

Here too, like Jerusalem for Jesus, a definite place is cited for Moses' death; three "predictions" of this death occur at the very end of Moses' life; and the fact that the Lord (God) Himself makes these statements

---

[3] The "lifting up" in the Johannine passages refers both to Jesus' Crucifixion and his exaltation. It should be noted that the Gospel of John also has three passion predictions: 3:14; 8:28; and 12:32-34.
[4] Cf. Jacob's blessing Joseph's sons in Genesis 48 and his final words to his twelve sons in chapter 49. This became the model for many later "testaments," not only of the Twelve Patriarchs.
[5] Cf. already 3:27 and 4:21-22, yet they do not belong to the very end of Moses' life. See also the three statements in Num 20:12; 27:13; and 31:2.
[6] It should be recalled that the numbering of individual verses is a modern phenomenon. Verses 14 and 16 would have been viewed together. It is also significant that *Pseudo-Philo* states in 19:6, "God spoke to Moses a third time [*tercio*], saying, 'Behold, you are going forth *to sleep with your fathers*' (Deut 31:16).... 7) 'Now I will show you the land before you die, but *you will not enter it*' (32:52)... (*SC* 229.158; *OTP* 2.327). Here Deut 31:16 is the third (and last) divine prediction of Moses' death in a first-century, Palestinian document originally written in Hebrew (Daniel Harrington in *OTP* 2.298-300).

shows that they are a divine necessity, like the "must" in the passion predictions of Jesus' death.[7]

I. 2 Jesus' Rebuke of Peter, and Moses' Rebuke of the Angel of Death / Sammael

A. *Jesus*

On the way to the villages of Caesarea Philippi, Jesus asked his disciples not only who the people say he is, but also: "Who do *you* (pl.) say that I am?" To this Peter alone responded: "You are 'the Messiah' (ὁ Χριστός)" (Mark 8:29 par.). At this point Jesus spoke the first passion prediction to all twelve disciples about what would happen to him in Jerusalem, including his death (v 31; see section I. 1 above). The only response to this again came from Peter:

32) And Peter took him aside and began to rebuke him.
33) But turning and looking at his disciples, he [Jesus] rebuked Peter and said to him, "Get behind me, Satan! For you are setting your mind not on divine things but on human things."

While Luke of the three Synoptics omitted this passage, and it is also lacking in John, Matthew appropriated the pericope from Mark and expanded it, first in Matt 16:16-19, including a wordplay on "Peter" (Πέτρος) and "rock" (πέτρα) in v 18. Then in vv 22-23 the First Evangelist writes:

22) And Peter took him aside and began to rebuke him, saying: "God forbid it, Lord! This must never happen to you."
23) But he turned and said to Peter: "Get behind me, Satan! You are a stumbling block to me; for you are setting your mind not on divine things but on human things."

While Matthew omits Jesus' "rebuking" Peter as found in Mark ("the rebuker" is "rebuked"), he spells out Peter's "rebuking" Jesus with direct speech on the part of the "first" disciple: 16:22b. He also omits Jesus' looking at his disciples (pl.) before rebuking Peter, yet adds: "You are a stumbling block to me" (23).

---

[7] The obvious difference, of course, is that while Jesus is represented as predicting his own suffering and death, for Moses it is the Lord who decrees his death.

Before pointing out in section B. how the above imagery derives from Judaic tradition on Sammael or the Angel of Death's taking Moses' soul at the very end of his life, several additional remarks are helpful in regard to the two Gospel accounts.

A. 1 Rebuking

Peter "rebuked" Jesus for saying that he, the Messiah, must suffer and be killed in Jerusalem. The latter was exactly the opposite of what the Messiah was supposed to do: to liberate the Jewish people from their (presently Roman) oppressors and, if necessary by force, establish an independent kingdom of peace and righteousness. Jesus in turn "rebuked" Peter for opposing the divine necessity (δεῖ) of his going to the capital to suffer and be killed.

The Greek verb for "to rebuke" here is ἐπιτιμάω.[8] In all eight occurrences in the LXX with a Hebrew equivalent, the original is גָּעַר.[9] Of the fourteen occurrences of this verb in the MT, only two deal with Satan,[10] and both are found in Zech 3:2, which reads: "And the Lord said to Satan: 'The Lord rebuke you, O Satan! The Lord who has chosen Jerusalem rebuke you!'" *Targum Jonathan* retains *gʿr* in both cases here, whereas the root elsewhere in the targums is always translated by other Aramaic verbs. This indicates that "the Hebrew original of this sentence had already acquired a semi-formulaic status...."[11]

"The Lord rebuke you, O Satan!" became an incantation formula and "is found in the Aramaic magic bowls from Nippur."[12] A good example of such an incantation is Michael's telling the devil, "The Lord rebuke you!" in Jude 9, from the first century CE, which I shall analyze in section B. below. Another example is *b. Ber.* 51a in the name of R. Joshua b. Levi,

---

[8] Cf. BAGD 303,1: *"rebuke, reprove, censure,* also *speak seriously, warn* in order to prevent an action or bring one to an end," and the art. ἐπιτιμάω , etc. by Ethelbert Stauffer in *TDNT* 2.623-27. See also Howard Kee, "The Terminology of Mark's Exorcism Stories" in *NTS* 14 (1967) 232-46.

[9] Cf. BDB 172; Jastrow 261; A. Macintosh, "A Consideration of Hebrew גער ," in *VT* 19 (1969) 471-79; and A. Caquot, art. גָּעַר , *gaʿar* in *TDOT* 3.49-53.

[10] Nor does Satan figure in the fifteen occurrences of the noun גְּעָרָה , or in the one occurrence of מִגְעָרֶת .

[11] Cf. Robert Gordon in *The Targum of the Minor Prophets* 190, n. 2. The Aramaic is found in Sperber 3.481.

[12] Cf. Carol and Eric Meyers, *Haggai, Zechariah 1-8* (AB 25B; Garden City, NY: Doubleday, 1987) 187, referring to Caquot in n. 9 (his p. 52, n. 4).

a first generation Palestinian Amora.[13] The Angel of Death informs him that in order to avoid harm from him when seeing women returning from a dead person, "let him turn his face away and say: 'And the Lord said to Satan, The Lord rebuke you, O Satan!' etc. (Zech 3:2) until they have passed by."[14] In 2 (Syriac) Baruch 21:23, Baruch prays to God: "reprove the angel of death,"[15] and in the *Life of Adam and Eve* (*Vita* 39), Seth tells the beast (serpent): "May the Lord rebuke you!"[16] In *Pseudo-Philo* 60:3 David tells the evil spirit plaguing Saul: "But let the new womb from which I was born rebuke you...."[17] At Qumran the verb גער is employed twice of "banishing" an evil spirit in 1QapGen ar 20:28-29. In 1QM 14:10 the author also thanks God in regard to Belial (= Satan): "You have chased away (גערתה) from [us] his spirits of [de]struction."[18]

It thus appears that the phrase "The Lord rebuke you, O Satan!", deriving from Zech 3:2, was employed *in toto* or in part in Palestine in the first and second centuries CE. The Palestinian Jewish Christian who first composed what is now Mark 8:32-33 in a Semitic language was certainly not the first person, nor the last, to borrow imagery from Zech 3:2. It had already become formulaic.

Another factor in Zech 3:2 appealed to the original author of what later became Mark 8:32-33. He interpreted "The Lord who has chosen Jerusalem rebuke you!" of his own Lord, Jesus.[19] "Has chosen" is the

---

[13] *Introduction* 92-93.

[14] Cf. Soncino 308-09. Similar advice is given by Satan to Pelimo (to drive him away) in *b. Qidd.* 81a-b. As in Zech 3:2, he should say: "The Merciful rebuke Satan" (Soncino 418). Pelimo was a Tanna; see the references in Jastrow 1182 under פְּלִימוֹ .

[15] Cf. *OTP* 1.628. A. Klijn places the writing, originally in Hebrew, at the beginning of the second century CE, and as probably from Palestine (1.616). On the Angel of Death as equivalent to Satan, see section 2. below.

[16] Cf. *OTP* 2.274. M. Johnson says the writing was originally in Hebrew, from the end of the first century CE, and from Palestine (2.251-52).

[17] Cf. *SC* 229.368-69; *OTP* 2.373. Daniel Harrington maintains that it was originally written in Hebrew at about the time of Jesus, and was from Palestine (*OTP* 2.298-300).

[18] Cf. *The Dead Sea Scrolls Study Edition* (Martínez and Tigchelaar) 1.42-43 and 136-37, respectively.

[19] This was facilitated for him by the similarity of "Jesus" in Hebrew (יֵשַׁ), and the "Joshua" (יְהוֹשֻׁעַ) of Zech 3:1 and 3. The LXX has Ἰησοῦς in both cases.

Hebrew הַבֹּחֵר , literally "the one choosing."[20] For the author, Jesus was now already choosing to suffer and be killed in Jerusalem (Mark 8:31; 10:32-33 explicitly names the city). He therefore "rebuked" Peter as Satan for opposing his choice to go there.

Finally, the nearby verse Zech 3:8 speaks of the Lord's "going to bring 'My servant, the Branch'" (אֶת־עַבְדִּי צֶמַח). The first Palestinian Jewish Christians considered Jesus to be the "servant of the Lord,"[21] and "branch" (צֶמַח) was a messianic designation, as in the Targum at this point and in other sources.[22] This nearby verse, interpreted messianically, thus probably facilitated the author's applying the "Lord" of 3:2 to his own Messiah, Jesus. It was then he, the Messiah, who rebuked Peter as Satan for proclaiming him as the Messiah.

A. 2 Satan

As a child and youth I was completely puzzled, indeed somewhat frightened, by Jesus' calling his main disciple, who had just confessed him as the Messiah, "Satan" (Σατανᾶ)[23] in Mark 8:33 and Matt 16:23. How could Jesus treat Peter so harshly so quickly? Only years later, having acquired a better understanding of early Judaism, was I able to appreciate how the Palestinian Jewish Christian who first composed the above scene could employ this seemingly offensive term for Peter.

First, he clearly borrowed it from Zech 3:2, "And the Lord said to Satan, 'The Lord rebuke you, O Satan!'" "Satan" here is the Hebrew הַשָּׂטָן both times, as also in v 1. The LXX has διάβολος instead, showing that the author here employed the Hebrew text as his background

---

[20] Cf. BDB 103 on בָּחַר , to choose. The LXX has an aorist participle here. The Targum expands to: "May the Lord 'who has been pleased to make His Shekinah dwell' in Jerusalem" (Sperber 3.481; Gordon 190-91).

[21] Cf. especially Isaiah 53 and the art. παῖς θεοῦ by Joachim Jeremias in *TDNT* 5.677-717.

[22] For the Targum, cf. Sperber 3.481, and Gordon 192 ("My servant the anointed One / Messiah"). See Gordon's references to other passages in n. 21, as well as Str-B 2.113 on Luke 1:78's ἀνατολή , also found in LXX Zech 3:8, as a messianic designation.

[23] Cf. שָׂטָן in BDB 966 and Jastrow 1554; the articles "Satan" by T. H. Gaster in *IDB* 4.224-28; σατανᾶς by Werner Foerster in *TDNT* 7.151-63; διαβάλλω , διάβολος also by him in *TDNT* 2.71-73, with "The OT View of Satan" by Gerhard von Rad on 2.73-75; "Satan" by Ludwig Blau in *JE* (1905/25) 11.68-70; and "Satan" by the Editorial Staff and "Satan, Post-Biblical" by Louis Rabinowitz in *EJ* (1971) 14.903-05.

model. In v 1 Satan stands at the right hand of the Lord (or angel of the Lord) "in order to accuse him" (לְשִׂטְנוֹ) - Joshua. The root שׂטן is thus employed four times within 3:1-2, showing its great importance here. While the verb can mean to accuse, it also can be translated as to be or act as an "adversary."[24] The same is true for the noun.[25] The LXX translates the verb in 3:1 with ἀντίκειμαι , " to be opposed."[26]

It is in the latter sense of "being opposed to something," of being a "hinderer," that Peter is rebuked by Jesus. Peter had himself just rebuked Jesus for saying he "must undergo great suffering," be rejected and killed in Jerusalem (Mark 8:31; Matt 16:21). His "opposing" Jesus, his attempt to be a "hinderer" of such a fate for the Messiah, (whom he had just before for the first time declared Jesus to be), lay in the dominant view of the time as to what functions the Messiah should have. As remarked above, it was hoped he would become King of the Jews, liberate them from their (now Roman) oppressors, and establish a kingdom of peace and righteousness. This is shown, for example, in John 6:15, where people forcibly want to make Jesus "king"; in the phrase "the King of the Jews," repeated four times by Pilate and the soldiers in Mark 15:2,9,12 and 18; and in the same inscription on the Cross in 15:26. Verse 32 also has the expression "the Messiah, the King of Israel," which reflects the very common Hebrew designation of the Messiah as "the Messianic King," מֶלֶךְ הַמָּשִׁיחַ , or its very similar Aramaic equivalent.[27]

The Palestinian Jewish Christian who first composed the episode of Mark 8:31-33 thus proleptically interpreted Jesus' later suffering and Crucifixion in Jerusalem already at this point. It was a divine "must" (δεῖ in v 31), and no one, including even Jesus' main disciple Peter, should try to "hinder" or "oppose" it. Only later, so the author, could Jesus triumph by rising from the dead after three days. This opposition to Jesus' suffering and dying is also shown at two other points in the Gospels, once before the beginning of his ministry, and once at the very end of his life.

Mark 1:13 states that Jesus "was in the wilderness forty days, tempted by 'Satan.'" The Q passage Matt 4:1-11 // Luke 4:1-13 expands this and instead employs the term "the devil" (ὁ διάβολος , also labeled "the tempter" (ὁ πειράζων) in Matt 4:3. One of the three temptations to

---

[24] Cf. BDB 966, with reference to Zech 3:1. See also סטן as "to hinder" in Jastrow 973.

[25] *Ibid.*, as well as שָׂטָן as "hinderer" in Jastrow 1554, and סָטָנָא 973: "hinderer."

[26] Cf. LSJ 156. II.

[27] Cf. Str-B 1.6-7.

which the devil subjects Jesus consists of his showing him all the kingdoms of the world and their glory, if only Jesus will worship him. That is, the devil offers him the possibility of (avoiding his future suffering and being killed, and instead) reigning as the (messianic) king. Yet Jesus is described as rejecting this; he only wants to serve God (Matt 4:10 // Luke 4:8, a quotation of Deut 6:13). Matthew, borrowing terminology from Mark 8:33 which he later also employs at 16:23, also has Jesus now say in 4:10, "Depart, Satan!" (Ὕπαγε , Σατανᾶ).[28] This shows how interrelated the two pericopes are.

The other narrative showing Jesus' opposition to Satan's temptation to avoid suffering and death is found at the very end of his life, in Gethsemane. There he is described as praying that "if it were possible, the hour might pass from him. He said, 'Abba, Father, for You all things are possible; remove this cup [of death] from me; yet, not what I want, but what You want'" (Mark 14:35-36 par.). The Jewish scholar David Flusser of Jerusalem aptly remarked here: Jesus at this point overcame the temptation to flee from Gethsemane in the darkness of the night in order to live an anonymous life in secret elsewhere.[29] Probably connected to this theme is the remark, in the Synoptics found only in Luke 22:3, that "Satan entered into Judas called Iscariot,"[30] who then actively began his preparations to betray Jesus, a task he completed in Gethsemane.[31] No satisfactory explanation for Judas' betrayal has ever been given.[32] One plausible proposal is that he attempted "to force Jesus into a display of power so that the religious and political authorities would be convinced of his messiahship."[33] To this extent he, like Peter in Mark 8:33 // Matt 16:23, was "satanically" opposed to the divine necessity of Jesus' suffering and being killed.

---

[28] Only later MSS add ὀπίσω μου from Matt 16:23 // Mark 8:33.

[29] Cf. his *Jesus* (Reinbek bei Hamburg: Rowohlt Taschenbuch Verlag, 1968) 115. See also his *Die letzten Tage Jesu in Jerusalem* (Stuttgart: Calwer Verlag, 1982) 84.

[30] Cf. the chapter "The Name Judas 'Iscariot' and Ahithophel in Judaic Tradition" in my *My Name Is "Legion." Palestinian Judaic Traditions in Mark 5:1-20 and Other Gospel Texts* (Studies in Judaism; Lanham, MD: University Press of America, 2003) 155-208.

[31] Cf. Luke 4:13's "until an opportune time" and Judas in 22:47 with "the power of darkness" in v 53, as well as John 6:70-71, 13:2 and 27.

[32] His ostensible greed, for example, is later embellishment (John 12:6; 13:29; Matt 26:14-16).

[33] Cf. E. P. Blair, art. "Judas," "7. Judas Iscariot," in *IDB* (1962) 2.1006-08, quotation p. 1007.

Finally, Satan is called by two other names of relevance to section B. below: the Angel of Death, and Sammael. Examples of the "Angel of Death"[34] are: Psalms of Solomon 7:4;[35] Test. Abraham A 8:9-10, 12 and 16-20, B 9:11 and 13-14;[36] 2 (Syriac) Baruch 21:23;[37] *b. Ber.* 51a;[38] *Gen. Rab.* Ḥayye Sarah 58/6 on Gen 23:3;[39] and *Exod. Rab.* Mishpatim 32/1 on Exod 23:20 in the name of R. Nehemiah, a third generation Tanna.[40] After a discussion of Satan's role in Job 1-2, Resh (Simeon b.) Laqish, a second generation Palestinian Amora, states in *b. B. Bathra* 16a that Satan and the Angel of Death are identical.[41] Examples of "Sammael"[42] are the Martyrdom and Ascension of Isaiah 1:8 ("Sammael 'Malkira' [king of evil]"); 1:13; 2:1 (= Satan); 5:15-16; 7:9 (= Satan); and 11:41 ("Sammael Satan");[43] 3 (Greek) Baruch 4:8 (= the devil) and 9:7;[44] 3 (Hebrew Apocalypse of) Enoch 14:2 ("Sammael, the prince of the Accusers");[45] *b. Soṭah* 10b;[46] *Gen. Rab.* Vayera 56/4 on Gen 22:7;[47] and *Exod. Rab.* Bo 18/5 on Exod 12:29, where he is identified with Satan.[48]

---

[34] Cf. Jastrow 786 on הַמּוּת מַלְאַךְ , and the articles "Angel of Death" by Ludwig Blau in *JE* (1903/25) 4.480-82, and by Dov Noy in *EJ* (1971) 2.952-56.

[35] Cf. *OTP* 2.658, where he is simply designated Death. See 2.644 on this, and R. B. Wright on the writing as originally in Hebrew, from Jerusalem, about the middle of the first century BCE (2.640-41).

[36] Here too he is simply labeled Death. Cf. *OTP* 1.892-95 and 900-02, and 1.875, where E. P. Sanders believes the work was originally in Greek (Hebrew is also proposed), from Egypt, and written ca. 100 CE.

[37] Cf. *OTP* 1.628, and A. F. Klijn on the writing as originally in Hebrew, and from Palestine at the beginning of the second century CE (1.616-17).

[38] Soncino 308-09.

[39] Theodor and Albeck 624; Soncino 2.512.

[40] Cf. the text in Mirkin 6.79-80 and Soncino 3.404. For Nehemiah, see *Introduction* 85.

[41] Cf. the text in Soncino 79, where he also adds the evil inclination (*yeṣer ha-ra'*). For the rabbi, see *Introduction* 95.

[42] Cf. Jastrow 998 on סַמָּאֵל , and the articles "Samael" by Ludwig Blau in *JE* (1905/25) 10.665-66, and "Samael" by Gershom Scholem in *EJ* (1971) 14.719-22.

[43] Cf. *OTP* 2.157, 160, 164, 166 and 176 respectively.

[44] Cf. *OTP* 1.666-67 and 673, respectively.

[45] Cf. *OTP* 1.266. See also the Testament of Solomon 7:1-6 (MS "D"), where he is "the chief Satan" (noted in *OTP* 1.937-38 and 987, n. "f"). See also "Sammael, the wicked angel, the chief of all the accusing angels" in *Deut. Rab.* 11/10, to be analyzed in section B. below.

[46] Soncino 48-49.

[47] Theodor and Albeck 598; Soncino 1.493-94.

[48] Mirkin 5.215; Soncino 3.222.

*   *   *

The Judaic sources cited above in regard to "rebuking" someone, with Satan, deriving from Zech 3:2, and Satan's function of opposing or hindering someone / something, together with his being called the Angel of Death and Sammael, help to appreciate the following analysis of Moses' rebuking the Angel of Death / Sammael when the latter attempts to take his soul at the end of his life. I suggest that this material, to which I now turn, is the basic background of Mark 8:32-33 and Matt 16:22-23.

B. Moses

B. 1   Jude 9, Zech 3:2, and Moses' Rebuke of the Angel of Death / Satan Just Before His Death

The motif of rebuking Satan with the words "The Lord rebuke you!" in connection with Moses' death is attested already in the first century CE. Jude 9 states that "when the archangel Michael contended with the devil [τῷ διαβόλῳ] and disputed about the body of Moses, he did not dare to bring a condemnation of slander against him, but said: 'The Lord rebuke you!' (Ἐπιτιμήσαι σοι κύριος)." The latter is clearly based on Zech 3:2, as shown in the Judaic traditions on this verse analyzed above in section A.[49]

The episode alluded to in Jude 9 is considered by many commentators to derive from a now lost work dealing with both the death and assumption of Moses, also called the "Assumption of Moses."[50] It may have been later appended to another writing which has survived, the "Testament of Moses."[51]

---

[49] On the date of Jude, cf. Jerome Neyrey, *2 Peter, Jude* (AB 37C; New York: Doubleday, 1993) 30: Although "The date of Jude remains a mystery...," "Some items in the document remain suggestive of an early second-century date...."

[50] Origen in his "Homilies on Joshua" 2.1 (*SC* 71.118-19) probably alludes to this "small book" (*libellus*), in which "two Moseses were seen: one alive in the spirit, and another dead in the body." In his "Stromata" 6.15.132 (GCS 52.498), Clement of Alexandria also relates that Joshua saw Moses in a twofold way: taken up, yet also thought to be buried in the ravines of mountains.

[51] Cf. R. H. Charles, "The Assumption of Moses," in *APOT* 2.407-24, especially 407-08, with notes 1-2. He bases this on his own edition, *The Assumption of Moses* (London: Black, 1897). See also Ginzberg, *Legends* 6.159-60, n. 946; the extensive analysis in Richard Baukham, *Jude, 2 Peter* (WBC 50; Waco, TX: Word Books,

An early example of Moses' rebuking the Angel of Death (= Satan) at the end of his life is found in the Tannaitic midrash *Sifre* Niṣṣabim 305 on Deut 31:14, which here comments on Num 27:18.[52] Shortly before Moses' death

> the Holy One, blessed be He, said to the Angel of Death: "Go and fetch me the soul of Moses." The Angel went and stood before Moses and said to him: "Moses, give me your soul." Moses replied, "You do not even have the right to be in the place where I dwell, and yet you dare to say to me: 'Give me your soul'?" Moses thus *rebuked* him, and the Angel left reprimanded.[53]

The phrase "rebuked him" here is the Hebrew גער בו , which also derives from Judaic tradition on Zech 3:2.

The above two passages, Jude 9 perhaps from the early second century CE, and the Tannaitic *Sifre* 305, show that there were early Judaic traditions on Michael's rebuking the devil and Moses' rebuking the Angel of Death in connection with the Israelite leader's imminent death. Other sources on the death of Moses, although now in rabbinic works which took their final form much later, contain variants of the same motif of Moses' rebuking the Angel of Death / Sammael / Satan, as well as other motifs and exact expressions which are of direct relevance to Jesus' rebuking Peter as Satan in Mark 8:32-33 and Matt 16:22-23.

According to *b. Meg.* 31a, in the early Palestinian triennial lectionary system Deuteronomy 33-34, the end of the Torah, were read on the day following the last day of the festival Sukkoth (Tabernacles).[54] This corresponded to the first Sabbath of Adar in the third year cycle of readings, which agrees with the traditional dating of Moses' death as the

---

1983) 47-48, 62, and 65-76: "Excursus: The Background and Source of Jude 9"; John Muddiman, "The Assumption of Moses and the Epistle of Jude," in *Moses in Biblical and Extra-Biblical Tradition*, ed. Graupner and Wolter, 169-80; and J. Priest on the *Testament of Moses* in *OTP* 1.919-25, where he maintains this writing is Palestinian, originally Hebrew, and in its final form from the first century CE (920-21).
[52] Finkelstein 326; Hammer 296, who on p. 488, n. 1, explains the relevance of the Numbers text at this point.
[53] I modify Hammer's translation slightly. "Reprimanded" is בנזיפה , which can also mean "angrily"; see Jastrow 891 on נְזִיפָה : "anger, rebuke."
[54] Soncino 189.

7th of Adar.[55] According to the third generation Palestinian Amora R. Isaac (II, Nappaḥa),[56] "a feast should be held after completing [the reading of] the Torah."[57] While it is unclear exactly when Simḥat (the "joy" of the) Torah later became a special festival by itself, such feasting / celebrating certainly contributed to its development. It was probably at this later stage that Joshua 1 became the haftarah or reading from the (former) prophets for this day.[58]

The midrash *Petirat Mosheh* (פטירת משה) or "Death of Moses"[59] was most probably composed for the occasion of Simḥat Torah, with the readings Deuteronomy 33-34 and Joshua 1.[60] It is now available primarily in four variants: 1) *Deut. Rab.* Ve'zot ha-Berakhah 11/5-10, especially 5 and 10.[61] 2) Jellinek, "Petirat Mosheh" A.[62] 3) "Petirat Mosheh" in the Parma MS.[63] 4) *Tanḥuma* Va'ethanan 6.[64]

---

[55] Cf. the articles "Triennial Cycle" by Joseph Jacobs in *JE* (1905/25) 12.257 ("the 7th of Adar, when the account of the death of Moses in Deut. xxxiv. was read") and the inserted two-page chart showing Deut 33:1 (to 34:12) for the first Sabbath in Adar in the third year; "Triennial Cycle" in *EJ* (1971) 15.1388 for Deut 33:1 on the first Sabbath in Adar and 34:1(-12) for the second Sabbath in Adar; "Triennial Cycle" in *EJ* (2007) 20.140-42, with Deut 34:1 on the second Sabbath of Adar (p. 142), which also states: "Deuteronomy 34, on the death of Moses, always read at the beginning of Adar [third year], tallies with the tradition that Moses died on the 7th of Adar"); "Simḥat Torah" by Schulim Ochser in *JE* (1905) 11.364-65; the same by Aaron Rothkoff in *EJ* (1971) 14.1571; and William Braude and Israel Kapstein, *Pesikta de-Rab Kahana* 445, n. 1, on the reading Deut 33:1(-34:12): "The reading of Deut. 33:1ff., which in the Land of Israel marked the completion of the triennial cycle, was an occasion for a Simḥat Torah, observed triennially." They call attention to an article by Ezra Fleischer on this topic. Their expression "a" Simḥat Torah should be noted. For Moses' death on the 7th of Adar, see for example the official chronography of early Judaism, *Seder 'Olam* 10 (Guggenheimer 100-01).

[56] *Introduction* 98.

[57] Cf. *Eccl. Rab.* 1:1 § 1 on 1 Kgs 3:15, where Solomon "provided a feast for all his servants" (Soncino 8.2).

[58] Cf. the articles in n. 55.

[59] The noun פְּטִירָה means departure, dismissal, but especially "departure from the world, death" (Jastrow 1155).

[60] Cf. Adolf Jellinek, *Bet ha-Midrasch* 1.XXI.

[61] Vilna 235-40 or 119a-120b; I employ the Mirkin edition in 11.152-60, English in Soncino 7.176-88.

[62] In his *Bet ha-Midrasch* 1.113-29; a second, abbreviated version (B), is found in 6.75-78. A German translation is given by August Wünsche in his *Aus Israels Lehrhallen* 1.134-62, with the variants from B in the notes. Rella Kushlevsky in *Moses and the Angel of Death* translates it on pp. 195-223. Her book itself was

In *Deut. Rab.* 11/5 R. Meir, a third generation Tanna,[65] speaks of the Angel of Death and Moses.[66] In 11/10 it is instead "Sammael, the wicked angel, the chief of all the accusing angels," who tries to take Moses' soul away.[67] This points to two different traditions which were placed side by side when this verse of the midrash on Moses' death was compiled. In addition, in 11/10 it is first stated: "there remained to Moses only one hour." Then later, "the moment of Moses' death arrived." Finally, "at the end of a moment" a heavenly voice declares that "the end, the time of your death has come."[68] This final part of a countdown only makes sense as an excerpt from the fuller form of the midrash, which moves consistently from five hours left to Moses to four, to three, to two, to one, to one-half, to a moment and a half, to half a moment, and finally to the last half moment, when "The last hour has come to an end," and God takes Moses' soul.[69] The above two examples show the seams and traditions from various sources which are also apparent in the *Deuteronomy Rabbah* version of the "Petirat Mosheh" midrash.

At this point I would like to point out four motifs and exact expressions, still found in the midrash on Moses' death, which (in an earlier form) were incorporated by the Palestinian Jewish Christian author of the unit Mark 8:32-33, and later by Matthew in 16:16-19.

As pointed out above, the Tannaitic midrash *Sifre* Niṣṣibim 305 on Deut 31:14 has Moses "rebuke" (נער) the Angel of Death when he tries to take his soul. This motif and verb are also found in *'Avot R. Nat.* A 12[70] and *'Avot R. Nat.* B 25.[71] Finally, in "Petirat Mosheh," Jellinek A, at

---

translated into English from modern Hebrew. She believes *Deut. Rab.* 11/10 "probably preceded the extended version typified by Jellinek-A" (p. 30, n. 2).

[63] Not available to me; Kushelevsky translates it in *Moses* 261-72. On p. 273, n. 1, she labels it Parma MS 327/37ff. 135b-138a. It is dated 1289 CE; she believes this version probably originated between the 11th and the 13th centuries. Strack and Stemberger in *Introduction* 362 speak of the various recensions as "to be dated between the seventh and the tenth or eleventh century."

[64] Eshkol 855-60. Kushelevsky also translates this short, homiletical version in *Moses* 251-58.

[65] *Introduction* 84.

[66] Mirkin 11.152; Soncino 7.176.

[67] Mirkin 11.157; Soncino 7.183.

[68] Mirkin 11.157, 158 and 159; Soncino 7.183, 184 and 186.

[69] Jellinek A in Kushelevsky, *Moses* 212-21.

[70] Schechter 50; Goldin 65.

[71] Schechter 51; Saldarini 149-50. The verb employed here is זעף (Jastrow 892: to be angry, *to rebuke*, to chide).

Sammael's final attempt to take Moses' soul, the latter struck him "and rebuked him with a rebuke (וגער בו בגערה)," so that Sammael then fled.[72]

Moses' rebuke of the Angel of Death / Sammael (= Satan) at the end of his life provides the basic background for Jesus' "rebuking" Peter as Satan. This is corroborated in the following.

B. 2 Moses' Words to the Angel of Death / Sammael: "Get away / depart from here!"

In *Deut. Rab.* Ve'zot ha-Berakhah 11/5 on "before his death" in Deut 33:1, the third generation Tanna R. Meir states that "The Angel of Death came to Moses and said to him: 'God has sent me to you, for you are to depart this life today.' Moses replied: 'Go away hence, for I desire to praise God' [by now blessing the twelve tribes in Deuteronomy 33]."[73] The antiquated English translation "Go away hence" is the Hebrew לֵךְ מִכָּאן , literally "Go [away] / depart from here!" It is also found as such in *Tanḥuma* Ve'zot ha-Berakhah 3 on the same verse.[74] In *Deut. Rab.* 11/10 a fuller form of Moses' words to Sammael is given: "'Get away, wicked one, from here!' You must not speak thus. 'Go, flee before me!' I will not surrender my soul to you."[75] The first sentence, "Get away, wicked one, from here!" is the Hebrew לֵךְ רָשָׁע מִכָּאן , and the phrase "Go away, flee before me!" is לֵךְ בְּרַח מִלְּפָנָי .

This is the background of Jesus' words to Peter in Mark 8:33 and Matt 16:23, "Get behind me, Satan!" (Ὕπαγε ὀπίσω μου, Σατανᾶ), which can also mean "Get out of my sight!"[76] In the *Deut. Rab.* 11/10 account, "Get away...from here" and "Go away, flee before me" are parallel. The Palestinian Jewish Christian who first composed the episode of Mark 8:32-33 purposely changed "from here," explained here as "'from before'

---

[72] Jellinek, *Bet ha-Midrasch* 1.128; Wünsche, *Aus Israels Lehrhallen* 1.160; Kushelevsky, *Moses* 221.
[73] Mirkin 11.152; Soncino 7.176.
[74] Eshkol 945.
[75] Mirkin 11.159; Soncino 7.186. Cf. the similar "Wicked one, flee before me!" in *Petirat Mosheh*, Jellinek A (*Bet ha-Midrasch* 1.128; Wünsche, *Aus Israels Lehrhallen* 1.159; Kushelevsky 220). After the episode just related from *Deut. Rab.* 11/10, Sammael returned and "placed himself at the side of Moses." This is similar to Peter's being "beside" Jesus when he rebukes him, whereupon Jesus in turn rebukes Peter by telling him to get "behind" him.
[76] Cf. BAGD 575 on ὀπίσω , 2.a.α .

me" (מלפני), to "behind me." Peter as Satan, the great opponent / enticer, should distance himself not only in thought, but also in space from opposing the necessity of Jesus' suffering and being killed in Jerusalem. He should not "set his mind...on human things" (v 33).[77]

B. 3 The Things of God and the Things of Man

In *Deut. Rab.* Ve'zot ha-Berakhah 11/5, Moses first struggles with the Angel of Death and then resigns himself to God's will that he must die. R. Abin, a fourth generation Palestinian Amora,[78] states at this point: "When Moses departed this world, 'the earthly beings' praised him, saying: 'Moses charged us with the law, as a possession for the assembly of Jacob' (Deut 33:4). 'The heavenly beings' also praised him, saying: 'he executed the justice of the Lord' (v 21). And God praised him, [saying]: 'Never since has there arisen a prophet in Israel like Moses' (34:10)."[79]

The Hebrew for "the earthly beings" here is הַתַּחְתּוֹנִים , from תַּחְתּוֹן , meaning "nethermost, lower." With the definite article, as here, it especially means "the lower creatures, *earthly things*, opposite to העליונים , the heavenly things."[80] Here in *Deut. Rab.* 11/5 the expression means mortals, humans. It is they who praise Moses just before his death with Deut 33:4. The phrase "the heavenly beings" is הָעֶלְיוֹנִים , from עֶלְיוֹן : uppermost, highest, most high. The plural, as here, especially means "heavenly creatures, angels,"[81] meant here. The angels praise Moses just before his death with the words of Deut 33:21. Yet the Hebrew can also signify "heavenly things."[82]

I suggest that the Palestinian Jewish Christian who first composed the episode of Mark 8:32-33 derived his imagery of τὰ τοῦ θεοῦ ("the things of God," "heavenly things"), and τὰ τῶν ἀνθρώπων ("the things of men," "earthly things"), from the above two Hebrew terms. They are still

---

[77] If the original of Jesus' "turning" in v 33, beginning, was "he turned 'behind him'" (אַחֲרָיו [cf. Delitzsch's Hebrew New Testament 78] or its Aramaic equivalent), there was a wordplay here with two usages of אַחֵר , "back of" (Jastrow 41 and BDB 29,2.a).

[78] *Introduction* 103.

[79] Mirkin 11.153; Soncino 7.177. The parallel in *Tanḥuma* Ve'zot ha-Berakhah 3 (Eshkol 946) has R. Abba as the speaker, perhaps R. Abba II, a third generation Palestinian Amora (*Introduction* 99).

[80] Jastrow 1662.

[81] Jastrow 1083.

[82] *Ibid.*

found in the late saying of R. Abin quoted from the midrash on the death of Moses just after Moses tells the Angel of Death, "Go away from here!" (see section 2. above). The Greek τὰ τῶν ἀνθρώπων can easily derive from התחתונים , "earthly things," "the things of men." The Greek τὰ τοῦ θεοῦ can also derive from העליונים , understood as "heavenly things." When a bilingual Jewish Christian translated this, he understood it as דִּבְרֵי הָעֶלְיוֹן : "the things of the Most High [God],"[83] and thus correctly rendered it as τὰ τοῦ θεοῦ .

Peter should not "set his mind on"[84] the normal human view of a Messiah who would not suffer or even be killed. Rather, he should learn to accept the divine necessity of the Messiah Jesus' suffering and death (δεῖ in Mark 8:31), just as Moses finally resigned himself at this point to the necessity of his own death in the midrash on the Death of Moses.[85]

B. 4 Stumbling, and "Heaven Forbid!"

The Evangelist Matthew employed in 16:22-23 the words of his source, Mark 8:32-33, almost completely. Yet he made two important additions. The first is an explanation in v 22 of how Peter rebuked Jesus. He said to him: "Heaven forbid, Lord! This must never happen to you!"[86] This is the Greek: "Ἵλεώς σοι, κύριε· οὐ μὴ ἔσται σοι τοῦτο . The second phrase merely spells out the first. Except for Heb 8:12, this is the only occurrence of "ἵλεως in the NT.[87] It is the Attic and later adverbial form of "ἵλαος , meaning in regard to the gods "propitious," "gracious."[88] Here it means *"May God be gracious to you, Lord,* i.e. may God in his mercy spare you this, *God forbid!"*[89]

---

[83] Cf. BDB 751 on this designation of God.

[84] Cf. BAGD 866 on φρονέω , 2.

[85] Cf. Moses' remarks in *Deut. Rab.* 11/5 when the Angel of Death comes to him a third time: "Seeing that this is from God, I must now resign myself to God's will, as it is said: 'The Rock, His work is perfect' (Deut 32:4)" - Mirkin 11.152; Soncino 7.176 (see also 11/10 on p. 184).

[86] The NRSV has *"God* forbid it, Lord!" Yet no first-century Jew would have openly used the term "God." Rather, a substitute would have been employed, or it would have been avoided, as I now propose. On the second addition, "stumbling," see below.

[87] In Heb 8:12 it has the meaning of being "merciful," different from Matt 16:22.

[88] LSJ 827.

[89] BAGD 376.

As Paul Billerbeck correctly pointed out over eighty years ago,[90] the equivalent in rabbinic Hebrew is חַס וְשָׁלוֹם . The Hebrew חַס means "sparing," "forbearance," and is only used in the above expression: "forbearance and peace!" "God forfend!" "Don't say that!"[91] Examples of the phrase are already found in the *Mishnah*[92] and the *Tosefta*.[93] Occurrences in connection with Moses' imminent death, however, are most important in regard to Matt 16:22.[94]

Midr. Pss. 5/10 on Ps 5:11 (Eng. 10) asks what Moses, the master of the prophets, said at the end of his praising (God). He spoke Deut 32:4, "The Rock, His work is perfect." "He said this lest men should declare that divine justice was too severe with him because he was not allowed to enter the Land of Israel. [Moses stated:] 'Heaven forbid (חס ושלום)! There is no partiality in the sight of God. The Rock, His work is perfect.'"[95] Here the first redeemer of Israel defends God's decision that he die before entering the Land of Israel with the expression "Heaven forbid!," connected to Deut 32:4.

The latter verse from Deuteronomy also plays an important role in the similar text *Midr. Pss.* 92/4 on Ps 92:16 (Eng. 15), "To declare that the Lord is upright, my Rock, in whom there is no unrighteousness." Moses was asked: "Who prevented you from entering the Land [of Israel]?" He replied to them: "I prevented it." They then asked him: "Was it not the Holy One, blessed be He, who did this to you?" He answered them: "Heaven forbid! (חס ושלום) Even if one should see the Holy One, blessed be He, appear to justify the wicked man and condemn the righteous man, 'The Rock, His work is perfect, and all His ways are just. A faithful God without deceit, just and upright is He' (Deut 32:4)."[96]

---

[90] Cf. Str-B 1.748. See also Adolf Schlatter, *Der Evangelist Matthäus* (Stuttgart: Calwer, 1929) 516-17.

[91] Jastrow 485. The Aramaic חס ל' means the same.

[92] Cf. *m. 'Ed.* 5:6 (Albeck 4.307; Danby 432; Neusner 654), and *m. Yad.* 3:5 (Albeck 6.481; Danby 782; Neusner 1127).

[93] Cf. *t. Ber.* 6:17 (Lieberman, *Zera'im* 38; Neusner 1.40), and *t. Soṭah* 6:6 and 7 (Zuckermandel -Liebermann 304; Neusner 3.173).

[94] The phrase is also connected to "rebuking" in *Eliyyahu Rabbah* 17 (Friedmann 88; Braude and Kapstein 234), with a parallel in *Eliyyahu Zuṭa* 7 (Friedmann 184; Braude and Kapstein 433).

[95] Buber 56; Braude 1.90, which I modify.

[96] Buber 412; I modify Braude 2.122-23, also citing the entire verse. Cf. also *Deut. Rab.* Ve'zot ha-Berakhah 11/10 for Moses' only citing Deut 32:4 when he realizes he must die (Mirkin 11.157-58; Soncino 7.184). It is also employed of submission to the divine judgment at the time of death in *b. 'Avodah Zarah* 18a (Soncino 91),

Here too Moses in connection with his imminent death accepts and defends as just God's decision not to allow him to enter the Land of Israel. To do so, he employs the phrase "Heaven forbid!" and Deut 32:4.

Deut 32:4 also plays an important role in *Deut. Rab.* Ve'zot ha-Berakhah 11/5 on Deut 33:1, "before his death." As pointed out above, the early Tanna R. Meir here first relates how Moses succeeded in blessing the twelve tribes in Deuteronomy 33 by seizing the Angel of Death and telling him: "Get away from here!" However, when the latter returned a third and final time, Moses stated: "Seeing that this is from God, I must now resign myself to God's will, as it is said: 'The Rock, His work is perfect' (Deut 32:4)."[97]

The continuation of this midrash follows in the name of R. Isaac, probably II, a third generation Palestinian Amora.[98] "The soul of Moses struggled to go forth, and Moses conversed with it, saying: 'My soul, do you perhaps think that the Angel of Death is seeking to gain dominion over you?' It replied to him: 'The Holy One, blessed be He, will [certainly] not do so!' [for it is said:] 'For You have delivered my soul from Death' (Ps 116:8).[99] [Moses continued:] 'Perhaps you have seen Israel weeping [because of my imminent death] and you have wept with them?' It replied to him: 'my eyes from tears' (*ibid.*). Moses said to it: 'Do you think then that they have attempted to thrust you into Gehenna?' It answered him: 'my feet from stumbling' (*ibid.*). He said to it: 'And where are you destined to go?' It replied to him: 'I will walk before the Lord in the land of the living' (v 9). When Moses heard [it speak] thus, he gave it permission [to leave] and said to it: 'Return, O my soul, to your rest, for the Lord has dealt bountifully with you' (v 7)."[100]

The Hebrew of the phrase, God "will [certainly] not do so!" above is לֹא יַעֲשֶׂה ... כֵּן . The Soncino translator, J. Rabbinowitz, correctly inserted "surely" at this point, for which I have "certainly." Its meaning is the same as the expression חַס וְשָׁלוֹם , "Heaven forbid!" *Midrash Tannaim* on Deut 34:5, identical with *Midrash Haggadol* on the same verse, relates the above narrative anonymously. When Moses' soul cites Ps 116:8 twice and

---

with parallels in *Sifre* Ha'azinu 307 on Deut 32:4 (Finkelstein 346; Hammer 312) and *Semaḥoth* 8:11, 47b (*Minor Tractates* 367-68).

[97] Mirkin 11.152; Soncino 7.176.

[98] *Introduction* 98.

[99] "Death" is thought of here as the (Angel of) Death.

[100] Mirkin 11.152-53; I modify Soncino in 7.176-77.

v 9 once, the midrash prefaces each quotation, however, with "Heaven forbid!"[101]

When Moses asks his soul in *Deut. Rab.* 11/5: "Do you think then that they have attempted to thrust you into Gehenna?"[102] the word for "thrust" is דָחוּ , from דחי , דחה , "to push away, thrust."[103] It is a wordplay with the term "stumbling" from Ps 116:8 cited just afterwards: דֶּחִי .[104] That is, "stumbling" occurs together with "Heaven forbid!" in Judaic tradition on Moses' imminent death, when he just before tells the Angel of Death (= Satan): "Get away from here!" It is exactly this combination of terms which occurs in Matt 16:22-23: Ἵλεώς σοι, Ὕπαγε ὀπίσω μου , and σκάνδαλον.

The latter Greek noun means "*stumbling-block, offence, scandal.*"[105] Peter (Πέτρος), whom Jesus had just labeled the "stone / rock" (πέτρα) upon which he will build his church, suddenly in v 23 becomes Satan, a "stumbling block" to Jesus, a stone / rock which could cause him to stumble. I suggest that the bilingual Palestinian or Syrian Jewish Christian Matthew,[106] who may even have been a converted scribe (13:52), was aware of an early form of the midrash on Moses' death, including the association of "Heaven forbid!" and "stumbling" (דֶּחִי). Because this Hebrew term was so rare, and was associated a number of

---

[101] Hoffmann 225 and Fisch 784, respectively.
[102] *Midrash Tannaim* and *Midrash Haggadol* on Deut 34:5 have instead: "from the Garden of Eden" (= Paradise). Cf. the previous note.
[103] Jastrow 291 and BDB 190-91.
[104] Cf. BDB 191. It occurs only here (= Ps 56:14) and is not found in rabbinic Hebrew.
[105] LSJ 1604. BAGD 753 do not even mention the first translation at this point, rendering here: "you are tempting me to sin." See also Gustav Stählin, art. σκάνδαλον, σκανδαλίζω in *TDNT* 7.339-58, especially p. 348.
[106] On his bilingualism, cf. for example Matt 1:21, where a wordplay between "Jesus" and "save" is only possible in Hebrew: יֵשׁוּעַ and the hiphil of יָשַׁע . See also W. D. Davies and Dale Allison, Jr., *The Gospel According to Saint Matthew* (Edinburgh: T & T Clark, 1988) 1.26,80,262 and 267, as well as my own studies "The Magi at the Birth of Cyrus, and the Magi at Jesus' Birth in Matt 2:1-12" in *New Perspectives on Ancient Judaism* 2, ed. Jacob Neusner et al. (Howard C. Kee Festschrift; Lanham, MD: University Press of America, 1987) 99-114; Peter's sinking in the Sea of Galilee in Matt 14:28-31 in "*Caught in the Act,*" *Walking on the Sea, and the Release of Barabbas Revisited* (SFSHJ 157; Atlanta: Scholars Press, 1998) 98-110; and "An Earthquake and Saints Rising from the Dead" (Matt 27:51b-53) in *Samuel, Saul and Jesus. Three Early Palestinian Jewish Christian Gospel Haggadoth* (USFSHJ 105; Atlanta: Scholars Press, 1994) 116-33.

times in the midrash with Deut 32:4's צוּר, "rock," "stone," he thought of
the expression צוּר מִכְשׁוֹל in Isa 8:14, "rock / stone" of "stumbling."[107]
Aquila, Symmachus and Theodotion all translate מִכְשׁוֹל here as
σκάνδαλον , which Matthew appropriated. In addition, *Targ.* Isa 8:14 has
כֵּיף for צוּר,[108] which also enabled him to think of Peter, whose
Aramaic name was כֵּיפָא , in Greek Κηφᾶς , Cephas.

The Jewish Christian evangelist Matthew thus recognized the episode
he found in Mark 8:32-33 as derived from the midrash on the death of
Moses. He then supplemented it with other expressions from the same
midrash.[109]

C. *The Question of Historicity*

W. D. Davies and Dale Allison, Jr. state in regard to Matt 16:21-23 (and
Mark 8:32-33) that they are impressed along with others "by the
difficulty of imagining who in the early church would have been so bold
as to create the allegedly pure fiction - which Luke felt moved to excise -
that Jesus called Peter Satan."[110]   In sections A. and B. above I have
argued that the scene was indeed first composed by a Semitic-speaking
Palestinian Jewish Christian who crafted it in light of widely-known
Judaic traditions (now only available in Hebrew) on the imminent death
of Israel's first redeemer, Moses. It was Moses' "rebuking" the Angel of
Death / Sammael / Satan, coupled with the expressions "Get away from
here!" and "earthly things" and "heavenly things," together with Moses'
finally resigning himself to the necessity of his death, which served him
as a "quarry" for the building stones found in his short narrative. The
bilingual evangelist Matthew, recognizing the midrash on Moses' death
as the background of the episode, then added two more expressions
from that midrash: "Heaven forbid!" and a "stumbling block."

As I will point out in chapter IV. below on the nature of "haggadah,"
the Palestinian Jewish Christian creation of such narratives in light of
Jewish heroes was customary, as other Jews had already been doing for

---

[107] Association through the same word was a legitimate exegetical method,
labeled *gezerah shawah*. Cf. *Introduction* 21.
[108] Stenning 28-29.
[109] There is no reason to think he received them from tradition and incorporated
them here.
[110] *The Gospel According to Saint Matthew*, II.655.

centuries. Two examples are Mary's virginal conception of Jesus[111] and the episode of the twelve-year-old Jesus in the Temple.[112] Such narratives were not created to present historical facts, but often to glorify a person, here Jesus: already at his birth he was someone very special, and already at the age of twelve he was a child prodigy, like twelve-year-old Samuel in Judaic tradition.

Yet the haggadic episode of Mark 8:32-33 and Matt 16:22-23 was not intended to glorify Jesus. Instead, it is an explanation in narrative form of why Jesus *must* (δεῖ) suffer and be killed in Jerusalem (Mark 8:31 and Matt 16:21), the first "passion prediction," ending with the "divine things" of 8:33. The older I get (and I have dealt with these texts for over forty years), the more I have come to believe that Jesus himself anticipated his suffering as a prophet, and perhaps even his being killed as such in Jerusalem, the fate of a number of his prophetic predecessors.[113] His voluntary journey to the capital, coupled with the so-called "cleansing of the Temple,"[114] and with the Temple authorities' shortly thereafter becoming thoroughly infuriated through his narrating the parable of the Wicked Tenants against them,[115] are concrete indications to me that Jesus intentionally provoked the spiritual leadership of his own nation so severely in order that they would repent and with the people prepare themselves for the kingdom of God, already now breaking in through his own activity. The prophet from Nazareth was well aware of the fate of his "predecessor," the prophet John the Baptist. It is thus possible that he reckoned not only with suffering in Jerusalem, bur also with his own death. This, in turn, makes it quite plausible that Jesus conveyed such thoughts to his disciples just before they started on the fateful journey to Jerusalem.

---

[111] Cf. my *Matthew 1-2 and the Virginal Conception in Light of Palestinian and Hellenistic Judaic Traditions on the Birth of Israel's First Redeemer, Moses.*

[112] Cf. "The Child Jesus in the Temple (Luke 2:41-51a), and Judaic Traditions on the Child Samuel in the Temple (1 Samuel 1-3)" in *Samuel, Saul and Jesus* 1-64.

[113] Cf. for example Zechariah b. Jehoiada in 2 Chron 24:21; Uriah b. Shemiah in Jer 26:23; and Isaiah in the "Martyrdom of Isaiah" 5 (*OTP* 2.163-64).

[114] Cf. Mark 11:15-19, especially v 18. The chief priests and scribes' then looking for a way to kill Jesus should be compared to 8:31, where the elders (also part of the Sanhedrin) are added.

[115] Cf. especially Mark 12:12, and "The Parable of the Wicked Tenants (Mark 12:1-9), The Song of the Vineyard (Isa 5:1-7), The Song at the Sea (Exod 15:1-18), and The Martyrdom of Isaiah" in my *The Wicked Tenants and Gethsemane*, 1-64.

The first "passion prediction" of Mark 8:31 thus may well have an historical core.[116] The disciples' reaction to it was certainly not only astonishment, but also incredulity. If they secretly or even openly now considered Jesus to be the long-awaited Messianic King, whose task was thought by almost all first-century Jews to rule politically and militarily over Israel, suffering and death would have been thoroughly incompatible with that idea. The disciples probably strongly objected to it over against Jesus, and Peter could very well have represented them in doing so. However, this would have been without the very harsh language of Jesus in Mark 8:33, a "rebuke" with "Get behind me, Satan!" An early Palestinian Jewish Christian later filled out this scene, employing materials from the early midrash on the imminent death of Israel's first redeemer, Moses, in order to do so.[117] His narrative was thus no "pure fiction," but based on core materials available to him, probably still from some of Jesus' original disciples.[118] It is this narrative, later translated into Greek, which was then appropriated by the first evangelist, Mark.

I. 3   Efforts to Kill Jesus, and Efforts to Kill Moses

A.   *Jesus*

Except for Herod the Great's non-historical attempt to murder the infant Jesus in Matt 2:1-12, based on Pharaoh's attempt to kill the newborn redeemer of the Israelites, Moses, in Egypt in Exod 1:15 -

---

[116] As pointed out above, however, it was without rising again after three days, a later, post-Resurrection addition on the part of the first Jewish Christians.

[117] Interestingly, Philo in *Mos.* 2.291 has Moses at the end of his life "prophesy with discernment" "the story of his own death," including telling "ere the end how the end came." This is an attempt to resolve the strange fact that Moses describes his own death and burial in Deut 34:5-12, also a conundrum for the early rabbis. See for example the Tannaitic *Sifre* Ve'zot ha-Berakhah 357 on Deut 34:5 (Finkelstein 427; Hammer 380-81), and *b. B. Bathra* 15a (Soncino 72). Judaic tradition on the first redeemer of Israel, Moses, who predicted his own death, thus may also in part have influenced the prediction of the death of the final redeemer of Israel, the Messiah Jesus.

[118] It is very difficult to decide whether Mark 8:31-33 originally also belonged to vv 27-30. Verse 31 suffices to explain a reaction such as found in vv 32-33, yet it also clarifies the function of a Messiah from v 29. The basis of the unit 8:27-30 may historically have occurred earlier, and vv 31-33 may then have been later attached to it in early Christian tradition before reaching Mark. On this difficulty, cf. also Davies and Allison, Jr., *The Gospel According to Saint Matthew*, II.654.

2:10;[119] the non-historical attempt of the inhabitants of Nazareth to hurl Jesus off a cliff to his death in Luke 4:29;[120] and some well-meaning Pharisees warning Jesus to "Get away from here, for Herod [Antipas] wants to kill you" (only in Luke 13:31), all efforts to kill Jesus related in the Synoptic Gospels occur only at the end of his public ministry.

Mark 11:18 par. states that after Jesus "cleansed" the Jerusalem Temple, "when the chief priests and the scribes heard it, they kept looking for a way to kill him...." After the prophet from Nazareth told the parable of the wicked tenants within the Temple precincts (Mark 12:1-9), the chief priests, scribes and elders (11:27) "realized that he had told this parable against them [and] wanted to arrest him..." (12:12).[121] Finally, Mark 14:1 par. states regarding Jesus that "The chief priests and the scribes were looking for a way to arrest him by stealth and kill him...." The result was his arrest in Gethsemane (Mark 14:43-50 par.).

The Gospel of John differs in this respect from the Synoptics by placing efforts to kill Jesus earlier in the narrative: 5:16,18; 7:1,19,25,30,32,44-45; 8:40; and 10:39. Efforts to stone him are also related in 8:59; 10:31-33; and 11:8.[122] Yet the Evangelist knew that the major efforts to kill Jesus occurred at the end of his ministry and stated after Jesus' raising Lazarus from the dead near Jerusalem: "So from that day on they planned to put him to death" (11:53; cf. 57). Jesus' entry into Jerusalem then follows in 12:12-15, and his arrest in Gethsemane in 18:1-12.

I suggest that the motif of attempting to kill Jesus, also by stoning, was *in part* influenced by attempts to kill Moses, which included stoning.

B. Moses

Numerous efforts to kill the first redeemer of Israel, Moses, are recorded both in the Bible and in Judaic tradition.

---

[119] See most recently my *Matthew 1-2 and the Virginal Conception in Light of Palestinian and Hellenistic Traditions on the Birth of Israel's First Redeemer, Moses* 19-29.

[120] Cf. my "Catchword Connections and Day of Atonement Imagery in Luke 4:16-30" in *My Name Is "Legion." Palestinian Judaic Traditions in Mark 5:1-20 and Other Gospel Texts* 101-53.

[121] Cf. my *The Wicked Tenants and Gethsemane* 1-64.

[122] The Q saying in Luke 13:34 // Matt 23:37 may be related: "Jerusalem, Jerusalem, the city that kills the prophets and *stones* those who are sent to it," although Jesus does not directly relate the latter to himself. Killing him as a prophet was more appropriate in his case.

Exod 1:1-15 - 2:10 describes Pharaoh's attempt to kill all male Hebrew children in Egypt, and the miraculous escape of the infant Moses (see A. above on Matt 2:1-12, partially based on this). After Moses as an adult killed an Egyptian who was beating a Hebrew, for which he is exonerated in Judaic tradition, Pharaoh "heard of it (and) sought to kill Moses" (Exod 2:15). *Cant. Rab.* 7:5 § 1 states regarding Moses at this point: "he was brought to trial on that same day, and he was condemned to be beheaded," yet he miraculously escaped.[123]

In Exod 10:28, after the ninth plague, Pharaoh tells Moses: "Get away from me! Take care that you do not see my face again, for on the day you see my face you shall die!" *Targum Neofiti 1* interprets at this point: "Take heed that my anger be not kindled against you and I deliver you into the hands of the people who sought your life and they kill you."[124] The *Fragment Targum* in both MSS "P" and "V"[125] and *Targum Pseudo-Jonathan*[126] are very similar here, showing that this was a common Palestinian tradition. Josephus in *Ant.* 2.310 has Pharaoh threaten to "behead" Moses here, another early variant.

When on their wilderness journey the Israelites camp at Rephidim and there is no water, the people not only quarrel with, and complain against, Moses. He cries out to the Lord: "They are almost ready to stone me" (Exod 17:4). The Tannaitic midrash *Mekilta de-Rabbi Ishmael* Vayassaʿ 7 on this verse has Moses say before God: "Between You and them I am being killed. You tell me: Do not get angry with them, for You say to me, 'Carry them in your bosom' (Num 11:12), yet they wish to kill me."[127] *Exod. Rab.* Beshallaḥ 26/2 also has Moses say in regard to Exod 17:4, "Lord of the Universe! Let me know whether they will kill me or not!"[128]

The Israelites later camped at Kadesh in the wilderness, and almost all the men sent to spy out the land of Israel severely warned against trying to take it by force (Num 13:25-33). The Israelites again complained against Moses and Aaron, preferring to return to Egypt. The latter two then "fell on their faces before all the assembly of the congregation of the Israelites" (14:5), and Joshua and Caleb, included among the spies (13:6-

---

123 Cf. Donsqi 157; Soncino 9.285. A similar narrative is related in *Deut. Rab.* Vaʾethanan 2/29 on Deut 4:41 (Mirkin 11.47; Soncino 7.58). See also Ginzberg, *Legends* 2.279-82, with the sources on the incident cited in notes 73-76 at 5.405-06.
124 Díez Macho 2.63; McNamara 44.
125 Klein 1.72 and 166; English in 2.37 and 125.
126 Rieder 1.96; English in Maher 187-88, with n. 28 calling attention to Mark 9:31. The verb for "deliver" is מסר (Jastrow 810-11).
127 I slightly modify the translation in Lauterbach 2.130-31.
128 Mirkin 5.288; I modify the Soncino translation in 3.318.

7), pleaded with the people not to rebel. Nevertheless, "the whole congregation said to stone them with stones" (14:10).[129] *Num. Rab.* Shelach Lecha 16/21 asks who is meant by "them" in the latter verse. It states: "Moses and Aaron."[130] Josephus in *Ant.* 3.307 also notes at this point that it was Moses and Aaron whom the people intended to stone.

Finally, in Deut 32:49 the Lord addresses Moses at the very end of his life: "Ascend this mountain of the Abarim, Mount Nebo...." Verse 50 continues: "You shall die there on the mountain that you ascend and shall be gathered to your kin...." *Targum Pseudo-Jonathan* on the latter verse relates that Moses now asks God in prayer:

> Master of the World, I beg of You, let me not be compared to a man who has an only son who was taken captive. He went to redeem him with much money; he taught him wisdom and skill; he betrothed a woman to him; put up for him a kingly dining hall, built him a marriage house, prepared for him a marriage bed on which he wreathed for him a canopy. He invited honored friends for him, baked his bread, prepared his feast, mixed his wine. When (the moment) arrived for his son to rejoice with his wife, his marriage friends sought to begin the meal; that man was required at the court, before the king, and was condemned to death, and they did not want to postpone it (his execution), so that he might see the enjoyment of his son. So I have worked for this people! I brought them out from Egypt by Your Memra, I taught them Your Law, I built for them a Tent for Your Name. When the time to cross the Jordan to possess the land arrived, I am condemned to death. Would that it be satisfactory before You, suspend (the sentence) for me that I may cross the Jordan and see the good of Israel; and after this, I shall die.[131]

Here Israel is compared to an only son, taken captive in Egypt. His "father" (Moses) redeemed him from there and with great efforts prepared him for the major event of entering the Land of Israel. At this critical point, however, the father (Moses) was required to appear before the king's (God's) court "and was condemned to death (וְאִתְקָנַס דִּין קְטוֹל)." His execution was not postponed so that he could view his son's marriage (Israel's entering the Land). Interpreting his own comparison, Moses states at this point: "I am condemned to death

---

[129] Cf. the bitterly disappointed people who consider stoning David in 1 Sam 30:6, as well as the actual stoning in 1 Kgs 12:18 (= 2 Chron 10:18).
[130] Mirkin 10.174; Soncino 6.688. *Num. Rab.* Korah 18:4 on Num 16:3 also states that the Israelites wanted to stone Moses (Mirkin 10.193; Soncino 6.712).
[131] Rieder 2.305; English in Clarke 96.

(אנא מתקנס למֶמֵת)."[132] He asks that the sentence be suspended long enough for him to cross the Jordan and view the good of Israel; then he would be willing to die. Rejecting Moses' plea bartering, the Lord nevertheless allows him to view the Land, but not to enter it (Deut 32:51-52). Moses must now die.

There is no way of knowing whether, and to what extent, this singular, Palestinian targumic tradition was known at an early time. If the latter was the case, however, it shows how at the very end of his life Moses is described as someone who is condemned by the king (God) to death. Even if it could be demonstrated that the tradition does not go back to the first century CE, the comparison shows how at least some Palestinian Jews could describe Moses' death in such judicial terms. It is very close in content to the verdict of the Sanhedrin in Jerusalem at the so-called "trial" of Jesus: "All of them condemned him as deserving death" (Mark 14:64 par.). The latter is reflected in the third passion prediction close to the end of Jesus' life in Mark 10:33, "See, we are going up to Jerusalem, and the Son of Man will be handed over to the chief priests and the scribes, 'and they will condemn him to death.'"

The above biblical and Judaic texts, some of the latter quite early (two from Josephus, one Tannaitic), show that Israel's first redeemer, Moses, could be described as one whom his own people at various times wanted to kill, in part by stoning him. In addition, he is once compared to a person condemned to death at the very end of his life. It appears that the first Christians, all Palestinian Jews, described the final redeemer of Israel, the Messiah Jesus, in similar terms, in part by using biblical and Judaic traditions regarding Moses as their model.

---

[132] Cf. also *Deut. Rab.* Ve'zot ha-Berakhah 11/10 on "Your time to die is near" (Deut 31:14) (Mirkin 11.155; Soncino 7.180), which notes that R. Yohanan (bar Nappaha, a second generation Palestinian Amora: *Introduction* 94-95) first records the ten references in Scripture to Moses' death. He interprets this to mean that "ten times it was decreed that Moses should not enter the Land of Israel. Yet the harsh decree was not finally sealed until the High Court [of God] revealed itself to him and declared: 'It is a decree before Me that you should not pass over,' [as it is said:] (Deut 3:27)." This is also found in *Petirat Mosheh* (Jellinek, *Bet ha-Midrasch* 1.120; Wünsche, *Aus Israels Lehrhallen* 1.144).

I. 4 Jesus' Farewell Address, and Moses' Farewell Address

A. *Jesus' Farewell Address*

Although one could view Jesus' remarks to his disciples while eating the Passover meal with them the evening before his death as a kind of abbreviated farewell address (Mark 14:17-25 par.), it is the Fourth Evangelist, John, who at the same point in his chapters 13-17 provides an extensive farewell address before Jesus goes out with his disciples beyond the Kidron Valley to a garden (18:1, called Gethsemane in the Synoptics). There he is apprehended, soon he dies and is buried.

Genesis 48-49 describe Jacob's blessing of Joseph's two sons and his final words to his own sons before his death and burial are related in 49:29-33. Jacob's words became the model for the later pseudonymous *Testaments of the Twelve Patriarchs.*[133] Joshua also delivered a farewell address in chapters 23-24 of that book before his death and burial are enumerated in 24:29-30. Yet it is Moses' farewell address to Israel which most directly influenced the Evangelist John in chapters 13-17.

B. *Moses' Farewell Address*

Moses recited Deut 32:1-43, the so-called "Song of Moses," before the whole assembly of Israel. Closely connected to this is his blessing of the twelve tribes in all of chapter 33. Directly after this, like Jesus' going off to his death in the Fourth Gospel, Moses proceeds to the site where he will die and be buried (34:1-12). Later Jewish tradition also provided him with his own farewell address at this point, the "Testament of Moses."[134]

The Tannaitic midrash *Sifre Ve'zot ha-Berakhah* 342 on Deut 33:1 says that at this time Moses spoke "words of comfort" to the twelve tribes.[135] These are enumerated in paragraphs 342-55.[136]

---

[133] Cf. *OTP* 1.775-828.

[134] Cf. *OTP* 1.919-34.

[135] Finkelstein 391; Hammer 349. This may be connected with Jesus' promise to send the Paraclete (παράκλητος), intercessor or helper, in John 14:16; 15:26; and 16:7. It is only found here in the farewell discourse. Interestingly, Moses is called "the good Paraclete" in *Exod. Rab.* Bo 18/3 on Exod 12:29 (Mirkin 5.212; Soncino 3.218). On this issue, see Nils Johansson, *Parakletoi. Vorstellungen von Fürsprechern für die Menschen vor Gott in der alttestamentlichen Religion, im Spätjudentum und Urchristentum* (Lund: Gleerup, 1940), especially his sections on Moses (5-11 and 161-66), as well as Str-B 2.561, "b."

[136] Finkelstein 391-423; Hammer 349-76.

The third generation Palestinian Amora, R. Levi,[137] also refers to Deuteronomy 33 as Moses' "farewell address." In *Lev. Rab.* Aḥare Moth 21/2 on Lev 16:3 he maintains the expression "in this" in Ps 27:3 means "in 'the farewell address' which Moses gave us in writing in the Torah, saying to the elders [thus to all twelve tribes]: "And *this* for Judah...' (Deut 33:7)."[138] This passage has a number of parallels.[139] The term "farewell address" here is the Hebrew אַנְסִיטְיְרִים , also found as אנסיטריון and אבסיטורין . Marcus Jastrow labels it a "farewell-address, bequest."[140] It probably derives from the Greek adjective ἐξιτήριος , meaning "*of* or *for departure*."[141]

Both the early "Testament of Moses" and the rabbinic traditions cited above support my suggestion that the farewell address Moses held for the twelve tribes just before he died was the model for the extensive farewell address Jesus directs to his twelve disciples in John 13-17 just before he himself dies.

I. 5 The Footwashing in John 13:1-20

A. *John 13:1-20*

According to the Fourth Gospel, the supper in 13:1-20[142] takes place a day earlier than the narrative of the "Lord's Supper" found in all three Synoptics.[143] The latter in contrast is definitely a Passover meal (Mark 14:17-26a par.), containing the "words of institution" (vv 22-25),[144] which are also strangely lacking in John. Yet the Johannine supper takes place just "before the festival of the Passover," when "Jesus knew that his hour had come to depart from this world and go to the Father" (13:1), i.e. to die through crucifixion. This imminent death is also alluded to in the

---

137 *Introduction* 98.
138 Mirkin 8.24; Soncino 4.267.
139 Cf. the end of 21/3 (Soncino 4.267); *Midr. Pss.* 84/4 on Ps 84:9 (Buber 371; Braude 2.66); 86/1 on Ps 86:1 (Buber 372; Braude 2.69); and 102/2 on Ps 102:2-3 (Buber 430; Braude 154). It is also found in Buber's edition of *Pesiqta de-Rab Kahana* (175a-b, with n. 158).
140 Cf. his *Dictionary* 6. See also Krauss, *Griechische und lateinische Lehnwörter im Talmud, Midrasch und Targum* 2.11,1). The term was frequently garbled.
141 LSJ 595.
142 Cf. δεῖπνον (BAGD 173) in vv 2 and 4; "bread" in v 18; "piece of bread" in vv 26-27 and 30; and "night" in v 30.
143 Cf. 18:28 and 19:14.
144 Cf. also 1 Cor 11:23-26.

phrase "to the end" in the same verse, and the mention of the betrayal by Judas Simon Iscariot in v 2 helps to prepare for remarks concerning him in vv 10-11 and 18-19.[145]

In the unit of John 13:1-20 Jesus is described as washing his disciples' feet.[146] He arose from reclining at the supper, which was typical of the Passover meal, indicating that even the poorest Jew did not eat standing like a slave, but reclining, in remembrance of the exodus from Egypt, from slavery to freedom.[147] Then Jesus removed his (outer) garments and tied a towel around himself (v 4). Verse 5 states: "Then he poured water into a basin and began to wash his disciples' feet and to wipe them dry with the towel that was tied around him." The Greek noun for "(wash)basin" here is νιπτήρ, found elsewhere only in a single Cyprian inscription.[148]

The timing here is very strange, which in addition to other factors points to the entire narrative as constructed.[149] Because of the dirt and

---

[145] This is developed in vv 21-31a, to be picked up again in 18:1-12 only after the long farewell discourses and "high priestly prayer."

[146] Cf. the Sheffield dissertation of John Thomas, *Footwashing in John 13 and the Johannine Community* (JSNTSup 61; Sheffield: Sheffield Academic Press, 1991), especially "A. Footwashing in the Old Testament and Early Judaism" (27-42). The latter is very limited because of his only considering sources "to the earliest layer of mishnaic tradition" (27, n. 1), a nebulous expression which he nowhere spells out. See also Christoph Niemand, *Die Fußwaschungserzählung des Johannes-evangeliums. Untersuchungen zu ihrer Entstehung und Überlieferung im Urchristentum* (Studia Anselmiana 114; Rome: Pont. Ateneo S. Anselmo, 1993). Neither of these monographs is aware of the major thesis I propose below.

[147] For Jesus and his disciples' reclining, see vv 12, 23 and 25. The basic text is *m. Pesaḥ.* 10:1 (Albeck 2.176; Neusner 249): "And even the poorest Israelite should not eat until he reclines at his table." Cf. Jastrow 948-49 on the hiphil of סבב , "to recline for dining in company." See also *b. Pesaḥ.* 99b (Soncino 532, with n. 3) and 108a (Soncino 560-61, with n. 5), but especially *y. Pesaḥ.* 10:1, 37b (Bokser in Neusner 13.475). There R. Levi, a third generation Palestinian Amora (*Introduction* 98), states: "Because it is the custom of slaves to eat standing, here [on Passover night, the Mishnah requires people] to eat reclining to proclaim that they have gone out from slavery to freedom." For theological reasons John has the meal with the footwashing take place on the evening *before* the evening of Passover. Yet at a normal meal no reclining took place (except at the banquets of the wealthy), another indication this was actually a Passover meal.

[148] BAGD 540. The cognate verb νίπτω , to wash, is employed eight times in vv 5-14, and of a widow's "washing" the feet of the saints in 1 Tim 5:10.

[149] Rudolf Bultmann could thus even speak of "the absurdity of the event" in vv 4-5. Cf. his *Das Evangelium des Johannes* (Meyer's; Göttingen: Vandenhoeck & Ruprecht, 1964) 355, as well as section C. below. See also Siegfried Schulz's

dust of Palestinian roads, streets and paths, water would be provided as a gesture of hospitality for a guest to wash one's own feet already upon arrival, not later in the midst of a meal.[150]

In addition, a Hebrew (Jewish) slave was not expected to wash his master's feet. This was one of the tasks of a non-Jewish slave.[151] However, one's "pupil" (תַּלְמִיד), in contrast, was "permitted" to do so.[152] This was almost an obligation. R. Joshua b. Levi, a first generation Palestinian Amora,[153] for example ruled: "All manner of service that a slave must render to his master (רב), a student (תלמיד) must render to his teacher (רב), except that of taking off his shoe."[154] That is, it was expected on the part of a student / disciple that he should wash the latter's feet on the appropriate occasions. R. Yohanan (bar Nappaha), a second generation Palestinian Amora,[155] even maintained that a teacher "who deprives his student of [the privilege of] attending on him acts as if he had deprived him of [an act of] kindness."[156] Elisha's "pouring water on the hands of Elijah," considered by the rabbis to be his "teacher" (2 Kgs 3:11), is interpreted by R. Simeon b. Yohai, a third generation Tanna,[157] as demonstrating that "the service of the Torah is greater than the study thereof."[158] Extreme examples of learning concrete aspects of

---

remark, "the apparently absurd performance of such slave service," in his *Das Evangelium nach Johannes* (NTD 4; Göttingen: Vandenhoeck & Ruprecht, 1978) 173.

[150] Cf. already Gen 18:4, where Abraham's three guests receive water and are expected to wash their own feet before eating. See also Luke 7:44. John 12:1-8, with Mary's anointing Jesus' feet, is a reworking of the tradition now found in Mark 14:3-9, an anointing of Jesus' head before Passover. In *Joseph and Asenath* 7:1 (*OTP* 2.210, with n. "b"), servants wash Joseph's feet before he eats. In 20:3 Joseph suggests that a maidservant wash his feet before a banquet (v 1); Aseneth as his future wife insists on doing this (vv 4-5). In *Test. Abraham* A 3:7-9 (*OTP* 1.883), Abraham washes the feet of his guest, tired from a long journey; see also B 3:8-9 (1.897). On these three texts, see especially Thomas, *Footwashing* 38-39.

[151] Cf. *Mek. R. Ish.* Nezikin 2 on Exod 21:1 (Lauterbach 3.5-6). See also *b. Qidd.* 22b bar. with "washing" (Soncino 109).

[152] Cf. the *Mekilta* passage in the preceding note, as well as Jastrow 1498 on רשאי.

[153] *Introduction* 92-93.

[154] Cf. *b. Keth.* 96a (Soncino 610, with n. 14).

[155] *Introduction* 94-95.

[156] Cf. n. 154, interpreting Job 6:14.

[157] *Introduction* 84.

[158] Cf. *b. Ber.* 7b (Soncino 38, with n. 3). See also the saying of R. Aqiba in *'Avot R. Nat.* A 36 (Schechter 109; Goldin 152): "He who, of the disciples of the Sages, does

the Torah by serving one's teacher are the following. R. Aqiba, a younger second generation Tanna, followed his teacher / master R. Joshua, an older second generation Tanna,[159] into the toilet in order to learn certain things from him in this regard.[160] The second generation Palestinian Amora Rab Kahana once even hid under his teacher Rab's bed while the latter had intercourse with his wife. He justified his behavior to him by saying: "It is a matter of Torah, and I require to learn."[161]

The above passages show that when Jesus washes his disciples' feet in John 13:1-20, he not only performs a task normally done for guests at a banquet by a non-Jewish slave. Above all, he is depicted here as reversing the roles of teacher and disciple. It was the disciple who considered it a privilege to attend / serve his teacher in concrete ways, for he then could learn by doing. This also included washing one's teacher's feet, for example after a journey.[162] Jesus, the teacher, in contrast insists on washing his disciples' feet.

The above discussion also forms part of the background of the teacher Jesus' remarks to his disciples in John 13:13-16a, a segment of the second sub-unit (12-20) of vv 1-20:

13) You call me teacher and Lord - and you are right, for that is what I am. 14) So if I, your Lord and Teacher, have washed your feet, you also ought to wash one another's feet. 15) For I have set you an example, that you also should do as I have done to you. 16) Very truly, I tell you, servants / slaves are not greater than their master....

"Teacher" in vv 13-14 is the Greek ὁ διδάσκαλος ; it corresponds exactly to רַב in the passages cited above.[163] "Lord" is ὁ κύριος , which

---

not serve has no share in the world to come." This "share" (חֵלֶק) should be compared with the "share" (μέρος) with Jesus in John 13:8.

[159] Cf. *Introduction* 79-80 and 77-78, respectively, on them.

[160] Cf. the baraitha in *b. Ber.* 62a (Soncino 388). Ben ʿAzzai does the same with his teacher R. Aqiba.

[161] Cf. *ibid.*, and *Introduction* 95.

[162] Raymond Brown misrepresents this basic attitude on the part of students by speaking of "an act of service that occasionally generous disciples might do for a rabbi" in his *The Gospel According to John XIII-XXI* (AB 29A; Garden City, NY: Doubleday, 1970) 569. Such service by disciples / students was not done occasionally, but on a regular basis, and not out of generosity but from the desire to learn from concrete actions.

[163] Cf. Str-B 2.258 and 1.916-17 with an example already from around 110 BCE, if the dating is correct.

could correspond to the Semitic מָר .[164] Yet it can also be אָדוֹן , meaning both "lord" and "Lord."[165] This double entendre is most probably what the Fourth Evangelist wishes to convey, especially if one understands εἰμί at the end of v 13 as an allusion to the term ἐγώ εἰμι , as found in v 19. The latter signifies the Tetragrammaton YHWH.[166] John, so fond of more than one meaning, appears to be describing Jesus in v 13 as not only the disciples' "lord," but also as their "Lord."

Finally, Peter's impetuousness is portrayed, as elsewhere,[167] in John 13:6-9. In v 6 Simon Peter as the representative of the disciples[168] asks Jesus: "Lord, are you going to wash my feet?" After Jesus answers in v 7, Peter replies in v 8, almost in terms of an oath: "You will never (οὐ μὴ ... εἰς τὸν αἰῶνα) wash my feet!" Here the disciple shows his incomprehension of the complete reversal of the normal teacher / disciple roles: If footwashing at all, he the disciple should be doing it. When Jesus replies in v 8: "Unless I wash you,[169] you have no share with me," Simon Peter says enthusiastically in v 9: "Lord, not my feet only, but also my hands and my head!" I propose that Peter's initial major objection to Jesus' serving him, the disciple, reflects the objection of Joshua, Moses' disciple, when the latter suddenly begins to serve him just before Moses dies in the "Petirat Mosheh." This midrash on the departure[170] of Moses, in an early form, also served the Evangelist John as a source for other imagery and motifs in 13:1-20, including Jesus' setting an example which his disciples should follow.

---

[164] *Ibid.* Cf. also the examples given in Jastrow 834, IV, for lord, master, and Mar as a title.

[165] BDB 10-11; Jastrow 16, with one example playing on κύριος .

[166] Cf. John 8:24 and other similar passages, as well as 17:11 and 22 for Jesus and the Father as one. See also the discussion in section B. a) 5. and b).

[167] Cf. 18:10 and 21:7. George R. Beasley-Murray aptly labels this Peter's "spluttering in astonishment and incomprehension." See his *John* (Word 36; Waco, TX: Word Books, 1987) 233.

[168] Another sign of this episode as being constructed is that, strangely, no disciple before Peter objected to Jesus' washing his feet (v 5); only Peter does. For him as "the representative disciple," see also R. H. Lightfoot, *St. John's Gospel. A Commentary*, ed. C. F. Evans (Oxford: Clarendon Press, 1957) 264, and Rudolf Bultmann, *Das Evangelium des Johannes* 355, n. 4: "representative and speaker" as so often in the ancient tradition.

[169] Probably "through the blood of the Cross" is meant by the Evangelist.

[170] Cf. the introduction to the footwashing scene in John 13:1 - "Jesus knew that his hour had come to 'depart' from this world and go to the Father." The Greek is μεταβαίνω , to go or pass over (BAGD 510). Passing from death to (eternal) life is found in 5:24.

B. Moses as Teacher / Master, and Joshua as Servant and Pupil / Disciple

a) Joshua

Before analyzing the relevant section of the "Petirat Mosheh" in b) below, it will first be helpful to sketch Joshua's servant and disciple / pupil role over against his teacher / master Moses in various Judaic sources. Since this material is also of major relevance to other later sections in this volume, the discussion here is more extensive.[171]

1. *The Bible.* Joshua ben Nun is called Moses' "servant" or "assistant" (מְשָׁרֵת)[172] in Exod 24:13; 33:11; Num 11:28; and Josh 1:1.[173] In Exod 33:11 he is labeled a "youth" (נַעַר) at this point. The phrase מִבְּחֻרָיו in Num 11:28 can either mean Joshua as "one of his [Moses'] chosen men,"[174] or "from his youth,"[175] the latter agreeing with Exod 33:11. The former may imply that Moses himself chose a number of men as disciples. It should be noted that Joshua addresses Moses in Num 11:28 with אֲדֹנִי , "*My lord* Moses...."[176] In Deut 1:38 the Lord also tells Moses: "Joshua son of Nun, 'the one who stands before you [to serve you],' shall enter" the Land of Israel to "secure possession of it."[177]

The above passages make it clear that Joshua already in the Hebrew Scriptures was considered to be Moses' "servant," and that from his youth on.

Just before Moses' death, he commissioned Joshua to be his successor. Moses himself had requested such a successor "so that the congregation of the Lord may not be like sheep without a shepherd" (Num 27:17). The Lord tells Moses that Joshua is "a man in whom is the spirit" (v 18), and

---

[171] Cf. the articles by E. Good, "Joshua son of Nun" in *IDB* 2.995-96; Emil Hirsch on "Joshua," "In Rabbinical Literature," in *JE* (1904/25) 7.282-83; Elimelech Hallevy on "Joshua," "In the Aggadah," in *EJ* (1971) 10.266-67; as well as the index of Ginzberg, *Legends* 7.265-67.

[172] BDB 1058, l.c. The piel of שָׁרֵת means to minister, serve.

[173] Elisha is described similarly in 1 Kgs 19:21, where he "follows / goes after" Elijah and "serves" him.

[174] NRSV; cf. BDB 103-04 on בָּחַר , to choose.

[175] BDB 104 on בְּחוּרִים . Cf. בָּחוּר as a young man.

[176] In Num 12:11 Moses' own brother, Aaron, addresses him similarly.

[177] Cf. BDB 764.1.e. on עבד לפני : attend upon, be(come) servant of, and 7.a.

Moses grants him some of his authority (v 20), laying his hands on him and commissioning him (v 23).[178] Joshua's being "full of the spirit of wisdom" is again stressed in the final verses of Deuteronomy, Moses' death scene. As such, the Israelites now obey him (34:9), and he can proceed to lead the people across the Jordan (Josh 1:2). The Lord then promises to be with him just as He had been with Moses (v 5; cf. 3:7).[179]

2. *Philo.* In his tractate "On the Virtues," the Alexandrian contemporary of Jesus extensively discusses the topic of "humanity" (φιλανθρωπία) by describing Moses' appointing Joshua as his successor just before he died (51-79, IX-XII).

Moses' friend (φίλος) Joshua had become his "pupil" (γνώριμος)[180] already at an early time. The mutual relationship was of divine, undefiled love (ἔρως). Joshua usually lodged and ate with Moses, being his "servant"[181] and rendering him "services"[182] different from those of the multitude. He was not only his lieutenant, but he also participated in governing (55). Moses asked God for a successor (διάδοχος) "who would care for his subjects as a father" (57), and he quotes Num 27:16-17 to emphasize this (58). Joshua, Moses' "disciple" (φοιτητής),[183] had "modeled himself on his master's characteristics with the love which they deserved," and was then divinely approved to govern (66). Joshua's being Moses' "successor" is emphasized by repetition in 56, 64, 68 and 70 (twice).

Philo shows that Hellenistic Judaism at the beginning of the first century CE clearly considered Joshua to be the "disciple" of Moses, who lived and ate with him except when the latter was receiving divine oracles. He was the epitome of virtue, a worthy successor to Moses because he had modeled himself after his master / teacher.

---

[178] For the commissioning of Joshua, cf. also Deut 31:7-8, 14-15 and 23. Is Jesus' commissioning Peter / Simon son of John to feed his lambs / sheep, to tend his sheep, in John 21:15-19 somehow connected to this?
[179] Cf. also Sir 46:1-8 on Joshua, including his being Moses' successor in the prophetic office (v 1).
[180] LSJ 355, 2.b. I disagree with F. H. Colson's translation in the LCL because of the noun's meaning "pupil" here, as in Josephus (see 3. below).
[181] Cf. LSJ 1872 on ὑπηρετέω , II., to be a servant, do service.
[182] Cf. LSJ 1872 on ὑπηρεσία , II., service.
[183] Cf. LSJ 1949: disciple, pupil.

3. *Josephus.* A native of Jerusalem with Aramaic as his mother tongue, Josephus also highly praised the character of Moses' disciple Joshua in his *Antiquities*, written at the end of the first century CE.

Moses appointed as the head of the army Joshua, "a man of extreme courage, valiant in endurance of toil, highly gifted in intellect and speech, and withal one who worshiped God with a singular piety" learned from Moses, his "teacher" (διδάσκαλος) (3.49; ii. 3).[184] Advanced in years, Moses appointed Joshua as his "successor" (διάδοχος), both in prophetical matters and as commander-in-chief (στρατηγός).[185] Joshua had been instructed by thorough instruction[186] in the laws and divine matters, "having been taught in detail"[187] by Moses (4.165; vii. 2). In 5.117 (i. 29) Josephus notes that Joshua died at the age of 110. Of these he had passed forty in the serviceable "instruction" (διδασκαλία)[188] of Moses. In 118 a view of Joshua similar to that in 3.49 is given. Finally, Joshua is labeled Moses' "disciple" (μαθητής) in 6.84 (v. 4).[189]

Having grown up in Palestine, Josephus here certainly reflects local first-century traditions on Joshua as Moses' disciple, who had enjoyed a thorough education from his teacher.

4. *The Pseudepigrapha and Qumran.* Two early writings in the Pseudepigrapha are important in regard to Joshua out of this vast corpus of material: "Pseudo-Philo," and the "Testament of Moses."

"Pseudo-Philo" is a Palestinian writing, originally in Hebrew and from the first part of the first century CE.[190] In 15:3 the author traces Joshua's lineage back nine generations to Joseph.[191] After an extensive description

---

[184] If the passage is genuine, cf. *Ant.* 18.63 for Jesus also as a "teacher."

[185] This is a reference to Num 27:18. Cf. 4.311 (viii. 46) on Joshua's prophesying in the presence of Moses.

[186] Cf. LSJ 1286, 2. on παιδεία .

[187] Cf. LSJ 504 on ἐκδιδάσκω .

[188] Cf. LSJ 421: teaching, instruction.

[189] Cf. *Ant.* 8.354, where Elisha was both Elijah's "disciple and attendant (καὶ μαθητὴς καὶ διάκονος)," showing the close relationship between learning from, and serving, a teacher; as well as 9.28 and 33 on Elisha. The combination of "teacher" and "disciple" is found in 17.334. In *Bell.* 4.460 Elisha is designated the "disciple" (γνώριμος) and successor of Elijah, a usage also found in 1.78 (parallel in *Ant.* 13.311) and 649.

[190] Cf. Daniel Harrington in *OTP* 2.298-300. George Nickelsburg in *Jewish Literature* 269 notes arguments for a dating "shortly before or after the Jewish War," i.e. ca. 70 CE.

[191] *SC* 229.140; *OTP* 2.323.

of Moses' farewell speech and death in nineteen, chapter twenty relates the first contents of the book of Joshua. God tells Joshua he should not continue to mourn and hope that Moses is still alive. "Take his garments of wisdom and clothe yourself, and with his belt of knowledge gird your loins, and you will be changed and become another man." God had already told Moses His servant that Joshua would lead His people after him, i.e. be his successor (20:2). This Joshua then does, and his "spirit" is moved to address the people (v 3).[192] Moses' "garments of wisdom" here recall the prophet Elijah's mantle, which his pupil Elisha picked up after his ascension in 2 Kgs 2:13, and Moses' "belt of knowledge" recalls Elijah's belt in 2 Kgs 1:8. After Elijah ascended, the company of prophets at Jericho also noted in regard to Elisha: "The spirit of Elijah rests on Elisha" (v 15). Joshua thus appears to be described by "Pseudo-Philo" as the prophetic successor of Moses,[193] just as Elisha was the prophetic successor of Elijah.

The "Testament of Moses," earlier called the "Assumption of Moses," was very probably originally written in a Semitic language, preferably Hebrew, in Palestine in the first century CE.[194] Chapter one already has Moses call Joshua in order for him to "become the minister [*successor*] for the people in the tent of testimony" and to "lead the people into the land which had been promised to their fathers...."[195] When Moses finishes his long farewell speech, announcing his imminent death, Joshua tears his garments, falls at Moses' feet, and weeps (11:1-2). Important for our purposes is the fact that Joshua now calls Moses "master" (*domine*) in 11:9, and addresses him as "master Moses" (*domine Monse*) three times (11:4, 14 and 19).[196] Thus this first-century Palestinian writing also clearly

---

[192] *SC* 229.166; *OTP* 2.329. Cf. also v 5 for the transfer of leadership, and 23:1 for Joshua as "mighty in virtue" (*SC* 229.182; *OTP* 2.332).

[193] It should not be forgotten that the Book of Joshua is one of the "Former Prophets" in the Hebrew Bible.

[194] Cf. J. Priest in *OTP* 1.919-21, who calls attention to its now only existing in a Latin translation from the fifth century CE. On p. 1.923, with n. 18, he correctly notes the great importance of Deuteronomy 31 and 34 for the writing. Unfortunately, the MS breaks off at 12:13, after which Moses' "assumption" may have been related, although perhaps in a different work attached here. See also Nickelsburg, *Jewish Literature* 74-77 and 247-48 for the first decades of the first century CE, the importance of Deuteronomy 31-34, and Hebrew or Aramaic as the original language.

[195] Cf. Tromp, *The Assumption of Moses* 7, and *OTP* 1.927. See also 10:15 for Joshua as Moses' "successor" (Tromp 20; *OTP* 1.933).

[196] *OTP* 1.933-34. For the Latin, cf. Tromp, *The Assumption of Moses* 20, 22 and 24.

presents Moses as the master / teacher, and Joshua as his servant / pupil.

In 4Q378 (4QapocJoshuaᵃ), also called the "Psalms of Joshua," fragment 22, col. I. 2 mentions "Joshua, minister of Your servant Moses."[197] I. 3-4 then presumably mentions God's covenant with Israel, which He established with Abraham and passed on "through the hand of Moses to Joshua." This appears to be the only non-biblical mention of Joshua at Qumran, certainly from a pre-Christian period. Here Moses is not only God's "servant" (עֶבֶד); Joshua is also described as his "minister" or "servant" (מְשָׁרֵת).

5. *Rabbinic Sources.* Of the countless references in rabbinic sources to Moses as Joshua's teacher / master (רַב), and to Joshua as Moses' servant (מְשָׁרֵת) and pupil / disciple (תַּלְמִיד), the following passages as examples help to elucidate the general background of the scene of the footwashing in the Gospel of John, and of other Gospel passages to be analyzed in later sections of this volume.

Num. Rab. Mattoth 22/4 on Num 31:13 speaks of "disciples of his [Moses'] disciples."[198] Yet Joshua is always considered "the" disciple of Moses. Because he "ministered" (שִׁמֵּשׁ) to Moses, the Holy Spirit rested upon him.[199] Joshua also "persistently begged" Moses to teach him at every moment, until the latter taught him the entire Torah; thus he was worthy of ruling after him.[200] In *b. Tem.* 16a Rab (Abba Arikha), a first generation Babylonian Amora who studied with Rabbi in Palestine,[201] states that when Moses "departed for the Garden of Eden" [= died, or was translated to heaven by God], Joshua asked him: "My master (רַבִּי), have I ever left you [even] for one hour and gone elsewhere?"[202] Because Joshua learned sections of the Torah from Moses, he even waited for him forty days and nights at the base of Mount Sinai while Moses was receiving the Ten Commandments.[203] In *Num. Rab.* Pinḥas 21 / 14 on

---

[197] Cf. Martínez and Tigchelaar, *The Dead Sea Scrolls Study Edition* 2.748-49.

[198] Mirkin 10.301; Soncino 6.856-57.

[199] *Mek. R. Ish.* Pisha 1 on Exod 12:1 (Lauterbach 1.14). Cf. Num 27:18; Deut 34:9; and Josephus above.

[200] Cf. *Midrash Tannaim* on Deut 34:9 (Hoffmann 227), and Jastrow 551, hiphil 3) of שׁמשׁ . This is also found in *Midrash Haggadol* on the same verse (Fisch 790).

[201] *Introduction* 93.

[202] This interprets Exod 33:11 (Soncino 109).

[203] Cf. *'Avot R. Nat.* B 11 (Schechter 28; Saldarini 90-91), found also in *Leqaḥ Ṭob* on Exod 32:19 (Buber 203).

Num 17:15-16, Joshua "rose early in the morning and remained late at night" at Moses' house of study. "He used to arrange the benches and to spread out the mats" there. Thus Moses was told by God, "Take Joshua the son of Nun" (Num 27:18 - as his successor). This illustrates Prov 27:18, "he who waits on 'his master' (אֲדֹנָיו) shall be honored."[204] Other comment on the latter verses maintains that Joshua "ministered to Moses by day and by night," which in addition interprets Exod 33:11 ("he did not depart from the Tent") and Num 11:28. Joshua employs "'My lord [אֲדֹנִי]' Moses" in this verse from Numbers. Because of Joshua's "serving his master" (שֶׁמֵּשׁ אֲדֹונָיו), he was worthy of receiving the Holy Spirit and prophesying.[205]

Finally, the third generation Tanna R. Eleazar b. Shammua[206] is recorded as saying in *m. 'Avot* 4:12, "Let the honor of your disciple be as dear to you as your own...."[207] The content of this saying is reflected in the Tannaitic midrash *Mek. R. Ish.* Amalek 1 on Exod 17:9, "And Moses said to Joshua, 'Choose us out men.'"[208]

> From this it is evident that Moses treated Joshua as his equal. Learn, all the world, proper conduct from Moses, who did not say to Joshua: "Choose me out men," but "choose us out men" - he treated him as an equal. From this we can learn that a teacher (רב) should hold his pupil / disciple (תלמיד) as dear as he holds himself. And how do we know that the respect for one's fellowman should be as dear to one as the reverence for one's teacher (רב)? It is said: "And Aaron said to Moses, 'Oh, *my lord*'"(אֲדֹנִי - Num 12:11). Was he not his older brother? What then does it mean by saying "Oh, *my lord*"? He treated him as though he were his master / teacher (רב). And whence do we know that the respect for his master / teacher (רב) should be as dear to a man as the fear of heaven [God]? It is said: "And Joshua the son of Nun, the minister / servant (מְשָׁרֵת) of Moses from his youth on answered and said: '*My lord* (אֲדֹנִי) Moses, shut them in'" (11:28). He said to him: "My teacher (רב) Moses, just as God would shut them in, so you should shut them in."[209]

---

204 Cf. Mirkin 10.288; Soncino 6.841.

205 Cf. *Num. Rab.* Naso 12/9 on Num 7:1 (Mirkin 10.29; Soncino 5.476).

206 *Introduction* 85.

207 Albeck 4.371; Danby 454; Neusner 683.

208 The emphasis is on "us" and not "me."

209 Lauterbach 2.140, which I modify. Part of this is also found in *'Avot R. Nat.* A 27 (Schechter 84-85; Goldin 115) on R. Eleazar ben Shammua's saying, as well as

Here Moses, while clearly the master / teacher (רַב) of his servant (מְשָׁרֵת) and pupil / disciple (תַּלְמִיד) Joshua, follows the advice later advocated by R. Eleazar b. Shammua and treats Joshua as his equal. Yet respect for one's fellowman should also be shown in addressing one's teacher / master, here Moses as אֲדֹנִי , "my lord."

The traditions cited above suffice to show that while Judaic sources usually portray Moses as the teacher / master of Joshua, his servant and pupil / disciple, one exception is made, at which Moses is also called "lord." This is important for another development of the midrash on Moses' death, the "Petirat Mosheh," to which I now turn.

b) Petirat Mosheh

The major background to the teacher Jesus' washing his disciples' feet, and not the reverse, as would be expected, is found in Judaic tradition on Moses' imminent death.[210] Here Moses attempts to barter with God: If he becomes Joshua's servant / pupil, then he hopes to live and not yet have to die.

Deut. Rab. Vayelech 9/9 on Deut 31:14, ("The Lord said to Moses, 'Your time to die is near;) call Joshua (and present yourselves in the tent of meeting so that I [God] may commission him),'" has Moses say to God: "'Master of the Universe, let Joshua take over my office and I will continue to live.' God then replied: 'Treat him as he treats you.' Moses immediately rose early and went to Joshua's house, and Joshua became frightened. Moses said to Joshua: 'My teacher [רַבִּי], come with me,' and they set out to go, Moses walking on the left of Joshua." Then Cant 8:6 is cited, "For love is strong as death," which is referred to "the love with which Moses loved Joshua."[211] As J. Rabbinowitz, the Soncino translator, points out, "the disciple walks on the left of his teacher."[212] Joshua is also frightened here because he did not go to Moses' house to serve him, but

---

in B 34 (Schechter 76; Saldarini 202). Joshua asks here that Moses stop Eldad and Medad from prophesying (Num 11:26-27).

[210] Masters who ostensibly serve their slaves at table at the feast of Saturnalia are hardly relevant here. Cf. Mauro Pesce and Adriana Destro, "La lavanda dei piedi di Gv 13,1-20, il *Romanzo di Esopo* e i *Saturnalia* di Macrobio" in *Bib* 80 (1999) 240-49. The Evangelist John, a bilingual Jewish Christian, was rather influenced here by Judaic traditions.

[211] Mirkin 11.137-38; correct in Soncino 7.162-63. Mirkin wrongly punctuates "And he [Joshua] said: 'Moses, my teacher, come with me.'" On Moses' love of Joshua, cf. the remarks of Philo cited in 2. above.

[212] Soncino 7.162, n. 4.

Moses came instead to him. Indeed, Moses even addressed him as "my teacher / master (רַבִּי)."[213] Joshua cannot comprehend this reversal of roles.

A similar tradition is found with some variants in *Tanḥ.* B Va'ethanan 6 on Deut 3:23, "I [Moses] entreated the Lord." Here the Lord tells Moses: "'Up to now it was your lot to serve. Now the lot of your disciple Joshua has come to serve.' Moses said to Him: 'Lord of the world, if I am to die before Joshua, I will go and be his disciple.' He replied to him: 'If you wish to do so, do it.'" Then Moses went to the door of Joshua's tent and remained standing while Joshua sat and expounded the Torah. Seeing this, the Israelites scolded Joshua severely for sitting while "Moses our teacher" stood. Joshua thus immediately rent his garments, cried out, wept and said: "My teacher, my teacher, my father, my father and my lord! (רבי רבי אבי אבי ואדני)."[214] When Moses tells the Israelites he no longer has the authority to teach them Torah, a heavenly voice proclaims: "Learn from Joshua!" This they then do.[215] A parallel tradition is found in *Tanḥ.* Va'ethanan 6 on the same verse.[216]

Here the teacher / master (רב) Moses also seeks to become the pupil / disciple (תלמיד) of his own pupil / disciple. Unwilling to accept this reversal of roles, Joshua calls out three expressions strongly reminiscent of Elisha's three expressions at the ascension of his teacher Elijah in 2 Kgs 2:12, "Father, father! The chariots of Israel and its horsemen!" *Targum Jonathan* on this verse has for example for "Father, father": "My master, my master (רבי רבי)...."[217] The midrash on Moses' death appropriately borrowed this imagery from the Elijah / Elisha complex because Moses is thought by some elements of Judaic tradition not to have died, but to have ascended to heaven like Elijah (see chapter III. B. 2. below).

---

[213] Cf. *b. Soṭah* 13b (Soncino 70) on Deut 3:26, "Let it suffice [*rab*] you" as applied to Moses: "You have a master [*rab*], Joshua."

[214] A variant in *Midr. Prov.* 14:34 has here: "My father, my father, my master, my master! My father who has raised me from my youth, my master who has taught me wisdom!" Cf. the Hebrew in Visotzky 118; English in Visotzky 74. This (without "from my youth") is already found in *Sifre* Niṣṣabim 305 on Deut 31:14, here on Num 27:18 (Finkelstein 327; Hammer 297), at the death of Moses.

[215] Buber 12-13; Bietenhard 2.454.

[216] Eshkol 858; English in Kushelevsky, *Moses* 255-56. It should be noted that this episode takes place directly after Moses expresses concern for the fate of his mother Yochebed, still alive, which is related to John 19:26-27, to be analyzed below in section I.8.

[217] Sperber 2.274; Harrington and Saldarini 267.

The third expression (after "teacher" and "father") Joshua employs for Moses is "my lord (אֲדֹנִי)." It is the same as in *Tanhuma* B and *Tanhuma*, cited above. Before I analyze it, other material relevant to the footwashing in the Gospel of John should first be noted.

The midrash on Moses' death / departure, "Petirat Mosheh" in the Jellinek A manuscript tradition, has God tell Moses when he barters with Him to remain alive and enter the Land of Israel: "It is enough for you, Moses; let this suffice you. The day has arrived for Joshua to lead Israel."[218] "Let this suffice you (רַב לְךָ)" is a quotation from Deut 3:26,[219] and shortly after this v 28 is cited to enforce not Moses' or Aaron's sons as leaders to succeed Moses, but Joshua. Submitting to the divine decree, Moses "went and spoke with all Israel" (Deut 31:1), i.e. he expounded the Torah for thirty-six days, from the first of Shevat (Deut 1:3) to the seventh of Adar, on which he was to die.[220] R. Yoshiyyah, a third generation Tanna,[221] states that at this time Moses bestowed great honor and much distinction upon Joshua in the sight of all Israel. A herald proclaimed him as the new prophet who had now arisen in Israel. Moses himself set up rows of benches for the Sanhedrin, the heads of the troops, and the priests.[222] As if he were his servant, he dressed Joshua and placed him on a golden throne. Then Joshua expounded the Torah to all Israel before Moses his master (רב).[223]

At this point a literary seam is visible in the midrash, showing the beginning of a different source. When Moses hears God's decrees in Deut 31:14 and 3:28, he attempts to continue to live and enter the Land of Israel by letting Joshua be Israel's leader: "From the first day of Shevat to the sixth of Adar, every morning and evening 'he would minister (משמש)' to Joshua as a 'disciple (תלמיד)' ministers to his 'master (רב).'" This lasted thirty-six days, a day for each year Joshua had served Moses in the wilderness (Exod 33:11).[224] It should be noted that Moses

---

[218] Jellinek, *Bet ha-Midrasch* 1.121; English in Kushelevsky, *Moses* 208; German in Wünsche, *Aus Israels Lehrhallen* 1.147. I omit much material which is irrelevant to the discussion here.

[219] Cf. n. 213 above.

[220] This is a very old chronology. On it, cf. *Seder ʿOlam* 10 (Guggenheimer 100).

[221] *Introduction* 83. Later on, R. Samuel bar Naḥman states something in the name of R. Jonathan (ben Eleazar), who was his teacher and a first generation Palestinian Amora (*Introduction* 92). All the other authorities are also Palestinian.

[222] Cf. the similar motif applied to Joshua in the house of study in *Num. Rab.* Pinḥas 21/14 on Num 17:15-16, cited above.

[223] Jellinek 1.122; Kushelevsky 209; Wünsche 1.148-49.

[224] Jellinek 1.123; Kushelevsky 210; Wünsche 1.150.

here also concretely serves Joshua "evenings / every evening (ערבית),"
which normally would have included washing the dust of the day off
Joshua's feet, especially during the greater part of the year when sandals
were worn and not shoes.[225] Moses' mode of serving Joshua is now
described in more detail, and it appears to be peculiar to the Jellinek A
account.

When Moses went daily to the door of Joshua's tent, in the middle of
the night, he served him by taking his shirt, shaking it, and putting it
next to his pillow. Then he would take Joshua's shoes,[226] clean them, and
place them next to the bed. Following this, Moses would take his cloak
(*tallith*),[227] garments, turban, golden helmet and crown of pearls,
examine, clean, and put them together and in order before him on the
golden chair there. "Then he would fetch a 'pitcher' (קִיתוֹן) of water and
a golden 'bowl' (קְעָרָה) and place them before the chair." After making
other preparations, Moses invited the Israelites to come to Joshua's tent
and greet him, for "according to the word of God, Joshua is the [new]
leader of Israel."[228]

A קִיתוֹן is a "ladle for drawing wine out of the mixing bowl into the
cup; also for washing hands." Another English translation is "pitcher," as
above.[229] A קְעָרָה is a dish, platter, charger, here meant as a "bowl."[230]
Moses is thus portrayed here as reversing his own normal role. Instead
of letting himself be served as a teacher / master by his servant and
pupil / disciple Joshua, he now acts as Joshua's servant and disciple.
This includes providing a pitcher full of water and a bowl with which he
would wash Joshua's hands when he awoke in the morning, the task of a
servant / disciple. Although not expressly stated, the same should be
assumed for the evening, for the text expressly states that Moses also

---

[225] Cf. my forthcoming article "Poverty, Hunger, Going Barefoot, and Home-
sickness in Luke 15:11-32" in the Maurice Casey Festschrift, *Judaism, Jewish
Identities and the Gospel Tradition*, ed. James Crossley (London: Equinox
Publishing, 2008).
[226] "Shoes" and "sandals" were often used interchangeably. Cf. the sources cited
in my article in n. 225.
[227] The טַלִּית can especially be the cloak of honor, a scholar's distinction (Jastrow
537), probably meant here to honor Joshua in his new position.
[228] Jellinek 1.123; Kushelevsky 211; Wünsche 1.150.
[229] Cf. Jastrow 1371, with the corrected text of Yalquṭ Samuel 124. Jastrow
maintains the Greek κώθων (LSJ 1016: Laconian drinking vessel) is confounded
here with κύαθος (LSJ 1003: ladle). Kushelevsky (211) has "jug," another
possibility. See also Krauss, *Lehnwörter* 1.89 and 192.
[230] Cf. BDB 891; Jastrow 1397-98. The root קער can mean to hollow out.

served Joshua "evenings," "every evening." As noted above, this would normally include washing the dust off Joshua's feet, even if he wore not sandals but shoes during the few rainy months of the year (Shevat and Adar). A teacher / master would not get into his bed with dirty or dusty feet.[231]

I suggest that the above motif of Moses' washing Joshua's hands (and feet) provided the bilingual Evangelist John (or the Palestinian Jewish Christian author of the narrative) with the concrete background for Jesus' washing his disciples' feet in John 13:1-20. As with Moses, it also took place just before Jesus' death. In the Fourth Gospel Jesus is represented as pouring water (from a pitcher) into a basin and washing the disciples' feet (v 5). The extremely rare word "basin," νιπτήρ , appears to be the attempt to render the Semitic קְעָרָה above: dish, platter, charger, "bowl." This suggestion is corroborated by the continuation of the narrative in the "Petirat Mosheh."

After assembling all the Israelites, at Joshua's waking up Moses entered his tent, took out his undershirt and wanted to dress him. When Joshua vehemently resisted, Moses explained to him why he was acting as his servant. "You served me with a pleasant countenance, so I shall serve you. It was I who taught you, 'Love your neighbor as yourself' (Lev 19:18). Have I not instructed you, 'Let the honor of your disciple be as dear to you as your own'?"[232] Finally, Moses did not cease until Joshua took his seat upon the golden throne. "And 'against Joshua's will' Moses served him in every needful way. 'Against his will' he laid upon him the beams of glory." When Joshua was fully dressed, Moses led him out from the middle of the tent. When the two arrived at the door of the tent, Moses led Joshua out "against his will." When the Israelites saw Joshua walking before Moses, they all trembled and stood up on their feet. The two walked on to the place of the notables next to the golden throne, and here Moses seated Joshua "against his will." Viewing this scene, all the Israelites began to weep, and Joshua also wept and asked: "Why this greatness and glory for me?" The narrative then continues by stating that at this point Moses has only five more hours to live. Thereupon Moses instructs Joshua to remain seated like a king before the people, and the

---

[231] Cf. already Cant 5:3, where a young woman lies in bed at night when her lover comes knocking at her door. She asks: "I had put off my garment; how could I put it on again? I had washed my feet; how could I soil them?" See again Joshua's "ministering to Moses by day *and by night*," his not leaving him even for an hour, interpreting Exod 33:11, in section a) 5. above.

[232] This is found in *m. 'Avot* 4:12, cited above (cf. n. 207).

two of them expound the Torah before Israel, Moses reading it aloud and Joshua interpreting it. When a heavenly voice proclaims that Moses at this point only has four more hours to live, he again attempts to barter with God for his life. Moses maintains that he is willing to act as Joshua's "pupil / disciple (תלמיד)." He can be a king, and Moses his "servant (עבד)." Yet God rejects this, informing him that he may not cross the Jordan (with Joshua and the other Israelites, but must die beyond the Jordan).[233]

It is striking that the expression "against his will ([ב]על כרחו)[234] is emphasized by being employed here four times by Joshua to convey his unwillingness as a pupil / disciple and servant to be served by his teacher / master. I suggest that this expression provided the bilingual Evangelist John (or the earlier author of the footwashing narrative) with the background for the main disciple Peter's vehement resistance to his master / teacher Jesus' desire to wash his feet, as if Jesus were now the servant, pupil / disciple. In John 13:6 Peter asks Jesus: "Lord, are you going to wash *my* feet?" After Jesus' answer in v 7, Peter passionately asserts in v 8a: "You will *never, ever* wash my feet!" My English here tries to reproduce the double negative in the Greek, Οὐ μή , which is coupled with εἰς τὸν αἰῶνα at the end of the sentence, "forever." The latter with a negative, usually together, means "never,"[235] and corresponds exactly to the Hebrew לֹא מֵעוֹלָם.[236] Although John employs the expression five

---

[233] Jellinek 1.123-24; Kushelevsky 211-13; Wünsche 1.150-52.

[234] Jastrow 666 on כֹּרַח , בּוֹרַח with על : "*against* or *without one's will.*" I know of only one other passage in rabbinic sources with somewhat similar imagery. *Mek. R. Ish.* Amalek 3 comments on Exod 18:12, "and Aaron came with all the elders of Israel to eat bread with Moses' father-in-law in the presence of God": Scripture teaches that "Moses was standing and serving them." He had learned this from Abraham (Gen 18:1-8). Then R. Isaac, a fourth generation Tanna (*Introduction 87*), relates that when Rabban Gamaliel II (a second generation Tanna: *Introduction 76*, in conversation with R. Ṣadoq and R. Joshua) gave a banquet for the Sages, all of them were reclining; yet Rabban Gamaliel II "stood up and served them." They then objected, saying: "We are not 'right' (בדין) in having Rabban Gamaliel serve us." R. Joshua counsels him to continue doing so, for one greater than he had already done so: Abraham with the angels (Lauterbach 2.177-78). Yet this anecdote is assumed to involve serving food, not washing the Sages' hands or feet. In *b. Ber.* 64a (Soncino 404), Exod 18:12 is interpreted to mean eating with a scholar such as Moses.

[235] BAGD 27,1.b.

[236] Jastrow 1052 on עוֹלָם. The opposite, לְעוֹלָם , means "always," "forever." The Aramaic is very similar, only with עלם or עלמא for עוֹלָם (Jastrow 1084).

times elsewhere,[237] I propose that it is here his attempt to reproduce the Semitic idiom for "never" which produced the strange Greek construction (οὐ μή - ל֔א), followed only at the end by "forever" (εἰς τὸν αἰῶνα - מְעוֹלָם) meaning "never."

Only after Jesus' explaining the necessity of his washing Peter's feet (John 13:8b) does the disciple allow his teacher / master to do so (cf. v 12). This is based on the servant, pupil / disciple Joshua, who first vehemently protests against his master / teacher's serving him, which included pouring water out of a pitcher into a bowl for the washing of Joshua's hands (and feet). Yet, since it is God's decision that Moses must die,[238] Joshua nevertheless allows his master Moses to serve him.[239]

In John 13:6 Peter asks: "Lord, are you going to wash my feet?" "Lord" here is the Greek κύριε , the vocative of κύριος . In v 13 Jesus states: "You call me Teacher and Lord - and you are right, for that is what I am." Here the Greek of "the Teacher" is ὁ διδάσκαλος,[240] of "the Lord" ὁ κύριος , emphasized by the definite article: not "a" or "any" teacher or lord, but "the" Teacher and "the" Lord. The latter phrase is repeated in v 14.[241] I suggest that the terminology of "teacher" and "lord / Lord" for Jesus here was borrowed by the Fourth Evangelist (or the Palestinian Jewish Christian who first composed this episode) from an early form of the midrash on Moses' death. In B. a) 5. above I pointed out that in the Tannaitic *Mek. R. Ish.* Amalek 1 on Exod 17:9, Aaron's addressing his own brother as "my lord" (אֲדֹנִי) in Num 12:11 is interpreted as his treating him as if he were his own master / teacher (רַב). There Num 11:28 is also quoted, where Joshua says: "My lord [אֲדֹנִי] Moses." This is then interpreted as his saying: "My teacher / master [רַב] Moses."[242] Here "lord" and "master" are synonyms, while the latter term can also

---

[237] Cf. 4:14; 8:51-52; 10:28; and 11:26.

[238] Jesus' death is most probably hinted at in John 13:7, "You do not know what I am doing, but later [after the Crucifixion] you will understand," and in v 8, "Unless I wash you [with the blood of the Cross], you have no share with me."

[239] John the Baptist's unwillingness to baptize Jesus, saying Jesus should rather baptize him (Matt 3:14), is thus not relevant here. Against Hermann Strathmann, *Das Evangelium nach Johannes* (NTD 4; Göttingen: Vandenhoeck & Ruprecht, 1959) 196.

[240] One should note that "rabbi" is interpreted as "teacher" (διδάσκαλος) in 1:38.

[241] Here it is without the addition of "your" as in the NRSV.

[242] Cf. n. 209. Other passages where Moses is meant by "my lord" are Exod 32:22; Num 32:25,27; and 36:2 (twice).

mean "teacher."[243] Because of the Fourth Evangelist's being bilingual and aware of Judaic haggadah on Joshua as a disciple serving his "lord" and "master / teacher" Moses, I suggest that he borrowed the two terms from this complex and applied them to Jesus. Another factor, however, also encouraged him to do so.

As noted above, one element recurring in all variants of the midrash on Moses' death, from the Tannaitic *Sifre* on Deuteronomy onwards, is Joshua's addressing him in a way similar to Elisha's expression at the ascension into heaven of his teacher / master Elijah.[244] Both *Tanḥ.* B and *Tanḥ* Va'ethanan 6 on Deut 3:23 have Joshua's words as: רבי רבי אבי אבי ואדוני , "My master / teacher, my master / teacher, my father, my father, and my lord!" Here אֲדוֹנִי is meant as "my lord" or "my master," as in numerous biblical examples.[245]   Yet the same consonants vocalized as אֲדוֹנָי mean "my Lord (*Adonay*)," one of the divine names.[246] It is this double entendre which the Fourth Evangelist most probably intends when he has Jesus say to his disciples: "You call me Teacher - and you are right, for that is what I am" (13:13). Here the Greek κύριος can mean not only "lord," but also "Lord," as does the Hebrew אָדוֹן . This agrees with passages in John such as 10:30, where Jesus openly states: "The Father and I are one," rightly interpreted in v 33 as his equating himself with God.[247]

Finally, Jesus states in 13:14-17:

> So if I, your lord / Lord and teacher, have washed your feet, you also
> ought to wash one another's feet. 15) For I have set you an example, that
> you also should do as I have done to you. 16) Very truly, I tell you,
> servants / slaves are not greater than their masters, nor are messengers
> greater than the one who sent them. 17) If you know these things, you
> are blessed if you do them.

---

[243] Thus "teacher and lord" in John 13:13 can be רַב וְאָדוֹן in Hebrew, as in Franz Delitzsch's Hebrew New Testament, p. 195. When "my teacher" / "rabbi" (רַבִּי) first became an official title (probably sometime in the late first century CE) is immaterial for the discussion here.

[244] In the Jellinek A version of "Petirat Mosheh," it is found in 1.127; Kushelevsky 218; and Wünsche 1.157.

[245] Cf. the texts in Buber 2.12 and Eshkol 859, as well as BDB 10-11.

[246] BDB 3. a. b.

[247] Cf. v 38, "so that you may know and understand that the Father is in me, and I am in the Father." See also 14:9-11,20; 17:21; and 20:28. This theme is present in the Gospel from 1:1 onwards.

Here, as their master / lord and teacher, Jesus gives his disciples a concrete "example" (ὑπόδειγμα)[248] of how they ought to treat each other. A servant / slave is obviously subservient to his "master" (κύριος , v 16). Yet Jesus the lord / master now just before his death reverses these roles and serves the servants, encouraging Simon Peter and others to do likewise. It appears that the Fourth Evangelist (or his source) also got the inspiration for this motif from an early form of the midrash on Moses' death.

As pointed out in the Jellinek A version of the "Petirat Mosheh" above, Moses reverses the roles of master and servant with his disciple Joshua when at the end of his own life and after having provided water in a basin for washing Joshua's hands (and feet), he again enters Joshua's tent and tells him: "You served me with a pleasant countenance, so I shall serve you. It was I who taught you, 'Love your neighbor as yourself' (Lev 19:18). Have I not instructed you, 'Let the honor of your disciple be as dear to you as your own'?"[249] Here Moses encourages Joshua to treat others as he, the master / lord, has now treated his servant and disciple, Joshua: by serving him in a concrete way. This is practical love of one's neighbors, one's fellow human beings.[250]

The above cluster of four motifs (the striking reversal of the master / teacher and servant, pupil / disciple relationship; the concrete action of washing another's hands (and feet) in a bowl; major resistance to this on the part of the main disciple; and the admonition to love one another in a similar way) makes it very probable that the Fourth Evangelist (or his Palestinian Jewish Christian source) borrowed these from an early form of the "Petirat Mosheh." He then adapted and embellished them to fit the special situation of the common meal taken by Jesus and his disciples shortly before his own death.

---

[248] BAGD 844: example, model, pattern.

[249] While the latter saying is now found in *m. 'Avot* 4:12 (see n. 207), in a general sense it could very well be much older than the Tanna who cites it.

[250] For this reason I do not consider John 13:14-17 to be a Johannine interpretation of Synoptic materials such as those found in Mark 10:43-45 par., 9:35 par., and Matt 24:11, but rather to be based on an early form of the midrash on Moses' death. On Jesus' "new commandment" to love one another as he has loved them (the disciples, and by implication now the hearers / readers of the Gospel), cf. 13:34-35 and 15:12 and 17.

C. The Source of the Narrative, and the Question of its Historicity

Various theories exist as to whether or not the Evangelist John himself composed the footwashing narrative in 13:1-20, or employed a source and modified it. Many commentators view vv 6-11 and 12-20 as two separate and independent units after the actual footwashing in vv 4-5. Yet they differ as to which verses derive from a pre-Johannine source.[251] In light of the conclusions reached above in sections A. and B., I propose instead that after the Evangelist's introductory remarks in 13:1-3, he first presents one modification of the startling reversal of the Moses / Joshua relationship just before the death of Israel's first redeemer Moses in vv 4-11. Then he presents the new relationship of the final redeemer of Israel, Jesus, to his disciples as one of mutual love in vv 12-20. The latter is based primarily on the citation of Lev 19:18 on loving one's neighbor as oneself, still found at the end of the similar unit in the "Petirat Mosheh" Jellinek A narrative on the new relationship of Moses to his main disciple, Joshua. Thus vv 12-20 are not from a new source, but are a continuation based on the same source employed in vv 4-11.

It is clear, however, that the Fourth Evangelist has himself added at least the introduction in 13:1-3 as well as vv 10b-11 and 18-20. Yet it is also possible that he himself could have composed the entire narrative of vv 1-20 on the basis of his knowledge of Moses' similar behavior towards his disciple Joshua at the end of his life in an early form of the midrash on Moses' death.

Others have noted numerous Semitisms in the footwashing narrative.[252] In his study of one aspect of the footwashing, Paul Fiebig already in 1930 recommended considering its Hebrew-Aramaic mode of expression.[253] C. K. Barrett even thought that the Fourth Evangelist "was accustomed to think and speak in Aramaic as well as in Greek."[254] Elsewhere in this study I have proposed that, like the Evangelist Matthew, John was bilingual. That is, he could not only read and

---

[251] Cf. the discussion in Brown, *The Gospel According to John, XII-XXI*, 559-62.
[252] Cf. the concrete remarks of Bultmann, *Das Evangelium nach Johannes* 352, n. 3; Joachim Jeremias, *Die Abendmahlsworte Jesu* (Göttingen: Vandenhoeck & Ruprecht, 1967) 94, n. 6; Adolf Schlatter, *Der Evangelist Johannes* (Stuttgart: Calwer Verlag, 1948) 281, 285; and Strathmann, *Das Evangelium nach Johannes* 196.
[253] He applied this to the entire Gospel in his article "Die Fußwaschung" in *Angelos* 3 (1930) 121-28, especially p. 127.
[254] Cf. his *The Gospel According to St John* (London: SPCK, 1962) 11. See also 107, where he states: "It is impossible to mistake the Hebraic cast of many of his dominating thoughts."

independently interpret the Hebrew Scriptures,[255] but was also conversant with early midrashim on them, whether these were (most probably) only oral at that time, or already at least in part written down.

The events just before Moses' death were a favorite theme in first-century CE Palestine, as shown for example in "Pseudo-Philo" 19, originally written in Hebrew. The midrash "Petirat Mosheh" most probably also existed in an earlier form or forms[256] already in the first century. It was from this very popular narrative that the Fourth Evangelist[257] borrowed in order to compose the episode of Jesus' washing his disciples' feet shortly before Passover.

Is the footwashing incident historical? Did it actually take place, or are the three Synoptic Gospels correct in not at least alluding to it? A large number of commentators favor its historicity, primarily by simply assuming it was so. Others cite their specific reasons. Raymond Brown thinks Jesus' prophetic action here was no more bizarre than those of Jeremiah and Ezekiel when they predicted the fall of Jerusalem.[258] George Macgregor correctly considers it strange that the footwashing did not take place before the supper, which would have been normal. Yet he thinks that Jesus may well have postponed the act to make it more impressive.[259] Finally, Rudolf Schnackenburg also maintains that the episode could be historical because the Synoptics certainly do not relate all that took place at the Last Supper.[260] Or, he proposes, it may originally have taken place at another meal and been transferred to its present position.[261]

---

[255] An example is John 13:18, which appears to cite Ps 41:10 (Eng. 9) in its MT, and not its LXX form (40:10).

[256] It is very clear that there are now various seams in the work, as well as a large number of later accretions.

[257] Or possibly his source. In light of the major influence of the "Petirat Mosheh" on the Gethsemane narrative and on Jesus' words to his mother and the beloved disciple from the Cross (see sections I. 6 and I. 8 below), I believe John himself could very well have composed all of 13:1-20.

[258] Cf. his *The Gospel According to John, XIII-XXI*, 568.

[259] Cf. his *The Gospel of John* (Moffatt's; London: Hodder and Stoughton, 1959) 274.

[260] This is clearly a form of harmonization. Craig Blomberg in *The Historical Reliability of John's Gospel. Issues & Commentary* (Downers Grove, IL: InterVarsity, 2001) 186-92 also considers the incident historical. He believes the author of the Gospel was "John, the apostle" (30).

[261] Cf. his *Das Johannesevangelium*, III. Teil (13-21) (Herder's; Freiburg, etc.: Herder, 1975) 46 and 48, respectively. While John Thomas appears to believe the Johannine community received the footwashing tradition from Jesus (*Footwashing* 148-49), he considers this a question for further consideration

Others such as Rudolf Bultmann,[262] C. H. Dodd[263] and C. K. Barrett[264] believe the footwashing is a dramatization of the saying found in Luke 22:27 ("For who is greater, the one who is at table or the one who serves? Is it not the one at the table? But I am among you as one who serves"). This statement by Jesus is made in Luke just after the "words of institution" at the Last Supper. [265]

Yet the footwashing scene in John is not historical for a different reason. It is an emphatic, convincingly appealing comparison of the first and last redeemers of Israel, Moses and the Messiah[266] Jesus, just before their deaths. The Fourth Evangelist was acquainted with an early version of the midrash on the "departure / death" of Moses, the "Petirat Mosheh." Here 1) the master / teacher Moses' relationship to his servant and pupil Joshua is also strikingly reversed: the master / teacher becomes the servant and pupil / disciple. This also includes 2) Moses' pouring water from a pitcher into a basin in order to wash Joshua's hands (and feet) with it; 3) Joshua's vehement objections to his master's strange behavior, but eventual reconciliation with it; and 4) the command to love one another. The Fourth Evangelist masterfully transferred these four motifs from the scene of Moses' imminent death to the scene of Jesus' last meal with his twelve disciples in Jerusalem, just before the Passover and his own death. In a manner very typical of Jewish haggadah,[267] he created a new scene, but one similar to that of the reversal of roles between Moses and Joshua in Judaic tradition. He had already done the same in other pericopes as well such as 2:1-11;[268]

(p. 189). Christoph Niemand cannot decide whether it is genuine Jesus tradition or a creation of the Christian community (*Die Fußwaschung* 399).

262 Cf. his *Das Evangelium des Johannes* 352, n. 2.

263 Cf. his *The Interpretation of the Fourth Gospel* (Cambridge: Cambridge University Press, 1968) 393.

264 Cf. his *The Gospel According to St John* 363.

265 In Mark, the earliest Gospel, Jesus speaks these words before arriving in Jericho (10:41-45; cf. Matt 20:24-28).

266 This would have appealed to the first Jewish-Christian hearers / readers of the Gospel, who were certainly also acquainted with many haggadic traditions on the death of Moses. It should also be noted that the only explicit occurrences of the title "Messiah" as Μεσσίας and not simply Χριστός in the NT are in John 1:41 and 4:25.

267 Cf. chapter IV. below on haggadah and the larger question of historicity.

268 Cf. my *Water into Wine and the Beheading of John the Baptist* (BJS 150; Atlanta: Scholars Press, 1988) 1-37.

8:56-58;[269] and 11:45-54.[270] His goal was not to dupe his hearers / readers by creating something "fictional" which was not true. Rather, in a masterful way[271] he, like so many other Jews, composed a new narrative, basing it on older materials. With great literary skill he here primarily emphasized Jesus' deep humility,[272] pointing to his vicarious death on the Cross as the "Servant of the Lord"[273] only shortly later, as well as to the necessity for the disciples of mutual service. Throughout the centuries these major motifs have inspired Jesus' "new" disciples to act likewise.[274]

---

[269] Cf. my *My Name Is "Legion." Palestinian Judaic Traditions in Mark 5:1-20 and Other Gospel Texts* 253-87 on this episode.

[270] Cf. my *Barabbas and Esther and Other Studies in the Judaic Illumination of Earliest Christianity* (SFSHJ 54; Atlanta: Scholars Press, 1992) 29-63.

[271] Adolf Schlatter in his *Der Evangelist Johannes* 281 also correctly speaks of the "geniale Kunst" of the footwashing narrative.

[272] Commentators fittingly call attention here to the early Christian hymn in Phil 2:7-8 where Jesus, though in the form of God (v 6), "emptied himself, taking the form of a slave," and "humbled himself, becoming obedient to the point of death - even death on the cross." "Eschatological hospitality" is hardly a major motif here. On it see Arland Hultgren, "The Johannine Footwashing (13:1-11) as Symbol of Eschatological Hospitality" in *NTS* 28 (1982) 539-45. The first Jewish hearers / readers of the footwashing incident, shortly before Passover, would also have recalled that the Messiah was expected to come during the night of Passover. When they themselves celebrated the Passover reclining, it reminded them that they were not "slaves" as in Egypt before the exodus. They realized that the Messiah Jesus is described in John as becoming a "servant / slave," washing the disciples' feet, thus performing the task of a non-Jewish slave, shortly before he died. In the Fourth Gospel this takes place just as the Passover lambs are slaughtered in the Jerusalem Temple (19:14,31; 1:29 - "the Lamb of God"). The latter was a major reason for John's changing Jesus' last meal with his twelve disciples from Passover evening to the evening before.

[273] Cf. the words of Herman Ridderbos in *The Gospel of John. A Theological Commentary* (Grand Rapids, MI: Eerdmans, 1997) 465: in the narrative "The shadows of the cross peep through again and again."

[274] The Pope's washing the feet of a select group of people annually on Maundy Thursday evening aids greatly in keeping this meaningful tradition alive today. I intentionally omit a discussion of the relevance of "washing" in this episode to baptism, although the Fourth Evangelist probably intends an allusion to it here, just as he alludes to the Lord's Supper in 6:11 and 23. In his own Christian community, knowledge of the two sacraments was apparently not for outsiders, who could also of course read his Gospel.

I. 6 Jesus' Struggle with Death and Arrest in Gethsemane, and Moses' Struggle with Death

In Judaic tradition, as stated before, Moses is considered the first redeemer of Israel because of his delivering the Israelites out of slavery in Egypt. The final or great redeemer of Israel will be the Messiah. For this reason Palestinian Jewish Christians compared the birth of Jesus with Judaic lore regarding that of Moses.[275] The same was true for the impending death of Jesus. The Gethsemane scene was modeled to a great extent upon Judaic traditions regarding Moses' imminent death.[276] The following twenty similarities in the setting, terminology and motifs speak very strongly in favor of this proposal.

6.1   The Setting

A.   After arriving at Gethsemane on the Mount of Olives with his (eleven) disciples, Jesus tells them to sit there while he prays. Then he takes with him Peter and the two sons of Zebedee, James and John. Going off a little further from them, he falls on the ground and prays by himself. Returning, Jesus finds the three sleeping. This sequence is then repeated two more times.

I suggest that the basic pattern of going off to a mountain first with a larger group, then having an inner circle of three, and finally being alone, derives from Judaic haggadic tradition regarding Moses' impending death.

B.   Deuteronomy 34 has Moses ascend Mount Nebo, to the top of Pisgah, where he dies.[277] Josephus, a native of Jerusalem whose mother

---

[275] Cf. the *Introduction* above, with n. 3; my study "Die Weihnachtsgeschichte im Lichte der jüdischen Traditionen vom Mose-Kind und Hirten-Messias (Lukas 2,1-20)" in *Weihnachtsgeschichte, Barmherziger Samariter, Verlorener Sohn* (ANTZ 2; Berlin: Institut Kirche und Judentum, 1988) 14-44, with many cross-references to the Matthean birth story; as well as *Matthew 1-2 and the Virginal Conception in Light of Palestinian and Hellenistic Judaic Traditions on the Birth of Israel's First Redeemer, Moses* 1-29.

[276] In *Legends* 3.417-73 and the respective notes, Louis Ginzberg has an almost encyclopedic listing of Judaic sources dealing with Moses' impending death. The length of this material in *Legends* shows how much attention was attributed to it. See also the additional secondary literature cited in the *Introduction*, n. 12.

[277] Cf. also 32:48-52. It should be noted that Deuteronomy 34 was read in the Palestinian triennial lectionary system in the third year at the beginning of Adar,

tongue was Aramaic, and who finished his *Antiquities* in 93-94 CE,[278] shows an acquaintance with Judaic expansion of this scene. In *Ant.* 4.320-31 he relates that all first follow Moses. Then only the elders (ἡ γερουσία) escort him, along with Eleazar and Joshua. When Moses arrives at Mt. Abarim,[279] he dismisses the elders. Then he bids farewell to Eleazar and Joshua,[280] and disappears before them in a ravine.

The "elders" here are the representatives of the twelve tribes of Israel,[281] similar to the full number of Jesus' disciples. They accompany Moses to the mountain, where he dismisses them and proceeds with his own inner circle. The basic pattern recalls that in the Gethsemane narrative.

In Judaic haggadah, Joshua is Moses' main "disciple" (תַּלְמִיד),[282] who after Moses' death assumes the leadership of the Israelites. The early Palestinian Jewish Christian describing Jesus' struggle with death in Gethsemane certainly thought here of Peter, Jesus' main "disciple" (μαθητής), who assumed the leadership of Jesus' adherents in Jerusalem some time after his death.[283] Therefore he had Peter accompany Jesus somewhat further when he prayed.

Josephus mentions only one other person, Eleazar (the son of Moses' brother Aaron). Since he and Joshua later distributed the land of Israel to the tribes,[284] his brother Ithamar was not as popular as he was in Judaic

---

and that Moses is thought to have died on the 7th of Adar. See the art. "Triennial Cycle" in *EJ* (1971) 15.1389, and other references in n. 54 in section I. 2 above. For the importance of "the top of Pisgah" in regard to Joseph of "Arimathea" and "the hewn out place" where Jesus was buried, see chapter II. B.

[278] Cf. *Vita* 7, *Ant.* 20.263, and 267 with note "c" in the LCL edition.

[279] Cf. Deut 32:49, where Mount Nebo is a mountain of the Abarim.

[280] A variant of this tradition may be found in the Greek fragments of the original, now lost *Assumption of Moses*, where Joshua and Caleb are mentioned. Cf. R. H. Charles in *APOT* 2.408, bottom, especially Clement of Alexandria, *Stromata* 6.15.132 (GCS 52.498).

[281] Cf. Deut 31:28 ("the elders of your tribes"), and the blessing of the twelve tribes in chapter 33, after which Moses ascends Mount Nebo.

[282] Cf. the extensive references cited in I. 5 B. a) *Joshua*, above.

[283] This begins already in Acts 1:13, where Peter, John and James are mentioned first among the eleven. It is probable that Peter, after fleeing to Galilee and receiving a vision of the resurrected Jesus (1 Cor 15:5; Mark 16:7; John 21), then returned to Jerusalem (Gal 1:18; Luke 22:32), from which the eschaton, including Jesus' parousia, was expected to proceed (see e.g. Zechariah 14).

[284] Cf. Josh 14:1; 17:4; and 19:51.

lore.[285] Yet the behavior of Joshua, Eleazar and Ithamar is described as being influential in finally making Moses resign himself to death.[286]

I suggest that the early Palestinian Jewish Christian author of the Gethsemane narrative mentioned not only Peter, but also the brothers James and John, because of his knowledge of the brothers Eleazar and Ithamar as present just before Moses' death. He intentionally chose Peter and the two brothers to make his original listeners aware of the similarities between the struggle with death on the part of the final redeemer of Israel, Jesus the Messiah, and that of Israel's first redeemer, Moses. This means, however, that the triad of Peter, James and John was not - as often maintained - appropriated by the Evangelist Mark from the scene of the Transfiguration in 9:2. Rather, he took it over from his source.

6.2   Intense Prayer Before One's Imminent Death

A.   In Gethsemane Jesus announces that he will pray (προσεύχομαι , in Mark 14:32); then he does so three times (vv 35, 39, 41 - assumed).[287] The prayer itself is related in vv 35-36. This intensity of Jesus' repeated praying also derives from Moses' doing so at the very end of his life.

B.   The following three examples show how strenuous and prolonged Moses' prayer was just before he died.

---

[285] For the predominance of Eleazar's descendents over those of Ithamar, cf. 1 Chron 24:4, quoted in *b. Ta'an.* 27a (Soncino 143-44). For Moses, Eleazar and Joshua on Mount Nebo, see 1Q Words of Moses (1Q22[1Q DM]), col. I, in Martínez and Tigchelaar, *The Dead Sea Scrolls Study Edition* 1.58-61. See also Num 27:12, 18-23.

[286] Cf. *Tanh.* B Va'ethanan 6 on Deut 3:23 (Buber 13, with "Eleazar and Ithamar"; Bietenhard 2.454, following Codex Vaticanus Ebr. 34, has "the sons of Aaron"); *Tanh.* Va'ethanan 6 (Eshkol 858); and *Midr. Prov.* 14 (Visotzky 118, Eng. 74). Leviticus 10 deals with the death of Aaron's other two sons, Nadab and Abihu, leaving only Eleazar and Ithamar. *Mek. R. Ish.* Amalek 2 on Exod 17:14 (Lauterbach 2.153), a midrash also on Deut 3:23-27 here, has Moses ask Eleazar to pray for mercy on his behalf, i.e. that he not have to die. This Tannaitic tradition presupposes his presence at this point, an early attestation of the basic topos here. 4QApocryphon of Joshua-b (4Q379), fragment 17 (*The Dead Sea Scrolls Study Edition* 2.750-51), interestingly lists: "Moses [...E]leazar and Ithamar." The name Joshua probably stood in the blank space.

[287] Jesus' exhortation that the disciples pray is mentioned in v 38.

1. *Pseudo-Philo*, probably written in Hebrew in Palestine about the time of Jesus,[288] relates in 19:8 that "Moses ascended Mount Abarim as God commanded him, and 'he prayed,' saying: 'Behold, I have completed my lifetime....'"[289] Moses' praying is an haggadic addition, not found at Deut 32:49, 34:1, or Num 27:12.

2.   Moses had been told by God that he may not go over the Jordan and see the good land beyond it before he dies (Deut 3:25-26; 31:2). Judaic tradition relates that he struggled greatly with God to obtain permission to go there and remain alive. R. Levi, a third generation Palestinian Amora,[290] comments in *Deut. Rab.* Va'ethanan 2/7 on Deut 3:27, "You shall not go over this Jordan": "When Moses saw how emphatic (הָיָאךְ ... חֲזָקִים) God's words were, he began to plead strenuously (מְדַבֵּר דְּבָרִים קָשִׁים)."[291]

3.   *Deut. Rab.* Ve'zot ha-Berakhah 11/10 on Deut 31:14 ("And the Lord said to Moses, 'Behold, the days approach when you must die'") notes that Moses' "prayer" (תְּפִלָּתוֹ) "was like a sword which tears and cuts its way through everything, and spares nothing...."[292] The great intensity of Moses' prayer for (delivery from death and) permission to enter the Land is also expressed in its quantity. The same midrash maintains that Moses "prayed" (הִתְפַּלֵּל) at this point 515 times, the numerical value of the term *va'ethanan* in Deut 3:25, "'And I besought' the Lord at that time, saying...."[293]

The above three examples of Moses' prayer, strenuous and prolonged, are typical of the Judaic haggadah which provided the Palestinian Jewish Christian author of the Gethsemane narrative with a model for portraying Jesus' intense, prolonged prayer that his life be spared.

6.3 Jesus' Prostration in His Prayer

A.   In Gethsemane, Jesus literally "falls on the ground" (ἔπιπτεν ἐπὶ τῆς γῆς - Mark 14:35), which should also be assumed for the second and

---

[288] Cf. Daniel Harrington's remarks in *OTP* 2.298-300.
[289] *OTP* 2.327. The whole chapter deals with "Moses' farewell, prayer, and death," showing the importance attached by *Pseudo-Philo* to this topic. The Latin has *oravit* for "he prayed" (*SC* 229.160).
[290] *Introduction* 98.
[291] Mirkin 11.33; Soncino 7.36.
[292] Mirkin 11.156; Soncino 7.182.
[293] *Ibid.*

third times he prays. This motif also derives from Moses' similar behavior while praying just before his death.

B.   The following three examples show Moses' prostration at the point of his imminent death.
1.   In *Deut. Rab.* Va'ethanan 2/1 on Deut 3:23 ("And I besought the Lord"), R. Yoḥanan, a second generation Palestinian Amora,[294] states that prayer is known by ten different terms. One of them is *nippul*, as in Deut 9:18 and 25, "Then 'I lay prostrate' before the Lord," from the root נפל , to fall.[295]
2.   In the same section, 2/3, R. Abin, a fourth generation Palestinian Amora,[296] states that Moses "supplicated and 'prostrated himself' (מִתְחַבֵּט)[297] to be permitted to enter the Land of Israel, yet it [his prayer] was not accepted [by God]." This is because Moses' hour was already past, as indicated by "And I besought the Lord 'at that time.'"[298]
3.   Moses' falling on his face in prayer before God is also related in "Petirat Mosheh," the "Midrash of Moses' Departure / Death." A voice from heaven asked Moses why he was so disturbed, for "the end of the hour has come." Moses then stood "in prayer" and asked the Lord of the world not to deliver him into the hand of Sammael (the Angel of Death). Having acknowledged that He has heard Moses' prayer, God then promised to concern Himself with his burial. When He then revealed Himself from heaven to take the soul of Moses, the latter literally "fell on his face" (נפל על פניו) and prayed.[299]

Moses' prostration or falling down to the earth on his face when praying that he may (be allowed to continue to live and) enter the Land of Israel thus appears to provide the background for Jesus' "falling upon

---

[294] *Introduction* 94.
[295] Mirkin 11.29; Soncino 7.29-30. On נִיפּוּל as "falling down for prayer," cf. Jastrow, *A Dictionary* 907, who calls attention to the Tannaitic midrash *Sifre* Deut. Va'ethanan 26 on Deut 3:23, where the tradition is anonymous (Finkelstein 39; Hammer 48).
[296] *Introduction* 103.
[297] Jastrow 417, hithpael: "to prostrate oneself (in prayer, in deep commotion)."
[298] Mirkin 11.31; Soncino 7.32, with n. 2.
[299] Version A in Jellinek, *Bet ha-Midrasch* 1.128, and version B in 6.77. An English translation is found in Kushelevsky, *Moses* 221, German in Wünsche, *Aus Israels Lehrhallen* 1.160-61. See also Str-B 2.260-61 on different forms of falling down to the earth in prayer. Moses' "falling down" to pray at the very end of his life is certainly more relevant to Jesus' similar behavior in Gethsemane than a passage in "an ancient novel, *Chaereas and Callirhoe*" (Adela Yarbro Collins, *Mark* 677).

the earth" and praying in Mark 14:35, then repeated twice. He too wishes to continue to live, if God will cause the hour to pass and remove the cup (of death) from him. Yet God does not accept Jesus' request, just as He rejected Moses'.

6.4   Jesus' Threefold Prayer

A.   In Gethsemane Jesus prayed the same prayer three times (Mark 14:35, 39 and 41 - assumed). This pattern of threefold prayer also reflects Moses' praying just before his death.

B.   Early Judaic tradition describes Moses as praying three times that he might not die, but continue to live and enter the Land of Israel. God then rejects his request three times, and Moses must resign himself to his fate of dying now. Four examples of this threefold prayer are the following.
1.   A remnant of this motif is found in *Pseudo-Philo* 19:6, where at the end of Moses' life "God spoke to him *a third time*, saying: 'Behold, you are going forth to sleep with your fathers...'" (Deut 31:16).[300] Although God will show Moses the Land before he dies, he may not enter it (19:7; cf. Deut 32:52 and 34:4).

The origin of this motif is probably 1 Sam 3:8, where only after the Lord's calling the boy Samuel "the third time" does Eli perceive that it is the Lord who does this. In the haggadah on Moses' death, this means that only after God tells him three times that he must die and may not enter the Land, does Moses acknowledge this as God's will. The following texts demonstrate this.
2.   *Mek. R. Ish.* Amalek 2 on Exod 17:14 states that on the very day Joshua became the successor to Moses, a hint of this was given to Moses, but he didn't comprehend it. Therefore at the end Moses continued to stand and beseech, as in Deut 3:23 : "And I besought the Lord...."[301] R. Joshua (b. Ḥananyah, a second generation Tanna,[302]) then notes that "Let it suffice you" in Deut 3:26 means it is enough for Moses to have the world to come. "Still he was standing and making all these petitions / prayers (בקשׁות)."[303] He first requests permission to enter the Land as a private person, which God rejects. "Still he was standing and making all these petitions / prayers." Secondly, Moses requests permission to enter

---

[300] *SC* 229.158: *tercio*; *OTP* 2.327.
[301] Lauterbach 2.149.
[302] *Introduction* 77.
[303] The term בקשׁה means both desire / request, and prayer. See Jastrow 188.

by way of the cave of Caesarion near Paneas, which God rejects with the words of Deut 34:4. Thirdly, Moses finally asks that at least his bones may go over the Jordan into the Land. This in turn God rejects in the words of Deut 3:27.[304] Only after the third request / prayer does Moses accept God's will for him.

3.   In *Deut. Rab.* Ve'zot ha-Berakhah 11/5 on Deut 33:1 ("before his death"), R. Meir (a third generation Tanna[305]) says the Angel of Death came to Moses and informed him that God had sent him to him, for he is to depart this life today. Moses tells him to go away, for he wants to praise God, as in Ps 118:17. When the Angel of Death came to him a second time, Moses pronounced over him the Ineffable Name, whereupon the angel fled. Only when he came "a third time" did Moses acknowledge that this is from God, and that he must accept it as God's will.[306]

4.   *Deut. Rab.* Ve'zot ha-Berakhah 11/10 on Deut 31:14 ("Behold, the days approach when you must die") states that Moses has only one more hour to live. He says that if God will not bring him into the Land, He should leave him in this world so that he can live and not die. This God rejects. Secondly, Moses asks God to let him become like the beasts of the field. This God rejects with the words of Deut 3:26, "Let it suffice you." Then Moses, thirdly, asks God to let him become like a bird. Again He answers him with Deut 3:26. When Moses sees that no creature is able to save him from the path of death, in that hour he acknowledges God's justice by quoting Deut 32:4.[307]

---

304 Lauterbach 2.151-52. Cf. also the parable in the same section of a king's son, who when he tries to enter the palace is rebuked by the guards "at the third" (בשל ישי) gate (Lauterbach 2.149-50). A similar parable is related in *Sifre* Deut. Va'ethanan 29 on Deut 3:27 (Finkelstein 48; Hammer 54).

305 *Introduction* 84.

306 Cf. Mirkin 11.152, and Soncino 7.176. This is anonymous in *Tanh.* Ve'zot ha-Berakhah 3 on Deut 33:1 (Eshkol 945). On the general phenomenon of struggling with the Angel of Death, see Eliezer Diamond, "Wrestling the Angel of Death: Form and Meaning in Rabbinic Tales of Death and Dying" in *JSJ* 26 (1995) 76-92.

307 Mirkin 11.157-58; Soncino 7.183-84. Moses' threefold prayer is thus the background of Jesus' prayer in Gethsemane, and not A. Loisy's proposal (*Marc* 416, as quoted in J. Warren Holleran, *The Synoptic Gethsemane.* A Critical Study [Analecta Gregoriana 191; Rome: Gregorian University, 1973] 46) that Mark intends the three prayers to correspond to the three watches of the night. Holleran's monograph mentions none of the proposals I make in this sub-chapter on Gethsemane.

The last three texts show that the motif of Jesus' praying "three times" in Gethsemane that his imminent death be averted, derives from the threefold request / prayer of Moses at the very end of his life. He wants to enter the Land and not die, but continue to live. This, however, God does not grant him, just as He does not remove the cup (of death) from Jesus in Gethsemane.

The pre-Markan, Palestinian Jewish Christian author of the Gethsemane narrative was not the only one to apply the "threefold prayer" motif from Judaic haggadah on Moses' imminent death to a new situation. The following remarks in regard to 2 Cor 12:7-9 are of relevance here.

Fourteen years before writing Second Corinthians, Paul was caught up to the third heaven, Paradise, where he experienced an abundance of revelations. To keep him from becoming too elated over this, a messenger of Satan, a thorn in the flesh, was given him. Paul besought the Lord "three times" (τρίς) that this should leave him (v 8), but He said to the apostle: "My grace is sufficient for you" (v 9). The latter is a Judaic interpretation of Deut 3:26, applied above to Moses.[308]

Paul's beseeching the Lord three times (in prayer) that something very negative should be taken away from him corresponds to Jesus' threefold pattern of prayer in Gethsemane. Both Paul and the Palestinian Jewish Christian author of the Gethsemane narrative appropriated this motif from Judaic haggadah on the end of Moses' life.[309]

6.5 If Possible

A.   In Mark 14:35 Jesus in Gethsemane falls on the ground and prays that "if it is possible (εἰ δυνατόν ἐστιν)," the hour should pass from him. The next verse (36) rephrases the petition: "Abba, Father, all things are possible (δυνατά) to You. Remove this cup from me. Yet not what I will, but what You (will)." The first expression, "if it is possible," (and indirectly also the second, together with "will") also reflects Judaic tradition on the last hour before Moses' death.

---

[308] Cf. especially *Deut. Rab.* Va'ethanan 2/1 on Deut 3:26 (Mirkin 11.29-30; Soncino 7.30), and a full discussion in "Paul's Calling and Re-Commissioning in 2 Cor 12:1-10 and Moses' Calling and Death Scene" in my *The Wicked Tenants and Gethsemane* 161-82.

[309] According to Christian Wolff, *Der zweite Brief des Paulus an die Korinther* (THNT 8; Berlin: Evangelische Verlagsanstalt, 1989) 248, n. 365, H. Windisch in 1934 had already called attention to the threefold prayer parallelism between Gethsemane and 2 Cor 12:8. Yet he was not aware of their mutual background.

B.   In the Tannaitic midrash *Sifre* Deut. Vaʾethanan 28 on Moses' petition in Deut 3:25, "Let me go over, I pray, and see the good land," the commentator asks: "'Is it possible that' (אי אפשר ש׳) Moses could have asked God to let him (continue to live and) enter the land? Is it not stated elsewhere, 'you shall not go over this Jordan' (3:27)?" This situation is illustrated by a parable, in which a king decrees that his servant should be without wine for thirty days. The servant responds: "'Is it possible that' I can be without wine for even a single hour?" This was to show "how precious to him were the words of his master. So also Moses demonstrated how precious to him were God's words by asking Him to let him enter the land," as in 3:25.[310]

Reuven Hammer notes that this servant actually pleads against the king's decree. Because he wants to do the king's will, he emphasizes how precious the wine is which he is now giving up. Hammer remarks that "Moses' repeated pleading is ... a demonstration of his complete obedience."[311]

Here Moses, in the hour of his death, is likened to someone who asks that "if it is possible," he may not be without wine even for one hour, although his king decreed he should be without it for thirty days. That is, Moses pleads that the entire decree of the king (God) be taken from him. He wants to continue to live and to enter the Land.

Jesus' situation in Gethsemane is depicted as being similar. He prayed three times that "if it were possible," the hour should pass from him, the cup (of death) be removed from him. By praying to the Father repeatedly, he acknowledged that God's will alone was determinative for him.

Another example of the expression "if it is possible" is found in *Tanh.* B Vaʾethanan 5 on Deut 3:23 ("And I besought the Lord at that time").[312] It begins by asking: "Why (did Moses beseech the Lord)? So that he could enter the Land (of Israel)." Although God tells him, "Let it suffice you" (3:26), and "Die on the mountain which you ascend!" (32:50), Moses continues to beseech God, saying: "I do not want to go forth and die."[313] Later Moses says: "Now I pray, 'Hear my cry, O God' (Ps 61:2, Eng. 1), 'and hide not Yourself from my supplication' (Ps 55:2, Eng. 1). The Holy One, blessed be He, said to him: It is not possible (אי אפשר), 'Let it

---

[310] Finkelstein 44; I slightly modify the translation of Hammer, 52.

[311] Hammer 401, n. 1.

[312] Buber 10; Bietenhard 2.450.

[313] Buber's text omits "go forth," apparently found in Codex Vaticanus Ebr. 34, which Bietenhard follows.

suffice you' (Deut 3:26). Your opponent in (the heavenly) court,[314] (the Angel of Death), has already issued a decree that you will die and all (human) creatures like you." Then "Let it suffice you" is quoted twice more.

In other words, in the "hour" when Moses besought the Lord[315] whether it was possible for him to remain alive and enter the Land, He responded: "It is not possible." The term אי here can be equivalent to אין , "not," certainly meant in this case.[316] Yet it can also be meant as אם , "if," "whether."[317] I suggest that the Jewish Christian author of the Gethsemane narrative was well acquainted with the haggadah on Moses' resistance to death in his last hour, and borrowed the term אי אפשר from it. He then changed its meaning from "it is *not* possible" to "*if* it is possible," which was later correctly translated into Greek as εἰ δυνατόν ἐστιν . This agrees with the formulation cited in the *Sifre* text above: "Is it possible that...?"

The next section in *Tanḥuma* B, 6, also on Deut 3:23,[318] has R. Simlai (b. Abba, a second generation Palestinian Amora,[319]) quote 3:26. Then God says: "Moses, I have sworn two oaths, one that you must die, and one to destroy Israel. To make both of them void 'is not possible' (אי איפשר). 'If it is your will' (אם תרצה אתה) to remain alive, Israel will be destroyed." Moses then accuses God of playing a trick on him. He states: "Moses and a thousand like him may be destroyed, but not one person from Israel should be destroyed!"

Here Moses is portrayed as sacrificing himself for the welfare of all Israel. His "will" may be to remain alive, but for both him and Israel to do so "is not possible" according to the divine plan. Precisely these two expressions appear in Jesus' struggling with God in the face of death in Mark 14:35-36.

Finally, the same motif of "if it is possible" is reflected in *Sifre* Num. Pinḥas 135, which deals with Deut 3:26 here, "Let it suffice you."[320] The background is again that Moses barters with God about entering the Land of Israel. He would prefer entering as Israel's leader, without

---

[314] Cf. Jastrow 182 on בעל דין .
[315] Cf. MS "V" of *Frag. Targ.* Deut 3:23, "in that hour," for "at that time" in the MT (Klein 1.212; 2.170). See also *Targum Neofiti 1 ad loc.* (Díez Macho 5.35 and 454).
[316] Jastrow 43, III.
[317] *Ibid.*, II.
[318] Buber 12; Bietenhard 2.453-54.
[319] *Introduction* 96.
[320] Horovitz 181-82; Kuhn 558-59.

placing the reins in Joshua's hands. The Tannaitic midrash states that he then tells God: "'If not' (אם לאו), I will enter as a plain man." This God rejects. The same is true for Moses' suggestions of entering as a disciple of Joshua, or through the air or a subterranean passage, or that at least his bones may cross over the Jordan.[321]

Here Moses means: "If it is not possible to enter the Land as I am, let me do so in a different way." As in the other haggadic passages cited above, this terminology is connected to Deut 3:26, "Let it suffice you." God informs Moses, who has prayed repeatedly to Him, that it is "not possible" to change His decision. Moses' death, like Jesus', has irrevocably come.

6.6   Your Will / My Will

A.   In Mark 14:36 Jesus prays for God to remove the cup (of death) from him. "Yet not what I will [θέλω], but what You [will]." The contrast here between Jesus' will and God's will also reflects Moses' last hour, his own struggle with death.

B.   The motif of the "will of God" at the time of Moses' impending death is already found in Josephus, *Ant.* 4.322. The Israelites' tears, their beating of the breast, grief, lamenting, sorrow, weeping and wailing on this occasion (321; cf. Deut 34:8) reduced Moses to tears. This was true although he had always been persuaded that one should not despair at one's approaching end and because this fate befalls man "in accordance with 'the will of God' and by a law of nature." The first phrase in Greek is κατὰ βούλησιν ... θεοῦ . Here Josephus emphasizes that Moses' death at this point is a part of God's will.

Four occurrences of Moses' will or God's will when the hour of Moses' death has arrived are found in *Tanḥ.* B. Va'ethanan 6 on Deut 3:23. After the citation of Deut 3:26, Moses continues to barter with God by saying: "Maybe the [coming] generations will maintain that I did 'Your will' [רצונך] in my youth, but in my old age [at the time of my death] I did not do 'Your will' [רצונך]. He spoke to him: I have already written, 'because you [pl.] did not revere Me as holy in the midst of the people of Israel' (Deut 32:51). [Moses] said before Him: If it is 'Your will' [רצונך], I will enter the Land and spend two or three years there, and afterwards

---

321 Here Deut 31:2 is quoted by God. The same pattern of "if not" is found in *Deut. Rab.* Ve'zot ha-Berakhah 11/10 (Mirkin 11.157; Soncino 7.183-84).

I will die. He said to him: It is a decree before Me that you may not enter!"[322]

Somewhat further on in the same section R. Simlai's exposition occurs, as described above in 5. B. There the expressions "it is not possible" and "if it is 'your will' to remain alive" are found together.

Finally, in Saul Liebermann's edition of *Deut. Rab.* Va'ethanan on Deut 3:26, Moses addresses God: "'And if it is not Your will' [ואם אינך רוצה], grant me permission, and I will go by the means I prayed for, on the condition that I not cross over the Jordan."[323]

The above five occurrences of Moses' will and God's will, once connected to "not being possible," all found in the context of the imminent death of Moses, make it very probable that the Palestinian Jewish Christian author of the Gethsemane narrative borrowed the expressions "my will" and "Your will" from this haggadic context.

6.7 Submission to God's Will

A.   Connected with the above discussion of Jesus' will and God's will in Mark 14:36 is the fact that only after his threefold prayer with the same contents, does Jesus ascertain: "It is enough / sufficient for me. The hour has come. The Son of Man is delivered into the hands of sinners. Rise, let us be going" (vv 41b-42a).[324] The Palestinian Jewish Christian author of the narrative creates the impression here of Jesus' submitting to God's will, his death at Golgotha the next afternoon, after struggling with God in prayer three times. This submission also reflects Judaic haggadah on the imminent death of Moses.

B.   In *Deut. Rab.* Ve'zot ha-Berakhah 11/5 on Deut 33:1 ("This is the blessing ... before his death"),[325] the third generation Tanna R. Meir[326] relates that the Angel of Death went to Moses three different times, informing him that God had sent him to him, for he was to depart from this life today. Only after the Angel of Death approached him a third time did Moses say: "Since this is from God, I must resign myself to

---

[322] Buber 11; Bietenhard 2.452. I follow the Vaticanus MS of Bietenhard here. However, all the "will" phrases are the same.
[323] Liebermann 47-48.
[324] Cf. section 6.8 below for my interpretation of "It is enough / sufficient for me."
[325] Mirkin 11.152; Soncino 7.176. A parallel is found in *Tanh.* Ve'zot ha-Berakhah 3 on Deut 33:1 (Eshkol 2.945).
[326] *Introduction* 84.

God's will." The phrase צדק את הדין employed here meaning resigning oneself to the divine dispensation as just, submitting oneself to God's will.[327] This is shown by the fact that Deut 32:4 is then quoted as a proof text: "The Rock [God], His work is perfect; for all His ways are justice. A God of faithfulness and without iniquity, just [צַדִּיק] and right is He." A variant of this tradition is found in Ve'zot ha-Berakhah 11/10, where Moses barters three times with God in order to remain alive, and God answers him with Deut 3:26. "When Moses saw that no creature could save him from the path of death, in that hour" he spoke Deut. 32:4.[328]

Finally, it should be noted that Ḥananyah b. Teradion, a second generation Tanna who became a martyr during the Hadrianic persecution of 132-35 CE,[329] is described in *b. 'Abod. Zar.* 18a as also submitting to the divine judgment / will and quoting Deut 32:4 when he went out to his death.[330]

The Palestinian Jewish Christian author of the Gethsemane narrative knew of the Judaic haggadic tradition of Moses' submitting to the divine will that he must die, even after he prays to God three times. For this reason he has Jesus say "It is enough / sufficient for me" after praying to God three times. To this expression I now turn.

6.8   It Is Enough / Sufficient

A.   After Jesus prays a third time in Gethsemane, he returns to the disciples and says to them: "Sleep from now on and rest! ἀπέχει . The hour has come. Behold, the Son of Man is delivered into the hands of sinners" (Mark 14:41).[331] Neither Matthew (26:45) nor Luke (22:46) understood the meaning of ἀπέχει here; they therefore omitted the expression. In his exhaustive commentary on the Passion Narrative,

---

[327] Jastrow 1263 on צדק .
[328] Mirkin 11.157-58; Soncino 7.184. Cf. also the emphasis on God's justice in "Petirat Mosheh" A (Jellinek 1.129) and B (Jellinek 6.78). In contrast to the haggadic Moses background here, Adela Yarbro Collins believes Jesus' "serene acceptance of God's will" is one aspect which rather calls to mind "Socrates and those who followed his example in meeting death with composure and courage" (*Mark* 635).
[329] *Introduction* 81.
[330] Soncino 91; here he speaks the first part of the verse, his wife the second. Cf. also *Sifre Niṣṣabim* 307 on Deut 32:4 (Finkelstein 346; Hammer 312).
[331] For this interpretation of sleeping and resting, see below, section 6.9.

Raymond Brown devotes a five-page appendix to the various possible meanings of it.[332]

Jerome, who had studied Hebrew extensively and had lived first in Antioch for some six years and then in Bethlehem from 386 until his death in 420, finished his translation of the New Testament into Latin, the "Vulgate," ca. 388 CE. It is known that local Bethlehem Jews helped him to translate the Old Testament from the Hebrew and the Aramaic, and he was also acquainted with many Judaic haggadic traditions.[333] Jerome translated the puzzling ἀπέχει as *sufficit*, "it is enough / sufficient."[334] There is no early lexicographical evidence for this interpretation.[335] Nevertheless, his interpretation has been adopted, for example, by the RSV ("It is enough"), NRSV ("Enough!"), and the 1985 Luther Bible ("Es ist genug"). Analysis of Judaic lore on the impending death of Moses, especially Deut 3:26 ("It is enough for you"), substantiates Jerome's translation, now adopted in many circles.

B.   The Book of Deuteronomy closes by having God show Moses the Land (of Israel) from Mount Nebo, opposite Jericho. Before he dies, God tells him: "I have let you see it with your eyes, but you shall not go over there" (34:4).[336] This scene is adumbrated already in chapter three, where Moses "beseeches" (v 23) the Lord (in prayer) to allow him to go over and see the good land beyond the Jordan (v 25). Yet He tells him: "Let it suffice you [רַב לְךָ]; speak no more to Me of this matter" (v 26). Moses is told to ascend the mountain and view the Land, but "you shall not go over this Jordan" (v 27).

As I have pointed out several times before, Judaic haggadah bases Moses' threefold prayer just before his death on Deut 3:23's "beseeching." *Deut. Rab.* Ve'zot ha-Berakhah 11/10, for example, states that when only one hour remained to Moses, he asked God if He would not let him enter the Land, to allow him to live in this world and not die. This God rejects. Moses' second request, if entering the Land is not possible, is to become

---

[332] Cf. his *The Death of the Messiah. From Gethsemane to the Grave* (ABRL; New York: Doubleday, 1994) 1379-83. See also Craig A. Evans, *Mark 8:27 - 16:20* (WBC 34B; Nashville: Thomas Nelson, 2001) 416-17, who prefers the meaning: "Is it far off?"

[333] Cf. Williston Walker, *A History of the Christian Church* (New York: Charles Scribner's Sons, 1959) 159, as well as the many references to Jerome in Ginzberg's *Legends*, as shown in the index (7.591-93).

[334] Cf. BAGD 84-85 on the Greek verb.

[335] Cf. Brown, *The Death* 1381-82.

[336] Cf. also 32:52 and 31:2.

like the beasts of the field. This God rejects by stating: "Let it suffice you." Moses' third attempt involves his becoming like a bird which can fly anywhere. God again rejects this request with "Let it suffice you." The midrash then asks: "What does 'Let it suffice you' mean? God said to him: 'You have spoken sufficiently / enough.' When Moses saw that no creature could save him from the path of death, in that hour" he quoted Deut 32:4, acknowledging God's justice, i.e. he submitted to the divine will.[337]

The Tannaitic midrash *Sifre Va'ethanan* 29 on Deut 3:26 explains Moses' words, "and did not hearken to me," as: "[God] did not accept my prayer."[338] *Sifre* then offers four different explanations of "Let it suffice you," showing how popular this motif was. The Palestinian Jewish Christian author of the Gethsemane narrative also employed this motif by having Jesus pray three times to be allowed to continue to live, but God did not accept his prayer either. Therefore Jesus says precisely at this juncture: "It is enough for me; the hour [to die] has come" (Mark 14:41).

In *'Avot R. Nat.* A 12, after Moses' persistent resistance to the Angel of Death's efforts to take his soul, God finally tells him: "Moses, 'you have had enough' [דייך] of this world; lo, the world to come awaits you."[339] *Mek. R. Ish.* Amalek 2 on Exod 17:14 has R. Joshua (b. Ḥananyah, a second generation Tanna[340]), say regarding Deut 3:26 : "'Let it suffice you' means 'it is enough for you' [דייך] to have the world to come."[341] In *Sifre* Num. Pinḥas 135, R. Ishmael (b. Elisha, a second generation Tanna,[342]) also comments on this phrase with a parable, showing very early rabbinic reflection on its meaning as applied to Moses' death scene.[343] As noted above, *Tanḥ.* B Va'ethanan 5 has God reject Moses' prayer and supplication not to die with the words: "It is not possible; 'let

---

337 Mirkin 11.157-58; Soncino 7.183-84.
338 Finkelstein 45; Hammer 53.
339 Schechter 50; Goldin 65.
340 Cf. n. 302.
341 Lauterbach 2.151. Before this another interpretation with דייך occurs.
342 *Introduction* 79.
343 Horovitz 181; Kuhn 556-57. In *b. Soṭah* 13b (Soncino 70) the "School of R. Ishmael" is cited. Cf. also the comments of R. Judah (b. Ilai) and R. Nehemiah, two third generation Tannaim (*Introduction* 84 and 85), on Deut 3:26 in the "Addition" to Deut 3:23 in Bietenhard, *Midrasch Tanḥuma B* 2.457, with n. 1.

it suffice you.'"[344] "If it is possible" is found in Mark 14:35, which strengthens my proposal for interpreting ἀπέχει in v 41 as deriving originally from "It is enough / sufficient [for me]."

In his Hebrew translation of the New Testament, Franz Delitzsch rendered ἀπέχει as רַב לִי.[345] This is similar to the phrase found in Deut 3:26. The United Bible Societies' Hebrew New Testament has מַסְפִּיק ! for ἀπέχει : "Enough!"[346] Both conform to Jerome's Vulgate translation of *sufficit*, "It is enough / sufficient."

Yet the Palestinian Jewish Christian author of the Gethsemane narrative most probably employed not the term רַב , but דַי in Mark 14:41, as in *'Avot R. Nat.* A 12 and *Mek. R. Ish.* Amalek 2 above. It also means "enough, sufficient." The form דַיִּי , pronounced almost the same, means: "It is enough for me."[347] In the context it means that, like Moses, after praying to God three times to be allowed to remain alive, Jesus finally submits to His will and acknowledges the Lord's decision as just. His strenuous struggling with his fate is now finished. Jesus resigns himself to his imminent death, for, as with Moses, his hour has come.

The Hellenistic Jewish Christian translator of the originally Semitic Gethsemane narrative[348] should have rendered דַיִּי by ἀρκεῖ μοι , similar to ἀρκεῖ σοι in 2 Cor 12:9. It too was based on Moses' death scene in Judaic sources. The translator may have puzzled at its meaning, however, considering it inappropriate on the lips of his Savior. He misunderstood דַיִּי , "It is sufficient / enough for me" as דַי , "Enough (of that)!" This was for him another reproach to the disciples for their still sleeping and resting instead of watching / keeping awake and praying. Not wanting Jesus on the night before his death to again reproach his

---

[344] Buber 10; Bietenhard 2.450. The next section, 6, also deals with Deut 3:23 and 26; it mentions Moses' "will" and God's "will" several times, a term also found in Mark 14:36.

[345] *The Hebrew New Testament* 93.

[346] Cf. *The Hebrew New Testament* 135. On *maspiq*, see Alcalay, *The Complete Hebrew-English Dictionary* 1402: "sufficient, adequate, enough."

[347] Jastrow 293. Cf. the modern Hebrew expression דַי ! , "Enough of that!" in Alcalay 427. It is also probably behind Matt 6:34, "Let the day's own trouble be 'sufficient' [ἀρκετόν] for the day." Both Delitzsch (344) and the United Bible Societies (466) have דַי לָךְ for ἀρκεῖ σοι in 2 Cor 12:9.

[348] See the discussion of this issue in my *The Wicked Tenants and Gethsemane* 152-53.

own disciples in such a way, however,[349] he deliberately translated the term as ἀπέχει . To him this probably meant: "full payment is being made."[350] That is, Judas would now perform the deed necessary to receive the money promised him (cf. Mark 14:11); he was already on his way to Gethsemane with a crowd to betray and have Jesus arrested. Jesus' hour had thus come; he was delivered into the hands of sinners (v 41). The translator's new term fit the context well.

The above proposal has the major advantage that it derives directly from early Judaic lore on Moses' imminent death in spite of his praying three times to God to allow him to continue to live. Jerome, living near Antioch and in Bethlehem, may have corrected ἀπέχει back to *sufficit* because he recognized Judaic motifs from the impending death of Moses in the Gethsemane narrative. Or, more probably, he had contact with Syrian or Palestinian Jewish Christians, a number of whom were bilingual, who in spite of the Gospel of Mark in Greek retained at least in oral tradition the earlier Syrian or Hebrew (possibly Aramaic) account of the Gethsemane incident, including דַּיִּי . This he preferred and (partially) correctly rendered as *sufficit*, which has been a favorite reading ever since.

6.9   Resting

A.   After praying for deliverance from death a third time, Jesus returned to the disciples and said: "Sleep from now on [in the future, but not now[351]], and take your rest! It is enough / sufficient for me. The hour has come. Behold, the Son of Man is delivered into the hands of sinners" (Mark 14:41). Here the first clause is a reproach to the disciples similar to Jesus' question of Peter in v 37; the same is implied for the disciples in v 40. If one conceives v 41a as a question, the same reproachful tone is implied: "Are you still sleeping and taking your rest?"[352] I shall mention a third alternative at the conclusion of B. below.

---

[349] The disciples' failure to watch with Jesus is nevertheless a major thrust in the narrative. See *The Wicked Tenants and Gethsemane* 142-43.

[350] Cf. LSJ 188, IV; BAGD 84 for "the account is (now) closed"; and Brown, *The Death* 1383, "The money is paid."

[351] For this meaning of τὸ λοιπόν , cf. BAGD 480, 3. a. α.: "from now on, in the future, henceforth." See also Delitzsch's translation in his Hebrew New Testament (p. 93): מֵעַתָּה , "from now on" (Jastrow 1129).

[352] On this meaning of τὸ λοιπόν , cf. BAGD *ibid.* It has been preferred in the United Bible Societies' Hebrew New Testament (p. 134): "Are you still [עוֹדְכֶם] sleeping and resting?"

It seems strange that "resting" (ἀναπαύομαι) is mentioned in addition to "sleeping" (καθεύδω) after the latter has occurred alone in vv 37 (twice) and 40. I suggest that "resting" has been mentioned here at the end of Jesus' praying three times because the Palestinian Jewish Christian author of the Gethsemane narrative knew of it in his Judaic model. There Moses, after praying three times before his imminent death, also spoke of "rest."

B.   In *Pseudo-Philo* 19:12 God tells Moses just before he dies: "I will give you 'rest' (*requiem*) in your sleep / slumber (*dormitione*) and bury you in peace."[353] *Sifre* Num. Pinḥas 135 also comments on Deut 3:26, "Let it suffice you," by stating: "You have toiled much, you have labored much. Depart, Moses, 'and rest' (וְנַח)."[354]

Here the emphasis is on Moses' resting. Yet the most important influence on Mark 14:41 derives from Moses' speaking the words of Ps 116:7 just before his death. As I have noted elsewhere, this Psalm was very important in the fashioning of the Gethsemane narrative.[355]

In *Deut. Rab.* Ve'zot ha-Berakhah 11/5 on "before his death" in Deut 33:1,[356] R. Isaac (probably II, a third generation Palestinian Amora,[357]) says the soul of Moses severely resisted[358] departing (from his body), and Moses conversed with it, saying: "My soul [נַפְשִׁי], do you think that the Angel of Death seeks to rule over you?" It answered him: "God will not do so [allow it]!" The soul then quotes Ps 116:8. This type of question and answer sequence is repeated two more times, with different quotations from the same verse. Then Moses asked his soul: "And where are you going to go?" It answered him: "I will walk before the Lord in the land of the living" (v 9). When (Moses) heard this, he gave it permission (to depart), saying to it: "Return, O my soul, to 'your rest' (מְנוּחָיְכִי)," etc. (v 7).

---

[353] Cf. *SC* 229.162; *OTP* 2.328.

[354] Horovitz 181; Kuhn 558. The last verse in Daniel is then quoted (12:13): "But go your way to the end; and you shall 'rest'...." Delitzsch's Hebrew New Testament on Mark 14:41 (p. 93) has the word play נוּמוּ וְנוּחוּ "[from now on] sleep and rest." The usual term for sleeping, however, is יָשֵׁן .

[355] Cf. *The Wicked Tenants and Gethsemane* 68-73, as well as 99-108.

[356] Mirkin 11.152-53; Soncino 7.176-77. A parallel is found in *Tanḥ.* Ve'zot ha-Berakhah 3 on Deut 33:1 (Eshkol 946). See also "Petirat Mosheh" in Jellinek 6.77, which is anonymous. After this God takes Moses' soul with a kiss (Deut 34:5).

[357] *Introduction* 98.

[358] Cf. Jastrow 1430 on the hithpael of קשה .

Here Moses' soul struggles greatly with the prospect of death. Only when it is reassured of being with God in the future, i.e. at the general resurrection, can it depart. Only then can Moses die. In *b. Pesaḥ.* 118a it is stated that the fourth of five reasons for reciting the Hallel is the resurrection of the dead, as found in the above verse, Ps 116:9.[359] This thought is presupposed in the haggadic narrative above.

Moses is described here as saying to his soul at the very end of his life: "Return...to your rest." I suggest that this motif influenced the Palestinian Jewish Christian author of the Gethsemane narrative. He too has Jesus, who has just submitted to God's will for him to die, say to the disciples: "Keep on sleeping and 'resting'" (Mark 14:41).[360] This appears strange in the context, where Jesus tells his disciples in the very next verse (42): "Rise, let us be going." The reason for the strangeness of the clause is that it has been adapted from the scene of Moses' impending death. The proposal above also explains why the puzzling expression τὸ λοιπόν in v 41 has produced so many different interpretations.

6.10 The Hour (of Death) Has Come

A.   In the Gethsemane narrative Jesus tells three of his disciples that his soul is deeply grieved, even to "death" (Mark 14:34). He prays that this "hour" (ὥρα) may pass from him (v 35). It includes "this cup" (of death) in v 36. Jesus then reproaches Peter for not being able to watch / keep awake this "one hour" (μίαν ὥραν - v 37). Finally, Jesus submits to God's will for him that he should die, by saying: "It is enough for me" (see the interpretation of ἀπέχει above). This is immediately followed by: "The hour (ἡ ὥρα - of death) has come. Behold, the Son of Man is delivered into the hands of sinners." "The hour" is thus a major motif in the Gethsemane narrative. It too reflects the scene of Moses' impending death in Judaic sources.

B.   *Deut. Rab.* Ve'zot ha-Berakhah 11/10 comments on Deut 31:14 ("Behold, your days have approached that you must die") up until the end of the biblical book with Moses' death in chapter 34. Examples from it show the major emphasis on the arrival of Moses' last hour.

---

[359] Soncino 608. Cf. the statement by Bar Qappara, a fifth generation Tanna (*Introduction* 90), in *y. Kil.* 9:3, 32c (Neusner 4.277), with parallels in *y. Keth.* 12:4, 35b (Neusner 22.352) and *Pesiq. R.* 1/4 (Braude 1.42).
[360] For "on and on," cf. BAGD 480, 3. a. α. on τὸ λοιπόν .

"The wicked angel Sammael, the chief of the accusing angels [lit. 'satans'], was awaiting the death of Moses 'every hour' [בכל שָׁעָה], saying: 'When will the end [קֵץ] or the moment [רגע] arrive [יַגִּיע] for Moses to die so that I can descend and take his soul from him?'"[361]

"Meanwhile there remained unto Moses [only] 'one hour' [שעה אחת]. 'In that hour' Moses said before God...." Moses then made three requests, ending with God's rejecting them with Deut 3:26, "Let it suffice you." "When Moses saw that no creature could save him from the path of death, he said 'in that hour'" Deut 32:4.[362] The "one hour" here before Moses is handed over to the Angel of Death should be compared with Jesus' asking his disciple Peter in Mark 14:37, "Could you not watch / stay awake 'one hour'?"[363] This means Jesus' final hour, which includes his being handed over to sinners to be killed by them.

"The moment for Moses' death then arrived. In that 'hour' [שעה] God said...."[364] Shortly after this a heavenly voice proclaims: "The end [סוֹף] has arrived, [the time of] your dying."[365] Then God tells Moses' soul: "Now your end has come [הגיע קצך] to depart [from this world]."[366] Here the term "end" (קֵץ)[367] is equal to "hour," which helps to explain the variant τέλος in several MSS of Mark 14:41, followed by "the hour has come / arrived."

These passages from *Deuteronomy Rabbah* could be supplemented by many others from the "Petirat Mosheh." One example is the following: "When 'the hour arrived' [הגיע שעה] in which he was to die...."[368] Another is: "The end 'has arrived' [הגיע], 'the hour' [שעה] for you to die."[369]

---

[361] Mirkin 11.157; Soncino 7.183.

[362] Mirkin 11.157; Soncino 7.183-84.

[363] Contrast *b. Tem.* 16a (Soncino 109), where Joshua, Moses' disciple, replies to him when Moses is about to depart from the world: "My master, have I ever left you for 'one hour' [שעה אחת] and gone elsewhere?"

[364] Mirkin 11.158; Soncino 7.184.

[365] Mirkin 11.159; Soncino 7.186.

[366] *Ibid.*

[367] On קֵץ , cf. Jastrow 1403-04: end, term, designated time. See also *'Avot R. Nat.* B 25 (Schechter 51; Saldarini 149): "When 'the appointed time came' [הגיע קצו] for Moses to depart from the world...."

[368] Cf. Jellinek 6.75.

[369] Jellinek 6.77. Other examples are found on pp. 76-77, and on 1.127-29 (see Kushelevsky, *Moses* 215-17).

All of the above citations from Judaic haggadic material on the last hour of Moses make it very probable that it provided the background for a Palestinian Jewish Christian when he described Jesus' last 'hour' (שָׁעָה) in Gethsemane, the hour of his impending death, in which Peter could not even watch / stay awake "one hour." After Jesus, like Moses, prayed three times to remain alive, but his prayer was rejected, he finally submitted to the will of God. This meant, as for Moses, that his hour had come / arrived (הגיע). This is also how the United Bible Societies' Hebrew New Testament translates Mark 14:41 : הִגִּיעָה הַשָּׁעָה , "The hour has come / arrived."[370]

6.11   Delivered into the Hands of...

A.   After Jesus finally submits to the will of God in Gethsemane, he says: "The hour [of my death] has come. The Son of Man 'is delivered into the hands' [παραδίδοται ... εἰς τὰς χεῖρας] of sinners (Mark 14:41). Rise, let us be going. Behold, 'he who delivers / betrays' [ὁ παραδιδούς] me has arrived" (v 42). "He who delivers / betrays" Jesus is Judas (vv 43-44), who already before the Passover meal had gone to the chief priests in order to "deliver / betray" him to them (vv 10-11; cf. also 3:19). At the meal Jesus is recorded as predicting that one of those present would "deliver / betray" him (14:18 and 21).

According to the Gospel of Mark, it was the chief priests who first "delivered" Jesus to the Romans to be tried and executed (10:33, with the scribes; 14:10-11; 15:1, with elders and scribes, the whole council; 15:10). Yet the "Gentiles," i.e. the Roman occupational power, were the ones who in the person of Pontius Pilate actually "delivered" Jesus to be crucified (9:31 - "men"; 10:33 - the Gentiles; 15:10). In Judaic sources "sinners" is almost a technical term for Gentiles.[371] For this reason the "sinners" (ἁμαρτωλοί) into whose hands the Son of Man is delivered in 14:42 are probably the Romans, and not just the (Jewish) troop sent by the Temple administration to arrest Jesus (v 43).

"To be delivered 'into the hands of'" in 14:41 is also found in 9:31. A variant of this phrase may also lie behind the expression "through whom" (δι᾽ οὗ) in 14:21 : "through whose hand(s)."[372]

---

370 In the 1979 edition, p. 135. Delitzsch has the simpler בָאָה , "has come" (p. 93).

371 Cf. the art. ἁμαρτωλός by Karl Rengstorf in TDNT 1.325-26, as well as Gal 2:15, "Gentile sinners," with Str-B 3.537 on this.

372 Cf. Delitzsch's translation in his Hebrew New Testament (p. 92): אֲשֶׁר עַל־יָדוֹ . An extensive study of the term "to deliver" is found in Wiard

Jesus' being "delivered into the hands of..." in Mark 14:41, while also being a major topos of the entire Passion Narrative, at this point reflects Moses' being "delivered into the hands of" Sammael, the Angel of Death, at the very end of his life.

B.   *Targ. Pseud.-Jon.* Gen 3:6 has Eve behold "Sammael, the Angel of Death."[373] *Deut. Rab.* Ve'zot ha-Berakhah 11/10 on the very end of Deuteronomy, including Moses' death, states that "the angel Sammael, the wicked [הרשע] - he is the chief of all the accusing angels [satans] -, was awaiting the death of Moses every hour." It adds that "there is no one among the accusing angels so wicked [רָשָׁע] as Sammael."[374]

Tannaitic midrashim deal with Moses' final hour by describing it so: "In that hour God told the Angel of Death: 'Go and bring Me the soul of Moses!'"[375] The *Deuteronomy Rabbah* passage above continues by saying that when Sammael came to Moses, the prophet told him: "'You shall not take away my soul!' He [Sammael] said to him: 'The souls of all who come into this world 'are delivered into my hand' [מְסוּרִין לְיָדִי]."[376] A bit later, when the time of his death has come, Moses addresses God as follows: "I implore You, 'do not deliver me into the hand' [אַל תִּמְסְרֵנִי בְּיַד] of the Angel of Death!" God then promises that He Himself will attend to Moses and his burial.[377]

Popkes, *Christus traditus*. Eine Untersuchung zum Begriff der Dahingabe im Neuen Testament (ATANT 49; Zurich and Stuttgart: Zwingli, 1967).

[373] Rieder 1.4; Maher 26. On Sammael, cf. Jastrow 998; the art. "Samael" by Ludwig Blau in *JE* (1905) 10.665-66; "Samael" by Gershom Scholem in *EJ* (1971) 14.719-22; and Str-B 1.136-49.

[374] Mirkin 11.157; Soncino 7.183.

[375] Cf. *Sifre* Niṣṣabim 305 (Finkelstein 326; Hammer 296-97), and *'Avot R. Nat.* A 12 (Schechter 50; Goldin 65-66; see also B 25 in Schechter 51-52; Saldarini 149-53). The latter also has two occurrences of "handing over my soul to you," and one of "handing over his soul to me."

[376] Mirkin 11.158; Soncino 7.185. Parallels are found in "Petirat Mosheh" A (Jellinek 1.128; Kushelevsky, *Moses* 219) and B (Jellinek 6.76).

[377] Mirkin 11.159; Soncino 7.186. Parallels are found in "Petirat Mosheh" A (Jellinek 1.128, with Sammael; Kushelevsky, *Moses* 221) and B (Jellinek 6.77). See also *Tanḥ.* B Va'ethanan 6 (Buber 11; Bietenhard 2.452 - "Do not hand me over to the throes of the Angel of Death!"). Jude 9 has the Archangel Michael contend with the "devil" (διάβολος) over Moses' body, not his soul. This Greek term already in the LXX translates "Satan"; see BAGD 182.

The biblical expression for "give into the power of, deliver over to" is נתן ביד.[378] Rabbinic Hebrew, however, employs here מסר ביד.[379] The latter verb especially means "to surrender a person to the authorities," which admirably fits Mark 14:41.[380]

The Palestinian Jewish Christian author of the Gethsemane narrative again borrowed here from haggadic lore on the last hour of Moses. The prophet fears that his soul will be "delivered over into the hand of the 'wicked' (רשע)" Sammael. The author transferred this imagery to Jesus at the very end of his struggle with death. In the Septuagint, ἁμαρτωλός is most frequently a translation of רשע.[381] The Hellenistic Jewish Christian translator of the Gethsemane narrative thus most probably employed ἁμαρτωλοί in Mark 14:41 because he found רשעים in his source. The original Palestinian author, in turn, most probably employed the latter because Moses' soul was to be "delivered into the hands of 'wicked' [רשע] Sammael," the Angel of Death and chief "satan."[382] To fit it into the new context, he simply changed the singular to the plural: "wicked men."

"Behold, he who delivers / betrays me has arrived" (= Judas) in Mark 14:42b continues the same thought as in v 41b. It probably derives from the Palestinian Jewish Christian author. "Rise, let us be going" (v 42a),[383]

---

[378] Cf. BDB 390 on יָד , 5.b.3).

[379] Jastrow 810-11: to hand over, to deliver. He cites *b. Giṭ.* 7a as one example: "It is within my hand [power] to deliver them to the kingdom" (= Roman government). Another is from the period of the (Hasmonean) war in *b. B. Qam.* 82b: "they will not be delivered into your hand."

[380] Jastrow 810.

[381] Cf. the concordance of Hatch-Redpath 1.64-65.

[382] In Luke 22:3 it is Satan who enters into Judas, who then consults with others on how to "betray" Jesus (v 4). John 13:2 has the devil (διάβολος ; see n. 377 for this as a translation of "Satan") put it into the heart of Judas to "betray" Jesus. In v 27 Satan then enters into him.

[383] The term ἄγωμεν is found once as a loanword in Hebrew. Cf. the parable by R. Levi, a third generation Palestinian Amora (*Introduction* 98), in *Gen. Rab.* Vayyishlaḥ 78/7 on Gen 33:1 (Theodor and Albeck 2.925, first line; Soncino 2.720). Here cattle and (other) animals say to a fox: "Let's go [to the lion]!" See Krauss, *Lehnwörter* 2.8. On the expression ἐγείρεσθε , said by Jesus to his disciples, see R. Aqiba's customary words to his disciples on the eve of Passover: "The time has come to rise [הגיע עת לעמוד]." This was spoken in the academy so that his disciples would not arrive home late and their children "fall asleep" (ישנו). Was it already a stock phrase at the time the Palestinian Jewish Christian author composed the Gethsemane narrative? See *b. Pesaḥ.* 109a, a baraitha

however, was part of an earlier tradition he incorporated into his narrative. This is shown by its odd occurrence in John 14:31.

6.12   Pass Over

A.   After partaking of the "Passover" (פֶּסַח) meal with his disciples in Jerusalem, which commemorated God's "passing over" the houses of the Israelites in Egypt (Exod 12:12 and 23 - עבר), Jesus went with eleven of them to Gethsemane. Taking Peter, James and John with him, he told them to remain there and watch / keep awake. "Proceeding" (προελθών) somewhat further, he prayed that if it were possible, the hour might "pass" (παρέλθη) from him (Mark 14:35). "Going on / proceeding" here can be expressed in Hebrew by עבר . The same is true for "passing."[384]

In the next verse (36) Jesus prays to God: ""Remove' this cup from me." This too can be expressed by the hiphil of עבר : "to cause to pass, remove."[385]

The Palestinian Jewish Christian author of the Gethsemane narrative displays his artistic ability here. Assonance and a difference in meaning of the same root within two verses would have been appreciated by his original audience(s). I suggest that the author employed the term עבר three times in his narrative not only because of the "Passover" festival, but also because it played such a major role in biblical and Judaic lore regarding the scene of Moses' impending death.

B.   Almost all the haggadic sources which I have cited in sections 6.1-11 above deal primarily with Moses' resistance to God's telling him he may not "pass over" (עבר) the Jordan and enter the Land of Israel (Deut 3:25,27; 31:2; 34:5; cf. 32:52). This is repeated in many variations. Instead, Moses is to ascend Mount Nebo and die there.

It seems probable, then, that the Palestinian Jewish Christian author of the Gethsemane account, which took place on the first evening of the "Passover" Festival, also borrowed the term "pass over" (עבר) from this and haggadic development of the above texts from Deuteronomy

---

(Soncino 563), as well as *b. Sukk.* 28a (Soncino 123, with notes 1-2) on Yoḥanan b. Zakkai.

[384] Cf. Delitzsch's Hebrew New Testament, p. 92. For עבר as also "pass on, go on, proceed," see BDB 718,5. For "passing a little" (further on), see עָבַר מְעַט in 2 Sam 16:1. Reference from Adolf Schlatter, *Der Evangelist Matthäus* 751.

[385] Cf. Delitzsch as in the previous note. On the verb, see Jastrow 1038.

dealing with the impending death of Moses. He then employed it three times.

6.13   *The Cup of Death*

A.   In Gethsemane Jesus told the inner circle of three disciples that his soul was very sad "unto death" (ἕως θανάτου ; Mark 14:34). Then he fell on the earth and prayed that if possible, the hour (of his death) might pass from him (v 35). This Jesus made into a direct request in v 36: "Remove / cause this 'cup' [ποτήριον] to pass from me." Every Palestinian Jewish Christian hearer acquainted with even the simplest form of the Gospel message knew this was the "cup of death" which Jesus was to taste at Golgotha the next afternoon. When Judas arrived in Gethsemane to deliver him over to others, Jesus also knew: "the hour [of death] has come" (v 41).

The "cup (of death)" also plays a role at the very end of Moses' life.

B.   Before analyzing the "cup of death" as associated with Moses, it will be helpful to make several other observations about the use of "cup" in the Hebrew Bible.

Lam 4:21 states that "to you [Edom] also the cup shall 'pass.'" Here the same verb, עבר , occurs for a cup as in the Semitic original (hiphil of עבר) of "'removing' this cup" in Mark 14:36.

Cups of judgment, wrath, staggering, horror and desolation occur numerous times in the MT, but not a cup of death.[386] It is another use of "cup" which is the general background for Jesus' cup and Moses' cup of death.

Ps 11:6 speaks of "'the portion' of their cup." Ps 16:5 also notes that "The Lord is my 'chosen portion' and my cup; You hold my 'lot.'" Here cup means the same as one's "fate": portion or lot.[387] When Jesus asks God in Gethsemane to remove "this cup" from him, it is not one of His negative judgment or wrath. Rather, it is Jesus' portion or lot, i.e. to die the next afternoon by crucifixion. For him it is "the cup of death."

The latter very rare expression is found in regard to only two biblical passages in Judaic sources. One of them is Deut 32:1, the beginning of the "Song of Moses," recited directly before he ascends Mount Nebo to die. *Targum Neofiti 1* on this verse reads:

---

[386] Cf. BDB 468.
[387] Cf. BDB on מנת , חלק and גורל : 584, 324 and 174 respectively.

When the appointed time [קִצָּה] of Moses the prophet arrived to be gathered in peace from the midst of the world [= to die], Moses thought in his heart and said: "Woe now is me, since I am being gathered from the midst of the world and I have not borne witness against the children of the Lord. If I bear witness against them before the sons of man who die and taste 'the cup of death,' the people die and their decrees are void. However, I shall bear witness against them before the heavens and before the earth, who never die and who do not taste 'the cup of death.' However, they will ultimately wear out in the world to come."

Here "the cup of death" (כַּסָא דְמוֹתָה)[388] is repeated twice in the context of the imminent death of Moses. "Tasting the cup of death" is synonymous here with dying. It is emphasized that (all) the sons of man die / taste the cup of death. This also included Moses, who very shortly thereafter in fact does die.

Again, it is the Judaic haggadic description of the scene of Moses' imminent death, as still found in *Targ. Neof. 1* Deut 32:1, which most probably inspired the Palestinian Jewish Christian author of the Gethsemane narrative to describe Jesus as asking God to remove "this cup (of death)" from him.[389]

6.14 Great Grief

A.   After taking Peter, James and John with him, Jesus in Gethsemane began to be greatly distressed and troubled. Then he said to them: "My

---

[388] Cf. Díez Macho, *Neophyti 1*, 5.265; McNamara 146-47, with n. 4. S. Speier in "'Das Kosten des Todeskelches' im Targum" in *VT* 13 (1963) 344-45 correctly defends the authenticity of these readings in Neofiti 1 over against R. Le Déaut, "Goûter le calice de la mort" in *Bib* 43 (1962) 82-86. The only other occurrence of the expression "the cup of death" in found in *Targ. Neof.* Gen 40:23 (Díez Macho 1.269, Eng. 609) in regard to "flesh that tastes the cup of death." The same is found in the *Fragment Targum* on the same verse (Klein 1.62 and 152; Eng. 2.26 and 114). The latter was pointed out by Matthew Black in "The Cup Metaphor in Mark xiv.36" in *ExpT* 59 (1957) 195. On "drinking the cup" that Jesus drinks, see Mark 10:38-39 par., and Acts 12:2 on the martyrdom of James the son of Zebedee. "The cup" and martyrdom are also related in *Mart. Isa.* 5:13, where Isaiah, while being sawed in two, says: "for me alone the Lord has mixed the cup" (*OTP* 2.164). I suspect Christian influence in the "Testament of Abraham," which speaks of the "bitter cup of death" in regard to Abraham in 1:3 and 16:11-12 (*OTP* 1.882 and 892).
[389] The cup imagery itself, however, was probably inspired by Judaic interpretation of Ps 116:13. Cf. *The Wicked Tenants and Gethsemane* 99-100.

soul is 'very sorrowful' [περίλυπος], even to death" (Mark 14:34). At this point Jesus began to pray that death might pass by him (vv 35-36: the hour, this cup).

I suggest that the Palestinian Jewish Christian author of the Gethsemane narrative also borrowed the expression of Jesus' being "very sorrowful" or "greatly grieved" from Judaic haggadah on Moses' great grief at the time of his impending death, when he too prayed that the Angel of Death should depart from him.

B.   In *Deut. Rab.* Va'etḥanan 2/7 on Deut 3:24, Moses pleads with God to be able to enter the Land of Israel for the sake of His mercy. God replies in the words of v 27: "for you shall not go over this Jordan." R. Levi, a third generation Palestinian Amora,[390] then comments: "And when Moses saw how emphatic God's words were, he began to plead strenuously," i.e. to speak v 24: "O Lord God, You have only begun to show Your servant...."[391] The Hebrew for "to plead strenuously" is "he spoke hard / difficult [קשה] words." The English translator in the Soncino edition, J. Rabbinowitz, correctly renders this as "to plead strenuously," for the phrase is designed to express Moses' strong inner feelings in light of his impending death.

In the same midrash, Va'etḥanan 2/3 on Deut 3:23 ("And I besought the Lord at that time"), R. Abin, a fourth generation Palestinian Amora,[392] noted that Moses now "supplicates and 'prostrates himself' to be permitted to enter the Land of Israel, and his prayers are not accepted. His hour is past," (as is indicated by) Deut 3:23.[393] The Hebrew for "prostrates himself" is the hithpael of חבט : "to prostrate one's self (in prayer, in deep commotion)."[394] The expression seeks to describe Moses' deep, inner feelings when he prays to (escape death and) be able to enter the Land.

Most importantly, the Tannaitic midrash *Sifre* Niṣṣabim 304 on Deut 31:14 ("And the Lord said to Moses: 'Behold, the days approach that you must die'") has Moses respond to this statement by replying: "Master of the world, since I am departing from the world 'in great grief,' show me a trustworthy man who can take charge of Israel."[395] This is his disciple

---

[390] See n. 290.
[391] Mirkin 11.33; Soncino 7.36 (cf. n. 2).
[392] See n. 296.
[393] Mirkin 11.31; Soncino 7.32 (cf. n. 2).
[394] Jastrow 417.
[395] Finkelstein 323; Hammer 293; Neusner 2.289.

Joshua. The Hebrew for "in great grief" is בנסים גדול . The Hebrew noun נָסִים means "falling away, grief," the Aramaic "evil, trouble."[396] I suggest that this expression lies behind the term περίλυπος in Mark 14:34. Moses' "strenuous pleading" and his prostrating himself in prayer, in deep inner commotion, were a part of his "great grief." Jesus was "greatly grieved" or "very sorrowful" in light of his upcoming death, so he, like Moses, prayed that his "hour" might pass by him.

For the above reasons I do not believe that the Palestinian Jewish Christian author of the Gethsemane narrative alluded in Mark 14:34 to the phrase "Why are you cast down / despairing, O my soul...?" in Ps 42:6, 12 and 43:5, as maintained by the commentators.[397] The Hebrew verb in these psalm passages is the hithpoel of שׁחח ,[398] which was not so employed in later Hebrew.[399] The Hellenistic Jewish translator of the original Semitic "my soul has great grief, unto death," could have employed λύπη πολλά or λύπη μεγάλη .[400] Yet he may also have been acquainted with the term περίλυπος in connection with both one's soul and prayer in Tob 3:1 (S), as well as with one's soul in LXX Ps 41:5, 11 and 42:5. They then encouraged him, the translator, to prefer the latter Greek term for "great grief." The origin of the term, however, lies in Judaic lore on Moses' departing from this world "in great grief."

6.15   The Contrast of God's Taking Away Moses' Soul Through a Kiss, and Judas' Handing Jesus Over to Certain Death Through a Kiss

A.   While Jesus was still speaking to his disciples, Judas entered Gethsemane with an armed crowd sent by the chief priests, scribes and elders. The "betrayer" had given this group a sign by which they could

---

[396] Jastrow 917. Hammer has "in great agony," Neusner "with great anguish." Cf. Luke 22:44, "And being in an agony [ἐν ἀγωνία], he prayed more earnestly."

[397] Cf. the margin of the Nestle / Aland Greek New Testament; Reinhard Feldmeier, *Die Krisis des Gottessohnes*. Die Gethsemaneerzählung als Schlüssel der Markuspassion (WUNT 2.21; Tübingen: Mohr, 1987) 156-62; Robert Gundry, *Mark*. A Commentary on His Apology for the Cross (Grand Rapids, MI: Eerdmans, 1993) 867; and Raymond Brown, *The Death* 154. In his monograph on Gethsemane, a revised Tübingen dissertation, Feldmeier does not have a single reference to Moses (see the index).

[398] BDB 1006.

[399] Jastrow 1546.

[400] For "great grief" in the LXX, cf. Jonah 4:1, Tob 3:6, and 1 Macc 6:4, 9 and 13. Sir 37:2 somewhat recalls the betrayer Judas: "Is it not a grief to the death when a companion and friend turn to enmity?"

recognize Jesus: "The one 'I shall kiss' [φιλήσω] is the man. Seize him and lead him off securely" (Mark 14:44). Then Judas proceeded to Jesus and addressed him as "Master!" "And 'he kissed' [κατεφίλησεν] him" (v 45). Recognizing the agreed upon sign, the armed crowd "laid hands on him and seized him" (v 46).

Matthew follows Mark closely at this point in regard to the kissing motif (26:48-49). Luke, in contrast, omits the agreed upon sign and has Judas approach Jesus "in order to kiss" (φιλῆσαι) him. This does not come about, however, for Jesus then asks him: "'By a kiss' [φιλήματι] you would deliver / hand over the Son of Man [= me]?" (22:47-48). The kiss is emphasized here by its position at the beginning of the question. In John 18:2-12 there is no kissing incident at all. Instead, when those who had come to arrest Jesus arrived, he went forth to meet them and identified himself (vv 4-8). He is here represented as himself determining the course of action (see section 6.19 below).[401]

Various suggestions have been made as to a possible background to Judas' kiss, including Prov 27:6 ("profuse are the kisses of an enemy") and 2 Sam 20:9 ("And Joab took Amasa by the beard with his right hand to kiss him." Then Joab struck his sword into Amasa's body, killing him - v 10). Rabbinic tradition on Esau's actually wanting to bite his brother Jacob instead of kissing him (Gen 33:4) is of no relevance here, nor are any of the other three or four types of kisses approved by the rabbis.[402]

B.   For the above reasons I would like to make a new proposal here as to the Judaic background of Judas' kissing Jesus, which led to his death the same day.[403] It is intimately connected to the portrayal of Jesus' praying three times in Gethsemane that God will remove the cup (of death) from him. As shown above in section 6.4, a Palestinian Jewish Christian described Jesus here in part with exact expressions and motifs from Judaic lore regarding Moses' threefold prayer that the Angel of Death would spare him at the very end of his life, even though his hour had now come. The climax of Judaic haggadic tradition on this scene portrays

---

[401] Cf. Brown, *The Death* 252-62 on this pericope. I agree with him that there is no increase in emotion between φιλέω and καταφιλέω (p. 253). The Hebrew, for example, is the same for both (נשׁק ; Jastrow 941-42), as shown in Delitzsch's Hebrew New Testament (p. 93).

[402] Cf. Str-B 1.995-96. Nor is the *Testament of Abraham* 20:9 applicable. It relates: "And he [Abraham] kissed his [Death's] hand, and immediately his soul cleaved to the hand of Death" (*OTP* 1.895).

[403] According to Judaic time reckoning, the day extended from sunset to sunset. Thus Jesus' Crucifixion the next afternoon was part of the same day.

God Himself as taking away Moses' soul with a kiss. The contrast would have been striking to Palestinian Jewish Christians acquainted with these traditions, and it is most probably intended.

In the last chapter of Deuteronomy (34), Moses ascends Mount Nebo, opposite Jericho. Then the Lord shows him all the land the Israelites are to inherit. Moses may view it, but may not go over there. Verse 5 then states: "So Moses the servant of the Lord died there in the land of Moab, 'according to the word of the Lord.'" Afterwards the Lord buried him in an unknown place.

The Hebrew for "according to the word of the Lord" is literally "'by the mouth' [עַל פִּי] of the Lord." The construct פִּי is from פֶּה , "mouth." While the Septuagint, *Targum Onqelos* and the *Fragment Targum* (MS "V") on Deut 34:5 simply have "the word of the Lord" here, *Targum Pseudo-Jonathan* reads: "by the kiss [עַל נְשִׁיקַת] of the word of the Lord."[404] The Lord's mouth is represented here as "kissing" Moses, who earlier had spoken "mouth to mouth" to God (Num 12:8).

Judaic haggadah concerned itself with the Lord's "mouth" here at an early time. *Pseudo-Philo* 19:16, for example, paraphrases Deut 34:5-6 regarding Moses in the following way: "and he died in glory [*in gloria*] according to the word of the Lord, and He buried him...."[405] Here "in glory" has been added by the Palestinian author, writing in Hebrew at about the time of Jesus.[406] He may have thought that God's kissing Moses was a "glorious" way to die, although he does not explicitly state this.

In *'Avot R. Nat.* A 12 God tells the Angel of Death to go and bring Him the soul of Moses. This he attempts to do, but in anger Moses drives him off. This occurs several times until God Himself addresses Moses: "Moses, you have had enough [דייך][407] of this world. Behold, the world to come is awaiting you." Then God "took the soul of Moses and stored it under the Throne of Glory. And when He took it, He took it only 'by a kiss' [בנשיקה], as Scripture states: 'By the mouth of the Lord' (Deut 34:5)." The narrative continues by noting that the souls of all the righteous are preserved under the Throne of Glory.[408]

---

[404] Rieder 2.308; English in Clarke 105. Cf. Michael Fishbane, *The Kiss of God. Spiritual and Mystical Death in Judaism* (Seattle: University of Washington Press, 1994) 17-19 on this motif.

[405] Cf. *SC* 229.164; *OTP* 2.328.

[406] Cf. n. 288.

[407] Cf. section 6.8 above on the relevance of this term for ἀπέχει in Mark 14:41.

[408] Schechter 50; Goldin 65. The dative φιλήματι in Luke 22:48, "by a kiss," corresponds exactly to the Hebrew phrase. In *b. Ber.* 8a (Soncino 40), a Tannaitic

A variant of this narrative is found in *Deut. Rab*. Ve'zot ha-Berakhah 11/10, where God informs Moses' soul: "Your end has come; depart, do not delay." To the soul's objections God replies: "Go forth, do not delay, and I will elevate you to the highest heavens, and I will place you under the Throne of My Glory with the cherubim, seraphim, and troops [of angels]." Moses' soul then maintains that Moses was purer than two angels. "'I implore You, let me remain in the body of Moses.' In that hour God 'kissed him' [וְשָׁקוֹ - Moses] and took away his soul 'by a kiss of the mouth' [בִּנְשִׁיקַת פֶּה]."[409]

Another variant, showing the great popularity of this tradition, is found in *Tanḥ*. B Va'etḥanan 6. The Israelites went to Moses and informed him that he had only another half moment to live. Moses then "placed both his arms on his heart and said to the Israelites: 'See the future of flesh and blood! These two hands, which received the Torah from the mouth of the Almighty, are falling into the grave!' In this moment his soul departed 'by a kiss' [בִּנְשִׁיקָה]," as is written in Deut 34:5.[410]

In *b. B. Bat.* 17a "our rabbis taught" that there were six persons over whom the Angel of Death had no dominion (since they died by a kiss of God). They are the Patriarchs, as well as Moses, Aaron and Miriam. "By the mouth of the Lord" (in Deut 34:5 and Num 33:38) applies to Moses and Aaron. R. Eleazar then adds that Miriam also died "by a kiss," deriving this from the occurrence of "there" both in Num 20:1 and Deut 34:5.[411]

Finally, Judaic tradition considered the Song of Songs to be a dialogue between God and Israel.[412] *Cant. Rab.* 1:2 § 5 on "Let Him kiss me with the kisses of His mouth," states for example: "The Rabbis say: The souls of these (viz. the righteous) will be taken away with a kiss." R. ʿAzariah,

---

tradition notes that the divine kiss is the easiest of the 903 forms of death in the world.

[409] Mirkin 11.159-60; Soncino 7.186-87. See also "Petirat Mosheh" A (Jellinek 1.129; Kushelevsky, *Moses* 222, with other references in n. 105 on pp. 247-48) and B (Jellinek 6.77).

[410] Buber 2.13; Bietenhard 2.456. A parallel is found in *Tanḥ*. Va'etḥanan 6 (Eshkol 2.860).

[411] Soncino 86. The text continues by stating that "our rabbis taught" that there are seven others over whom the worms had no dominion. "By the mouth of the Lord" here also applies to Moses, Aaron and Miriam. A parallel to the first tradition is found in *b. Moʿed Qaṭ.* 28a (Soncino 181).

[412] Cf. Shimʿon Donsqi's remarks in his edition of *Midrash Rabbah. Shir ha-Shirim* 29-30.

a fifth generation Palestinian Amora,[413] then explains this in regard to Aaron (Num 33:38), Moses (Deut 34:5), and Miriam (Num 20:1 and Deut 34:5). Cant 1:2 is cited to show that this also applies to *all* righteous persons (כל הצדיקים).[414]

The latter is already implied in *'Avot R. Nat.* A 12. After stating that God took the soul of Moses by a kiss (Deut 34:5), the midrash says He stored it under the Throne of Glory, where the souls of all the righteous are preserved (see above).

Jesus was considered by early Palestinian Jewish Christians to be not only the Righteous One (ὁ δίκαιος in Acts 3:14; 7:52; 22:14), and thus also deserving of having God take his soul from him by a kiss. As the Messiah, he was also thought to be the final or great redeemer, the successor of Israel's first redeemer, Moses.[415]

I therefore propose that, as in the Gospel of John, historically there was no kiss by Judas in Gethsemane as a sign of recognition.[416] Judas most probably simply pointed Jesus out to the troop / band that accompanied him. The enigmatic figure of Judas was then quickly developed in an haggadic style by early Palestinian Jewish Christians.[417] Jesus was portrayed in Gethsemane with expressions and motifs derived from Judaic tradition on the hour of Moses' death. Palestinian Jewish Christians also knew how Moses died. The Angel of Death had no authority over him, therefore God Himself took his soul "with a kiss." They therefore described Jesus, the "new" Moses (final redeemer), in similar terms: Judas' kiss of Jesus in Gethsemane meant his death the next afternoon on a cross at Golgotha. A great contrast was intentionally made: God Himself gave Moses the kiss of death, ending his (mental) suffering. This He did not do, however, with His Son Jesus. Instead, acting as the agent of wicked Sammael, the Angel of Death and the chief satan, it was Judas who gave Jesus a kiss, beginning his suffering and leading to his terribly painful death. Paradoxically, however, the narratives of the Resurrection on Easter Sunday and the empty tomb

---

[413] *Introduction* 104.

[414] Cf. Donsqi 16; Soncino 9.28.

[415] Cf. n. 275.

[416] Many elements in John's presentation are, however, patently late, as will be shown shortly.

[417] For an overview of the relevant passages in the NT, cf. E. Blair, art. "Judas," 7, in *IDB* 2.1006-08, as well as "The Name Judas 'Iscariot' and Ahithophel in Judaic Tradition" in my *My Name Is "Legion." Palestinian Judaic Traditions in Mark 5:1-20 and Other Gospel Texts*, 155-208.

show that God would indeed take Jesus to Himself at the time of his death.

Introduction to Sections 6.16-20

There is no reason to doubt the historicity of Jesus' being taken captive in Gethsemane (Mark 14:43-50 par.), which was on the Mount of Olives (v 26; Matt 26:30; and Luke 22:39). John 18:1 basically agrees with this location, saying Jesus and his (eleven) disciples went "across the Kidron Valley to a place where there was a garden." Both John (18:2) and Luke (22:39) state that Jesus went there often, so Judas knew of the site.

When Judas arrived with "a crowd with swords and clubs, from the chief priests, the scribes, and the elders" (Mark 14:43),[418] Judas is represented as betraying Jesus by kissing him, a pre-arranged sign. Thus "they laid hands on him and arrested him" (v 46) and took him to the high priest (v 53).

At Jesus' arrest in Gethsemane, "all of them [the eleven disciples] deserted him and fled" (14:50).[419] The preceding verse (49) says the arrest (and the disciples' fleeing) revealed that the Scriptures were fulfilled. This refers back to v 27, where Jesus tells the eleven disciples upon arriving at the Mount of Olives: "You will all become deserters; for it is written, 'I will strike the shepherd, and the sheep will be scattered' (Zech 13:7)." Big-mouth Peter is then described as bragging: "Even though all become deserters, I will not!" (Mark 14:28). It should be noted that after Jesus is portrayed as quoting Zech 13:7, he immediately refers to his Resurrection: "But after I am raised up, I will go before you to Galilee" (Mark 14:28; cf. 16:7). That is, the eleven disciples were originally thought of as fleeing for their lives at this point - back home to Galilee, where the first Resurrection appearances occurred.[420] Peter's vehement assertion that he would never become a deserter, and the other disciples' similar statement (vv 29-31), appear to have been composed later by a

---

[418] Matthew modifies this at 26:47. See also Luke 22:47 and 52, as well as John 18:3.

[419] This would certainly not have been possible for the disciple who ostensibly cut off the ear of the high priest's servant / slave. If the incident were historical, he would have been immediately apprehended.

[420] Cf. 1 Cor 15:5 for the first appearance as being to Cephas (Peter), then to "the twelve," etc. (vv 6-8). Paul does not state where these appearances took place.

Palestinian Jewish Christian as a foil to illustrate the meaning of Zech 13:7.[421]

There are other indications in the Gospels that all the eleven disciples fled (back home to Galilee) when Jesus was taken captive and did not remain in Jerusalem for his Crucifixion because they feared they also would be arrested as his accomplices and be killed. Already in Gethsemane Jesus is represented as saying to Peter: "Keep awake and pray that you may not come into the time of trial; the spirit indeed is willing, but the flesh is weak" (Mark 14:38). The "time of trial" here primarily means Jesus' subsequent arrest, yet in the Gospel it also points to 14:66-72.

Before departing for the Mount of Olives, Jesus is also portrayed in Luke as telling Peter at the "Last Supper": "Simon, Simon, listen! Satan has demanded / obtained permission to sift you [pl.] like wheat, but I have prayed for you [sing.] that your [sing.] own faith may not fail; and you [sing.], when once you [sing.] have turned back, strengthen your [sing.] brothers" (22:31-32). Peter's response in v 33 is then that also found in Mark 14:29 and 31. I suggest that Satan's "sifting" the disciples refers to their terribly heart-rending decision whether to remain with Jesus at his arrest, or to abandon him. In the Semitic original of Peter's "turning back," Hebrew שׁוּב or Aramaic תוּב , this meant his "repenting"[422] of his behavior in Gethsemane. After Jesus' later appearances, first to him and then to the other eleven disciples in Galilee, Peter "strengthened" them to believe that Jesus was indeed the Messiah in spite of his being killed, and to form together with him the first Christian community, the "church."

This is also meant in John 21:15-17, where after Jesus appears to the disciples at the Sea of Galilee, he commissions Peter: "Feed my lambs"; "Tend my sheep"; and "Feed my sheep." In spite of his also abandoning Jesus in Gethsemane, Peter is represented here as being commissioned by the resurrected Jesus to gather the scattered sheep, now including all his previous followers and not just the other disciples, and to feed / tend them, i.e. to assume the leadership of the earliest Christian community. The narrative indicates this began in Galilee, from which it very soon spread to Jerusalem.

---

[421] That is, I also do not consider Peter's later threefold denial of Jesus in the courtyard of the high priest (14:66-72) as historical. He was already on his way home to Galilee, running for his life.

[422] Cf. Jastrow 1528: "Esp. to return (to God); to repent." On תוּב , see p. 1649, I, 3).

In his farewell discourse in John (chapters 13-16, and his prayer in 17), before Jesus goes to Gethsemane (18:1) he also tells his disciples in 16:32, "The hour is coming, indeed it has come, when you will be scattered, each one to his home, and you will leave me alone." This is an allusion to Zech 13:7, as found in Mark 14:27 (cf. vv 49-50). The disciples will leave Jesus alone when he is taken captive in Gethsemane, and each (ἔκαστος - meant as everyone) will be scattered "to his home" (εἰς τὰ ἴδια).[423] This was originally meant literally, and the disciples' homes were not in Jerusalem,[424] but in Galilee, primarily on or near the Sea of Galilee.

All of the above texts point to Jesus' eleven disciples' abandoning him in the Garden of Gethsemane and fleeing for their lives back to their homes in Galilee, where the first Resurrection appearances later took place and not in or by Jerusalem.[425] Jesus' words at his arrest in Mark 14:46-50 par., as well as John 18:4-11, are later haggadic embellishments of the episode. The following sections, 6.16-20, now describe this encounter.

6.16 Judas Accompanied by Soldiers and Temple Servants / Slaves at Jesus' Arrest

A.   When Judas went to Gethsemane to have Jesus arrested, he brought with him "a crowd with swords and clubs, from the chief priests, the scribes, and the elders" (Mark 14:43). Verse 47 mentions "the servant / slave [δοῦλος] of the high priest" as one of those in the crowd.[426] Jesus

---

[423] Cf. εἰς τὰ ἴδια in LXX Esth 5:10 and 6:12 as rendering the Hebrew אֶל־בֵּיתוֹ , "to his home."

[424] This is in spite of John 20:10. The Evangelist's own Christian community had a special interest in resurrection appearances in Jerusalem (vv 11-29), with this form of the Gospel then ending with v 31.

[425] The Evangelist Luke omits Mark 14:28 and 16:7 because he (alone) describes Jesus' ascension in 24:50-53, which he connects with the Pentecost event in Jerusalem in his second volume at Acts 1:1-12. The "walk to Emmaus" in Luke 24:13-35 is not historical, but instead expresses the Evangelist's interest in the first Resurrection appearance as taking place in Jerusalem. Cf. "The Road to Emmaus (Luke 24:13-35)" in my *The Stilling of the Storm*. Studies in Early Palestinian Judaic Traditions (ISFCJ; Binghamton, NY: Global Publications, Binghamton University, 2000) 137-229. This is followed by another appearance in Jerusalem itself (Luke 24:36-49).

[426] It is known that the chief priests sent their servants / slaves, armed with clubs or staves as in Gethsemane (the "swords" derive from elsewhere; see section 6.17 below), to forcibly collect their share of the tithes. See *b. Pesaḥ.* 57a (Soncino 285), as well as other references cited by Joachim Jeremias, *Jerusalem in the Time of Jesus*

asked them: "Have you come out with swords and clubs to arrest me as though I were a bandit / insurrectionist [ληστής]?" The latter term[427] prepares the hearer / reader for Jesus' being crucified the next afternoon between two bandits / insurrectionists (15:28).

Matthew makes Mark's crowd into a "large crowd" and omits the scribes, but adds elders "of the people" (26:47). In v 55 the First Evangelist has "crowds," plural, yet retains the singular for the high priest's servant / slave in v 51.

In 22:47, Luke speaks only of Judas' leading a crowd.[428] Yet in v 52 Jesus addresses "the chief priests, the officers of the Temple police (στρατηγοί),[429] and the elders," who themselves had come to take him captive. Luke also has the singular "servant / slave" of the high priest in v 50.

John's version of Jesus' arrest is very different from the above in numerous ways. In 18:3 he states that Judas brought along "a detachment of soldiers" (ἡ σπεῖρα), and from the high priests and the Pharisees "servants" (ὑπηρέται),[430] in the plural, arriving there with lanterns, torches and "weapons" (ὅπλα).[431] In v 12 he notes that a χιλίαρχος was present with the *speira*. Literally, a *chiliarch* is an officer over 1000 soldiers, yet later the term was also used to describe the commander of a Roman cohort, i.e. ca. 600 men.[432] In v 10 John labels the servant of the high priest a δοῦλος and even gives him a name, Malchus.

Those accompanying Judas thus develop in the four Gospels from a crowd, to a large crowd, to crowds, to officers of the Temple police, to a detachment of soldiers, and from a servant / slave to servants in the plural. The term σπεῖρα in John 18:3 corresponds to a Roman *cohors*. A cohort was the tenth part of a legion, thus between 420 and 600 soldiers, corresponding to the ca. 600 men under a *chiliarch* (v 12).[433]

(London: SCM Press, 1969) 180-81. The "crowd" of v 43 would have been primarily made up of such servants / slaves. Josephus in *Bell.* 4.293 notes that at least some of the Temple guards were armed. Perhaps they too could have been employed for police duties by the high priests.
[427] BAGD 473: 1. robber, highwayman, bandit; 2. revolutionary, insurrectionist.
[428] Cf. also Acts 1:16 for Judas as the "guide" of those who arrested Jesus.
[429] BAGD 770,2.
[430] BAGD 842, with examples from Josephus for them as servants / assistants of the Jewish Law Court, the Sanhedrin.
[431] BAGD 575,2.
[432] BAGD 881.
[433] Chambers Murray 122 and 395, respectively, on *cohors* and *legio*, as well as BAGD 761 and LSJ 1625, II., on σπεῖρα . For σπεῖρα in Krauss, *Lehnwörter*, see

John's terminology at this point borders on the fantastic. As will be shown in section B. below, it is due to his dependence here on the "host" or "army" (troops) of Sammael.

It is important to note that for the traditions behind the Evangelists Luke and John, when Judas decides to betray Jesus (leading to his arrest in Gethsemane), he is labeled "Satan." Luke in 22:3 states: "Then Satan entered into Judas called Iscariot...." Verse 4 then relates that Judas "conferred with the chief priests and officers of the Temple police[434] about how he might betray him [Jesus] to them." The only time "Satan" occurs in the Fourth Gospel is at 13:27, where John states: "After [Judas] received the piece of bread, Satan entered into him." In v 2 "The devil [διάβολος] had already put it into the heart of Judas son of Simon Iscariot to betray him." Already in 6:70 John had noted that Jesus said to the twelve: "Yet one of you [v 71 - Judas] is a devil."[435]

Satan, also called in Judaic sources the devil, Sammael, and the Angel of Death, is here described as causing Judas to betray Jesus in Gethsemane. Indeed, Satan enters Judas, making him become the latter. This aids in understanding how the Fourth Evangelist borrowed terminology connected with Sammael in order to describe the "troops" which accompanied Judas when he went to have Jesus arrested in the garden of Gethsemane. It also offers an explanation for Jesus' question in Mark 14:48 par.

B.   *Test. Dan.* 1:7 states that "one of the spirits of Beliar was at work within me."[436] In 6:1, Beliar is called Satan: "be on guard against Satan and his spirits."[437] The *Martyrdom of Isaiah* speaks at 2:2 of "Satan and his angels," whereby he is equivalent to Sammael in v 1.[438] The Tosefta on

---

2.93, 408 and 497. It is doubtful that the reference is to a *manipulus*, "a company, maniple of foot soldiers (one third of a cohort)" (Chambers Murray 421). Yet that would still mean either 140 or 200 soldiers. See also Matt 26:53 with "more than twelve *legions* of angels." The "whole *speira*" is more logically present at the praetorium in Mark 15:16 // Matt 27:27. See also Acts 21:31 for the time of Paul.
[434] The same Greek word as in 22:52.
[435] Cf. also 17:12 for Judas as "the son of ἀπώλεια ," destruction, an activity of Satan.
[436] *OTP* 1.808.
[437] *OTP* 1.810.
[438] *OTP* 2.158. Within the Christian part of the work, 7:9 has "Sammael and his hosts" (*OTP* 2.166). See also Matt 25:41 for "the devil and his angels," as well as the *Life of Adam and Eve* 16:1, where the devil speaks of "me and my angels" (*OTP* 2.262).

Šabb. 17:3 also deals with "angels of Satan."[439] *Lev. Rab.* Aḥare Moth 21/4 on Lev 16:3 enlarges Ps 27:3 somewhat. Israel says to God here: "'Though a host' of Sammael 'should encamp against me....'" Here Sammael is described as having his מַחֲנֶה,[440] "army," "host."[441] *Deut. Rab.* Ve'zot ha-Berakhah 11/10 notes that "Sammael, the head of all the satans / accusing angels, was awaiting the death of Moses every hour...."[442] Finally, *Pirq. R. El.* 13 (12) states that Sammael "took his band and descended" from heaven, and it notes that the serpent (= Sammael) was most skilled to do evil. Gerald Friedlander explains "his band" here as a "troop of angels obeying him."[443] The Hebrew of "band" is כַּת.[444] It is also used of Sammael and his band / troop in *Pirq. R. El.* 14 and 27.[445] The double plural כִּתּוֹת כִּתּוֹת is found in the phrase "many bands / troops" of לִסְטִים in *Lev. Rab.* Ṣav 9/8 on Lev 7:11-12.[446] The latter Hebrew term is the plural of the loanword לִיסְטִים, Greek λῃστής,[447] employed in Mark 14:48 par.

I suggest that the Palestinian Jewish Christian who first composed the narrative which is now Mark 14:43-50 knew of the certainly frequent association of "band / troop" of "bandits / insurrectionists" as above. Aware of the tradition which represented Jesus as crucified between two bandits / insurrectionists, he then had Jesus ask those arresting him in Gethsemane: "Have you come out with swords and clubs to arrest me as though I were 'a bandit / insurrectionist'?" (v 48).

In addition, the crowd's swords and clubs (Mark 14:43; Matt 26:47; Luke 22:52) are generalized into "weapons" in John 18:3. The same verse speaks of a *speira*, composed of 420 to 600 soldiers, an incredible number. I propose that John, or the Palestinian Jewish Christian tradition behind him, was thinking here of Sammael's coming to take the soul of Moses as

---

[439] Cf. Zuckermandel / Liebermann 136; Neusner in 2.67 translates "adversary angels."

[440] Mirkin 8.25; Soncino 4.268.

[441] BDB 334, 3.c.

[442] Mirkin 11.157; Soncino 7.183.

[443] Cf. Friedlander 92. The Hebrew is in Eshkol 41.

[444] Jastrow 678. For other "bands" (of angels), cf. *Pesiq. R.* 20/4 (Friedmann 97a; Braude 406). A "troop" (גְּדוּד , Jastrow 210) of angels is also found four times in the same section (Friedmann 97b and 98b; Braude 408 and 410), as well as in *Deut. Rab.* 11/10 (Mirkin 11.160; Soncino 7.187).

[445] Cf. Eshkol 45 and 87, and Friedlander 99 and 193-94.

[446] Mirkin 7.96; Soncino 4.114. This is said by R. Aḥa, a fourth generation Palestinian Amora (*Introduction* 103).

[447] Jastrow 708. Cf. n. 427 above.

described above in an early form of the midrash "Petirat Mosheh." While no mention is made at this point of others being with him, elsewhere, as illustrated above, Sammael is frequently described as having a band / troop / army / host of evil angels who accompany him. This military term, entailing a very large number, could explain the exaggerated term *speira* which John employs in 18:3 very well. Satan / the devil/ Sammael/ the Angel of Death had entered into Judas, Jesus' betrayer. He then came to Gethsemane with his very large military escort, his band or troop, in order to arrest Jesus and have him die.

6.17   Swords at the Arrest of Jesus

A.   In Mark 14:43 Judas arrived in Gethsemane with "a crowd with 'swords' and clubs." "Swords" is the plural of the Greek μάχαιρα .[448] Verse 47 states that when they laid hands on Jesus and arrested him, "one of those [disciples] who stood near drew his 'sword' and struck the servant / slave of the high priest, cutting off his ear." In v 48 Jesus then reproaches those who have taken him captive with the question: "Have you come out with 'swords' and clubs to arrest me as though I were a bandit / insurrectionist?"

The threefold mention of "swords" in the scene of Jesus' arrest shows the term's importance here. Even for one of the disciples to have been armed and to have drawn[449] his sword (out of its sheath) and to have cut off the ear of another person at this point (or at any other time) is unthinkable in light of the prophet from Nazareth's ethical teachings such as those now found in the Beatitudes: Matt 5:9; Matt 5:11 // Luke 6:22; and Matt 5:39 // Luke 6:29. As Jesus' disciples they would have practiced non-retaliation at his arrest in Gethsemane.[450] Historically, it is

---

[448] BAGD 496.
[449] BAGD 761 on σπάω , middle. It occurs elsewhere in the NT only in Acts 16:27.
[450] Cf. John 18:36. In addition, the pericope of the two swords in Special Luke, just before Gethsemane (22:35-38), is not historical. Jesus says that Isa 53:12 ("he was numbered with the transgressors") must be fulfilled in him. That is, he (and his disciples) must be considered to be like the bandits / insurrectionists between whom he is crucified. These certainly employed swords. Nor should Simon "the Cananaean" (ὁ Καναναῖος), the disciple of Mark 3:18 // Matt 10:4, be thought of as having a sword, although this stands for קַנְאָן , a Zealot (Jastrow 1388; cf. Luke 6:15 and Acts 1:13 for him as "the Zealot"). He most probably was an adherent of this movement earlier, but no longer. Jesus himself would not have tolerated such behavior in his inner circle. Finally, the sword of Matt 10:34 is only metaphorical; Luke in 12:51 has "division."

most probable that they now simply abandoned him and ran into the darkness for their lives (Mark 14:50), hoping to escape what they now knew would definitely be his fate: death.[451]

Matthew repeats the "swords" and clubs of Mark 14:43 in his 26:47. In v 51 he expressly states that it was "one of those [disciples] with Jesus" who cut off the ear of the servant / slave of the high priest with his "sword." Peculiar to Matthew are the words which Jesus now directs to this disciple in v 52: "Put your 'sword' back into its place; for all who take the 'sword' will perish by the 'sword.'" This appears to be a comment by the Evangelist on the tragic fate of thousands of his fellow Jews who rose up against Rome and were killed in the Jewish-Roman war of 66-70 CE. In v 55 Matthew repeats Jesus' saying from Mark 14:48 with "swords." He thus intensifies the use of sword imagery in his retelling of the Markan narrative.

In 22:49 Luke changes the singular of Mark to the plural, implying that all of Jesus' disciples bore a sword: "When those who were around [Jesus] saw what was coming, they asked, 'Lord, should we strike with the sword?'"[452] When one of them does so without Jesus' first answering the question, he cuts off the "right" ear of the high priest's servant / slave (v 50), an added detail. Jesus then instructs his disciples: "'No more of this!' And he touched his ear and healed him" (v 51). Here Jesus, the great opponent of violence, is described as miraculously making up for the violence one of his disciples engaged in without his approval. The saying of Mark 14:48 with "swords" and clubs is then reproduced in v 52. In v 53 Jesus addresses the chief priests, the officers of the Temple police and the elders: "this is your hour, and the power of darkness!" This "hour" recalls the Johannine usage of the term not only in regard to the disciples' fleeing at Jesus' arrest in Gethsemane (16:32), but also in regard to Jesus' death.[453] The "power" of darkness in Luke 22:53 is the Greek ἐξουσία, which can mean this, but also "authority," "warrant."[454] I suggest that it represents here from the pre-Lukan tradition the Hebrew רְשׁוּת or Aramaic רְשׁוּתָא, also meaning "power," "authority."[455] It could very well be influenced by God's commissioning or authorizing Sammael twice to go and fetch Moses' soul in an early form of the "Petirat

---

451 Cf. the introductory remarks above to 6.16-20.
452 Cf. Luke 22:38.
453 Cf. for example John 13:1.
454 BAGD 278, 2. and 3.
455 Jastrow 1499.

Mosheh." Sammael, equivalent to Satan, the prince of darkness,[456] thus now has not only the power, but also the authority to do so.[457]

John, like Luke, notes that it was the right ear of the high priest's servant / slave which was cut off, and he alone of the four Evangelists identifies the perpetrator: it was "Simon Peter, who had a sword" (18:10). This implies for John that the others did not. Jesus then tells Peter: "Put your sword back into its 'sheath' (θήκη)"[458] (v 11), similar to Matt 26:52, "Put your sword back into its place."

All four Evangelists thus emphasize what a large role the sword plays in the narrative of Jesus' arrest. While it is historically probable that Judas came to Gethsemane with a small troop armed with "swords and clubs" (Mark 14:43), the further development of the sword motif is typical of Judaic haggadah. I suggest that it is due to the great role Sammael's sword plays when he comes to take the soul of Israel's first redeemer, Moses.

B. In *b. 'Avod. Zar.* 20b it is related that the Angel of Death stands above a person about to die "with his sword drawn out in his hand and a drop of gall hanging on it." Shocked at this figure, the person opens his or her

---

[456] Cf. *Pesiq. R.* 20/2 for the "Prince of Darkness" (שׂר החחשׁך), who is (as black) as a bull (Friedmann 95a; Braude 400, with n. 11). In Acts 26:18 the power of Satan is in "darkness"; in 2 Cor 11:14 he can even disguise himself with the opposite, light; and Barn 4:9 labels him "the Black One." *Lev. Rab.* Meṣora 18/3 on Lev 15:1-2 (Mirkin 7.207; Soncino 4.231) also labels the Angel of Death (= Satan) "Darkness," based on Deut 5:20(23). A parallel is found in *Cant. Rab.* 8:6 § 1 (Donsqi 169; Soncino 9.306), also in the name of R. Eliezer b. R. Yose the Galilean, a third generation Tanna (*Introduction* 85; the Soncino translation should be corrected accordingly). Here God appoints the Angel of Death as an "executioner" and "cosmocrator," that is, with power over all of God's creatures.

[457] Cf. for example *Deut. Rab.* Ve'zot ha-Berakhah 11/10 in Mirkin 11.158, Soncino 7.184 ("Go and bring Moses' soul"), and the same divine imperative in 7.186 (Mirkin 11.159). See also Sammael's statement in 7.185: "The souls of all who come into this world are delivered into my hands." The Angel of Death (= Sammael) believes God has given him the "authority" (רְשׁוּת) to take Moses' life in comment on Deut 33:1, "before his death." See *Tanh.* B Berakhah 2 (Buber 54; Bitenhard 2.510); *Tanh.* Berakhah 3 (Eshkol 945); and *Pesiq. Rav Kah.*, Suppl. 1/14 (Mandelbaum 448; Braude and Kapstein 456). On God's twofold command to the Angel of Death, "Go and fetch Me the soul of Moses," connected with Moses' telling him he has no "authority" to stand where he does, see already *Sifre* Niṣṣabim 305 on Deut 31:14, here Num 27:18 (Finkelstein 326; Hammer 296).

[458] BAGD 360, only here in the NT.

mouth in fright, the gall enters and takes its deathly effect.[459] His sword is typical of the Angel of Death, who in turn is equated with Sammael.[460]

Deut. Rab. Ve'zot ha-Berakhah 11/10 first relates that God charged Sammael the Wicked: "'Go forth and bring Moses' soul.' He immediately clothed himself with anger, 'girded on his sword,' wrapped himself with ruthlessness, and went forth to meet Moses." Moses reacted to his words by saying: "Away from here, Wicked One, you must not speak thus. Go, flee before me. I will not surrender my soul to you." When Sammael returned to God, He again commanded him: "Go and bring Moses' soul." "Immediately 'he drew his sword from the sheath' and placed himself at the side of Moses."[461] The latter Hebrew phrase is

462. שָׁלַף חַרְבּוֹ מִתַּעְרָה

This is also found in the Jellinek A version of "Petirat Mosheh."[463] The Parma MS of the midrash mentions the Angel of Death's sword four times at this point, including his dropping it, and not being able to pick it up again until Moses gives him permission.[464]

I suggest that the above haggadic description of the Angel of Death / Sammael's attempt to take the soul of Israel's first redeemer, Moses, at the end of his life, coupled with extensive sword imagery, provided the impetus for the large amount of sword imagery found in the four Evangelists' accounts of the arrest of Jesus, the last redeemer of Israel, in Gethsemane (except for the initial "swords and clubs" from tradition). Only Luke explicitly states that all the eleven disciples ("they") had

---

[459] Soncino 105. One source of the sword image may be 1 Chron 21:15-16, where the "destroying angel" of the Lord stands between earth and heaven (thus in the air), "and in his hand 'a drawn sword' stretched out over Jerusalem." *Targ.Ps.-Jon.* Exod 12:13 labels the destroyer the Angel of Death; see v 23 (Rieder 1.97-98; Maher 191-92).

[460] One example is *Targ. Ps.-Jon.* Gen 3:6, which states: "And the woman [Eve] saw Sammael the Angel of Death, and she was afraid" (Rieder 1.4; Maher 26).

[461] Mirkin 11.158-59; Soncino 7.184 and 186. The midrash ends by God's taking Moses' soul by a kiss and burying him Himself.

[462] Cf. Jastrow 1587 on שָׁלַף, 2) to draw (a sword), and 1684 on תַּעַר, 2) sheath.

[463] Cf. his *Bet ha-Midrasch* 1.127-28; English in Kushelevsky, *Moses* 219-20; German in Wünsche, *Aus Israels Lehrhallen* 1.158 and 160.

[464] Cf. the text in Kushelevsky, *Moses* 270. This is just before Moses entrusts his family, including his mother, to his disciple Joshua. *Tanḥuma* here notes the sword of the Angel of Death twice, the second time also before Moses' concern for his mother (Kushelevsky, *Moses* 253 and 255, with n. 6 on p. 260). *Ḥarbo*, "his sword," is definitely the better reading in light of *Deut. Rab.* 11/10, Jellinek A, and the Parma MS.

swords (22:49), yet this is due to his special material just cited in 22:35-38. Otherwise it is only one of the disciples (Mark 14:43; Matt 26:51; John 18:10, naming Peter), like the single Angel of Death / Sammael. In Matt 26:52 Jesus tells the disciple who had "drawn" his sword in v 51: "Put your sword back into its place." John 18:11 specifies this "place": "its sheath." These two passages appear to reflect imagery from Sammael when he attempts to take Moses' soul, i.e. cause him to die: "he drew his sword from the sheath." Here in the Gospel account, however, it is not Judas (into whom Satan / Sammael had entered) who draws his sword, but one of Jesus' disciples. Part of Judas' "troop / band" should be thought of as already having drawn their swords in order to achieve Jesus' arrest without resistance from him or his disciples. The single disciple then responds to this by drawing his own sword, an object which - viewed historically - he certainly did not have with him.

6.18   Jesus' Special Knowledge in Gethsemane

A.   In the Markan version of the Gethsemane scene, Jesus first told his eleven disciples to sit down while he prays (14:32). Then he took with him a bit further Peter, James and John (v 33). Returning from praying separately, Jesus addressed these three: "Are you still sleeping and taking your rest? Enough! The hour has come; the Son of Man [= I] is betrayed into the hands of sinners. 42) Get up, let us be going. See, my betrayer is at hand" (vv 41-42). Then "immediately, while he was still speaking," Judas arrived with "a crowd with swords and clubs" (v 43). Here foreknowledge of Judas' coming is attributed to Jesus. Matthew basically reproduces this incident in 26:44-45, while Luke omits most of it at 22:45-46. The Fourth Evangelist at this point states: "Jesus, 'knowing' [εἰδώς] all that was to happen to him, came forward" (18:4) and spoke with Judas and the "detachment of soldiers together with police" (v 3). [465] I suggest that Jesus' special knowledge of who was coming to arrest him is also based on an early form of the midrash on Moses' death.

B.   *Deut. Rab.* Ve'zot ha-Berakhah 11/10 on Deut 31:14, "Your time to die is near," states: "Now before Sammael showed himself to Moses [to take his soul], Moses knew of his coming...."[466] The "Petirat Mosheh,"

---

[465] On this special foreknowledge in John, cf. 13:1-2. However, it has nothing to do with the Evangelist's emphasizing other foreknowledge of Jesus, for example in 6:6 in regard to Philip.
[466] Mirkin 11.158; Soncino 7.184.

Jellinek A version, also notes: "And when Moses, who had known of his [Sammael's] coming, lifted his eyes...."[467]

It thus appears that the traditions behind both Mark (followed by Matthew) and John derive from an earlier form of the midrash on Moses' death. Just as the first redeemer of Israel knew in advance of Sammael / the Angel of Death's coming to take his soul, so the second or final redeemer of Israel, Jesus, knew in advance of Judas' coming to arrest him (and have him killed).

6.19   Jesus' Directing His Arrest by Judas with His Troop / Band

A.   In contrast to the Synoptic accounts of Jesus' arrest, John portrays him as being in charge the entire time.[468] Although he knew everything that was to happen to him, he nevertheless went forward and asked Judas and those accompanying him: "Whom do you seek?" (18:4). When they replied: "Jesus the Nazorean [of Nazareth]," Jesus told them: "I am he" (v 5). Then they went backwards and "fell to the ground" (v 6). Therefore Jesus asked them (ostensibly still on the ground) again: "Whom do you seek?" Their response is then the same as before. Reproaching them, Jesus answered: "I told you I am he. So if you are seeking me, let these men [the disciples] depart" (v 8). The Evangelist then adds in v 9 that this fulfils Jesus' words (in 17:12, which in turn speak of Scripture being fulfilled).[469] After the incident of Jesus' healing the ear of the high priest's servant / slave cut off by Peter, the pericope ends by Jesus' asking: "Am I not to drink the cup that the Father has given me?" (v 11). His arrest then follows. John thus intentionally omits a reference in the narrative to Judas' betraying Jesus to the band / troop accompanying him by means of a kiss, which is found in all three Synoptics. In addition, in the Johannine account Jesus himself directs the entire scene.[470] Much of the above imagery, peculiar to John, is also derived from an earlier form of the midrash "Petirat Mosheh."

B.   *Deut. Rab.* Ve'zot ha-Berakhah 11/10 comments on Deut 31:14, "Behold, your days approach that you must die." When told by God to

---

[467] Cf. *Bet ha-Midrasch* 1.127; English in Kushelevsky, *Moses* 219; German in Wünsche, *Aus Israels Lehrhallen* 1.159. The Parma MS at this point speaks of the Angel of Death, whom Moses "instantly recognized" (Kushelevsky, *Moses* 270).
[468] Jesus' role in the Synoptics consists only of his speaking Mark 14:48-49 par.
[469] Jesus' statement in John 18:9 probably refers back to 16:32, which in turn echoes "the sheep will be scattered" in Zech 13:7.
[470] Cf. his words already in 10:17-18.

go and bring Him Moses' soul, Sammael put on his sword and went forth to meet Moses. Before he showed himself to him, Moses (miraculously) knew he was coming. Afraid of Moses' great radiance, Sammael did not dare to speak to Moses first. Thus Moses asked him: "What are you going to do here?"[471] Sammael replied: "I have come to take away your soul." Then Moses asked him: "Who sent you?"[472] He answered: "He who created all the creatures." After further dialogue, Sammael states: "The souls of all who come into the world are 'delivered into my hands.'" When Moses resists, not wanting to be handed over or delivered to the Angel of Death, God finally promises to bury him Himself.[473]

This narrative is also found in the Jellinek A version of "Petirat Mosheh." Here too Sammael puts on his sword and goes forth to meet Moses, who knows of his coming. It continues with Moses' asking Sammael: "Why are you standing opposite me?" and "Who sent you to me?"[474]

The Parma MS of "Petirat Mosheh" paints this scene somewhat differently, yet includes Moses' question of Sammael, who has approached him "with his sword drawn out of its sheath": "What do you want?" When Sammael replies that he wants his soul, Moses tells him: "[Try and] come and get it." Then the Angel of Death's sword drops out of his hand.[475]

In all three recensions of the "Petirat Mosheh," Moses is thus described as being in full control of the scene. It is he who directs two questions to Sammael (= the Angel of Death), who has come to seize him and "deliver / hand him over" to Him who sent him, God, so that Moses' life can be taken. I propose that this imagery has also influenced the tradition behind John, or the Evangelist himself. For him too, Jesus does not wait for Judas or his fantastically large army to ask the first question. Instead, in spite of "knowing all that was to happen to him," he asks: "Whom do you seek?" This is then repeated. Jesus here poses the questions, as in Judaic tradition on Moses, the first redeemer of Israel.

---

[471] Is the phrase ἐφ' ὅ πάρει used of Judas in Matt 26:50 related here? The RSV translates it as a question: "Why are you here?"

[472] Jastrow in 1522 on שָׁגַר , pi., 2) to send, cites a passage with "arrest them and send them."

[473] Mirkin 11.158; Soncino 7.184-85.

[474] Cf. Jellinek, *Bet ha-Midrasch* 1.127-28; Kushelevsky, *Moses* 219-20; Wünsche, *Aus Israels Lehrhallen* 1.158-59.

[475] Kushelevsky, *Moses* 270.

Like him, Jesus, the final redeemer of Israel, is in full charge in the Johannine scene of his arrest. In fact, he directs it.

6.20 *Jesus as "I Am," and Those Arresting Him as Falling*

A.   According to the Evangelist John, Judas came to Gethsemane with "a detachment of soldiers together with police from the chief priests and Pharisees" (18:3). Jesus himself went forth to meet them, asking them whom they were seeking. When they answered, "Jesus the Nazorean / of Nazareth," he replied: "I am he" (v 5). After Jesus said to them, "'I am he,'" "they stepped back and fell to the ground" (v 6). This same interplay is repeated in v 7, whereupon Jesus answered: "I told you that 'I am he'" (v 8).

The phrase "I am he" (ἐγώ εἰμι) thus occurs three times within the span of only four verses, showing its great importance here. It is also connected with Jesus' opponents, including Judas, who "stepped backwards and fell to the ground" in v 6: ἀπῆλθον εἰς τὰ ὀπίσω καὶ ἔπεσαν χαμαί .[476]   For John, Jesus' adversaries are actually powerless before him. Both of these motifs, "I am" and "falling" to the ground, also derive from Judaic haggadah on Sammael's trying to take the soul of Moses at the very end of his life.

B.   *Deut. Rab.* Ve'zot ha-Berakhah 11/10 deals with Deut 31:14, "Behold, your days approach that you must die," up to the end of Deuteronomy. It notes that when the moment of Moses' death arrived, God told Sammael the Wicked:

> "Go forth and bring Moses' soul!" Immediately he clothed himself in anger, and girded on his sword, and wrapped himself with ruthlessness, and went forth to meet Moses. When Sammael saw Moses sitting and writing down the Ineffable Name, and how the radiance of his appearance was like unto the sun and he was like an angel of the LORD of hosts, he became afraid of Moses and declared: "Of a surety, angels [like Gabriel, Michael and me] cannot take away Moses' soul." Now before Sammael showed himself to Moses, Moses knew of his coming, and when Sammael caught sight of Moses, trembling and anguish took hold of him, as of a woman in travail, and he did not have the affrontery to speak to Moses until he said to Sammael: "There is no

---

[476] Cf. BAGD 875 on χαμαί 2., to the ground. In the NT it is only found here and in 9:6.

peace, says my God, for the wicked" (Isa 57:21 = 48:22). [Then Moses asked Sammael:] "What are you doing here?" and "Who sent you?"[477]

The same narrative is found in the Jellinek A version of "Petirat Mosheh." It states that "fear and trembling seized Sammael. And when Moses, who had known of his coming, lifted his eyes and saw him, at once Sammael's eyes grew dim before the radiance of Moses' countenance, 'and he fell upon his face.' Fear took hold of him as of a woman in travail, so that he lost his power of speech."[478]

The Parma MS of "Petirat Mosheh" at this point states: "By the time the Angel [of Death] reached him, Moses had uttered the Ineffable Name, and instantly the Angel's sword dropped out of his hand. He wanted to retreat, but was too feeble to move. He tried to pick up his sword, but was incapacitated." After a short dialogue between Moses and God, Moses blessed the twelve tribes (Deuteronomy 33). "When he concluded his blessing, Moses gave him [Sammael] permission, and the Angel picked up his sword and went away."[479]

While *Deut. Rab.* 11/10 and Jellinek A have Moses writing down the Ineffable Name when Sammael approaches him with his sword,[480] the Parma MS notes that Moses himself had spoken it distinctly, causing the Angel of Death to drop his sword. "The Ineffable Name" here is שֵׁם הַמְפֹרָשׁ.[481] Exod 20:7 states: "You shall not make wrongful use of 'the *name* of the LORD' [אֶת־שֵׁם־יְהוָה] your God, for the LORD [יְהוָה] will not acquit anyone who misuses His *name*." Out of great reverence for the "name of the LORD," substitute expressions were used for it.[482]   The term יְהוָה was only pronounced on one occasion during the entire year and by only one person while the Temple was still standing, up to 70 CE. On the Day of Atonement the high priest confessed the people's sins over the scapegoat and spoke Lev 16:30, including the term "the LORD." The Mishnah at *Yoma* 3:8 notes regarding this: "And when the priests

---

[477] Mirkin 11.158; Soncino 7.184-85, which I slightly modify.

[478] Cf. Jellinek, *Bet ha-Midrasch* 1.127; Kushelevsky, *Moses* 219; and Wünsche, *Aus Israels Lehrhallen* 1.158-59.

[479] Kushelevsky, *Moses* 270. Note the Angel of Death's desire to "retreat," i.e. to step back, as in John 18:6.

[480] *Deut. Rab.* 11/10 later also notes that Moses drives Sammael away with "the staff on which was engraven the Ineffable Name" (Mirkin 11.159; Soncino 7.186).

[481] Cf. Jastrow 1590: "Esp. הַשֵּׁם or שֵׁם , the Divine Name, the Tetragrammaton." See also 1242 on פָּרַשׁ , piel 4): to specify, express clearly.

[482] Cf. *m. Šebu.* 4:13 (Albeck 4.258; Danby 415; Neusner 629), as well as *b. Šebu.* 35a (Soncino 204) with a list of ten substitutes.

and the people who stood in the Temple Court heard the Expressed Name come forth from the mouth of the High Priest, they used to kneel and bow down and 'fall on their faces,'" saying a blessing.[483] This reverential "falling on their faces" stands behind the imagery of Sammael's "falling upon his face" when he encounters Moses, who had just written the Ineffable Name. One falls upon one's face when hearing / encountering it. The Parma MS of "Petirat Mosheh" has the important variant here that Moses himself clearly expressed the Ineffable Name. It should be noted that this is highly unusual because of the strong tradition which developed on the basis of Exod 20:7.

An early form of the "Petirat Mosheh" narrative in turn influenced the Palestinian Jewish Christian who first composed the Johannine version of Jesus' arrest in Gethsemane, or the bilingual Evangelist John, if he himself did so. When Judas, into whom Satan had entered (13:27; cf. v 2 and 6:70), and his troop / band came to arrest Jesus, the latter went forward to meet them and identified himself as Jesus of Nazareth twice[484] by stating "I am he," the Greek ἐγώ εἰμι . His opponents then "stepped back and fell to the ground" (18:6), precisely because "I am he" was thought to stand for the expressed divine name. The following aids in understanding this.

When Moses requests God to reveal His "name" to him at the burning bush in Exod 3:13, God tells him in v 14: "I am who I am," labeled "the LORD" (יהוה) in v 15. The LXX has for the first in v 14: Ἐγώ εἰμι ὁ ὤν .[485] Thus the ἐγώ εἰμι of John 18:5, 6 and 8 can also be understood as an abbreviation of the divine name. The Fourth Evangelist's use of the term elsewhere (4:26; 6:20; 8:24, 28, 58; and 13:19) makes this clear. While John does not employ it in the "trial" scene, this Gospel presupposes the hearer / reader is acquainted with other basic Gospel traditions, which it varies and plays upon so much. One of them is found in Mark 14:61, where the high priest, who alone was allowed to utter the divine name once a year in the Temple, asks Jesus: "Are you the Messiah, the Son of the Blessed One?"[486] In v 62 Jesus then answers:

---

[483] Albeck 2.240; Danby 165; Neusner 275. This influenced the Moses scene with Sammael, which in turn influenced the arrest scene in John. Against Craig Blomberg, *The Historical Reliability of John's Gospel* 231, who maintains traditional material from Pss 35:4; 27:2; and 56:9 is employed here by the Fourth Evangelist. See the following.

[484] Actually a threefold mention since v 6 is repetitious.

[485] Cf. Isa 41:4 and 43:10.

[486] Here "the Blessed One" is also one of the reverential substitutes for the divine name. Cf. n. 482.

"I am [' Εγώ εἰμι]; and you will see the Son of Man seated at the right hand of the Power,[487] and coming with the clouds of heaven." The high priest thereupon tears his clothes, charging Jesus with blasphemy,[488] and all (the chief priests, elders and scribes - v 53) condemn Jesus as deserving death (vv 63-64). According to Lev 24:16 "one who blasphemes the name of the LORD shall be put to death." In *m. Sanh.* 7:5, however, "the blasphemer is not culpable unless he pronounces the Name itself." If upon examining him witnesses attest this, the judges rend their garments, as the high priest above did.[489]

While Jesus does not pronounce the divine name expressly when he says "the Power" in Mark,[490] and thus does not blaspheme,[491] the term "I am" in John 18:5, 6 and 8 is certainly meant to connote this.[492] The Evangelist John clearly points to this in 10:30, where Jesus says: "The Father and I are one." Thus people want to stone him (v 31) because of blasphemy: "you, though only a human being, are making yourself God" (v 33; cf. v 36). Jesus' threefold use of "I am" in the scene of his arrest thus already points to what "the Jews" tell Pilate at Jesus' so-called "trial" in 19:7, "We have a law, and according to that law he ought to die because he has claimed to be the Son of God."

---

[487] Another reverential substitute for the divine name.

[488] Ironically, this charge comes from the high priest, who when in full regalia on the Day of Atonement wore a turban on his head, on which the Tetragrammaton was inscribed. Cf. Exod 28:36; 39:30; but especially Josephus, *Ant.* 3.157-58 with "the name of God," and n. "a"; *Bell.* 5.235 and n. "j"; and Philo, *Mos.* 2.114-15. Both Josephus, himself a priest from Jerusalem, and Philo imply that "Holy to" as in Exodus was no longer used in their time, only the Tetragrammaton itself. Knowledge of the Tetragrammaton on the high priest's turban can be assumed for the first Jewish Christians, who would have appreciated this irony.

[489] Albeck 4.191; Danby 392; Neusner 597.

[490] Mark's ἐγώ εἰμι in 14:62 simply means "Yes" and does not allude to the Tetragrammaton. Cf. for example Craig A. Evans, *Mark 8:27 - 16:20* 450, citing *Test. Job* 29:3-4. The Hebrew הוא אני is similar in meaning.

[491] Contrast the third generation Tanna, R. Meir (*Introduction* 84), who maintains in *m. Sanh.* 7:8 that one is liable to being stoned to death for cursing his father or mother even with a substitute (divine) name (Albeck 4.193; Danby 393; Neusner 598). R. Meir may reflect an earlier, stricter tradition in effect in the early first century CE in regard to all situations employing the divine name or a substitute for it. It should be recalled that the aristocratic priests in the Sanhedrin were Sadducees, noted for their heartlessness in judging legal cases. See Josephus, *Ant.* 20.199, and the opposite for the Pharisees in regard to punishments in 13.294.

[492] Cf. also 17:11-12, where Jesus states that the Father has given him His name.

In conclusion one can correctly maintain that in the scene of Jesus' arrest in Gethsemane the Fourth Gospel has appropriated Judaic tradition from an early form of the "Petirat Mosheh" in regard to Sammael and his sword. When he comes to take the soul of Israel's first redeemer, Moses, the latter has either just written the divine name or pronounced it himself. At this, Sammael fell upon his face and became speechless. The Palestinian Jewish Christian who first composed the episode of Jesus' arrest, or the Fourth Evangelist himself, then borrowed this imagery to describe how Jesus, the final redeemer of Israel, reacted in regard to Judas, coming to lead him off to death, and how the latter and his troop / band then fell to the ground. Here a phenomenon typical of the rest of John's Gospel, double entendre, is also found. Jesus' response "I am [he]" concomitantly points to him as the Son of God, indeed, that he and the Father are one.

*   *   *

One may question the validity of one or even more of the above twenty comparisons made between Jesus' stay in Gethsemane and his arrest there, and Moses' final hours, including Sammael / the Angel of Death's attempt to take his soul, in Judaic tradition. Yet the cumulative force of the argument is very strong. The Palestinian Jewish Christian who first composed the Gethsemane narrative patterned it to a great extent upon materials known to him from an early form of the midrash on Moses' death, the "Petirat Mosheh." The latter, very popular, probably circulated orally in various forms. The Gethsemane narrative, also originally oral, was then translated from Aramaic or Hebrew into Greek in one of the bilingual Jewish Christian congregations. Only in this final, Greek form did it become available to the first Evangelist, Mark, who shows no major signs of editing the pericope.

The Fourth Evangelist, bilingual himself, also seems to have been well acquainted with the Judaic haggadic narrative(s) of Moses' final hours and death. A number of his special emphases in the Gethsemane account (described primarily within sections 6.16-20 above) can now be better understood in light of this background. He later also incorporated material from the same source in his description of Jesus' special care for his mother Mary in the Crucifixion scene (see section I. 8 below), which corroborates the basic proposal I have made above. It is to the scene of Jesus' suffering and dying to which I now turn.

I. 7 Suffering, Giving One's Life, Jesus and Moses
as the Servant of the Lord, and Isaiah 53

A. *Jesus*

According to the Gospels, at the end of his life Jesus was given a hearing before the assembled chief priests, elders and scribes (Mark 14:53; "the whole council" - 55; 15:1). All of these condemned the prophet from Nazareth as deserving death (v 64). At this point some spit on him, struck and beat him (vv 65-66).[493] After Jesus' second hearing, now before Pontius Pilate, the Roman procurator had Jesus flogged (15:15). Then soldiers in the praetorium mocked him, putting a wreath / crown of thorns on him, striking his head with a reed, and spitting on him (vv 16-20). Following this he was led out to be crucified, a passerby being forced to carry his cross to the site of execution, apparently because Jesus was already too weak from the flogging to do so himself (v 21).[494]

Roman crucifixion in the first century CE was purposely an extremely painful, drawn-out procedure, the victim usually being nailed to the crossbeam with outstretched arms, his feet nailed to the upright beam.[495] The heel bone, including a nail driven through it, of a crucified first-century Jew was discovered in 1968 at Give'at ha-Mivtar near Jerusalem, adding archaeological evidence to numerous literary sources.[496] There is thus no doubt that Jesus suffered tremendously, especially from the lack of sleep all night, the preliminary flogging, and the crucifixion itself.

The earliest Christians, all Jews, interpreted Jesus' death in terms familiar to them, for example by means of verses from Psalm 22 for his crucifixion. Another favorite scriptural passage was the fourth Servant of the Lord song in Isa 52:13 - 53:12.[497] This figure is described as "a man of

---

[493] On the servant of the Lord as being struck and spit at, cf. Isa 50:6.

[494] John presents an additional detail in 18:22 - a Temple policeman strikes Jesus in the face for his answer to the high priest.

[495] Cf. especially the many references in the chapter "Crucifixion as a 'Barbaric' Form of Execution of the Utmost Cruelty" in Martin Hengel, *Crucifixion* (Philadelphia: Fortress Press, 1978) 22-32.

[496] Cf. the description, illustration and literature cited by Max Küchler, *Jerusalem. Ein Handbuch und Studienführer zur Heiligen Stadt* (Orte und Landschaften der Bibel, IV,2: Göttingen: Vandenhoeck & Ruprecht, 2007) 424-25, and on the site 1011-12.

[497] On this, see especially the art. παῖς θεοῦ by Joachim Jeremias in *TDNT* 5.677-717; עֶבֶד by Helmer Ringgren, U. Rüterswörden and H. Simian-Yofre in *TDOT* 10.376-405, esp. 394-403; and Bernd Janowski and Peter Stuhlmacher, eds., *Der*

suffering," "despised" (53:3), and "wounded for our transgressions" (v 5). Upon him the Lord "has laid the iniquity of us all" (v 6). Oppressed and afflicted, "he did not open his mouth" (v 7).[498] "By a perversion of justice he was taken away,"[499] "stricken for the transgression of my people" (v 8). "They made his grave with the wicked and his tomb with a rich person" (v 9).[500] He "poured out himself to death[501] and was numbered with the transgressors;[502] yet he bore the sin of many,[503] and made intercession for the transgressors" (v 12).[504]

This short selection of references shows how Jesus' first followers interpreted his suffering and death to be the fulfillment of Scripture. He was for them the suffering "servant of the Lord" of Isaiah, who voluntarily gave his life for the sins / transgressions of others. One major reason they applied this imagery to Jesus was that Moses was also described in biblical and Judaic sources as suffering and as *the* servant of the Lord. This is now shown in the following sections.

B. Moses

B. 1 Suffering.   The obvious difference, of course, between Jesus' and Moses' death is that in contrast to Jesus', that of Moses was peaceful and at the advanced age of 120 (Deut 34:5,7). Nevertheless, in Judaic sources Moses is also described as suffering: in part during the long period of his leading the Israelites up to their entry into the Land, but especially at the

---

leidende Gottesknecht. Jesaja 53 und seine Wirkungsgeschichte mit einer Bibliographie zu Jes 53 (FAT 14; Tübingen: Mohr, 1996). The English, trans. Daniel Bailey, *The Suffering Servant: Isaiah 53 in Jewish and Christian Sources* (Grand Rapids, MI: Eerdmans, 2004), has not been available to me.

[498] Cf. Jesus' silence before the high priest in Mark 14:61.

[499] Cf. the many studies of the questionable nature of a nocturnal "trial," for example Paul Winter, *On the Trial of Jesus* (SJ 1; Berlin: de Gruyter, 1974) 28, 36, 38-39.

[500] Matthew clearly alludes to this verse in Isaiah by calling Joseph of Arimathea "a rich man" in 27:57.

[501] Cf. Phil 2:7, with the entire very early hymn in vv 6-11.

[502] Cf. Mark 15:27, with some MSS citing Isa 53:12 here, as well as Luke 22:37.

[503] Cf. Jesus' words at the Lord's Supper in 14:24, "This is my blood of the [new] covenant, which is poured out 'for many.'" According to Jewish reckoning, this meal took place at the beginning of the same day on which Jesus was crucified. See also Heb 9:28.

[504] Cf. Luke 23:42-43.

end of his life when he is told by God that he has to die without being allowed to enter the Land.[505]

The *Testament of Moses*, a Palestinian document from the first century CE, maintains in 3:11 that Moses "'suffered many things' (*multa passus est*) in Egypt and at the Red Sea and in the wilderness for forty years...."[506] One example for Egypt is Moses' sharing his fellow Israelites' extremely strenuous task of having to carry clay there. *Exod. Rab.* Shemoth 1/27 on Exod 2:11 says that when Moses saw their burdens, he wept, saying: "Woe is me for you! Would that I could die for you!" He therefore helped each individual.[507] When he also killed an Egyptian who was beating a Hebrew, Pharaoh heard of it and "sought to kill Moses" (2:15). Pharaoh again threatened Moses with death after the ninth plague: "on the day you see my face again, you shall die!" (10:28). When the Israelites later camped at Rephidim and there was no water, they complained to Moses that he wanted to kill them through thirst. He therefore cried out to the Lord: "They are almost ready to stone me!" (17:4). *Mek. R. Ish.* Vayassaʿ 7 on the latter verse has Moses tell God: "Between You and them I am being killed. You tell me, Do not get angry with them, for You say to me, 'Carry them in your bosom' (Num 11:12), while they would kill me!"[508]

Moses' "suffering" is also emphasized in regard to his receiving the Torah from God at Mount Sinai. The Tannaitic midrash *Sifre* Debarim 14 on Deut 1:14 raises the question of from whom it is best to learn Torah. The Israelites should have said to Moses: "Is it not from you, who 'have suffered' [נצטערת] for it?" Two verses are then adduced to confirm this, first Exod 34:28 ("He was there with the Lord forty days and forty nights; he neither ate bread nor drank water"), then Deut 9:9 ("I remained on the mountain forty days and forty nights. I neither ate bread nor drank

---

[505] Cf. Renée Bloch's section on Moses, "Die Bedeutung seiner Leiden und seines Todes für Israel," in her essay on "Die Gestalt des Moses in der rabbinischen Tradition" in the volume *Moses in Schrift und Überlieferung*, ed. Friedolin Stier and Eleonore Beck (Düsseldorf: Patmos-Verlag, 1963) 130-40. She points out that Moses' suffering reaches its high point at the moment of his death because he may not enter the promised land and thereby share in the joy of his people (131). The original is *Moïse, l'homme de l'Alliance* (Tournai: Desclée & Cie., 1955).

[506] Cf. Tromp, *The Assumption of Moses* 10; *OTP* 1.928.

[507] Mirkin 5.42; Soncino 3.34. God then rewarded his "sharing the sorrow of Israel" with them by calling him from the burning bush (Exod 3:4).

[508] Lauterbach 2.130-31.

water").[509] This is basically repeated in Ha'azinu 306 on Deut 32:2, where "The Sages say that Moses said to Israel: Perhaps you do not know 'how much I suffered' [כמה צער נצטערתי] for the sake of the Torah, how much I toiled in it, how much I labored in it." Then Exod 34:28 and Deut 9:9 are also cited. The midrash continues: "I went among the angels, among the [heavenly] beasts,[510] among the seraphim, each one of which is capable of burning the entire world over its inhabitants, as it is said: 'Above him stood the seraphim' (Isa 6:2). I gave my soul for the Torah, I gave my blood for it. Just as I learned it 'in suffering' (בצער), so shall you learn it in suffering."[511] Here Moses' "suffering" is coupled with his "giving his blood," his "soul / life" for the Torah.

B. 2 Giving One's Life. A large number of Judaic texts express Moses' willingness to offer / give his soul / life for Israel and the Torah. In *Mek. R. Ish.* Pisha 1 on Exod 12:1 Moses is cited as one of the prophets who "offered their lives" (נתנו נפשם) in behalf of Israel. Two biblical texts are cited to substantiate this. The first is Exod 32:32, "But now, if You will only forgive their sin - but if not, blot me out of the book that You have written." It should be noted that this is in the context of Israel's major sin with the Golden Calf, when Moses tells the Israelites in v 30: "Perhaps I can *make atonement* for your sin." The second text cited is Num 11:15, where Moses, the "servant" of the Lord (v 11), pleads to Him in regard to the Israelites who are dissatisfied with only manna: "If this is the way You are going to treat me, put me to death at once - if I have found favor in Your sight - and do not let me see my misery."[512] *Eccl. Rab.* 2:15 § 2 on "why was I then more wise" has Moses ask: "Why did I 'give my life'

---

[509] Finkelstein 23; Hammer 38. The verb is the nithpael of צער , Jastrow 1294: to feel pain; to suffer privation. Cf. Jesus as the "new" Moses, who is tempted forty days in the wilderness by Satan (Mark 1:12-13). The Q tradition adds that he was hungry and was tempted to turn stones into bread (Luke 4:1-4 // Matt 4:1-4).

[510] I suggest that these dangerous (for Moses) heavenly "beasts" (חיות - BDB 312,b. "wild animal," although they originally may refer to the beings surrounding the cherubic chariot of Ezekiel 1, 3 and 10 [1.c.]) stand behind the earthly θηρία of Mark 1:13 - "(wild) animal, beast" (BAGD 361 on θηρίον). They are omitted in Q.

[511] Finkelstein 337; Hammer 305, with n. 33 on p. 492 referring to Gershom Scholem's study of the dangers involved with ascending to heaven.

[512] Lauterbach 1.10.

[נתתי נפשי] for the Torah?"[513] Other texts repeat the same motif of Moses' giving his life.[514]

The midrashim dealing with Moses' death scene emphasize how Moses was willing to do anything just to be allowed to enter the Land with the other Israelites. He suffered all the more for God's refusing him permission to do this.[515] Two texts illustrate this. In *Sifre* Niṣṣabim 304 on Deut 31:14 Moses tells God: "Master of the world, since it is in great agony that I depart from this world...."[516] Here Moses knows of his imminent death, which will take place "in great agony" for him. The second is *Pesiq. Rav Kah.* Suppl. 1.12, which deals with Deut 33:1, "This is the blessing with which Moses, the man of God, blessed the Israelites before his death." It states: "It was fitting for Moses to bless Israel [at the end of his life] because [his love for them was so strong that] at every instant he was ready to 'give up his life' for their sake."[517] William Braude and Israel Kapstein, the English translators, aptly remark here: "The words 'before his death' may have suggested to the commentator the idea that Moses was ever ready to lay down his life for Israel, whom he loved."[518]

B. 3   Moses as the Servant of the Lord.   While other figures in the Hebrew Bible can also be called a "servant of the Lord" (עֶבֶד יהוה),[519] it is Moses

---

[513] Vilna 15 or 8a; Soncino 8.64.

[514] Cf. *Sifre* Ve'zot ha-Berakhah 344 on Deut 33:3 (Finkelstein 400; Hammer 356); *Pesiq. R.* 5/2 on Num 7:1 (Friedmann 14b; Braude 1.94); *Tanḥ.* B Shofetim 4 on Deut 16:18 (Buber 2.29; Bitenhard 2.479), with a parallel in *Exod. Rab.* Mishpatim 30/4 on Exod 21:1 (Mirkin 6.37; Soncino 3.351); *Deut. Rab.* 'Eqeb 17 on Deut 10:1 (Mirkin 11.68; Soncino 7.88); and *b. Ber.* 32a, with Moses' "handing himself over to death" for the Israelites (Soncino 197).

[515] Cf. for example *Sifre* Va'etḥanan 28 and 29 on Deut 3:25-28 (Hammer 52-55); Niṣṣabim 305 on Deut 31:14, but dealing here with Num 27:18 (Hammer 294-97); and Ha'azinu 339 on Deut 32:50 (Hammer 347), as well as *Deut. Rab.* Ve'zot ha-Berakhah 11/10 at the end of the midrash on Moses' death (Soncino 7.180-88).

[516] Finkelstein 323; Hammer 293.

[517] Mandelbaum 448; Braude and Kapstein 456. The content of the first brackets is from me.

[518] Braude and Kapstein 456, n. 46.

[519] Cf. a listing of them in BDB 714. One factor which contributed to the application of "servant" texts such as Isaiah 53 to Jesus the Messiah is the fact that the messianic designation "the Branch" of Zech 3:8 is "My [the Lord's] servant." It is he who will rebuild the Temple (6:12). It should also be noted that of the eighteen biblical figures called "servants," *'Avot. R. Nat.* B 43 lists two of them as

who is overwhelmingly labeled so: thirty-six times.[520] It is also striking that of these occurrences, six are found in the last chapter of Deuteronomy, concerned with Moses' death, and in the first chapter of the book of Joshua, immediately following, which deals with Joshua, Moses' successor after his death. In regard to Mount Nebo, the top of Pisgah (Deut 34:1), v 5 states: "Then Moses, 'the servant of the Lord,' died there in the land of Moab, at the Lord's command." That is, a major designation of Moses, at this point summing up his entire life, is "the servant of the Lord."[521] This is underlined by the opening words of the succeeding writing, the book of Joshua: "After the death of Moses, 'the servant of the Lord,' the Lord spoke to Joshua son of Nun, Moses' assistant, saying: 'My servant Moses' is dead. Now proceed to cross the Jordan...'" (1:1-2). Verse seven also has "My servant Moses," and vv 13 and 15 "Moses the servant of the Lord." That is, a major cluster of six out of the thirty-six occurrences of Moses as "the servant of the Lord" occurs at the time of his death. This helps to explain the later application of Isaianic servant imagery to him in Judaic sources. Before discussing it in section B. 4.4 below, a review of Moses as the servant of the Lord in other Judaic sources will aid in showing how easily Isaianic servant imagery could be applied to him: it was part of a long tradition, from the Bible on.[522]

B. 3.1   *The Apocrypha.*   The Book of Baruch, probably from the second century BCE and originally in Hebrew,[523] mentions "His servant Moses" in 1:20, and "Your servant Moses" in 2:28, both παῖς in the Greek. The first is in connection with "the Lord," the second with "O Lord our God."

B. 3.2   *The Pseudepigrapha.*   Very important for the first-century CE Palestinian designation of Moses as "the servant of the Lord" is *Pseudo-Philo*, originally written in Hebrew in Palestine and in that century. It has

---

Moses (Num 12:7) and the Messiah (Isa 42:1) (Schechter 121; Saldarini 262-64). On this, see B. 3.10 below.

[520] This includes the variants "My servant," "His servant," "Your servant," and "Moses, the servant of God" (the latter in Neh 10:30, Eng. 29, and Dan 9:11).

[521] This is true in spite of his even greater role as "prophet" in v 10.

[522] Cf. n. 520 for the variations I include here, a listing which is not intended to be complete. Passages which contain a scriptural reference to Moses as the servant of the Lord, without comment, are usually not cited.

[523] Cf. Nickelsburg, *Jewish Literature* 97.

"Moses My servant" in 20:2; 30:2; 53:2; 53:8; and 58:1.[524] In addition, "Moses Your servant" occurs in 47:1,[525] and "my lord Moses, the servant of God" in 57:2.[526] All these references are *famulus*, "servant,"[527] in the Latin, with the one exception of 20:2, which has the synonym *servus*. In addition, apparently Hellenistic Jewish synagogue prayers from the second or third century CE have Moses as the servant of the Lord. *Apos. Con.* 7.33.6 speaks of "Moses, Your faithful and holy servant," and 8.12.25 of "Your holy servant Moses."[528]

B. 3.3   *Qumran.* Moses is labeled "Your servant" three times in the Dead Sea Scrolls: 4Q378 (4QapocJoshua^a) 22, col. 1.2; 4Q504 (4QDibHam^a), Frag. 6 (Puech, col. 2), 12; and the same, Frags. 1-2, col. 5 (Puech, col. 16), 14.[529]

B. 3.4   *The Mishnah.* In the Jerusalem Temple before its destruction in 70 CE, the high priest on the Day of Atonement (Yom Kippur) placed both hands upon his own bullock and spoke a prayer of extensive confession. Before citing Lev 16:30, ending with the fully pronounced divine name YHWH, he introduced this scriptural verse with the words: "as it is written in the Torah of Moses, Your servant" (*m. Yoma* 3:8).[530] This occurs a second time in 4:2.[531] Later on the high priest laid his two hands upon the scapegoat and spoke a prayer of extensive confession for all the iniquities, transgressions and sins of Israel. This also concluded with Lev 16:30, also introduced by "as it is written in the Torah of Moses Your servant" (6:2).[532] On each of these three different occasions, both the

---

[524] Cf. *SC* 229.166 and *OTP* 2.329; *SC* 229.232 and *OTP* 2.343; *SC* 229.340 and *OTP* 2.367; *SC* 229.344 and *OTP* 2.368; and *SC* 229.360 and *OTP* 2.371, respectively.
[525] *SC* 229.312 and *OTP* 2.361.
[526] *SC* 229.358 and *OTP* 2.371.
[527] Chambers Murray 264.
[528] Cf. *OTP* 2.678 and 693. On the dating, see D. Fiensy on p. 673.
[529] Martínez and Tigchelaar, *The Dead Sea Scrolls Study Edition* 2.748-49, 1008-09, and 1016-17. Interestingly, Moses is also called "His Anointed One" in 4Q377 (4QapocPentB), Frag. 1, col. 2.5 (*Study Edition* 2.744-45). It may also be noted that (presumably) the Teacher of Righteousness speaks of himself twenty-four times in 1QHodayoth as "Your servant." See 4:11,21,23,25-26; 5:24; 6:8,25; 8:16,18,22,26; 13:15,28; 15:16; 17:11; 18:22,30; 19:27,30,33; 22:16; and 23:6,10 in the *Study Edition* 1.146-203.
[530] Albeck 2.231; Neusner 269.
[531] Albeck 2.233; Neusner 271.
[532] Albeck 2.240; Neusner 275. The Jerusalem and Babylonian Talmuds merely repeat the statements of the Mishnah here.

priests and all those assembled in the Temple Court at hearing the expressly pronounced divine name knelt, bowed down, fell on their faces and said: "Blessed is the name of the glory of His kingdom forever and ever."[533]

It can be assumed that the high priest's prayers, spoken publicly within the liturgy of Judaism's holiest day and including three of the very rare explicit pronouncements of the divine name, were very widely known. As such, the introductory phrase "as it is written in the Torah of 'Moses, Your servant,'" was very probably also well-known in both Judea and Galilee.

B. 3.5 *Seder 'Olam.* In the earliest Jewish chronography, *Seder 'Olam*, chapter ten quotes Deut 34:5 and Josh 1:1-2, all on the death of Moses, the servant of the Lord, to show that he was born and died on the seventh of Adar.[534]

B. 3.6 *Mekilta of Rabbi Ishmael.* In Beshallaḥ 7 on Exod 14:31c, "His servant Moses" is interpreted as the shepherd of Israel.[535] In Shirata 1 on Exod 15:1, the statement is made: "There were three things to which Moses devoted himself with his whole soul, and they were all named after him. He devoted himself with his whole soul to the Torah, and it is named after him. For it is said: 'Remember the Torah of Moses, My servant' (Mal 3:22)."[536]

B. 3.7 *Sifre Numbers*, and *Sifre Zuṭa* on Numbers. *Sifre* Beha'aloteka 103 on Num 12:7 and 8 interprets the phrase "My servant Moses" there.[537] The same is true for *Sifre Zuṭa* on these verses.[538]

---

[533] *Ibid.* It is directly followed by 6:3, "He gave [the scapegoat] over / delivered it to the one who was to lead it out." This should be compared to similar imagery in Mark 15:15b and 20b (the soldiers' mocking is a later addition; see the excursus in III. below). On the high priest on the Day of Atonement as expressing the divine name, see also *m. Soṭah* 7:6 (Albeck 3.250; Neusner 458); *Tam.* 3:8 (Albeck 5.300; Neusner 867); *t. Yoma* 2:2 (Zuckermandel / Liebermann 183; Neusner 2.192); and *y. Yoma* 3:7, 40d (Neusner 14.95).

[534] Cf. Guggenheimer 100-101.

[535] Lauterbach 1.252 and 255.

[536] Lauterbach 2.3-4.

[537] Horovitz 101-02; Neusner 2.123 and 125.

[538] Horovitz 276; Börner-Klein 144-45.

B. 3.8   *Sifre Deuteronomy.*   Va'ethanan 27 on Deut 3:24 states: "Moses called himself 'servant,' as it is said: 'to show Your servant,' and the Holy One, blessed be He, also called him a servant, as it is said: 'My servant Moses is not so' (Num 12:7)."[539]

B. 3.9   *Soferim* and *Kallah Rabbathi.*   These two writings are now included in the "Minor Tractates" of the Babylonian Talmud. According to *Soferim* 13:9, 40a the conclusion of the benediction spoken before one reads from the Prophets in the synagogue service is: "Blessed are You, O Lord, who have chosen the Torah and Moses Your servant, and Israel Your people, and the prophets of truth and righteousness."[540] While it is notoriously difficult to date liturgical materials, if this benediction spoken before the *haftarah* or reading from the prophets is relatively old, as seems probable, it would be another indication that the phrase "Moses Your servant" was also known from the synagogue liturgy.

   Kallah Rabbathi 3:4, 52b says that "Our Rabbis taught: From where [do we know that a disciple of the wise should be] meek? From Moses our teacher, as it is stated: 'Now the man Moses was very meek' (Num 12:3). And on that account Moses was praised, as it is stated: 'My servant Moses is not so' (v 7)."[541]

B. 3.10   '*Avot de Rabbi Nathan* A and B.   Version A 12 states that "Joshua was sitting and worrying about Moses [after his death] until the Holy One, blessed be He, said to him: Joshua, why are you worried about Moses? 'Moses My servant' is dead (Josh 1:2)."[542] In chapter 36 "Moses the servant of the Lord" in Deut 34:5 is also interpreted as one of the righteous with whom the word "there" is used.[543]

   Version B in chapter 1 interprets Num 12:7-8, with "My servant Moses" in both verses, as the King of kings' glorifying and sanctifying Moses.[544] Closely related to the subject of this book is the tradition recorded in chapter 25: "The Angel of Death went to the Almighty and said to Him: 'Master of the World, Moses Your servant does not want to

---

[539] Finkelstein 42; Hammer 50.
[540] Soncino, *Minor Tractates* 273. Cf. the set liturgical phrases employed before and after the reading of the Epistle and the Gospel in many Christian denominations.
[541] Soncino, *Minor Tractates* 444.
[542] Schechter 51; Goldin 66.
[543] Schechter 107-08; Goldin 150.
[544] Schechter 1; Saldarini 21.

hand over his soul to me.'"[545] Finally, chapter 43 states that Moses (Num 12:7) is one of the eighteen called "servant" in the Hebrew Bible. Another is the Messiah (Isa 42:1),[546] at the beginning of the first Isaianic servant song.[547]

B. 3.11   *Midrash Rabbah.*   *Gen. Rab.* Ḥayye Sarah 62/4 on Gen 25:11 interprets Josh 1:1, "After the death of Moses the servant of the Lord," to mean that "immediately thereafter the well, the manna, and the clouds of glory ceased."[548]

Exod. Rab. Bo 18/1 on Exod 12:29 interprets the clause "Who confirms the word of His servant" in Isa 44:26 to mean Moses.[549] Mishpatim 30/4 on Exod 21:1 relates the same tradition as found in *Mek. R. Ish.* Shirata 1 on Exod 15:1, noted in B. 3.6 above.[550] Teṣaveh 37/2 on Exod 28:1 employs Num 12:7 with "My servant Moses" to explain that the Lord made Moses the superintendent of the palace.[551] In Ki Thissa 40/1 on Exod 30:1, it is stated that "The reward of fear is Torah, for the Lord raised from Jochebed Moses, who had the distinction of having the Torah ascribed to him, as it says: Mal 3:22."[552] Pequde 51/1 on Exod 38:21 interprets the "faithful man" of Prov 28:20 as Moses, a confidant of God, as in Num 12:7.[553] In 51/6 on the same verse it is stated that although God trusted Moses implicitly (Num 12:7), he made an account to others.[554]

Num. Rab. Bemidbar 4/1 on Num 3:40 interprets "the member of His house" as Moses (Num 12:7).[555] Naso 12/9 on Num 7:1 also relates the same tradition found in *Mek. R. Ish.* Shirata 1 on Exod 15:1, noted in

---

[545] Schechter 51; Saldarini 150.
[546] Schechter 121; Saldarini 263.
[547] These are usually defined as Isa 42:1-7; 49:1-7; 50:4-11; and 52:13 - 53:12.
[548] Theodor and Albeck 675-76; Soncino 2.553. According to rabbinic tradition (see chapter II. below), the well temporarily ceased at Miriam's death, and the clouds of glory at Aaron's; then they returned again. However, at Moses' death they, in addition to the manna, ceased forever.
[549] Mirkin 5.211; Soncino 3.217.
[550] Mirkin 6.37; Soncino 3.351.
[551] Mirkin 6.112; Soncino 3.445.
[552] Mirkin 6.126; Soncino 3.460-61.
[553] Mirkin 6.205; Soncino 3.562.
[554] Mirkin 6.210; Soncino 3.567.
[555] Mirkin 9.68; Soncino 5.96.

B. 3.6 above.[556] Ḥuqqath 19/21 on Num 21:5 notes in regard to Moses and God: "They put the servant on the same level as his Master."[557]

Finally, *Deut. Rab.* Va᾽etḥanan 2/18 on Deut 4:25 states: "it is through Moses, My servant, that I forewarned them."[558]

B. 3.12   *Pesiqta Rabbati and Pesiqta de Rav Kahanah.*   In *Pesiq. R.* 5/2 on Num 7:1 there is a tradition similar to that found in *Mek. R. Ish.* Shirata 1 on Exod 15:1 noted in B. 3.6 above.[559] In 12/1 on Deut 25:17, commenting on Prov 10:7, Moses' name is interpreted as one of the righteous. God spoke well of him, for which Isa 63:11 is cited.[560] In 14/11 on Num 19:2 it is related that the Torah is inscribed to Moses with his name, as in Mal 3:22.[561] Finally, 17/2 on Exod 12:29 cites Isa 44:26, "Who confirms the word of His servant," and interprets it to mean the word of Moses (Num 12:7). Exod 11:4 is quoted in regard to midnight as the time the Israelites departed from Egypt. "Long since have I assured Moses and said to him: 'He is trusted in all My house' (Num 12:7). Shall My servant Moses be made out to be a liar? Since Moses said: 'At the time of midnight,' I will act 'at midnight.'"[562]

Pesiq. Rav Kah. 5/4 on Exod 12:2 relates the expression "Your truth" in Ps 43:3 to Moses, as in Num 12:7.[563] In 7/3 on Exod 12:29 the same tradition is given as in *Pesiq. R.* 17/2 above.[564] In Suppl. 1/20 on the death of Moses, the name "Moses" is interpreted to mean both the man and the Torah (Mal 3:22).[565]

B. 3.13   *Eliyyahu Rabbah.*   In (6) 7 it is stated that "there were none who knew how to pour out [pleas for] mercy and utter supplications as Moses did." Thus Mal 3:22 is quoted of him. "But is it Moses' Torah? Is it not Yours, kept by You for 974 generations before the world was created? Was it not You who refined it and gave it to Israel Your servants? Why then is it said: 'Remember the Torah of Moses My servant'? Because on

---

[556] Mirkin 10.29; Soncino 5.477.
[557] Mirkin 10.236; Soncino 6.770.
[558] Mirkin 11.39; Soncino 7.45.
[559] Friedmann 14b; Braude 94.
[560] Friedmann 47a; Braude 219. Friedmann's text has the reading "Moses His servant," while the present MT differs.
[561] Friedmann 64a; Braude 286.
[562] Friedmann 85b; Braude 363, following Rashi (n. 6).
[563] Mandelbaum 85; Braude and Kapstein 97.
[564] Mandelbaum 123; Braude and Kapstein 141.
[565] Mandelbaum 451; Braude and Kapstein 460.

four and five occasions Moses stood up in prayer and saved Israel from death, the Holy One credited him with the writing of the Torah as though it had actually been wrought by him - as though, in fact, it belonged to him. Hence 'Remember the Torah of Moses My servant.'"[566]

B. 3.14 *Midrash Psalms.* In 1/16 on Ps 1:2, it is explained that "because Moses went on high and meditated there for forty days and nights, almost dying for its sake, the Written Law came to be called after Moses, for it is said: Mal 3:22."[567] In 18/4 on Ps 18:1, "David the servant of the Lord," the midrash explains that "whenever a man calls himself a servant, God also calls him a servant." For Moses this is shown by Deut 3:24 and Num 12:7.[568] In 19/13 on Ps 19:8, it is maintained that only one who occupies himself with Torah "will be able to hide himself in the time-to-come." This is shown by Mal 3:22 following v 21.[569] In 30/4 on Ps 30:1 it is stated that Moses "suffered grief" (נצטער) for the Torah, as in Exod 34:28; therefore it came to be called after his name (Mal 3:22).[570] In 42/43 on Ps 43:2, the author asks: "Did You not send redemption at the hand of two redeemers [גואלים] to that generation, as it is said: 'He sent Moses His servant, and Aaron whom He had chosen' (105:26)? Send two redeemers like them to this generation." "Your light" in Ps 43:3 is Elijah, and "Your truth" is the Messiah, son of David. "Likewise Scripture says: 'Behold, I will send you Elijah the prophet' (Mal 3:23), who is one [redeemer], and speaks of the second in 'Behold My servant, whom I uphold' (Isa 42:1)."[571] It should be noted here that the Messiah, son of David, is the redeemer meant by "Your truth" in Ps 43:3, interpreted elsewhere of Moses (see *Pesiq. Rav Kah* 5/4 in B. 3.12 above). Here the Lord's servant in Isa 42:1 is meant of the Messiah, son of David,[572] as in *'Avot R. Nat.* B 43 cited above in B. 3.10. In *Midr. Pss.* 90/5 on Ps 90:1, Moses is interpreted to be God's director of the palace, for He spoke Num 12:7 of him.[573] Finally, in 101/2 on Ps 101:2 and 6, R. Judah (b. Ilai, a third generation Tanna,[574]) says Moses asked God whether he should

---

[566] Friedmann 33; Braude and Kapstein 117.
[567] Buber 15; Braude 1.23.
[568] Buber 136; Braude 1.232.
[569] Buber 170; Braude 1.282-83.
[570] Buber 235; Braude 1.389-90.
[571] Buber 267; Braude 1.445.
[572] This is true although Mal 3:22 (Eng. 4:4) mentions "My servant Moses."
[573] Buber 388; Braude 2.89. Braude derives the garbled מייסטרופולין from *magister palatii* (494, n. 13) and translates "seneschal."
[574] *Introduction* 84-85.

appoint a high priest from the tribes of Reuben, Simeon, Dan, Joseph and Judah. This God adamantly refused. Then Moses asked Him about the tribe of Levi, and God approved it, quoting "the *faithful*" of Ps 101:6. "For what you are, so is your tribe [Levi], and of you it is said: 'My servant Moses...is *faithful* / trusted in all My house' (Num 12:7)."[575]

B. 3.15   *Midrash Proverbs.*   Commenting on Prov 14:34, R. Nehemiah, a third generation Tanna,[576] says that Moses taught Israel Torah, laws and righteousness. For the Torah he cites Mal 3:22.[577] There is no reason to doubt the authorship of R. Nehemiah here. He was often in debate with R. Judah b. Ilai, quoted above in *Midr. Pss.* 101/2. These are two examples of how midrashim which were compiled at a very late date can also contain quite early material.

B. 3.16   *The Babylonian Talmud.*   In *b. Šabb.* 89a God tells Moses that "since you have [humbly] disparaged yourself, it [the Torah] shall be called by your name," with Mal 3:22.[578] In *b. Yebam.* 96b, R. Jacob b. Idi attempts to conciliate R. Yohanan, who was annoyed that R. Eleazar said something in the schoolhouse without naming him as the author. R. Jacob b. Idi cites Josh 11:15 with "Moses His servant" and maintains that "Joshua was sitting and delivering his discourse without mentioning names, and all knew that it was the Torah of Moses. So did your disciple R. Eleazar sit and deliver his discourse without mentioning names, and all knew that it was yours." This then conciliated R. Yohanan.[579] A baraitha in *b. Qidd.* 38a notes that Moses was born and died on the seventh of Adar, for which Deut 34:5 and Josh 1:2 are cited.[580] Another baraitha in *b. B. Bath.* 15a cites Deut 34:5 and maintains that from then on Joshua did the writing.[581] Basically the same is maintained in *b. Menah.* 30a, but it then also suggests the alternative that God dictated as of Deut 34:5, and Moses continued to write.[582]

---

575   Buber 427-28; Braude 2.151.
576   *Introduction* 85.
577   Visotzky Heb. 121; Eng. 75-76.
578   Soncino 423.
579   Soncino 660-61. R. Yohanan (bar Nappaha) was a second generation Palestinian Amora active in Tiberias, where this episode appears to take place. Cf. also *y. Šeq.* 2:5, 47a (Neusner 15.52-53) and *y. Peah* 1:1, 15b (Brooks / Neusner 2.44).
580   Soncino 186.
581   Soncino 72.
582   Soncino 194.

* * *

The above survey of Moses designated as "the servant of the Lord," or variations of this such as "Your servant" and "His servant," reaches from the Hebrew Bible through the Apocrypha, Pseudepigrapha and Qumran, to the Mishnah, the Tannaitic midrashim, and later midrashic compilations, which in part include Tannaitic traditions. There is thus very good reason to maintain that Moses was thought of as *the* servant of the Lord in first-century CE Palestine, as the thirty-six occurrences of the expression in the Hebrew Bible already indicate.[583] This is of major importance for the interpretation of Moses as the Isaianic servant of the Lord, to which I now turn.

B. 4 Isaiah 53.   Isa 53:12 reads in the Hebrew Bible:

> Therefore I [the Lord] will allot him a portion with the great,
> and he shall divide the spoil with the strong,
> because he poured out his soul to death,
> and was numbered with transgressors;
> yet he bore the sin of many,
> and made intercession for the transgressors.

As pointed out in section A. above, this verse was interpreted by the earliest Jewish Christians to apply to Jesus' sufferings and death by crucifixion. The Judaic messianic interpretation of the fourth and last servant song in Isa 52:13 - 53:12 encouraged them to do so.[584] Yet its

---

[583] In this respect cf. especially the sevenfold mention of Moses as such in *Pseudo-Philo* in B. 3.2 above, from first-century CE Palestine.

[584] Cf. for example *Targ. Isa.* 52:13 with "My servant, the Messiah," and 53:10 with "the kingdom of their Messiah" (Stenning 178-81). These messianic references have remained in the Targum in spite of a general tendency to eradicate them because Christians appropriated the servant songs for their Messiah Jesus. They would certainly not have been inserted later, for they provided too good "ammunition" (proof from Scripture and its interpretation) for Christians. See also *Ruth Rab.* 5/6 on Ruth 2:14 with the Messiah's sufferings derived from Isa 53:5, with 11:4 also cited (Vilna 18; Soncino 8.64); *Tanḥ.* B Toledoth 20 with the messianic interpretation of Isa 52:13 (Buber 139; Townsend 1.166); and other passages cited in Str-B 1.481-83. On the Isaiah Targum, see now especially Jostein Ådna, "Der Gottesknecht als triumphierender und interzessorischer Messias. Die Rezeption von Jes 53 im Targum Jonathan untersucht mit besonderer Berücksichtigung des Messiasbildes" in *Der leidende Gottesknecht* 129-58, especially 156 in regard to Moses. He is dependent in part on the works of

application to Moses also encouraged this. Before I deal with this, it is important to note that v 12 could also be applied to other figures in early Judaism, showing that the Messiah and Moses were not alone.

B. 4.1 *The Israelites.*   *Num. Rab.* Naso 13/2 on Num 7:12 interprets Cant 5:1 in light of Isa 53:12. The Israelites exposed their souls to death in exile, yet busied themselves with the Torah, for which God will reward them in the time to come.[585] The verse is thus applied here to the Israelites *in toto.*

B. 4.2 *Rabbi Aqiba.*   In *y. Šeq.* 5:1, 48c it is R. Aqiba, a second generation Tanna,[586] who is meant by Isa 53:12, certainly because of the great suffering involved in his execution.[587] In *b. Ber.* 61b it is related for example that Aqiba had intentionally disregarded the Roman government's "decree forbidding the Jews to study and practice the Torah." Therefore his flesh was combed with iron combs.[588] Aqiba's reciting the Jewish confession of faith, the Shema', at his death is considered here to be an example of "hallowing / sanctifying the divine Name," or martyrdom.[589]

B. 4.3 *Phinehas.*   Numbers 25 relates that during the wilderness wandering, Israelite men began to have sex with Moabite women, even bowing down to their god Baal of Peor. When the Simeonite Zimri was so bold as to even bring the female Midianite Cozbi into his family in the sight of all Israel, the only one who manifested great zeal in preventing this was Phinehas the son of Eleazar, son of Aaron the priest. He went into their tent and speared them both through the belly. This stopped the Lord's plague, which by then had cost 24,000 lives.[590] As a reward for Phinehas, the Lord said: 12) "I hereby grant him My covenant of peace. 13) It shall be for him and for his descendants after him a covenant of

---

J. Bowman, O. Betz and O. Hofius, and unfortunately not aware of the work of Renée Bloch (see n. 505 here).

[585] Mirkin 10.46; Soncino 6.501.

[586] *Introduction* 79.

[587] Cf. Neusner 15.97.

[588] Soncino 385-87.

[589] Cf. Jastrow 1314 on קְדוּשַׁת הַשֵׁם . Did Jesus allude to this aspect, willingness to martyrdom, in the first petition of the "Lord's Prayer" he taught his disciples?

[590] This figure from Num 25:9 should be compared to that of "about 3000" in Exod 32:28 in regard to the Golden Calf. The idolatry in connection with the Baal of Peor was considered even more disastrous.

perpetual priesthood, because he was zealous for his God, and made atonement for the Israelites." Ps 106:30-31 comments on this in the following way: "Then Phinehas stood up and interceded, and the plague stopped. 31) And that has been reckoned to him as righteousness from generation to generation forever." Finally, Sir 45:23 says that Phinehas was third in rank in Israel; only Moses and Aaron are superior to him. This is "for being zealous in the fear of the Lord, and standing firm, when the people turned away, in the noble courage of his soul; and he made atonement for Israel."[591]

Phinehas' risking his own life in order to sanctify God's Name at this point is emphasized in various ways in rabbinic sources. The Tannaitic midrash *Sifre* Balak 131 on Num 25:6 has Phinehas ask: "Is there no one [else] here who is willing to kill [Zimri] and be killed [in the process]?"[592] This is repeated in *y. Sanh.* 10:2, 28d.[593] In *Exod. Rab.* Terumah 33/5 on Exod 25:2, R. Yose, perhaps a third generation Tanna,[594] notes that "Phinehas reasoned to himself [in regard to Prov 21:31]: 'If the horse risks its life in the day of battle, prepared to die for its master, then how much more should I be prepared to do in order to sanctify God's name?'"[595] *Midrash Haggadol* on Num 25:7 also accentuates the latter motif by stating that God performed many miracles for Phinehas at this time "because 'he risked his life' (מסר עצמו) for the sanctification of the Name."[596] *Num. Rab.* Balak 20/25 on the same verse states that "Phinehas rose up from among the congregation of judges and, 'volunteering' to do the deed, 'he took a spear in his hand,' etc. (*ibid.*)."[597] The "voluntary" character of Phinehas' action is also stressed in *Tanḥ.* B Balak 29 on Num 25:6[598] and *Tanḥ.* Balak 21.[599] The voluntary character of Phinehas' risking his own life in order to sanctify God's Name is thus emphasized in a number of rabbinic sources, showing its importance.

---

[591] On the large number of Judaic interpretations of this entire episode, cf. Ginzberg, *Legends* 3.380-91 and its notes. For its influence on the narrative of the woman "caught in the act" of adultery in John 7:53 - 8:11, see my "*Caught in the Act*," *Walking on the Sea*, and the Release of Barabbas Revisited 6-15.
[592] Horovitz 172; Kuhn 521.
[593] Neusner 31.340.
[594] *Introduction* 84.
[595] Mirkin 6.93; Soncino 3.420.
[596] Rabinowitz 440.
[597] Mirkin 10.274; Soncino 6.824. The nithpael of נדב is employed here for "volunteering"; cf. BDB 621, hithpael 1, and Jastrow 877.
[598] Buber 149; Bietenhard 2.384.
[599] Eshkol 806.

The Tannaitic *Sifre* Phinehas 131 on Num 25:13 comments on Phinehas as follows: "'because he was zealous for his God.' [This means:] 'because he poured out his soul to death' (Isa 53:12)."[600] Phinehas' voluntary behavior, his willingness to risk his own life for the sanctification of the divine Name, that is, to become a martyr, is interpreted here in light of a scriptural verse describing similar behavior on the part of the Suffering Servant. The same verse, Isa 53:12, was employed of R. Aqiba at his martyrdom, described above in section B. 4.2.

It is important to note how the *Sifre* Phinehas 131 passage on Phinehas now continues. It cites the end of Num 25:13, "and made atonement for the Israelites," and then comments: "It is not written here: 'and he made atonement (כִּפֶּר)[601] for the Israelites,' but 'and he makes atonement (יְכַפֵּר) for the Israelites.' [This means] that he has not ceased [to do so] up to now. Rather, he [continually] stands and makes atonement (מכפר) until the resurrection of the dead."[602]

A rabbinic passage which corroborates the above is found in *Num. Rab.* Phinehas 21/3 on Num 25:12, "I hereby grant him My covenant of peace." "This means that he [Phinehas] is still alive at the present time. In this strain it says: 'My covenant with him was a covenant of *life* and peace, and I gave them to him, and of reverence, and he revered Me, and stood in awe of My name' (Mal 2:5)."[603] Judah Slotki correctly notes here that "Phinehas is identified with Elijah, and is thus said to have passed alive into heaven."[604] Phinehas' voluntarily risking his own life for the sanctification of the divine Name at the incident of Baal Peor can thus be described not only as being rewarded by God with Phinehas' continually making atonement for Israel, as in *Sifre* Numbers on Num 25:13b. He also is portrayed here as ascending into heaven, just as Elijah did in 2 Kgs 2:11. Elijah was "very zealous" (קַנֹּא קִנֵּאתִי) for the Lord in 1 Kgs 19:10, and Phinehas was very zealous (בְּקַנְאוֹ and קַנֹּא) for the Lord in the incident of Peor (Num 25:11 and 13).[605] This certainly aided early Jewish commentators in associating the two.

Pseudo-Philo, written in Hebrew in Palestine in the first century CE, shows how early the ascension of Phinehas was thought of in terms of

600 Horovitz 173, (who falsely still labels the section Balak); Kuhn 527.
601 I follow Kuhn, n. 193, in reading וכפר from *Yalquṭ* 1.771 (see Kook, *Numbers* 512) instead of לכפר.
602 Horovitz 173; Kuhn 527, with notes; Börner-Klein 295.
603 Mirkin 10.280; Soncino 6.829.
604 Soncino 6.829, n. 7.
605 Phinehas even becomes the biblical model for the later Zealots.

the ascension of Elijah. In chapter 48 the Lord tells Phinehas to "dwell in Danaben on the mountain" for many years (v 1).[606] There the Lord will nourish him by means of a bird (*ibid.*), as He did by means of birds for Elijah in 1 Kgs 17:4. Later Phinehas will both shut up and open the heaven (in regard to rain), as Elijah did in 1 Kings 17 and 18. The Lord then instructs him: "And afterward 'you will be lifted up' (*elevaberis*) into the place where those who were before you 'were lifted up' (*elevati sunt*),[607] and you will be there until I remember the world" (48:1). "And Phinehas 'went up' (*ascendit*) and did all that the Lord commanded him" (v 2). "Now in that time when he 'went up' (*ascenderet*), then the sons of Israel were celebrating Passover..." (v 3).[608]

*   *   *

The above Judaic texts, in part Tannaitic and from the first century CE, show how another figure who voluntarily risked his own life for Israel in order to sanctify the divine Name, was thought of as presently making atonement for Israel in heaven, to which he had ascended without dying. The application of Isa 53:12 to Phinehas is very similar to its being employed of Moses, to whom I now turn.

B. 4.4   *Moses.*   In Deut 3:24 Moses describes himself as "Your [the Lord's] servant." In *Midrash Tannaim* on the next verse, 25, Moses is portrayed as wishing to enter the Land and perform the commandments so as to receive a reward in the time to come for doing so. God then reassures him that he should not worry about this matter, for everyone who has performed them (including, of course, Moses,) will have a "portion" (חלק) in the time to come, as it is written: "Therefore 'I will allot [him] a portion' (אחלק) with the many" (Isa 53:12).[609]

In the same midrash on Deut 31:14, dealing with Moses' imminent death, he is compared to a shepherd. He wishes to enter the Land of Israel. God again reassures him that he will receive his reward in the

---

[606] On "Danaban on the mountain" as possibly the "mountain of the Abarim, Mount Nebo," where Moses dies, cf. Deut 32: 49-50 and chapter II. below.

[607] Enoch in Gen 5:24 and Elijah in 2 Kgs 2:11 are most probably meant here because of their ascensions into heaven. If my proposal below is accepted, Moses is also included in this group.

[608] *SC* 229.320; *OTP* 2.362.

[609] Hoffmann 17. The same material is found in *Midr. Haggadol* Deut 3:25 (Fisch 63).

time to come, more than all Israel, as it says: "Therefore I will allot him [Moses] a portion with the many" (Isa 53:12).[610]

The Tannaitic midrash *Sifre* Ve'zot ha-Berakhah 355 on Deut 33:21,[611] "And there came the heads of the people," interprets this to mean that "in the future Moses will enter [the Land] at the head of every group - at the head of Bible scholars, at the head of the group of Mishnah scholars, at the head of the group of Talmud scholars - and take his reward with each one of them, as it is said: 'Therefore I will allot him a portion with the great, and he shall divide the spoil with the mighty' (Isa 53:12)."[612] Here "the great" and "the mighty" are various groups of Torah scholars, and Moses will be at their head.

In light of the above three texts it is not surprising to find that *b. Soṭah* 14a also applies Isa 53:12 to Moses. There definitely was Judaic tradition for doing so. The Mishnah states in *Soṭah* 1:8, "We have none so great as Moses, for only the Holy One, blessed be He, took care of his [burial], since it is said: 'And He buried him in the valley' (Deut 34:6)."[613] In *b. Soṭah* 14a on this biblical verse, R. Simlai (שְׂמְלַאי), a second generation Palestinian Amora,[614] maintains: "Torah begins with an act of benevolence and ends with an act of benevolence. It begins with an act of benevolence, for it is written: 'And the Lord God made for Adam and for his wife coats of skin, and clothed them' (Gen 3:21). And it ends with an act of benevolence, for it is written: 'And He buried him in the valley' (Deut 34:6)."[615] Here R. Simlai connects Deut 34:6 on Moses' death with the base text in the Mishnah. Elsewhere he cites a more extensive version of this haggadic tradition, which is reproduced here in an abbreviated form.[616]

---

[610] Hoffmann 179. The same material is found in *Midr. Haggadol* Deut 31:14 (Fisch 179).

[611] It should be noted that the catchword חל קה is also employed in this verse: a commander's "allotment / portion."

[612] Finkelstein 418; I slightly modify Hammer 372-73. Cf. also *Midrash Tannaim ad loc.* (Hoffmann 219) and *Midrash Haggadol ad loc.* (Fisch 772), as well as *Yalquṭ* Isaiah 338.

[613] Albeck 3.236; I slightly modify Neusner 449.

[614] *Introduction* 96.

[615] Soncino 73.

[616] Cf. *Gen. Rab.* Bereshit 8/13 on Gen 1:28 (Theodor and Albeck 67; Soncino 1.63). See also *Midr. Pss.* 25/11 on Ps 25:10 (Buber 213-14; Braude 1.353-54), as well as *Tanḥ.* B Vayyera 1 on Gen 18:1ff. (Buber 83-84; Townsend 87), and *Tanḥ.* Vayyera 1 (Eshkol 1.72; Berman 112-13). R. Ḥama b. R. Ḥanina, a second generation

It is thus known that R. Simlai definitely concerned himself with the death of Moses. The text of *b. Soṭah* 14a now continues with an extensive account by him explaining why Moses sought to enter the Land. It is somewhat similar to the two accounts found in *Midrash Tannaim* quoted above. Because it refers Isa 53:12 to Moses in a major way, it deserves to be quoted *in toto* here:

> Why did Moses our teacher yearn to enter the land of Israel? Did he want to eat of its fruits or satisfy himself from its bounty? But Moses spoke so: "Many precepts were commanded to Israel which can only be fulfilled in the land of Israel. I wish to enter the land so that they may all be fulfilled by me." The Holy One, blessed be He, said to him: "Is it only to receive the reward [for obeying the commandments] that you thus seek? I ascribe it to you as if you performed them, as it is said: 'Therefore I will allot him a portion with the great, and he shall divide the spoil with the strong; because he poured out himself to death, and was numbered with the transgressors; yet he bore the sin of many, and made intercession for the transgressors' (Isa 53:12)." "Therefore I will allot him a portion with the great" - is it possible [to think that his portion will be] with the [great of] later generations and not former generations? Therefore there is a text to declare: "and he shall divide the spoil with the strong," that is, with Abraham, Isaac and Jacob who were strong in the Torah and the commandments. "Because he poured out himself to death" - because he surrendered himself to die, as it is said: "but if not, blot me out," etc. (Exod 32:32). "And was numbered with the transgressors" - because he was numbered with them who were condemned to die in the wilderness. "Yet he bore the sin of many" - because he secured atonement for the making of the Golden Calf. "And made intercession for the transgressors" - because he begged for mercy on behalf of the sinners in Israel that they should turn in penitence. And the word *pegiʿah* [intercession] means nothing else than prayer, as it is said: "As for you, do not pray for this people, do not raise a cry or prayer on their behalf, and do not intercede with Me" (Jer 7:16).[617]

Here R. Simlai takes up and develops a motif already emphasized by his rabbinic predecessors. Moses reasons that since many precepts / commandments can only be fulfilled in Israel, he too wishes to enter the Land and fulfill all of them. It is the same type of "bartering" with God he is portrayed as doing elsewhere so as not to die now: "if..., then...." God

---

Palestinian Amora as well (*Introduction* 96), is also quoted before R. Simlai with a more extensive version of this tradition in *b. Soṭah* 14a (Soncino 72-73).
[617] Soncino 73-74, which I modify.

here counters that if Moses is only interested in receiving the reward for such behavior, He can ascribe it to him as if he did them, (although he must die outside the Land and not enter it). The exposition of individual parts of Isa 53:12 serves to confirm this. Most interesting for our purposes are four aspects of R. Simlai's explanation of the Isaianic verse.

B. 4.4.a   "'Because he poured out his soul to death': because he surrendered himself to die [שמסר עצמו למיתה], as it is said: 'but if not, blot me out of the book that You have written' (Exod 32:32b)." This is part of the Golden Calf incident, just after the Levites had killed about 3000 Israelites (v 28). "On the next day Moses said to the people: 'You have sinned a great sin. But now I will go up to the Lord; perhaps I can make atonement for your sin' (v 30)." The Hebrew of "I can make atonement" here is אֲכַפְּרָה . Moses thus informs the sinful Israelites that he is willing to sacrifice his own life for them[618] in order to "atone" for their great sin of the Golden Calf idolatry, so that this may be "forgiven" by God. Verse 32a states: "But now, if You will only 'forgive' (תִּשָּׂא) their sin...." The Lord did not accept Moses' offer, however, deciding on other consequences (vv 33-35). What is important here is Moses' voluntary decision to sacrifice his own life in order to atone for the Israelites' sins, so that they could be forgiven by the Lord. Isa 53:12's "because he poured out his soul to death" was admirably suited to express this thought.

B. 4.4.b   "'And was numbered with the transgressors' - because he [Moses] was numbered with them who were condemned to die in the wilderness." Because of their rebellious and sinful behavior, the Lord had

---

618 On this in connection with Exod 32:32, cf. *Mek. R. Ish.* Pisha 1 on Exod 12:1 (Lauterbach 1.10), which also cites Num 11:15; *Sifre* Ve'zot ha-Berakhah 344 on Deut 33:3 (Finkelstein 400; Hammer 356); *Exod. Rab.* Ki Thissa 47/9 on Exod 34:27 (Mirkin 6.188; Soncino 3.545); and *b. Ber.* 32a (Soncino 197). Moses' linking his own fate with those Israelites who had sinned with the Golden Calf is also explained via various parts of Exod 32:32 in *Exod. Rab.* Ki Thissa 46/1 on Exod 34:1 (Mirkin 6.175; Soncino 3.527). That is, he associates himself here with sinners, being willing to share or bear the results of their sin. In *Mos.* 2.166, Philo maintains that Moses at this point "took the part of mediator and reconciler" (μεσίτης καὶ διαλλακτής), making prayers and supplications, "begging that their sins might be forgiven." Here he was not only a protector, but also an "intercessor" (παραιτητής : LSJ 1311). In 4Q504, frags. 1-2, col. II, lines 9-10 (Martínez and Tigchelaar, *The Dead Sea Scrolls Study Edition* 2.1012-13), which probably refers to the Golden Calf incident and Exod 32:30, the text states: "for Moses atoned for (כפר ... ב) their sin."

decreed that none of the Israelites who had participated in the exodus from Egypt and the wilderness wanderings should see the Land He had promised their ancestors (Num 14:22-23).[619] R. Simlai says that out of solidarity, Moses was numbered with such transgressors and shared their fate: like them, he may not enter the Land.

B. 4.4.c   "'Yet he bore the sin of many' - because he secured atonement for the making of the Golden Calf." "Because he secured atonement for" here is the Hebrew שׂכיפר על . It refers back to Moses' offer in Exod 32:30, just before v 32b, which R. Simlai cited. Here it is assumed that Moses' offer of giving his own life for the sake of God's forgiving the Israelites' great sin in itself atones for them, leading to God's forgiving them. Unlike the other 3000, whom the Levites killed, they are now spared by God and may continue to live.

B. 4.4.d   "'And made intercession [יַפְגִּיעַ] for the transgressors' - because he [Moses] begged for mercy on behalf of the sinners in Israel that they should turn in penitence. And the word *pegi'ah* [intercession] means nothing else than prayer, as it is said: 'As for you, do not pray for this people, do not raise a cry or prayer on their behalf, and do not make intercession [תִּפְגַּע] with Me' (Jer 7:16)." R. Simlai here connects the verb פגע , translated as "to make intercession," but actually more in the sense of to request, entreat, interpose,[620] in Isa 53:12 with that in Jer 7:16. He also employs the cognate noun פְּגִיעָה , "entreaty," "prayer,"[621] to mean that Moses prayed for the sinful Israelites. They should "return [to God] in repentance [תְּשׁוּבָה]." As in sections B. 4.4.a and c above, the reference here is to the incident of the Golden Calf, where Moses pleads in Exod 32:31-32[622] for the Lord to forgive Israel's sin.

In comparison with the three passages cited above from *Midrash Tannaim* and *Sifre* Deuteronomy, R. Simlai's exposition of Isa 53:12 in regard to Moses is more extensive. Yet it has the same basic intention as there: it reassures Moses just before his death (Deut 34:6) that although he may not enter the Land, God will ascribe it to him as if he had fulfilled the precepts / commandments which normally could only be

---

[619] Caleb and Joshua were the only two exceptions: v 24 and Deut 1:36-38.
[620] Cf. BDB 803, qal 4. and hiphil 3., and Jastrow 1135: to beseech, entreat; to intercede, pray.
[621] Jastrow 1133.
[622] Moses' "praying" before the Lord in vv 30-31 is emphasized in *Targum Pseudo-Jonathan* on these verses (Rieder 1.132; Maher 255).

performed there. It differs from the other three passages, however, in also emphasizing Moses' willingness to sacrifice his own life for the sake of Israel. A similar thought prevailed in the account of R. Aqiba's voluntary death as a martyr. He is portrayed as sanctifying the divine Name, and Isa 53:12 is also applied to him. In addition, the verse is applied to Phinehas, who, like Moses, did not actually die as a martyr, but voluntarily risked his own life "for the sanctification of the Name." R. Simlai thus stands at the end of a long chain of Judaic tradition when he connects Moses' imminent death (Deut 34:6) and Isa 53:12 with his willingness to die on behalf of Israel. When R. Simlai cites "bearing the sins of many," he refers it to Moses' making atonement for the Golden Calf in Exod 32:30. He had already quoted v 32, and his hearers knew the incident so well they certainly also had it in mind at this point. The motif of Moses' procuring atonement for Israel is thus both biblical and Judaic, and should by no means be considered anti-Christian here, as has been suggested by some interpreters.[623]

*   *   *

The above analysis of Moses as portrayed in Judaic sources as greatly suffering, willing to sacrifice his own life for Israel, with Isa 53:12 applied to him, shows that the earliest Palestinian Jewish Christians could also logically apply such imagery to Jesus, their Messiah. As Moses, the first redeemer of Israel, was considered to be *the* servant of the Lord in biblical and Judaic texts, such as *Pseudo-Philo* from Palestine and from the first century CE, so the Messiah, the great or final redeemer of Israel, was also described by them with servant of the Lord imagery, including Isa 53:12. For these Jewish Christians, who thus portrayed Jesus in terms

---

[623] Cf. Jacob Lauterbach, art. "Moses," "In Rabbinical Literature," in *JE* (1905/25) 9.51 (his reference to a different tradition in the *Yalquṭ*, ostensibly deriving from *Tanna debe Eliyyahu*, cannot be found in modern editions, yet is probably anti-Christian), and George Foot Moore, *Judaism in the First Centuries of the Christian Era, the Age of the Tannaim* (Cambridge, MA: Harvard University Press, 1959) III. 166, n. 254. R. Simlai's debating with *minim* about the plurality of the godhead, for example in *y. Ber.* 9:1 (Zahavy / Neusner 1.307-08), is not relevant to the present passage, which can be explained very well on the basis of previous traditions on Moses. For the larger issue, see Alan Segal, *Two Powers in Heaven. Early Rabbinic Reports about Christianity and Gnosticism* (SJLA 25; Leiden: Brill, 1977), with a list of the "dangerous" biblical passages on pp. 128-29. Isa 53:12 is nowhere mentioned, although R. Simlai also dealt with messianic passages, such as in *b. Sanh.* 97b (Soncino 659) and 98a (Soncino 662).

already familiar to them, the Messiah Jesus as *the* servant of the Lord was not only willing to sacrifice his life for his own people, thereby atoning for them. In contrast to Moses, through his crucifixion at Golgotha he actually did so.

I. 8   Jesus' Concern for the Welfare of His Mother After His Death in John 19:25-27, and Moses' Concern for the Welfare of His Mother After His Death

A.   *Jesus*

Peculiar to the Gospel of John is the pericope after the soldiers divide up Jesus' clothes among themselves at the Crucifixion. John 19:25-27 reads:

> Meanwhile, standing near the cross of Jesus were his mother and his mother's sister, Mary the wife of Clopas, and Mary Magdalene. 26) When Jesus saw his mother and the disciple whom he loved standing beside her, he said to his mother, "Woman, here is your son." 27) Then he said to the disciple, "Here is your mother." And from that hour the disciple took her into his own home.

Here Jesus, his mother's first child and the oldest of five sons (Matt 1:18 and Luke 2:7; Mark 6:3), even at his death shows his concern for the well-being of his mother, who most probably had already been a widow for some time.[624] This passage led to the later belief that Jesus' "beloved disciple" John took Mary along with him to Ephesus, where her tomb is displayed and visited also by Moslems even today.[625]

In the oldest account, Mark 15:40 has three women view Jesus' Crucifixion "from a distance"; they are not "near" the Cross, as in John 19:25. It also would have been proper in first-century Palestinian Jewish society for James, Jesus' oldest brother, to demonstrate filial piety by

---

[624] Cf. the fact that Joseph is already not mentioned in Mark 3:31-35. See also 6:3, John 2:12, and Acts 1:14. The most extensive analysis of John 19:25-27 is found in Raymond Brown, *The Death of the Messiah* 2.1019-30.

[625] Cf. Selahattin Erdemgil, *Ephesos* (Istanbul: Net Turistik Yayinlar, 1989) 118-20. Mary is also, however, thought to be interred with Joseph and her parents Joachim and Anna just north of the present Garden of Gethsemane at the base of the Mount of Olives. See Max Küchler, *Jerusalem* 683-97.

assuming responsibility for the care of their mother after Jesus' death.[626] Yet here Jesus strangely does not entrust the care of his mother to James or another of his brothers, nor to one of his originally twelve disciples,[627] but to another disciple, the "beloved" one. I suggest that this is due to the Fourth Evangelist's modeling this (non-historical) episode on Moses' entrusting his own mother Yochebed to the care of his disciple Joshua just before his own death. It too derives from an earlier form of the midrash on Moses' death, the "Petirat Mosheh."

B.   Moses

Before he was called by God in the burning bush, Moses "was keeping the flock of his father-in-law Jethro" (Exod 3:1). Philo notes in *Mos.* 1.60-62 that this activity helped him learn to govern / be a king, "the shepherd of his people." *Mek. R. Ish.* Beshallah 7 on Exod 14:31 speaks of the Israelites' having faith in, and speaking against, the "shepherd of Israel."[628] The third generation Tanna R. Nehemiah[629] compares Moses to a "faithful shepherd" in *Ruth Rab.*, proem 5,[630] a title also given to him elsewhere.[631] In Numbers 27 the Lord tells Moses to ascend a particular mountain (Nebo) of the Abarim range and to view the land of Israel, for then he will be gathered to his people / die (vv 12-13). Moses at this point petitions the Lord to appoint someone over the Israelites "so that the congregation of the Lord may not be like sheep without a shepherd" (v 17). This implies that he himself has been Israel's shepherd up until then. The Lord then tells him to commission Joshua as his successor,

---

[626] This may be implied in Acts 1:14. James' importance in the early Jewish Christian community in Jerusalem is noted in 12:17; 15:13; and 21:18, as well as in Gal 1:19. See also the pseudepigraphical letter of "James."

[627] Out of fear for their own lives, except for Judas they had all fled when Jesus was taken prisoner in Gethsemane. This is implied in John 18:8 and 17:12, and it is explicitly stated in 16:32 and in Mark 14:27 ("you will all become deserters") and 50 ("And all of them deserted him and fled"). See the extensive discussion of this in I.6 above on Gethsemane.

[628] Lauterbach 1.252.

[629] *Introduction* 85.

[630] Soncino 8.8.

[631] Cf. *Lam. Rab.*, proem 24 (Soncino 7.46), where Moses says to God: "Was I not a faithful shepherd to Israel for forty years, running before them like a horse in the desert?"; *Esth. Rab.* 7/13 on Esth 3:9 (Soncino 9.99); and *Pirq. R. El.* 42 (Friedlander 333, n. 6 on the reading of the first editions and MS Gaster). The image of Jesus as the "good shepherd" in John 10:1-18 may be influenced by this.

which he does (vv 18-23). Joshua, Moses' main "disciple,"[632] thus becomes the new leader or shepherd of Israel. *Sifre* Phinehas 138 on Num 27:15 (-17) describes Moses' positive behavior at this point as making known "the excellency of the righteous, for when they depart from the world, they put aside their own needs and occupy themselves with the needs of the community."[633]

Moses' primary concern at his imminent death was thus with the entire people. Yet Judaic tradition also describes him as worried at this point about the fate of his own family members. With his wife Zipporah Moses had two sons, Gershom (Exod 2:22 and 18:3) and Eliezer (Exod 18:4). They were numbered among the tribe of Levi and themselves later had sons (1 Chron 23:14-17; 26:24-25). *Sifre* Niṣṣabim 305 inserts regarding the subject of Moses' imminent death in Deut 31:14 comment on Num 27:18. R. Nathan, a fourth generation Tanna,[634] said: "Moses was saddened by the fact that one of his sons had not been appointed leader." God comforts him by informing him that Joshua, his successor, will have to go to Eleazar, one of his brother Aaron's sons, who should be like his own to him.[635] In *Num. Rab.* Phinehas 21/14 on Num 27:15-18, Moses also expresses the wish that his sons should "inherit his glory." Yet God answers him by saying: "Your sons sat idly by and did not study the Torah. Joshua served you much, and he showed you great honor."[636] This is the reason Moses' sons do not succeed him, but rather his disciple Joshua.

Moses' concern at his death, however, was especially for his aged mother, Yochebed. The oldest Jewish chronography, *Seder ʿOlam*, notes in chapter 9 that she "was of those who came to Egypt, and of those who left it," after which Num 26:59 is quoted.[637] In regard to Exod 2:1, *b. Soṭah* 12a states that Yochebed was conceived on the way (to Egypt), but was

---

[632] For Joshua as Moses' "disciple" and Moses as his "teacher," cf. the many sources cited in section I.5.B.a) Joshua, above.

[633] Horovitz 184; Kuhn 567. The cross-reference to Deut 34:9 should be noted. See also *Cant. Rab.* 1:7 § 2, together with Num 27:16, on Moses' concern with whom God will appoint as shepherd(s) over the Israelites (Soncino 9.63). In the Tannaitic *Sifre* Niṣṣabim 305 on Deut 31:14, dealing here with Num 27:18, Moses tells his successor Joshua: "This people that I am giving into your care are still as young kids, still mere infants" (Finkelstein 324; Hammer 295).

[634] *Introduction* 88.

[635] Finkelstein 324; Hammer 294.

[636] Mirkin 10.287-88; Soncino 6.840-41. On the sons' behavior, cf. also *Tanh.* Phinehas 11 (Eshkol 816).

[637] Guggenheimer 96, with the Hebrew on p. 95; see also his n. 11 on p. 98.

born between the walls (of Egypt).[638] When she bore Moses, she was 130 years old.[639] Since he was 120 years old when he died (Deut 34:7), Yochebed was 250 years old at this time, and Aaron and Miriam, Moses' older siblings, had already died. Who should now take care of her when she entered the Land of Israel at such an advanced age?

Tanḥ. B Va'ethanan 6 on Deut 3:23 has Moses address God in the following manner: "Sovereign of the worlds, my mother Yochebed, who suffered grief during her lifetime through her two sons, should she also suffer grief through my death?"[640] This is also found in *Tanḥ.* Va'ethanan 6.[641] Yochebed had personally observed all the sorrows and tribulations connected with persecution in Egypt, the Israelites' exodus from there, and their wandering in the wilderness for forty years, during which her two older children, Aaron and Miriam, had died. Moses, seeking to postpone his own death, here asks whether his aged mother should have to endure further severe grief through also experiencing his own death, that of her last living child.

In the midrash on Moses' death, "Petirat Mosheh," Moses first blessed the tribes of Israel in Deuteronomy 33 and then finally gave the Angel of Death permission to take his soul, i.e. he resigned himself to God's taking his soul. At this point according to the Parma MS, Moses said to Joshua before all the Israelites:

> I know that you have to carry a burden too heavy for three persons. This burden of taking care of the people of Israel was hitherto shared by Aaron, Miriam and me. Now you are the only one to bear it. May God be with you. I entrust you with her [Yochebed] whose world is shattered, being fated to bury those who in the natural order of things were supposed to bury her. From now on she has no other son but you. On the day of her death [later in the Land of Israel], wear black clothes and rend them, and walk before her bier until you place her in the grave. I also entrust you with this proselyte [his wife Zipporah], whose world is also shattered. See that no evil is done to her. I further entrust

---

[638] Soncino 60-61, with notes 1-3. Cf. the other texts I cite on this in my *Matthew 1-2 and the Virginal Conception* 52, n. 62.

[639] Cf. also *Exod. Rab.* Shemoth 1/19 on Exod 2:1 (Mirkin 5.33; Soncino 3.26).

[640] Buber 12; Bietenhard 2.454. The expression "dulling one's teeth" is meant as grieving. Cf. BDB 874 and Jastrow 1321 on קהה .

[641] Eshkol 858. Kushelevsky in *Moses* 255 also translates this version. See also Ginzberg, *Legends* 3.436, with n. 897 in 6.150. He cites another parallel found in the version of "Petirat Mosheh" in *'Oṣar ha-Midrash*, ed. Jehudah Eisenstein, 2.375 (left column, middle).

you to treat my orphans, to whom it was not granted to be my successors, as members of your household.[642]

The Hebrew of "From now on she [Yochebed] has no other son but you [Joshua]" is: ואין לה מעתה בן אלא אלא אותך.[643] Moses here makes Joshua into Yochebed's son. I suggest that the Fourth Evangelist was acquainted with this version of the "Petirat Mosheh" in an earlier form and borrowed this motif of Moses, the first redeemer of Israel, as entrusting at his imminent death his own mother Yochebed to his disciple Joshua, and not to a relative still living (e.g., Moses' two sons). John applied the motif to Jesus, the final redeemer of Israel, the Messiah, also about to die, yet on the Cross. He entrusts his own mother Mary to the "beloved disciple," and not to James or another brother, with words similar to those of Moses: "Woman, here [is] your son," and "Here [is] your mother" (John 19:26-27).[644] Here the "beloved disciple" becomes Mary's son, just as Joshua becomes Yochebed's son.[645]

---

[642] Since I have no access to the Parma MS, I basically reproduce Kushelevsky's translation in *Moses* 270. Moses then goes on to give further instructions regarding priests and judges. Kushelevsky notes that both in the Ethiopic version of the "Petirat Mosheh" ("Mota Musē"), and in the Faitlovitch Arabic Muslim version, Moses is also represented as being concerned with the welfare of his family members (*Moses* 138 and 152). This address of Moses to Joshua, however, has nothing to do with medieval *piyyut*, liturgical poems, which describe Yochebed's searching for her son after his death. On this, see Leon Weinberger, "A Lost Midrash" in *Tarbiz* 38 (1968) 285-93.

[643] I quote from the version of "Petirat Mosheh" printed by Eisenstein, *'Oṣar ha-Midrashim* 2.380, bottom of the left column. Ginzberg in *Legends* 6.153, n. 909, translates this as "Now thou art to be her son." He refers to this version as "2 Petirat Mosheh," which should not be confused with the second recension of the midrash printed by Jellinek in his *Bet ha-Midrasch* 6.71-78.

[644] The εἰς τὰ ἴδια in v 27 (NRSV correctly: "into his own home"; see LXX Esth 5:10 and 6:12 for אֶל־בֵּיתוֹ) may also have been influenced by Moses' request to Joshua in regard to his sons: he should treat them "as members of your household" (Kushelevsky, above). The Hebrew of Eisenstein has instead: "that they not be coupled from you." Finally, the Fourth Evangelist may also be indicating a contrast to 16:32, where Jesus tells his disciples: "you will be scattered [at Gethsemane], each one 'to his home,' and you will leave me alone." Yet the beloved disciple remains faithful to Jesus even to the end.

[645] According to Raymond Brown, *The Gospel According to John, XIII - XXI*, 924, dependent on an article by T. Koehler, only Ephraim the Syrian noted a parallel between Moses' commissioning Joshua to care for the Israelites at his death, and the beloved disciple's being appointed to care for Mary, who for him represents

Raymond Brown may be correct in proposing that the Fourth Evangelist's main interest was not in the literal meaning of 19:25-27, i.e. that the text does not primarily express Jesus' concern for the further well-being of his mother Mary after his death on the Cross. He suggests rather: "The fact that the mother of Jesus is now the disciple's mother and that he has taken her to his own is a symbolic way of describing how one related to Jesus by the flesh (his mother who is part of his natural family) becomes related to him by the Spirit (a member of the ideal discipleship)."[646] This is a far cry from reading into the text the idea of Mary's perpetual virginity, or her as Lady Zion or the new Eve, as is done by some interpreters.[647]

C. Historicity

Brown seriously considers the possibility that in John 19:25-27 "the Johannine community draws on a tradition that has come down from the Beloved Disciple...."[648] Elsewhere he thinks the Fourth Evangelist may have transferred a scene such as that found in Mark 3:31-35 from Jesus' public ministry and adapted it to the Cross, while conceding that the Johannine verses are "the most difficult element to verify historically among the activities at the cross...."[649]

C. K. Barrett cites plausible reasons why he believes "the historical foundation of the incident is slight; and we note that in Acts 1.14 the mother of Jesus appears in company with his brothers."[650] Yet there is no historical foundation to the narrative whatsoever, and there is good reason none of the three Synoptic Evangelists included it. John may have received this short episode from his own Jewish Christian community, yet I consider it more probable he borrowed it from a well-known earlier version of the "Petirat Mosheh" and edited it himself.[651] There the first

---

the Christian church. Yet no mention of Yochebed is made, so Ephraim probably only had the biblical text in mind.

[646] Cf. his *The Death of the Messiah* 2.1024.

[647] Cf. Brown, *The Gospel According to John, XIII-XXI*, 922-27.

[648] *Op. cit.*, 922.

[649] Cf. his *The Death of the Messiah* 2.1029, n. 106, and 1028, respectively. In *The Gospel According to John, XIII-XXI*, 922, Brown states that "the historical question is probably insoluble...."

[650] Cf. his *The Gospel According to St John* 459.

[651] Cf. for example the designation "Woman" for Mary also in 2:4. I consider it extremely improbable that a Jewish author of one version of the "Petirat Mosheh" knew the Fourth Gospel in Greek well enough to have modeled his portrayal of

redeemer of Israel, Moses, is described just before his death as entrusting all of his family members to his disciple, Joshua. This is especially true for his aged mother Yochebed, whom he cannot place into the care of his dead brother Aaron. Thus he tells Joshua: "From now on she has no other son but you." Here Joshua becomes Yochebed's son, and thus a brother to Moses. In the Fourth Evangelist's masterful adaptation of this incident to the Cross scene, Jesus, the final redeemer of Israel, the Messiah, just before his death causes the beloved disciple to become his mother Mary's son, and thus his brother. It is thus he who will now "take her into his own home" (19:27). John meant this not only literally to show the dying Jesus' concern for the welfare of his mother, but also primarily symbolically (cf. Brown at the end of section B.), which was typical of the Fourth Evangelist.

Like the changing of water into wine at Cana in 2:1-11,[652] Jesus' walking on the water in 6:16-21,[653] Abraham's seeing the Messiah in 8:56-58,[654] and the incident of 11:45-54,[655] the short narrative of 19:25-27 is not historical. Its historicity is not only very improbable because it is not found in the three Synoptics, where women rather view Jesus' Crucifixion "from a distance" (Mark 15:40 par.). It is also typical of early Palestinian Jews and Jewish Christians who were accustomed to the retelling and rewriting of the biblical narratives (here the scene of Moses'

Moses, Yochebed and Joshua on Jesus, Mary and the beloved disciple. The figure Yochebed makes very good sense within the context of Moses' concern for the welfare of *all* his family members, including his wife and children, and within the broader context of his concern with the fate of all the Israelites after his death. If in turn a Jew who had converted to Christianity composed the scene, would it appear as it does now? There are no indications of Christian or anti-Christian (e.g., Moses is somehow better than Jesus) influences at any point in the "Petirat Mosheh," including here, nor in the short segment of it preserved in the *Tanḥuma* midrashim analyzed above in section B. Geza Vermes' statement is particularly applicable here: "it is most unlikely, indeed unthinkable, that the Jewish sages would borrow directly from the Gospels." See his *The Religion of Jesus the Jew* 8.

[652] Cf. "The Wedding Feast at Cana (John 2:1-11), and Ahasuerus' Wedding Feast in Judaic Traditions on Esther 1" in my *Water into Wine and the Beheading of John the Baptist* 1-37.

[653] Cf. "Walking on the Sea" in my *"Caught in the Act," Walking on the Sea, and the Release of Barabbas Revisited* 53-133.

[654] Cf. "Abraham's Prophetic Vision of the Messiah: The Judaic Background of John 8:56-58" in my *My Name Is "Legion"* 253-87.

[655] Cf. "The Death of One for All in John 11:45-54 in Light of Judaic Traditions" in my *Barabbas and Esther, and Other Studies in the Judaic Illumination of Earliest Christianity* 29-63.

commissioning his disciple Joshua to be his successor at the very end of his life, now including Moses' concern for the welfare of his aged mother) in an haggadic manner in order to express new religious meanings. The Jewish Christian John was well-acquainted with this method, as shown in my studies on the other four Johannine pericopes enumerated above. Here too the question of historicity was simply not posed by those in his Jewish Christian community who now may have first heard the incident narrated in their worship services, or later read it in the Greek Gospel form. They as Jews did not shout: "That's all nonsense!" The opposite was certainly the case. They deeply appreciated John's haggadic narrative artistry in recasting material known to him and to them from Judaic tradition on the death of Israel's first redeemer, Moses.[656]

I. 9 Death in the Afternoon, in Public, and on a Friday

A.   Mark 15:25 says Jesus was crucified at nine o'clock in the morning.[657] It was Friday, the day before the Sabbath (v 42; cf. 14:16-18, 26). At noon (lit., "the sixth hour") "darkness came over the whole land until three in the afternoon" (lit., "the ninth hour" - v 33),[658] when Jesus cried with a loud voice: "My God, my God, why have You forsaken me?" (v 34). Shortly thereafter he "gave a loud cry and breathed his last" (v 37). In biblical and rabbinic Hebrew, Jesus was crucified at "noon," צָהֳרַיִם.[659] According to Mark, the oldest Gospel, Jesus had been led out (of Jerusalem - v 20) and crucified at a public site where people passed by (v 29), and some of his female followers looked on from a distance (v 40).

---

[656] For a much more extensive discussion of haggadah and its relation to the question of historicity, cf. chapter IV. below.

[657] Lit., "Now it was the third hour." On the division of the day into twelve hours, beginning at sunrise, cf. Str-B 2.442 and 543 (on John 11:9 - "Are there not twelve hours of daylight?") as well as Josephus, *Vita* 279.

[658] For Judaic sources on God's mourning by causing a solar eclipse when His son dies, cf. the section "The Sun's Eclipse" in "The Prodigia at Jesus' Crucifixion..." in my *Samuel, Saul and Jesus* 134-47, esp. pp. 143-44. A basic text on God's mourning for an "only son" in Amos 8:10 was the preceding verse, 9: "I will make the sun go down 'at noon' [בצהרים], and darken the earth in broad daylight" (p. 137). On the unit of three hours, see Peter Kuhn, *Gottes Trauer und Klage in der rabbinischen Überlieferung (Talmud und Midrasch)* (AGJU 13; Leiden: Brill, 1978) 339, n. 7.

[659] BDB 843: midday, noon; Jastrow 1265: noon-time.

It was the first day of Passover, the fifteenth of Nisan,[660] which extended from Thursday evening until Friday evening.[661] It was precisely on this day that first-century Palestinian Jews expected the Messiah to come.[662]

The Fourth Evangelist maintains that "the place where Jesus was crucified was near the city" (19:20). In contrast to the Synoptics, John says this was the Day of Preparation, the fourteenth and not the fifteenth of Nisan.[663] In 19:14 he notes that it was three hours later than in the Synoptics, "about noon" (lit., "about the sixth hour"), when Pilate handed Jesus over to be crucified (v 16). For the Fourth Evangelist, Jesus is "the Lamb of God, who takes away the sin of the world" (1:29), the Passover lamb[664] whose bones should not be broken (19:36, alluding to Exod 12:46). For John, Jesus was therefore killed at the same time the Passover lambs were killed / slaughtered in the Jerusalem Temple, i.e. during the afternoon of the fourteenth of Nisan.

The above afternoon death of the Messiah Jesus, the final redeemer of Israel, in public, on a Friday (the preferable Synoptic dating), may in part have been described in terms of the afternoon death of Moses, Israel's first redeemer, also in public, on a Friday.

B.   Deut 34:6 states in regard to God's burying Moses: "And He buried him in a valley in the land of Moab, opposite Beth-Peor, but no one knows his burial place to this day." There are no witnesses to Moses' death here. Perhaps to counter one Judaic view that Moses did not die,

---

[660] Cf. Exod 12:14 for the Passover lamb as being slaughtered on the fourteenth of the first month (v 2), "at twilight" - to be eaten after that on the evening of the fifteenth.

[661] Cf. Mark 14:12b,16; 15:6; and Joachim Jeremias, *Die Abendmahlsworte Jesu*, for Jesus' last meal with the disciples as clearly a Passover meal.

[662] Cf. for example the Tannaitic *Mek. R. Ish.* Pisha 14 on Exod 12:42 in Lauterbach 1.115-16: "In that night they were redeemed, and in that night they will be redeemed in the future." *Exod. Rab.* Bo 18/12 on the same verse states that "on that night Messiah and Elijah will appear" (Mirkin 5.219; Soncino 3.227, adapting Radal's emendation of changing a ד into an א - n. 7). See also: "on that very night know that I will redeem you" (Soncino 3.228). For the Jerusalem authorities as wanting to arrest Jesus "by stealth," see Mark 14:1-2 and the darkness of the arrest scene in Gethsemane (vv 43-50). This was because of fear of a riot on the first day of Passover, when messianic expectations were very high.

[663] Cf. 19:14, 31 and 42.

[664] Cf. Paul's similar imagery in 1 Cor 5:7, "our paschal lamb, Christ, has been sacrificed."

but instead was translated bodily to heaven,[665] some Judaic traditions stress how public his death scene was.

The first-century CE Palestinian work, the *Testament of Moses*, has Moses state in 1:15, "The years of my life have come to an end, and 'in the presence of the entire community' I am going to sleep with my fathers."[666] *Pseudo-Philo*, also Palestinian and from the first century CE, states in 19:16 regarding God: "'And He buried him' [Deut 34:6] with His own hands on a high place and 'in the light of the whole world.'"[667] Both these early works stress the public character of Moses' death and burial. Many people witnessed them, just as many people witnessed Jesus' Crucifixion according to the Gospels.[668]

Deut 32:48-50 states: "'On that very day' the Lord addressed Moses as follows: 49) 'Ascend this mountain of the Abarim, Mount Nebo...50) you shall die there on the mountain that you ascend and shall be gathered to your kin....'" "On that very day" or "that selfsame day" in v 48 is the Hebrew בְּעֶצֶם הַיּוֹם הַזֶּה.[669] The early rabbis linked together various biblical passages via the phrase "that selfsame day,"[670] one of them dealing with Moses' death in public, at noon. To illustrate this, the Tannaitic midrash *Sifre* Ha'azinu 337 on Deut 32:48 deserves to be quoted here *in toto*:

> The phrase "that selfsame day" is used in three places. "That selfsame day" (Gen 7:13) refers to Noah, showing that the generation of Noah said: "By our oath, if we see him [going into the ark], we will not let him go. Rather, we will take picks and axes and wreck his ark over him!" Said the Holy One, blessed be He: "Behold, I will bring him into [the ark] 'at midday' [בחצי היום], and if anyone wants to stop him, let him come and try."
>
> Concerning [the exodus from] Egypt, what was Scripture's purpose in saying: "That selfsame day it came to pass that all the hosts of the Lord went out from the land of Egypt" (Exod 12:41)? The reason was that the Egyptians said: "By our oath, if we see them [preparing to leave], we will not let them go. Furthermore, we will take hold of our

---

[665] See chapter III. below.

[666] Tromp, *The Assumption of Moses* 6-7; *OTP* 1.927.

[667] *SC* 229.164; *OTP* 2.328.

[668] Nevertheless, as in the *biblical* account of Moses' burial by God alone, only Joseph of Arimathea concerns himself with Jesus' burial in the Synoptics (John adds Nikodemus in 19:39-42).

[669] Cf. BDB 783 on עֶצֶם , 3., esp. "this selfsame day."

[670] This is called in Hebrew *gezerah shawah* and is the second of Hillel's seven rules of exegesis (*Introduction* 21).

swords and cutlasses and slay them!" Said the Holy One, blessed be He:
"Behold, I will bring them out [of Egypt] 'at midday' [בחצי היום], and
if anyone wishes to stop them, let him come and try."

And what was Scripture's purpose in saying "that selfsame day" here
[in Deut 32:48]? The reason was that Israel said: "By our oath, if we see
Moses [leaving us], we will not let the man who had brought us out of
Egypt, had split the [Red] Sea for us, had brought down manna for us,
had supplied us with the quail, had performed miracles and wonders
for us - we will not let him go!" Said the Holy One, blessed be He:
"Behold, I will bring him into the cave 'at midday' [בחצי היום], and if
anyone wishes to stop [Me], let him come and try." Thus Scripture says:
"And the Lord spoke to Moses 'that selfsame day.'"[671]

Here it is clearly assumed that the generation of Noah could publicly
witness his entering the ark, just as the Egyptians could publicly witness
the Israelites' exodus from Egypt, (which both actually did). Most
important for our purposes, however, is that in direct contrast to
Deuteronomy 34, in this Tannaitic account the Israelites are assumed to
be present at Moses' death. It is a public affair. They witness it, as in the
above passages from the *Testament of Moses* and *Pseudo-Philo*.

Secondly, all three events (Noah's entering the ark, the Israelites'
departing from Egypt, and Moses' dying) here take place "at midday."
The Hebrew phrase בחצי היום literally means "at half the day,"[672]
i.e. at noon. Thus Moses' death is here described as occurring at noon.[673]
Yet it can be made more precise because of its comparison with the
exodus event.

The Tannaitic Tosefta has the House of Hillel state in *Pesaḥ.* 10:9 that
the Israelites "did not go forth from Egypt until the sixth hour," i.e. until
noon.[674] The Tannaitic *Mek. R. Ish.* Pisḥa 5 on Exod 12:6, "at twilight"[675]

---

[671] Finkelstein 386-87; I slightly modify Hammer, 346. On ʿeṣem, "selfsame," see
Hammer 504, n. 2: it is "understood as meaning at the very height of the day." On
the episode with Noah's ark, see also *Gen. Rab.* Noah 32/8 on Gen 7:13 (Theodor
and Albeck 294; Soncino 1.253). The same motif is applied to Abraham's
circumcision in Lech Lecha 47/9 on Gen 17:26 (Theodor and Albeck 476; Soncino
1.404).
[672] Cf. BDB 345 on חֲצִי : half. See also Exod 12:29, just before the first Passover,
which has the Lord strike down all the firstborn in Egypt "at midnight," lit. "at
half the night." The construction is similar for "noon" and "midnight."
[673] This would appear to agree more with John 19:14, "about noon," for the
beginning of Jesus' crucifixion. However, no indication is made here of its length.
[674] Zuckermandel / Liebermann 173; Neusner 2.165. At issue is when the Prayer
of Redemption should be said.

(the Passover sacrifice should be slaughtered on the fourteenth of Nisan by the whole assembled congregation of Israel), has Rabbi or Judah the Prince, a fifth generation Tanna,[676] state: "Behold, it says: 'there you shall offer the Passover sacrifice, in the evening at sunset' (Deut 16:6). I might take this literally, i.e. in the evening [after dark]. But Scripture goes on to say: 'the time of day when you departed from Egypt' (*ibid.*). When did Israel go forth out of Egypt? From the sixth hour and beyond. And so it says: 'And it came to pass the selfsame day that the Lord brought the Israelites out of the land of Egypt' (Exod 12:51)."[677] At this point R. Nathan, a third generation Tanna,[678] also interprets "at twilight" in Exod 12:6 as meaning "from the sixth hour and beyond."

"From the sixth hour and beyond" is the Hebrew מששׁ שעות ולמעלה.[679] Thousands of Passover lambs could not be slaughtered simultaneously in the Herodian Temple of Jerusalem at the time of Jesus precisely "at twilight."[680] Therefore the rabbinical authorities pushed the beginning time for this action upwards to the sixth hour, i.e. noon, on the fourteenth of Nisan. According to *m. Pesaḥ.* 5:3 the Passover offering was valid if slaughtered after "noon" (חֲצוֹת).[681] In *Spec. Leg.* 2.145, Philo also notes that myriads of victims are offered by the whole people at Passover "from noon [ἀπὸ μεσημβρίας] till eventide."

If Tannaitic tradition maintained that Israel went forth from Egypt on the fifteenth of Nisan "from the sixth hour and beyond," i.e. after twelve noon, it seems probable that the same analogy was made to apply to Moses on the day of his death, labeled "that selfsame day," as in *Sifre* on Deut 32:48 above. There God brings Moses into a cave "at midday" -

---

675 Lit., "between the evenings."
676 *Introduction* 89; he was the editor of the Mishnah.
677 Lauterbach 1.42-43. He explains in n. 15 that "Rabbi takes the expression מוֹעֵד צֵאתְךָ in Deut 16.6 to designate the day when they came out, and not the season." R. Simeon b. Yoḥai, a third generation Tanna (*Introduction* 84), then interprets similarly (see n. 17). The *Mekilta of R. Simeon b. Yoḥai* on Exod 12:51 (Epstein / Melamed 37) also interprets: "'That very day' only means at the height [power - תוֹקֶף] of the day."
678 *Introduction* 85. Unfortunately there is no separate entry for him.
679 On the latter noun, cf. Jastrow 817 on מעלה with ל , c) (of time) "further on."
680 For a description of this, cf. *m. Pesaḥ.* 5:5-7 (Albeck 2.158-59; Neusner 238; Danby 142).
681 Albeck 2.157; Neusner 237; Danby 142. "At twilight" in Exod 12:6 is then cited. See also Jeremias, *Die Abendmahlsworte Jesu* 17, with n. 1.

noon. His death is assumed to take place sometime after this, i.e. after noon. The same was true for Jesus.

Finally, it should also be noted that the earliest rabbinic chronography, *Seder 'Olam*, maintains in chapter five that the Israelites entered Egypt and left it centuries later "at the same time," that is, on the fifteenth of Nisan (Exod 12:41).[682] On the fourteenth of Nisan, a Thursday, they slaughtered their Passover sacrifices there. Then they departed on the next day, the fifteenth of Nisan, which was a Friday.[683] Since Moses is represented as dying on "that selfsame day" (of the week)[684] as that on which the Israelites left Egypt, this was also a Friday. The same result was reached by later commentators in regard to traditions recorded in *Seder 'Olam* 10.[685]

Both Jesus and Moses in Judaic tradition are thus described as dying in public, on a Friday, and after noon. This also confirmed for early Jewish Christians the common analogy: As the first redeemer of Israel (Moses), so the final or great redeemer of Israel (the Messiah).

---

[682] On this, cf. also *Exod. Rab.* Bo 18/11 on Exod. 12:41 (Mirkin 5.219, with parallels listed in n. 2; Soncino 3.227).

[683] Cf. Guggenheimer 58 and his notes on p. 59. His text wrongly has הפסח on p. 59, which makes no sense. Chaim Milikowsky in his 1981 Yale dissertation, "Seder Olam: A Rabbinic Chronography," 243 and 462, rightly omits it in his critical edition.

[684] The month, however, was not Nisan but Adar.

[685] Cf. Ratner's edition of *Seder Olam Rabba*, 42, n. 11, and Ginzberg, *Legends* 6.162, n. 952. Ginzberg calls attention to a similar tradition contained in the Arabic "Mota Musa," ed. Faitlovitch. It also alludes to Moses' concern with the question of who will care for his mother Yochebed at his death. On this, see section I. 8, with n. 642 above.

II. The Burial of Jesus, the Burial of Moses, and the Well

A. The Burial of Jesus

Mark 15:42-47 describes the burial of Jesus in the following way:

42) When evening had come, and since it was the day of Preparation, that is, the day before the sabbath, 43) Joseph of Arimathea, a respected member of the council, who was also himself waiting expectantly for the kingdom of God, went boldly to Pilate and asked for the body of Jesus. 44) Then Pilate wondered if he were already dead; and summoning the centurion, he asked him if he had been dead for some time. 45) When he learned from the centurion that he was dead, he granted the body to Joseph. 46) Then Joseph [he] bought a linen cloth, and taking down the body [it], wrapped it in the linen cloth, and laid it in a tomb that had been hewn out of the rock. He then rolled a stone against the door of the tomb. 47) Mary Magdalene and Mary the mother of Joses saw where the body [it] was laid.

This account is reproduced with variations in Matt 27:57-61 and Luke 23:50-56; John 19:38-42 has its own version of the narrative.

Mark 15:43 introduces a new character in the Passion Narrative, "Joseph of Arimathea," called in Greek Ἰωσὴφ [ὁ] ἀπὸ Ἀριμαθαίας . The Fourth Gospel employs the same expression in 19:38. Matt 27:57 speaks instead of "a rich man from Arimathea, whose name was Joseph." Luke 23:51 explains that Joseph was "from Arimathea, a town of the Jews." That is, in all four Gospels the place name is Ἀριμαθαία. Its identification is uncertain,[1] yet the initial A betrays the Aramaic prothetic א , often

---

[1] Cf. the art. "Arimathea" by K. W. Clark in *IDB* (1962) 1.219. The "consensus" of which he speaks certainly does not prevail today. He notes among the many variants "Ramatha," important in my discussion below. For bibliography on the entire section, see Craig A. Evans, *Mark 8:27 - 16:20*, 512-14, and Raymond Brown, *The Death of the Messiah* 2.1201-04.

added to Hebrew place names.[2] The Hebrew place name רָמָתַיִם , which can take an initial הָ , is the dual of רָמָה , thus "heights."[3] The home of Samuel in the hill country of Ephraim, for example, is called Αρμαθαιμ in the LXX.[4]

Mark 15:43 states that Joseph of Arimathea was "a respected member of the council" (εὐσχήμων [5] βουλευτής [6]), the latter referring back to the Jewish council or Sanhedrin (συνέδριον) in v 1. In v 43 the Evangelist Mark notes that Joseph "was also himself waiting expectantly for the kingdom of God." Luke in 23:50-51 labels him "a good and righteous man, who...had not agreed to their [the council's] plan and action." While Matthew and John do not refer here to Joseph's membership in the council, both Matthew in 27:57 and John in 19:38 make Joseph into a disciple of Jesus. The Fourth Evangelist also notes that he was "a secret one because of his fear of the Jews." He is assisted in burying Jesus here by Nicodemus (v 39), described in 3:1 as "a leader of the Jews"[7] and thus presumably a member of the council.

Only Matthew calls Joseph "a rich man" in 27:57. This bilingual Jewish Christian Evangelist alludes at this point to Isaiah 53, which plays such an important background role in the Crucifixion scene. The Hebrew of 53:9 states regarding the Lord's treatment of the Suffering Servant: "He made his grave with the wicked, and at his death 'with a rich person' (אֶת־עָשִׁיר)."[8] Matthew or the tradition behind him is also the only evangelist to note that Joseph laid Jesus' body "in his *own* new tomb" (27:60). Presumably only a wealthy person could afford such a tomb directly next to the city of Jerusalem, the nation's capital, and not further away. Luke notes in 23:53 that it was a tomb "where no one had ever been laid," and John 19:41 also describes it as "a new tomb in which no one had ever been laid." All of these are haggadic additions to the simple statement in the oldest Gospel. Mark 15:46 only notes that Joseph laid

---

[2] For the addition of א to Hebrew place names, cf. the "Namenwörterbuch zu Flavius Josephus" by Abraham Schalit under A in the Josephus concordance. Examples are Ἀβουμᾶ for רוּמָה , Ἄδαμα for דָּמִין , Ἀμμαοῦς for מוֹצָא , Ἀραβλαθά for רִבְלָתָה , Ἀσωφών for צָפוֹן , and Ἀσωχις for שִׁיחִין .
[3] BDB 928 on רָמָה II.
[4] *Ibid.*, 2.
[5] Cf. BAGD 327: 2. prominent, of high standing or repute, noble.
[6] Cf. BAGD 145: member of a council.
[7] Cf. 7:49 for him as "one of them," and possibly 12:42.
[8] The LXX and the Isaiah Targum (Stenning 180-81) both have "the rich" as plural, showing Matthew's use of the Hebrew text here.

Jesus' body "in a tomb that had been hewn out of the rock." It could thus have been used many times before, as was customary for a preliminary burial before the bones were later gathered and placed elsewhere in an ossuarium.[9]

After Joseph of Arimathea took Jesus' body down from the Cross, he wrapped it in a linen cloth he had just bought and laid it "in a tomb that had been hewn out of the rock" (Mark 15:47). This is the Greek ἐν μνημείῳ ὃ ἦν λελατομημένον ἐκ πέτρας. Matt 27:60 has the variant ἐν τῷ ... μνημείῳ ὃ ἐλατόμησεν ἐν τῇ πέτρᾳ ("in the tomb, which he had hewn in the rock"). That is, here it is Joseph himself (or workers commissioned by him) who hewed out the tomb, which is not the case in Mark. Luke has a different paraphrase in 23:53 : Joseph laid Jesus' body ἐν μνήματι λαξευτῷ , "in a rock-hewn tomb." The Fourth Evangelist does not note how the tomb was fashioned.

The Greek verb employed in Mark 15:47 and Matt 27:60 is λατομέω , "to hew out [of a rock or quarry]."[10] In the NT it is only found in these two verses. The adjective λαξευτός in Luke 23:53 means "hewn out of the rock"[11] and also only occurs here in the NT.

I have suggested elsewhere that Matt 27:51b-53 is a remnant of the very early belief that at Jesus' death the general resurrection of the dead had already begun. Luke 23:43 also implies that, since the repentant criminal will be with Jesus "today," Jesus' soul ascended to heaven at the time of his death and not three days later, on Easter Sunday.[12] Other

---

[9] Cf. the sources cited in Str-B 1.1049-51, as well as the articles "Burial" and "Ossuaries" by W. L. Reed in *IDB* 1.474-76 and 3.610-11, respectively.

[10] LSJ 1031. A λατομεῖον is a stone quarry (*ibid.*). Cf. BAGD 467, "hew out of the rock."

[11] LSJ 1029, and BAGD 466, "hewn in the rock."

[12] Cf. "An Earthquake and Saints Rising from the Dead," and "Jesus' Promise to the Repentant Criminal of Participation in Paradise Today (Luke 23:39-43)" in my *Samuel, Saul and Jesus* 116-33 and 158-73, respectively. In regard to the latter, see also the episode of Yose b. Yoezer, a martyr at the time of the Maccabean persecution (see 1 Macc 7:9 and 16). From his cross he sees the bier of the repentant high priest Yakim flying in the air: "See, this man by a brief hour precedes me into the Garden of Eden" (*Midr. Pss.* 11/7 on Ps 11:7, "The upright shall behold His face" [Buber 103-04; Braude 1.166-67]). A parallel is found in *Gen. Rab.* Toledoth 65/22 on Gen 27:27 (Theodor and Albeck 744; Soncino 2.600). This tradition of a martyr's soul being taken up immediately to heaven is also found at the time of the Hadrianic persecution, 132-35 CE, as shown in *b. 'Abodah Zarah* 18a (Soncino 90-93) and *Sifre* Ha'azinu 307 on Deut 32:4 (Finkelstein 346; Hammer 312) regarding R. Ḥaninah b. Teradion. In his art. "Das leere Grab" in *ZNW* 23 (1924) 281-92, Elias Bickermann also states that an early stage of belief in

factors such as a Palestinian Jewish Christian reading of Isa 52:13 and 53:8 on the Suffering Servant as being "exalted and lifted up" and "taken away," and the ascension of the souls of Jewish martyrs to heaven immediately after their death, also contributed to this belief.[13] The tradition of Jesus' rising from the dead only after "three days," although very early as shown in 1 Cor 15:4, is nevertheless a later development based primarily on Hos 6:2 and the other texts I analyze below in chapter III. C.

The narrative of Joseph of Arimathea's burying Jesus' body "in a tomb that had been hewn out of the rock" and then "rolling a stone against the door of the tomb" (Mark 15:46) was composed to prepare for Jesus' Resurrection three days later on Easter Sunday in 16:1-8. It is extremely improbable that a respected member of the council / Sanhedrin, which had just demanded that Pilate have Jesus killed, would concern himself with the body of a man condemned and executed as a criminal, a messianic pretender, "The King of the Jews" (15:26). Yet the Roman Pilate may indeed have asked the Sanhedrin, which wanted to be rid of the very uncomfortable prophet Jesus, to take care of his burial. Pilate may have reasoned: "The Jews also wanted his death, let them then relieve the Roman soldiers of an unpleasant task, that of disposing of the corpse." In addition, he may have found it politically convenient not to offend Jewish sensibilities in regard to leaving a corpse overnight "on a tree" (Deut 21:22-23), especially at the major pilgrimage festival of Passover.

A Jewish servant / slave of the Sanhedrin (thus neither a Roman soldier nor a member of the council) would then have placed Jesus' body in one of the "two 'burying places' (בָּתֵּי קְבָרוֹת) ... kept in readiness by the court, one for them that were beheaded or strangled, and one for them that were stoned or burned" (*m. Sanh.* 6:5).[14] The *Tosefta* states here

---

Christ maintained "the direct exaltation, the translation / rapture [Entrückung] of Jesus" (p. 290). Yet he strangely holds that Paul's description of the resurrection in 1 Corinthians 15 derives from Hellenistic circles acquainted with the dying and rising figures of the mysteries (p. 292). On the motif of translation / Entrückung, see chapter III.

[13] Cf. a discussion of these in "The Ascension of Jesus' Soul from the Cross" (*Samuel, Saul and Jesus* 173-87).

[14] Cf. Albeck 4.189; Danby 391; Neusner 595. See also *Ruth Rab.* 2/24 on Ruth 1:17 (Soncino 8.40), as well as *Num. Rab.* Masse 23/13 on Num 35:11 (Mirkin 10.316; Soncino 6.878). I thus disagree with Alfred Loisy, who maintained that it was the Roman soldiers who "removed the body from the Cross before evening and put it in some common grave, where the remains of executed criminals were thrown helter-skelter." After some days it would have been impossible to recognize

(9:8-9) that criminals may not be buried in their ancestral burying grounds but have to be placed in those of the court. This is justified by quoting a psalm of David: "Do not gather my soul with the sinners" (26:9).[15] In *b. Sanh.* 47a it is stated in this respect that "a wicked man may not be buried beside a righteous one."[16] The earliest Palestinian Jewish Christians could have seen in Jesus' body being placed in such a burial site the fulfillment of Isa 53:9, "And they [here the Sanhedrin] made his grave with the wicked."

Jesus' remains. See his *Les Évangiles Synoptiques* (Ceffonds: published by the author, 1907) 1.223, where he also refers to his commentary on Matt 27:8. John Dominic Crossan also believes that if Jesus' body was not left on the Cross for the wild beasts to devour, but taken down by the Roman soldiers, they would have buried him in "a hurried, indifferent, and shallow grave barely covered with stones from which the scavenging dogs would easily and swiftly unbury the body...." This is part of his chapter "The Dogs Beneath the Cross" in *Jesus. A Revolutionary Biography* (San Francisco: Harper, 1994) 156 (see also 154). It should also be noted that Paul in Pisidian Antioch is represented as saying in Acts 13:29 that "they [the residents of Jerusalem and their leaders - v 27] took him down from a tree and laid him in a tomb." Here the Sanhedrin or Council causes Jesus' burial to be carried out. In their art. "Did Joseph of Arimathea Exist?" in *Bib* 75 (1994) 235-41, Gerald O'Collins and Daniel Kendall reject Crossan's view that the Gospel of Peter predated and greatly influenced the Gospel of Mark, and that the Evangelist himself created the figure of Joseph of Arimathea. Instead, the language used of the latter figure in Mark 15:43 "may indicate a rich property owner and member of some local council" (p. 240, n. 14). Yet see section B. 4.3 below on this. See also William Lyons, "On the Life and Death of Joseph of Arimathea" in *JSHJ* 2 (2004) 29-53, who believes one should see "the Markan Joseph as reflecting an earlier tradition about a Jewish council member who condemned Jesus, buried him for reasons of either personal piety or communal duty, and died without ever becoming a follower of Jesus" (p. 53). Yet what was this "earlier tradition"? My own proposal is found in section B. 4.2-4 below.

[15] Zuckermandel / Liebermann 429; Neusner 4.228. In *y. Sanh.* 6:9 (11), 23d (Neusner 31.193), Ps 26:9's "sinners" and "bloodthirsty men" are applied to the first and last two kinds of criminals mentioned in *m. Sanh.* 6:5. Byron Mc Cane in his art. "Where No One Had Yet Been Laid: The Shame of Jesus' Burial" in *Authenticating the Activities of Jesus*, ed. Bruce Chilton and Craig A. Evans (NTTS 28.2; Leiden: Brill, 1999) 431-52, also believes Jesus' body was placed "within a burial cave reserved for criminals," but by "one or more of the Jewish leaders in Jerusalem - later personified by Christian tradition as Joseph of Arimathea..." (p. 452). His reference to *m. Sanh.* 6:6 (p. 440) should be 6:5. The essay is now included in his *Roll Back the Stone*. Death and Burial in the World of Jesus (Harrisburg, PA: Trinity Press International, 2003) 89-108.

[16] Soncino 311.

Although archaeological remains have been found of burials in the Kidron Valley from the time of the First Temple, including the "public cemetery" (בְּנֵי עָם [ין]קבר) in 2 Kgs 23:6,[17] the public burial site for criminals at the time of the Herodian Temple is unknown.[18] *All* of Jesus' followers forsook him and fled when he was arrested in Gethsemane (Mark 14:50 par. and v 27). They first returned home to Galilee, where Jesus appeared to them (16:7; 14:28; John 21). No one knew any longer where Jesus was buried near Jerusalem because, out of fear for their lives, all his adherents had fled far north to escape the same fate as their master.[19]

The short narrative of Joseph of Arimathea in Mark 15:42-47 was therefore composed by a Palestinian Jewish Christian to serve as a concrete prelude to the Resurrection account with an empty tomb in 16:1-8. To do so, I suggest that the author borrowed the terminology of "Arimathea," a "prominent man" from the "council," "kingdom," and "a tomb that had been hewn out of the rock," from Judaic tradition on the site of the death of Israel's first redeemer, Moses. To this I now turn.

B. The Burial of Moses, and the Well

Deut 34:6 states regarding Moses: "no one knows his burial place to this day." That is, just as the burial site of the first redeemer of Israel, Moses, remained unknown, so the burial site of Israel's great or final redeemer, the Messiah Jesus, remained unknown (see section A. above).

According to Deut 34:1, just before his death Moses "went up from the plains of Moab to Mount Nebo, to 'the top of Pisgah (רֹאשׁ הַפִּסְגָּה),'[20] which is opposite Jericho." From the top of Pisgah the Lord showed him the entire Land of Israel, but did not allow him to enter it. It was also here that Moses died (v 5). Yet "he was buried in a valley in the land of Moab, opposite Beth-Peor," at an unknown site (v 6). After the Song of Moses in 32:1-43, the Lord had already told him: "Ascend this mountain of the Abarim, Mount Nebo, which is in the land of Moab, across from

---

[17] Cf. T. R. Hobbs, *2 Kings* (WBC 13; Waco, TX: Word Books, 1985) 333. See also Jer 26:23, where King Jehoiakim threw Uriah's "dead body into the burial place of the common people."

[18] *Sifre* Shelaḥ 114 on Num 15:35 states that "all those who are to be executed are put to death outside of the court house" (Horovitz 123; Neusner 2.174). Unfortunately, it too does not name the site.

[19] Cf. especially the Introduction to I. 6.16, III. A and C. 1 below.

[20] On Pisgah, cf. the art. "Pisgah, Mount" by E. Grohman in *IDB* 3.819, and his art. "Nebo, Mount" on pp. 528-29.

Jericho, and view the land of Canaan" (v 49). It is on that mountain where he should die (v 50).

Here Moses is described as dying on Mount Nebo, a mountain of the Abarim range; it is associated with "the top of Pisgah" in 34:1. The uncertain location of Pisgah makes it understandable that the Tannaitic midrash *Sifre* Ha'azinu 338 on Deut 32:49 states regarding "this mountain of Abarim": It is "known by four names: Mount Abarim, Mount Nebo, Mount Hor, and the Top of Pisgah." It adds that it is called Mount "Nebo" because "three prophets (*nebi'im*)[21] were buried there: Moses, Aaron and Miriam."[22] This clear contradiction of the biblical data[23] shows how important it was for Judaic tradition to have Miriam's burial site be the same at that of her younger brother Moses. The Tannaitic tradition of Mount Abarim, Mount Nebo, Mount Hor, and the Top of Pisgah as being equivalent is attested elsewhere, showing its general acceptance.[24]

The "Top of Pisgah" in Judaic tradition also provided the Palestinian Jewish Christian who in a Semitic language first composed the narrative which later became Mark 15:42-47 with the designation "Arimathea" for Joseph. To appreciate this, it is first necessary to sketch Judaic tradition on the well which accompanied the Israelites for forty years until at the death of Moses it stopped forever at the Top of Pisgah. Since a variant of the well tradition also plays a major role in chapter III. in regard to the empty tomb, it is appropriate to describe it extensively here.

B. 1   The Well in Biblical and Judaic Tradition

The Fourth Evangelist alludes to the incident of the bronze serpent in Num 21:4-9 when he compares the Son of Man's being "lifted up" (crucified, but also exalted) to Moses' "lifting up" the serpent in the wilderness (3:14). Just after this incident the Israelites are described as setting up camp north of the Arnon River at the boundary of Moab

---

[21] This is a wordplay with "*Nebo*."
[22] Finkelstein 387; Hammer 346-47.
[23] According to Num 20:22 and 28 (see also 33:38-39 and Deut 32:50), Aaron was buried on Mount Hor. Cf. the art. "Hor" by J. Mihelic in *IDB* 2.644. Num 20:1 states that Miriam died and was buried in Kadesh.
[24] Cf. also *Midrash Tannaim* on Deut 32:49 (Hoffmann 206) and *Midrash Haggadol ad loc.* (Fisch 739); and *Sifre* Zuṭa on Num 27:12 (Horovitz 318; Börner-Klein 257). *Sifre* 'Eqeb 37 on Deut 7:12 and 11:10 (Finkelstein 72; Hammer 72) says there were three names: Mount Abarim, Mount Nebo, and the Top of Pisgah.

(Num 21:13).[25] The Numbers narrative continues with the "Song of the Well," inserted at this point because of the place name "Beer" (בְּאֵר). Num 21:16-20 reads:

> 16) From there they continued to Beer; that is the well [בְּאֵר] of which the Lord said to Moses:
> "Gather the people together, and I will give them water."
> 17) Then Israel sang this song: "Spring up, O well! - Sing to it! -
> 18)   the well that the leaders sank,
>   that the nobles of the people dug,
>   with the scepter, with the staff."
> From the wilderness to Mattanah, 19) from Mattanah to Nahaliel, from Nahaliel to Bamoth, 20) and from Bamoth to the valley lying in the region of Moab by the top of Pisgah that overlooks the wasteland [Jeshimon].

In Judaic tradition this narrative was combined with the incident of the waters of Meribah in the chapter just before it.[26] Numbers 20 describes how Moses struck the rock (סֶלַע) before the Israelites with his staff, which then produced abundant water for the congregation and its livestock (vv 2-13).[27] Two passages in the Psalms, and one in the prophet Isaiah, reflect this.

Ps 78:15-16 says of God: "He split rocks open in the wilderness, and gave them drink abundantly as from the deep. 16) He made streams come out of the rock, and caused waters to flow down like rivers." Verse 20 also maintains that God (through Moses) "struck the rock so that water gushed out and torrents overflowed...." The text continues by speaking of the gift of manna and quails.

---

[25] Cf. the place name Iye-abarim in v 11, certainly somehow related to the "Abarim" mentioned above.

[26] Cf. the extensive description of this incident in Ginzberg, *Legends* 3.50-54 and the relevant notes. Paul Billerbeck also notes a number of passages on the well in Str-B 3.406-08. For other secondary literature on the well, especially as related to John 4:1-42, see III. B. 1.11 with n. 105. In *Num. Rab.* Ḥuqqat 19/26 on the Song of the Well in Num 21:17, the waters of Meribah are interpreted as being the cause of Moses' being punished (by not being allowed to enter the Land, but having to die). They are his "executioner" (a Hebrew loanword from the Latin *speculator*, Greek σπεκουλάτωρ : LSJ 1626). See Mirkin 10.240, with parallels in n. 1 on p. 239; Soncino 6.775.

[27] A doublet of this narrative is found in Exod 17:1-7, just after God's giving manna to the people in chapter 16.

Ps 105:40 also mentions God's bringing quails and "food from heaven" (manna) to the Israelites in the wilderness. Verses 41-43 continue: "He opened the rock, and water gushed out; it flowed through the desert like a river. 42) For He remembered His holy promise, and Abraham, His servant. 43) So He brought His people out with joy, His chosen ones with singing."[28]

Isa 48:21 also refers to the above incident: "They did not thirst when He led them through the deserts; He made water flow for them from the rock; He split open the rock and the water gushed out."

The above two psalm passages are employed to describe the well in the Tannaitic account found in the Tosefta at *Sukkah* 3:11-13. Because of its great importance in regard to other passages, it deserves to be quoted extensively here.

> 11)   The well which was with the Israelites in the wilderness was a rock, the size of a large round vessel, surging and gurgling upward, as from the mouth of this little flask,[29] rising with them up onto the mountains, and going down with them into the valleys.
>
> Wherever the Israelites would encamp, it made camp with them, on a high place, opposite the entry of the Tent of Meeting.
>
> The princes of Israel come and surround it with their staffs, and they sing a song concerning it: "Spring up, O well! Sing to it; [the well which the princes dug, which the nobles of the people delved with the scepter and with their staves]" (Num 21:17-18).
>
> And the waters well upward like a pillar on high, and each one [of the princes] draws water with his staff, each one for his tribe, and each one for his family, as it is said: "The well which the princes dug."
>
> 12)   "And from Mattanah to Nahaliel, and from Nahaliel to Bamoth, and from Bamoth to the valley [lying in the region of Moab by the top of Pisgah, which looks down upon the desert]" (vv 19-20).
>
> This surrounds the entire camp of Israel and provides water for the whole desert, as it is said: "Which looks down upon the desert" (v 20).
>
> And this is turned into mighty streams, as it is said: "The streams overflow" (Ps 78:20).
>
> They sit in small boats and come together, as it is said: "It flowed through the desert like a river" (Ps 105:41).
>
> 13)   He who goes up on the right goes up on the right, and he who goes up on the left goes up on the left.

---

[28] The latter noun could be thought of as alluding to the "Song" of the Well, although a different Hebrew term is employed.

[29] This refers to the "flask of water for the water libation on the Festival" in 3:3(4) (Neusner 2.218).

So the water which flows forth from it is made into a great river and flows into the Great Sea [the Mediterranean].

And they derive from it all necessary goods, as it is said: "For the Lord your God has blessed you in all the work of your hands; He knows your going through this great wilderness; these forty years the Lord your God has been with you; you have lacked nothing" (Deut 2:7).[30]

The well provided the Israelites in the wilderness not only with water for themselves and their livestock. The Tannaitic midrash *Sifre* Beha‛alothekha 95 on Num 11:22 states for example that the well also provided them with "fat fish," more than they needed.[31]

Deut 8:4 notes regarding this wilderness period: "The clothes on your back did not wear out, and your feet did not swell these forty years." In *Midr. Pss.* 23/4 on Ps 23:2, R. Eliezer (b. Hyrcanus, a second generation Tanna,[32]) asked R. Simeon (b. Yoḥai, a third generation Tanna,[33]): "But since the Israelites did not change their garments, did they not reek of sweat?" R. Simeon answered: "The well brought up various herbs and various spices for them, and in these they were made to lie down," as Ps 23:2 is interpreted. Thus "the fragrant smell of them was carried from one end of the world to the other," as Cant 4:11 and 14 are meant. All of these came out of "the fountain of gardens, the well of living waters" (v 15).[34]

R. Yoḥanan (bar Nappaḥa, a second generation Palestinian Amora,[35]) also maintained that the Israelites procured the wine necessary for drink-offerings for forty years in the wilderness from the well. "Most of their enjoyments" came from there: "various kinds of herbs, vegetables and trees," as Num 20:5 is interpreted.[36]

---

[30] Lieberman, *Mo‛ed* 268-69; Zuckermandel / Libermann 196-97; Neusner 2.220-21, which I slightly modify.

[31] Horovitz 95; Neusner 2.105. It then cites Ps 78:20 regarding the rock and water, and notes bread (manna) and meat (quails). On the well's bringing up for the Israelites "various kinds of exceedingly fat fish," cf. also *Gen. Rab.* Toledoth 66/3 on Gen 27:28 (Theodor and Albeck 747; Soncino 2.602).

[32] *Introduction* 77.

[33] *Ibid.* 84.

[34] Buber 200; I modify Braude in 1.331. A variant of this tradition is found in *Pesiq. Rav Kah.* 11/21 (Mandelbaum 196; Braude and Kapstein 219), and in *Cant. Rab.* 4:11 § 2 (Soncino 9.216-17).

[35] *Introduction* 94-95.

[36] *Cant. Rab.* 4:13 § 3 (Soncino 9.223; cf. vv 14-15). See also the Rabbis' and R. Yoḥanan's comments on women's attractive clothes from the well in 4:14 § 1 (Soncino 9.225).

The well according to Tannaitic tradition is one of the ten things created at twilight before the first Sabbath; another is Moses' grave, which allowed them to be associated with each other.[37] The Song of the Well in Num 21:17-18 according to Tannaitic tradition is also the third song of ten recited by Israel, the fourth being Moses' song in Deut 31:24-30 just before his death.[38] The Song of the Well appears to have had special benedictions spoken before and after it,[39] and to have been read at the afternoon service on the Sabbath of Rosh ha-Shanah (New Year's).[40] Josephus also reports in *Ant.* 3.38 that "A writing deposited in the [Jerusalem] Temple attests that God foretold to Moses that water would thus spring forth from the rock." In his English translation of Josephus, H. St. John Thackeray thinks this refers "to a separate collection of chants made for the use of the temple singers, and that the allusion here is to the little song of the well in Numb. xxi. 16ff., with the introductory promise 'Gather the people together, and I will give them water.'"[41] If he is correct, which seems very probable, this is another sign of the liturgical usage of the Song of the Well.

There were professional well-diggers in Palestine such as Simeon of Siknin, who "used to dig wells, trenches and caves in Jerusalem." In *Eccl. Rab.* 4:17 § 1, he is represented as proudly telling R. Yoḥanan b. Zakkai, a

---

[37] Cf. *Sifre Ve'zot ha-Berakhah* 355 on Deut 33:21 (Finkelstein 418; Hammer 372); *b. Pesaḥ.* 54a as a baraitha (Soncino 264); *m. 'Avot* 5:6 (Albeck 4.376; Danby 456; Neusner 686; this has the "mouth of the well," and "some say" the grave of Moses); and *'Avot R. Nat.* B 37 (Schechter 95; Saldarini 217, with his comparative table on pp. 306-10).

[38] Cf. *Mek. R. Ish.* Shirata 1 on Exod 15:1 (Lauterbach 2.2); *Mekilta de R. Šimeon b. Yoḥai* on the same verse (Epstein / Melamed 71); and *Tanḥ.* Beshallaḥ 10 on Exod 14:16 (Eshkol 285; Berman 419). According to *Num. Rab.* Ḥuqqat 19/25 on Num 21:17, although given to the Israelites at the beginning of their forty year wilderness journey, the Song of the Well was only sung at the end of this period (Mirkin 10.238, with parallel traditions in n. 1; Soncino 6.773).

[39] Cf. *Soferim* 12:4, 39b (*Minor Tractates* 1.265). It is, of course, very difficult to date such liturgical traditions.

[40] Cf. *b. Roš. Haš.* 31a (Soncino 147).

[41] Cf. LCL 4.336-37, n. "a." He also calls attention to the Song of Moses (Deut 32:1-43) so described in 4.303, with n. "a," which also mentions the Song at the Red Sea in Exod 15:1-18 in 2.346, as well as to the sun's standing still, prolonging the day (Josh 10:12-13) in 5.61. These were three of the ten "Songs" according to *Mek. R. Ish.* Shirata 1 on Exod 15:1 (Lauterbach 2.2), greatly strengthening Thackeray's thesis. Philo relates the Song of the Well after the Song at the Red Sea in *Ebr.* 111-13. In *Mos.* 1.255 he calls it "a new song." See also n. 51 below.

first generation Tanna,[42] that he was equal to him by providing the wells to which the rabbi sent those who sought his advice.[43] This incident also speaks of a well "whose waters are 'pure and cold,'" the Hebrew זַכּוּ and צוֹנֵן.[44] Jer 6:7 already notes that a well keeps its water "cold."[45] Prov 20:5 maintains that "Counsel in the heart of man is like deep water; but a man of understanding will draw it out." Commenting on this, *Gen. Rab.* Vayyigash 93/4 remarks: "This may be compared to 'a deep well full of cold and excellent water,' yet none could drink of it."[46] Jacob's Well near Shechem in John 4 is an example of such a well in Palestine. Verse 11 states that it is "deep," and its depth is estimated to be 32 meters (105 feet).[47] Verses 10-11 speak of the well's "living" (ζῶν) water, which is the Hebrew חַי , "flowing," "fresh."[48] Such water was greatly preferred to that of the motionless, flat water of a cistern.

---

[42] *Introduction* 74-75.

[43] Vilna 27; Soncino 8.125-26. The Hebrew for "wells" here is the plural of בּוֹר , actually a pit or cistern, but meant as בְּאֵר , well. The latter two terms were often used to mean the same thing. Cf. BDB 91 on בְּאֵר , well, pit, and בֹּאר and בּוֹר 92: cistern, pit, well; Jastrow 149; and Krauss, *Talmudische Archäologie* 1.179, with n. 13. The whole section "Wasser" on pp. 78-83 with its notes is helpful. See also "Neḥonia the digger of wells, ditches and caves" in *b. B. Qam.* 50a (Soncino 287, with n. 9) and *t. B. Qam.* 6:5 (Neusner 4.28). In *Plant.* 79, Philo of Alexandria notes that well-diggers search for hidden springs.

[44] Jastrow 399 and 1268, respectively.

[45] Cf. BDB 903 on the hiphil of קָרַר , to be cold, as well as קַר , cool, of water in Jer 18:14 and Prov 25:25 ("like cold water to a thirsty soul"). See also the Haqqar Well, employed by the Exiles when coming to Jerusalem on pilgrimages: *m. 'Erub.* 10:14 (Albeck 2.126; Danby 136, with n. 6; Neusner 229).

[46] Theodor and Albeck 1153; Soncino 2.858.

[47] Cf. Zev Vilnay, *Israel Guide* (Jerusalem: Daf-Chen Press, 1979) 182. Over forty years ago an Orthodox priest kindly gave me a very refreshing drink from it. Although Philo of Alexandria allegorizes as usual, he refers positively to a well which is very deep in *Post.* 130; *Somn.* 1.6 and 11; and 2.271 in regard to Num 21:17.

[48] BDB 312, 1.f. In regard to Moses and the Messiah, *Eccl. Rab.* 1:9 ("That which has been is that which shall be") § 1 states that "As the former redeemer made a well to rise [Num 21:17-18], so will the latter Redeemer bring up water," for which Joel 4:18 is quoted (Soncino 8.33). Jesus as the "living water," the Messiah of John 4:25-26 and 29, is related to this motif. See also 7:37-38. For an analysis of the influence of Judaic tradition on Gen 28:10 and the "Jacob's well" narrative in 29:1-14 on the narrative of John 4:4-42, see chapter III., B. 1.11 below.

Because of the rocky terrain of Palestine, a well was simply "dug out," from the root חפר .[49] A baraitha in *b. B. Bath.* 64a states that (because of the rocky terrain), a well did not have to be faced with stone, which was, however, necessary for a cistern.[50] Following the LXX, Philo of Alexandria thought that the well of Num 21:16-18 "had been dug by the hands of no common men, but of kings, whose ambition was not only to find the water but so to build the well that the wealth lavished upon it should show the royal character of the work and the sovereignty and lofty spirit of the builders."[51]

B. 2   1 Cor 10:1-4

Before discussing the relevance of early Jewish views of how the well of Num 21:17-18 was constructed, I wish to call attention at this point to the significance of Judaic tradition on the well in regard to what is often considered by lay people and beginning students of theology to be one of the most puzzling passages in the NT, 1 Cor 10:1-4. It reads in the NRSV:

> I do not want you to be unaware, brothers and sisters, that our ancestors were all under the cloud, and all passed through the sea, 2) and all were baptized into Moses in the cloud and in the sea, 3) and all ate the same spiritual food, 4) and all drank the same spiritual drink. For they drank from the spiritual rock that followed them, and the rock was Christ.

The Jewish Christian Paul wrote his first (surviving) letter to the Corinthians from Ephesus (16:8) around 54 CE.[52] Here in chapter 10 he means the Israelites with "our fathers / ancestors" in v 1. The Apostle to the Gentiles now expressly also includes non-Jewish Christians in this designation ("our"). He first refers to the sacrament of baptism in v 2,

---

[49] Cf. BDB 343, 1.a., including Num 21:18 from the Song of the Well; and Jastrow 493: to dig, hollow out.
[50] Soncino 258. On this, cf. Krauss, *Talmudische Archäologie* 1.79-80.
[51] Cf. *Mos.* 1.256 with n. "c" in the LCL edition regarding the sides of the well. Living in the soft soil of the Nile Delta, the Alexandrian philosopher simply assumed that the biblical well needed stone walls, as there. Philo also refers to the well in *Ebr.* 112-13 and *Somn.* 2.270-71 (269 quotes Miriam's song in Exod 15:1, and the well is often referred to as "Miriam's Well").
[52] Cf. Anthony Thiselton, *The First Epistle to the Corinthians* (NIGTC; Grand Rapids, MI: Eerdmans, 2000) 31-32: 54 to 55 CE. On this pericope, see also the fine analysis of Christian Wolff in *Der erste Brief des Paulus an die Korinther*, Zweiter Teil, 7/II (ThHKNT; Berlin: Evangelische Verlagsanstalt, 1982) 38-43.

"the sea" alluding to the Re(e)d Sea through which the Israelites passed in Exodus 14. Then (in the wilderness) they ate manna, the same "spiritual food" of v 3. It corresponds to the bread of the second sacrament, the Lord's Supper (v 16; 11:23, 26). The Israelites also drank there the same "spiritual drink" (v 4a), meant as the wine of the Lord's Supper, the blood of Christ (v 16; 11:25-26). The Apostle continues in v 4b by maintaining that the Israelites continually drank[53] from the spiritual "rock" (πέτρα) (which was) following (them). Now "the rock" (ἡ πέτρα) was the Christ.

Paul's reading the two Christian sacraments back into the time of the wilderness wandering, with manna as heavenly food satisfying the Israelites' hunger, the well continually satisfying their thirst, as in the (at least weekly) celebration of the Lord's Supper in early Christian congregations, may go back to a Hellenistic Jewish-Christian tradition which he appropriated here. Yet if Paul (as Saul) in fact did study in Jerusalem at the feet of Gamaliel (I, a first generation Tanna[54] : Acts 22:3),[55] he may just as well have later appropriated the basic content of 1 Cor 10:1-4 from a Palestinian, Aramaic-speaking Jewish-Christian congregation with former scribes and other Scripture experts in it. They were constantly searching the Scriptures for allusions to Jesus as the Messiah.[56]

One very early motif in Judaism aided them in associating Christ, literally "the Anointed One" or "the Messiah" (הַמָּשִׁיחַ), with the Israelites in their forty year wandering in the wilderness. The pre-Christian LXX Ps 71(72):17 already states that "his name endures before the sun." In a baraitha in *b. Pesaḥ.* 54a the name of the Messiah is one of the seven things which were created before the world was created. Ps 72:17 is cited to prove this: "His name shall endure for ever, and has existed before the sun."[57] *Gen. Rab.* Bereshith 1/4 on Gen 1:1 also

---

[53] This is the connotation of the imperfect ἔπινον .

[54] *Introduction* 73.

[55] This seems quite probable to me because of his knowledge of Judaic traditions both in Hebrew and in Aramaic reflected elsewhere. For an example of this, cf. my *Imagery of Triumph and Rebellion in 2 Corinthians 2:14-17 and Elsewhere in the Epistle. An Example of the Combination of Greco-Roman and Judaic Traditions in the Apostle Paul* (Studies in Judaism; Lanham, MD: University Press of America, 2005) 47-79.

[56] Cf. Psalm 22 as applied to him at the Crucifixion in numerous ways, as well as Jesus considered the Servant of the Lord in Isaiah 52-53.

[57] Soncino 265.

employs Ps 72:17 for the name of the Messiah at this point,[58] as do many other passages.[59] Palestinian Judaism, which conceived of the name of the Messiah as already created or contemplated by God before the creation of the world, could thus have provided Palestinian Jewish Christians with a thought pattern for describing Christ (ὁ Χριστός), the Messiah, as already present with the Israelites in the wilderness.[60]

The pre-Christian Qumranites, writing in Hebrew, applied the well in the Song of the Well in Num 21:18 to themselves: "The well is the Torah. And those who dug it ... are the converts of Israel, who left the land of Judah and lived in the land of Damascus, all of whom God called 'princes'.... And 'the staff' is the interpreter of the Torah.... And 'the nobles' of the people are those who came to dig the well with the staves that 'the scepter' decreed...."[61] Here the Qumranites describe themselves in terms of the very popular well imagery from Num 21:(17-)18. It is thus not hard to imagine that Aramaic-speaking Jewish Christians, some also fluent in Hebrew, could also appropriate the same imagery to themselves and the new Christian sacrament of the Lord's Supper. Paul then borrowed this from them, or after it had been passed on to Hellenistic Jewish-Christian congregations.

What is most startling is Paul's statement in 1 Cor 10:4 that the rock which followed the Israelites (in the wilderness) was Christ (ὁ Χριστός). How could Christ possibly be considered "the rock" (ἡ πέτρα)? To understand this, Judaic tradition on the section just before the Song of the Well in Num 21:16-20 must be taken into account. After Miriam died and was buried in Kadesh (20:1),[62] there was no water, so the Israelites "quarreled" with Moses (v 3), leading to vv 2-13 being regarded as the incident of the "waters of 'Meribah' (quarreling / strife)"[63] in v 13. After the people's complaining, Moses and Aaron went

---

[58] Theodor and Albeck 6, with parallels in n. 4; Soncino 1.6.

[59] Cf. Str-B 2.334-35, including those with the "Yinnon" / "Yinnin" of Ps 72:17 as the Messiah. See also Enoch 48:3 and 6 for the Son of Man (*OTP* 1.35), as well as John 1:1 on the Word.

[60] This could then have entered Hellenistic Jewish-Christian communities, from where Paul appropriated it. Yet this is not necessary, nor is there any evidence of a wisdom christology at this point (cf. Prov 8:22-23).

[61] Cf. CD-A 6:3-9 (Martínez and Tigchelaar, *The Dead Sea Scrolls Study Edition* 1.558-59). See also CD-B 19:34 (1.578-79), as well as CD-A 3:16 (1.554-55).

[62] This is assumed to be in the fortieth or last year of wandering in the wilderness. See the commentaries.

[63] Cf. מְרִיבָה in BDB 937. See Num 27:14, where the site is connected to the reason for Moses' death.

to the entrance of the tent of meeting, where the glory of the Lord appeared to them (v 6). They should take the staff, assemble the congregation, "and command 'the rock' before their eyes to yield its water" (v 8). This they did, Moses striking "the rock" twice with his staff, so that water came out abundantly. Then the congregation and their livestock could drink (v 11).

In this episode "the rock" is mentioned five times, showing its importance (20:8 [twice], 10 [twice], and 11). In the Hebrew it is always הַסֶּלַע.[64] In the LXX it is always ἡ πέτρα , as in 1 Cor 10:4.[65] Judaic tradition greatly embellished this incident. The "staff" or "rod" of Num 20:8, mentioned again in vv 9 and 11, was a "staff of 'miracles' (ניסיא)" according to the popular Palestinian *Targum Pseudo-Jonathan* on vv 8-9.[66] It was the same staff with which Moses had turned the waters of the Nile in Egypt into blood. God told him then in regard to Exod 4:20, "Take this rod in your hand, and all the 'miracles' (נסים) you wish you can do with it." This included the incident of Num 20:2-13.[67] In regard to the expression "before the rock" in v 10, *Numbers Rabbah* comments that "all the Israelites were standing there and watching all the 'miracles' (נסים) performed through the rock."[68] The miraculous nature of the rock is thus emphasized in Judaic tradition.

God had told Moses and Aaron to "speak" (דבר ; NRSV: "command") to the rock before the congregation's eyes in order for it to yield its water (20:8). *Targum Pseudo-Jonathan* on this verse notes that this speaking was

---

[64] Cf. BDB 700-01, "crag, cliff, synon. צוּר ." It was later understood, however, as "rock" (Jastrow 996, also the NRSV translation).

[65] The Greek πέτρα is also employed in the related passages LXX 77(78):16-17; 104(105):41; and Isa 48:21.

[66] Rieder 2.222-23; Clarke 244.

[67] Cf. *Tanḥ.* Shemoth 23 (Eshkol 2.228; Berman 342-44, who mistakenly has "Gen" 20:8 at the end instead of Num 20:8).

[68] Cf. Ḥuqqath 19/9 on Num 20:10 (Mirkin 10.228-29; Soncino 6.758). A parallel is found in *Tanḥ.* B Ḥuqqath 29 on Num 20:8 (Buber 120; Bietenhard 2.348). *Deut. Rab.* 'Eqeb 3/8 on Deut 9:1 (Mirkin 11.61; Soncino 7.76) has "the Rabbis say" that there were "miracles" (נסין) performed by God for the Israelites at the rock. This is related to Num 20:8, and miracles are also noted for the well in regard to 21:17. Before this it is stated that the Tetragrammaton (יהוה) was engraved upon Moses' staff. Josephus notes on the parallel tradition in Exodus 17 that when Moses struck the rock (ἡ πέτρα) with his staff and great amounts of water streamed forth, the Israelites were "amazed at this marvelous prodigy" (*Ant.* 3.38; see BAGD 615 on παράδοξος : wonderful, remarkable). He omits an account of the same incident at 4.85.

to be "by the great and precise Name [Yahweh]."[69] Because Moses lost his temper, called the Israelites "rebels" in v 10, and instead struck the rock "twice" with his staff (v 11), he first caused it to bring forth drops of blood. This is explained by the same Hebrew root (זוב) which occurs in Ps 78:20 (of water) and in Lev 15:25 (of blood), which verses are quoted here. The second time Moses struck the rock, however, it brought forth water abundantly (Num 20:11). Because of this disobedience to God's command, Moses was to die before entering the Land of Israel. Numerous sources relate this incident, with variants.[70]

I suggest that this Judaic tradition on the rock's yielding both blood and water informed the Palestinian Jewish Christian who first composed the basic content of what later became 1 Cor 10:1-4. The Jewish Christian Paul later appropriated it. The Israelites are described there as not only drinking the same spiritual drink in the wilderness. They also drank from the same spiritual rock that followed them, Christ. Christ, the rock, first yielded blood (the red wine of the Eucharist or Lord's Supper), then water. The Evangelist John may also have this tradition in mind when he states that after Jesus died on the Cross, a soldier "pierced his side with a spear, and at once blood and water came out" (19:34). This recalls Moses' striking the rock (for Paul, Christ), and blood and water coming out. The latter two may symbolize the Lord's Supper[71] and baptism for John, just as the two sacraments are meant in 1 Cor 10:1-4.

The early Jewish-Christian appropriation of Judaic traditions on the wilderness well in 1 Cor 10:1-4 points to the possibility that such well imagery could also be employed in the narrative of Jesus' burial. This is indeed the case. To understand it better, the shape of the well and its final disappearance at the top of Pisgah should first be described.

---

[69] Rieder 2.222; Clarke 244. Cf. the emphasis on God's "Name" in *Targum Neofiti 1* on v 12 (Díez Macho 4.183; McNamara 111).

[70] Cf. *Exod. Rab.* Shemoth 3/13 on Exod 4:9 (Mirkin 5.70; Soncino 3.73); *Num. Rab.* Ḥuqqath 19/9 on Num 20:10 (Mirkin 10.228-29; Soncino 6.758-59); *Midr. Pss.* 78/2 on Ps 78:20 (Buber 344-45; Braude 2.22-23); 105/12 on Ps 105:41 (Buber 452; Braude 2.185-86); *Tanḥ.* B Ḥuqqath 29 and 30 (Buber 120-21; Bietenhard 2.348-49); *Tanḥ.* Ḥuqqath 9 on Num 20:8 (Eshkol 770); *Tanḥ.* Shemoth 23 on Exod 4:20 (Eshkol 228; Berman 342-44); and *Targ. Pseud.-Jon.* Num 20:1-13 (Rieder 2.222-23; Clarke 244). The latter notes on v 2: "And for Miriam's merit a well was given; when she died the well was hidden away." The following incident of water from the rock thus represents its return. It is specifically mentioned in v 13: "concerning the well which was hidden," and "when it had been given to them."

[71] Cf. John 6:55 for Jesus' blood as "true drink," (to be drunk as red wine at the Lord's Supper: vv 53-54), whereby his flesh is compared to the manna.

B. 3 The Shape of the Well

The Tannaitic writing *t. Sukk.* 3:11 states that "the well which was with the Israelites in the wilderness was like a rock (סֶלַע), 'the size of a large round vessel,' surging and gurgling upward..., rising with them onto the mountains and going down with them into the valleys."[72] The "large round vessel" here is the Hebrew כְּבָרָה.[73] In *Midr. Pss.* 24/6 on Ps 24:2, R. Ḥiyya bar Abba, a fifth generation Tanna,[74] comments on Num 21:20, "the top of Pisgah, it is seen upon the face of Jeshimon": "This verse implies that when a person comes to the top of Mount Nebo, he sees in the Sea of Tiberias something of the shape and size of 'a large round vessel' (כברה)."[75] *Tanḥ.* Bemidbar 2 on Num 1:1 also asks how the well was constructed. It states: "It was like 'a rock' (סֶלַע), like 'a large round vessel' (כַּוֶּרֶת)[76] or 'a globe' (כַּדּוּרֶת),[77] and it 'rolled along' (מִתְגַּלְגֶּלֶת) and accompanied them on the stations [of their wilderness journey]."[78] Commenting on Num 21:20, "(by the top of Pisgah that) overlooks the wasteland," *Num. Rab.* Ḥuqqath 19/26 says "this alludes to the well, which accompanied them until it entered the Sea of Tiberias. One who

---

[72] Lieberman, *Moʿed* 268; Zuckermandel / Liebermann 196-97; Neusner 2.220.

[73] Jastrow 609,1).

[74] *Introduction* 90.

[75] Buber 206; I modify Braude in 1.341. A parallel is found in *Lev. Rab.* Aḥare Moth 22/4 (Mirkin 8.37; Soncino 4.283). R. Yoḥanan b. Nuri, a second generation Tanna (*Introduction* 80), then relates earlier rabbinic opinion on the exact location of Miriam's well. In *b. Šabb.* 35a (Soncino 164), R. Ḥiyya maintains the former tradition in regard to the top of (Mount) Carmel. MS "M" correctly adds to "Sea": "of Tiberias," because the Mediterranean is not meant. In *y. Kil.* 9:3, 32c (Neusner / Mandelbaum 4.281), also dealing with Num 21:20, the author has become R. Ḥiyya b. Ba. The same is true for *y. Keth.* 12:3, 35b (Neusner 22.351). In *Eccl. Rab.* 5:8-9 § 5 (Vilna 30; Soncino 8.144), R. Ḥiyya b. Abba comments on Num 21:20 with a "small rounded vessel (כברה קטנה)."

[76] Jastrow 617, 1).

[77] Jastrow 613: ball, globe.

[78] Eshkol 646. *Tanḥ.* B Bemidbar 2 on Num 1:1 has the same without these two Hebrew words (Buber 3, yet cf. his n. 21; Bietenhard 2.193). *Num. Rab.* Bemidbar 1/2 on the same verse says "it was a rock (סֶלַע) like a large round vessel (כַּוֶּרֶת), which rolled along..." (Mirkin 9.12; Soncino 5.4). *Seder ʿOlam* 8 (Guggenheimer 90) states that there were altogether forty-two stations. This is based on the number of sites found in Numbers 33 (91, n. 7).

stands 'overlooking the wasteland'[79] sees in the middle of the Sea [something] shaped like 'an oven' (תַּנוּר).[80] This is the well which is seen when 'overlooking the wasteland.'"[81] *Tanh.* Huqqath 21 on the same verse speaks of something "the shape of the mouth of an oven."[82]

All of the above descriptions of the well, whether in the shape of a large round vessel, a globe, or an oven, begin by stating that the well was (like) "a rock" (סֶלַע). This makes the at first very strange expression, Christ as "the rock" (ἡ πέτρα) in 1 Cor 10:4, easier to understand, for the rock in Judaic sources was another designation for the well, from which the Israelites drank.[83]

B. 4   The Disappearance of the Well at the Top of Pisgah

The Tannaitic passage *t. Sotah* 11:1 states: "So long as Miriam was alive, the well provided ample water for all Israel. Once Miriam had died, what does it say? 'And Miriam died there, and there was not enough water for the congregation' (Num 20:1-2) - for the well dried up."[84] In 11:8, R. Yose b. R. Judah, a fourth generation Tanna,[85] notes in regard to the merits of Moses, Aaron and Miriam for the Israelites: "On their account three gifts were given to them: the pillar of cloud, manna and the well - the well through the merit of Miriam, the pillar of cloud through the merit of Aaron, and the manna through the merit of Moses. When Miriam died, the well ceased, but it came back through the merit of Moses and Aaron. When Aaron died, the pillar of cloud ceased, but both of them came back through the merit of Moses. When Moses died,

---

[79] Jastrow 1625 on שָׁקַף translates: "he that stands on the face (plateau) of Jeshimon sees...."

[80] Jastrow 1680.

[81] Mirkin 10.241; Soncino 6.777.

[82] Eshkol 781.

[83] For a Judaic tradition which relates that God Himself was at the well, upon the rock, cf. *Exod. Rab.* Beshallah 25/4 on Exod 16:4 (Mirkin 5.278; Soncino 3.304). Interpreting the double "behold" of Isa 65:1, God says: "Behold, it was I at the well, for it says: 'Behold, I will stand before thee there upon the rock in Horeb' (Exod 17:6), and behold, it was I who gave the manna, for it says: 'Behold, I will cause to rain bread from heaven for you' (16:4)." Early Jewish Christians thus could have thought the "Son of God," Jesus the Messiah, was also present with his heavenly Father at the well, deriving from the rock. John 6:22-59 portrays him as the bread of life, the true manna.

[84] Zuckermandel / Liebermann 314; Neusner 3.193.

[85] *Introduction* 88.

all of them came to an end and never came back, as it is said: 'In one month I destroyed the three shepherds' (Zech 11:8)."[86] This Tannaitic tradition is found in numerous early sources, showing its popularity.[87] One of the earliest is *Pseudo-Philo* 20:8, a Palestinian text from the first century CE written in Hebrew.[88]

The latter also states in 11:15 that the water (of the well) "followed them [the Israelites] in the wilderness forty years and went up to the mountain with them and went down into the plains."[89] This is a very early haggadic rendering of the place names at the end of the Song of the Well in Num 21:17-18. Verses 18-20 read of the well's route:

> 18) From the wilderness to Mattanah, 19) from Mattanah to Nahaliel, from Nahaliel to Bamoth, 20) and from Bamoth to the valley lying in the region of Moab by the Top of Pisgah that overlooks the wasteland / Jeshimon.

It is significant that all four targums, including the usually quite literal *Onqelos*, interpret these place names in almost exactly the same way. This shows how widespread and firm the basic tradition was. *Targum Neofiti 1* on vv 19-20 states, for example:

> 19) And after the well had been given to them as a gift, it went on to become for them swelling torrents; and after it had become swelling torrents, it went on to go up with them to the tops of the mountains and to go down with them to the deep valleys. 20) And after it had gone up

---

[86] Zuckermandel / Liebermann 315-16 as 11:10; Neusner 3.195.
[87] Cf. the parallel in *b. Ta'an.* 9a (Soncino 38-39), which states that although Miriam died in Nisan, Aaron in Ab, and Moses in Adar, they were nevertheless regarded as all dying in one month. See also *Seder 'Olam* 10 (Guggenheimer 102-03; here the well disappeared "on the day of Moses' death"); *Gen. Rab.* Ḥayye Sarah 62/4 on Gen 25:11, which states that "after the death of Moses the servant of the Lord" (Josh 1:1), the well ceased "immediately" (Theodor and Albeck 675-76; Soncino 2.553); *Mek. R. Ish.* Vayassaʿ 6 on Exod 16:35 in the name of R. Yose (b. Ḥalafta, a third generation Tanna), and R. Joshua, a second generation Tanna (*Introduction* 84 and 77, respectively); and *Sifre* Niṣṣabim 305 on Num 27:18 (Deut 31:14) in Finkelstein 326, Hammer 295-96. See also the other sources cited in Ginzberg, *Legends* 6.19, n. 113.
[88] Cf. *SC* 229.170 and *OTP* 2.329.
[89] Cf. *SC* 229.124 and *OTP* 2.319. It refers to the water of Marah, made sweet in Exod 15:22-25. This takes the water of the well back even farther than 17:1-7, the parallel version to Num 20:2-13. The well is also referred to in *Pseudo-Philo* 10:7 (*SC* 229.118 and *OTP* 2.317).

with them to the tops of the high mountains and had gone down with them to the deep valleys, it was hidden for them in the valley which is at the boundary of the Moabites, the top of the height which looks out opposite Beth Jeshimon.[90]

The well is described here in v 20 as being hidden away (forever)[91] for the Israelites "in the valley which is at the boundary of the Moabites, the top of the height which looks out opposite Beth Jeshimon." "The top of the height" here interprets "the top of Pisgah" in the Hebrew text. Strange to us today, it did not disturb the early Jewish interpreters of the expression "the top of Pisgah" to equate it with "'the valley' which is at the boundary of the Moabites." This is because Moses died "in the land of Moab" (Deut 34:5), and the Lord buried him "in 'a valley' in the land of Moab" (v 6). He had gone up "from the plains of Moab to Mount Nebo, to the top of Pisgah, which is opposite Jericho" (v 1). This common mention of "the top of Pisgah" enabled early commentators to combine Num 21:20 and Deut 34:1(-6).

The same was true for the term "the valley" in Num 21:19 and Deut 34:6. R. Judah (b. Ilai), a third generation Tanna,[92] interpreted "from 'Bamoth' (במות) to the valley" in Num 21:19 to mean that (the Israelites) were the cause in regard to him who was righteous (Moses), that (the Lord) "buried [him] in the valley" (Deut 34:6). R. Judah views the מות of the term בָּמוֹת as the Angel of "Death" (מָוֶת , Aramaic מוֹת),[93] who "came" (בָּא) for Moses.[94] *Num. Rab.* Ḥuqqath 19/33 on Num 21:17 also has Moses quarrel with God about his upcoming death. Here "Bamoth" means for him that after the inheritance (Nahaliel) "came death" (בָּ מוֹת). "And from Bamoth to 'the valley' that is in the field of Moab"

[90] Díez Macho 4.197; McNamara 119-20 with explanatory notes. Cf. also these verses in *Onqelos* (Sperber 1.259; Grossfeld 126, with notes); *Pseudo-Jonathan* (Rieder 2.225; Clarke 248-49, with notes); and the *Fragment Targum*, MSS "P" and "V" (Klein 1.101 and 199; 2.72 and 157).
[91] Another, independent tradition has "Miriam's Well" later proceed to the middle of the Sea of Tiberias, where it can be seen from Jeshimon, i.e. from the top of Pisgah (see the texts cited above with notes 75-81).
[92] *Introduction* 84-85.
[93] Jastrow 752.
[94] Cf. *Midr. Pss.* 5/1 on Ps 5:1 (Buber 50, with n. 5; Braude 1.80 translates very loosely).

in v 20 also means: "And He buried him in 'the valley' in the land of Moab" (Deut 34:6).[95]

It is important to note here that "the top of Pisgah," where the well finally resided before disappearing immediately and forever on the day of Moses' death, is exactly the same place where he died and was buried (Deut 34:1 and 6). Because of the Judaic dictum of "as the first redeemer of Israel (Moses), so the final or great redeemer of Israel, the Messiah," I suggest that Jesus' burial by Joseph of Arimathea was described in at least four respects by the first Palestinian Jewish Christians in terms of Moses' burial in biblical and Judaic tradition.

B. 4.1   An Unknown Burial Site

a) Moses. Deut 34:6 clearly states of Moses: "no 'man' knows his burial place to this day." To emphasize this, the Tannaitic midrash *Sifre* ha-Berakhah 357 on this verse notes that some maintain: "Even Moses himself does not know the place of his sepulcher, and 'man' always refers to Moses, as it is said: 'Now the man Moses was very meek' (Num 12:3)." Even the imperial house of Caesar, which sent two commissioners to find the grave, saw the bier but could nowhere locate it.[96] Josephus avoids a description of Moses' burial site, stating that "a cloud suddenly descended upon him and he disappeared in a ravine" (*Ant.* 4.326) of the mountain called Abaris (Abarim) (325). *Deut. Rab.* Vayelech 9/5 on Deut 31:14 notes that one's relatives and friends usually attend to the burial of a person, but in the case of Moses, God and His Court (of angels) did so, as Deut 34:6 is interpreted.[97] That is, Moses is considered here to be alone at his own burial so that the grave site was also unknown. This is also meant by R. Ishmael (b. Elisha), a second generation Tanna,[98] who taught in regard to the same scriptural verse that Moses buried himself.[99] Philo of Alexandria states in *Mos.* 2.291 that in Deuteronomy 34, Moses

---

[95] Mirkin 10.246; Soncino 6.785. A parallel is found in *Tanḥ.* Ḥuqqath 21 on Num 21:20 (Eshkol 781).

[96] Finkelstein 428-29; Hammer 381-82. A similar tradition is found in *b. Soṭah* 13b-14a (Soncino 72).

[97] Mirkin 11.136; Soncino 7.160. One Armenian narrative on the death of Moses states that it was the archangel Michael who buried him. Cf. Michael Stone, "Three Armenian Accounts of the Death of Moses" 120. See also the paraphrase of Deut 34:6 as "And the angel buried him" on p. 118.

[98] *Introduction* 79.

[99] Cf. *Sifre* Naso 32 on Num 6:13 (Horovitz 39; Neusner 1.171), and *Num. Rab.* Naso 10/17 on the same verse (Mirkin 9.272; Soncino 5.397).

prophesied "how he was buried with none present, surely by no mortal hands but by immortal powers [angels]." He "was not laid to rest in the tomb of his forefathers but was given a monument of special dignity which no man has ever seen." For the Alexandrian philosopher, Moses' burial site was thus also unknown, as in the biblical and Palestinian Judaic traditions cited above.

b) Jesus. As pointed out in section A. above, after his death by crucifixion Jesus' body was most probably placed by a servant / slave of the Council / Sanhedrin in one of the two public "burying places" for criminals outside the Jerusalem city limits. Since *all* of his followers had abandoned him, first fleeing for their lives back home to Galilee with the accompanying women whom they would not have left behind alone, they did not know where Jesus had been buried, although they may have later assumed it was in one of the two public burying places for criminals. But where, especially because the burial would have been carried out anonymously, in haste because of the soon to begin Sabbath, and most probably also with others crucified by Pilate?[100] Like the burial site of Israel's first redeemer, Moses, that of Israel's final or great redeemer, the Messiah Jesus, was simply unknown.[101]

---

[100] These would have included at least the two insurrectionists crucified with Jesus (Mark 15:28), but probably more.

[101] On the site of Hadrian's second-century CE pagan temple, the emperor Constantine had a splendid church erected, which was dedicated in 335 CE. Before Hadrian's temple, what are now considered by many to be Golgotha and Jesus' grave lay outside of Jerusalem to the NW, where there was presumably a quarry earlier. The area became a part of the city in 40-44 CE, causing the site of Jesus' ostensible grave to be hardly identifiable even as of then. The great devastation caused by the Jewish-Roman War some two decades later at precisely this place makes the later, fourth-century accounts of Eusebius of Caesarea concerning finding the original "holy sites" through divine inspiration very suspect. For these dates and a general discussion of the subject, cf. Küchler, *Jerusalem* 415-33. He also mentions a beam from the original Cross of Jesus displayed as of ca. 350 CE (p. 440). The Greek Orthodox Monastery of the Cross, lying between the present district of Reḥavia and the Israel Museum, is the site where Constantine's mother Helena maintained the tree grew which later was made into the two beams of Jesus' Cross. See *Jerusalem* 440 and Vilnay, *Israel Guide* 100-01. Legends developed very fast when they were needed for practical purposes, for example the building of a church.

B. 4.2   Joseph of "Arimathea"

Moses died in the land of Moab (Deut 34:5) and was buried in a valley in the land of Moab, opposite Beth-peor (v 6), in Judaic tradition thought to be the same site as Mount Nebo, "the top of Pisgah" (v 1).[102] The latter is the Hebrew רֹאשׁ הַפִּסְגָּה . In Num 23:14 Balak took Balaam "to the field of Zophim, to the top of Pisgah," where he uttered his second oracle. *Num. Rab.* Balak 20/19 on this verse states: "It was there that Moses died, as is borne out by the text: 'Go up to the top of Pisgah' (Deut 3:27)."[103] Philo of Alexandria comments on Num 23:14 by saying that Balak "led the way to another spot, and from 'an exceedingly high hill' showed the seer a part of the enemy's host" (*Mos.* 1.282). The latter expression is the Greek λόφου πάνυ περιμήκους .[104] In describing the site of Moses' death (Mount Nebo, the top of Pisgah in Deut 34:1), Josephus avoids these two names. Instead, he states that Moses "arrived on the mountain called Abaris[105] - 'a lofty eminence' situated over against Jericho..." (*Ant.* 4.325). "A lofty eminence" is the Greek ὑψηλόν .[106] Also from Palestine in the first century CE and written in Hebrew, *Pseudo-Philo* comments on Deut 34:1 and 6 by stating regarding God and Moses: "And He buried him on 'a high place' and in the light of all the world." "A high place" is the Latin *excelsam terram*.[107]

The latter three first-century CE passages show that "the top of Pisgah" in Deut 34:1 as the site of Moses' death and burial (v 6) was strangely no longer designated by this term. Instead, "the top of Pisgah" was paraphrased as "an exceedingly high hill," "a lofty eminence," and "a high place." All of these reflect a strong early Judaic tradition, which has also survived in the targums.[108]

"Pisgah," which may mean the "cleft" in a mountain,[109] occurs eight times in the Hebrew Bible. "The slopes of Pisgah" is found in Deut 3:17; 4:49; Josh 12:3; and 13:20. "The top of Pisgah" also occurs four times: in the Song of the Well episode in Num 21:20; the Balak / Balaam incident in 23:14 noted above; Moses' viewing the Land of Israel (also thought to

---

[102] Cf. n. 22.

[103] Mirkin 10.265; Soncino 6.811.

[104] On λόφος as a crest of a hill, a ridge, cf. LSJ 1062, II.

[105] This is Mount Abarim of Deut 32:49. Cf. n. 22.

[106] On ὑψηλός as high, lofty, cf. LSJ 1909.

[107] Cf. SC 229.164 and *OTP* 2.328.

[108] On its already influencing the LXX, cf. section B. 4.4 below.

[109] Cf. BDB 820, as well as the verb פסג on p. 819, which in rabbinic Hebrew means "to divide" (Jastrow 1191).

be just before his death) in Deut 3:27; and finally in 34:1, the site where he dies and is buried (v 6).

Targums *Onqelos, Pseudo-Jonathan,* and the *Fragment Targum* where available always have רמתא for פסגה in the above passages. *Targum Neofiti 1* has the variant רמתה , with an *he* instead of an *aleph* as the final letter. Two of the relevant passages demonstrate this.

Targ. Pseud.-Jon. Num 21:20 states that the well "disappeared from them [the Israelites] at the border of the Moabites, at the top of 'the height' (רמתא) which is oriented in the direction of Beth Jeshimon."[110] This is the same site as the Pisgah of Deut 34:1.

Targ. Pseud.-Jon. Deut 34:1 states: "Then Moses went up from the plains of Moab to Mount Nebo, the summit of 'the height' (רמתא) that is opposite Jericho."[111] This is where he then died and was buried (v 6). Martin McNamara translates the very similar formulation in *Targum Neofiti 1* as "to the top of 'Ramatha' (רמתה)."[112]

The Aramaic noun רָמָא in the singular means "height."[113] The form רָמָתָא , always found in the targums for "Pisgah," is translated by Clarke and McNamara above with the singular, as in the tradition behind *Pseudo-Philo,* Josephus and Philo of Alexandria noted above. However, it is actually the feminine plural,[114] and could be translated as "heights."[115] The term רמתא can also be considered a place name. McNamara, for example, translates the term as (the top of) "Ramatha" in *Targum Neofiti 1* on Deut 3:27; 4:49; and 34:1.[116] This may be because the place name "Beth-Ramatha" occurs at 3:17.[117]

---

[110] Rieder 2.225; Clarke 249. *Neofiti 1* (Díez Macho 4.201; McNamara 120) is very similar, and both *Onqelos* (Sperber 1.259; Grossfeld 126) and MSS "P" and "V" of the *Fragment Targum* also have רמתא (Klein 1.101 and 199, and 2.72 and 157).

[111] Rieder 2.308; Clarke 104.

[112] Díez Macho 5.295; McNamara 174. *Onqelos* (Sperber 1.352; Grossfeld 113) and the *Fragment Targum* ("VN" in Klein 1.235 and 2.192) have רמתא .

[113] Jastrow 1481, II.

[114] *Ibid.* Cf. also Franz Rosenthal, *A Grammar of Biblical Aramaic* (Wiesbaden: Otto Harrassowitz, 1963) 23.

[115] Klein inconsistently translates so on Num 21:20 and Deut 34:1 (2.72 and 192). Grossfeld has the plural at Deut 3:17 and 27 (26), as well as 4:49 (31). Harrington and Saldarini have the plural both at *Targ. Jon.* Josh 12:3 and 13:20 (*Targum Jonathan of the Former Prophets,* 37 and 39).

[116] Cf. his pp. 34, 42 (strangely with "Resh-Ramatha"), and 174.

[117] Cf. Díez Macho 5.35.

In light of the above evidence I suggest that the early, Aramaic-speaking, Palestinian Jewish Christian who first formulated the narrative of Jesus' burial borrowed the term (Joseph of) "Arimathea" from Judaic tradition available to him on the site of the death and burial of Israel's first redeemer, Moses. It was the top of "Pisgah," in Aramaic the plural רָמָתָא , "Ramatha," "the heights." It was also the same form employed for the top of "Pisgah" at the end of the Song of the Well in Num 21:20. As noted above, early Judaic tradition maintained that the well followed the Israelites to the site of Moses' death and burial, that is, the Pisgah of Deut 34:1 (with v 6). The author of Jesus' burial probably himself added an initial *aleph*, often done to place names, as shown in section A. above, n. 2. The Aramaic ארמתא was then basically correctly translated into Greek as Αριμαθαια .[118]

While this at first seems somewhat far-fetched to a modern person, it becomes more plausible if it can be shown that other terms employed to describe Joseph of "Arimathea" and his burial activity also derive from early Judaic traditions on the well and the site of Moses' death and burial. To these I now turn.

B. 4.3 A Respected Member of the Council, Waiting Expectantly for the Kingdom of God

As noted in section A. above, Mark 15:43 describes Joseph of Arimathea as "a respected member of the council (εὐσχήμων βουλευτής)," who "was also himself waiting expectantly for the kingdom of God." The "council" here refers to the Jewish council or Sanhedrin (συνέδριον) in v 1 and in 14:55. I suggest that three terms here, "respected," "member of the council," and "kingdom of God" derive from Judaic interpretation of the Song of the Well, associated via Pisgah / Ramatha in Num 21:20 with the site of Moses' death and burial, Pisgah / Ramatha, in Deut 34:1 (and 6).

a) Respected

Mark 15:43 is the only occurrence within the four Gospels of the adjective εὐσχήμων , meaning "prominent, of high standing or repute,

---

[118] This is without the rough breathing, lacking in the original Greek text, but inserted in modern NT editions because of the influence of *ha*-Ramah and *ha*-Ramatha (BDB 928, II).

noble."[119] Acts 13:50 employs it of "the leading men of the city," and 17:12 has "men of high standing" (in Thessalonica). Josephus uses the adjective in the latter sense for a faction in the city of Tiberias who were "men of high standing" (*Vita* 32).[120]

I suggest that the adjective εὐσχήμων, respected / prominent / noble, derives from Judaic interpretation of Num 21:18. It speaks of "the well that 'the leaders' sunk, that 'the nobles of the people' dug." The two terms are used here synonymously.

"The leaders" here is the plural of the Hebrew שַׂר , which can mean in biblical Hebrew "chieftain, leader," and "noble, official."[121] *Targum Onqelos* speaks here of רברביא , the plural of רַבְרְבָא : great man, prince, officer.[122] *Targum Pseudo-Jonathan* has the variant רברבניא , the plural of רַבְרְבָנָא , great man, prince.[123] *Targum Neofiti 1* reads רברבני עלמא , the great men of the world.[124] Finally, the *Fragment Targum* has רברבני עמא , the great men of the people.[125] An example of the use of רברבא in the above sense is also found in *Eccl. Rab.* 2:2 § 4. It states that once "the son of one of 'the eminent men (רברבי)' of Kabul married on the fourth day of the week."[126] This is close to the meaning of εὐσχήμων in Acts 13:50 and 17:12 and in Josephus, and would speak for the meaning "prominent" in Mark 15:43.

"The nobles of the people" in Num 21:18 is the Hebrew נְדִיבֵי הָעָם . The adjective נָדִיב can mean "*noble, princely*, in rank."[127] *Targum Onqelos* translates this phrase as רישי עמא , "the heads of the people,"[128] as does *Pseudo-Jonathan*.[129] *Neofiti 1* reads more expansively: "the intelligent ones

---

[119] BAGD 327,2.

[120] H. St. John Thackeray translates here as "respectable citizens." The word is not found in Philo and only once in the LXX (Prov 11:25), but in a different sense.

[121] BDB 978, 1. and 2. It is also employed of tribal heads (6.), and as a term of rank and dignity (7.). In rabbinic Hebrew it usually means "prince, chief" (Jastrow 1627).

[122] Jastrow 1446. Cf. Sperber 1.259 and Grossfeld 126.

[123] Jastrow 1446. Cf. Rieder 2.225 and Clarke 248-49.

[124] Díez Macho 4.199.

[125] MS "P" in Klein 1.101. MS "V" has רברבי עלמא , the great men of the world (1.199).

[126] Vilna 13; Soncino 8.54 mistakenly has Babylon, reading בבל for כבל .

[127] BDB 622, 2. Cf. for example Ps 47:10 (Eng. 9) for "the princes of the peoples," and 83:12 (Eng. 11) with "their nobles." It is not found in rabbinic Hebrew.

[128] Sperber 1.259. Grossfeld 126 has "the leaders of the people."

[129] Rieder 2.225 and Clarke 248-49.

of the people perfected it, the seventy sages who were 'distinguished.'"[130]
The latter is the Aramaic מפרשׁיּין, "distinguished ones."[131]

I suggest that the image of "the nobles of the people" in Num 21:18,
meant as a head person, a noble, a distinguished person, combined with
the meaning of its synonym in the same verse, "the leaders," "the great
men," to suggest the Aramaic רברבא or מפרשׁ to describe Joseph of
Arimathea as a great man, an eminent man, a distinguished man. This
was then appropriately translated by the relatively rare adjective
εὐσχήμων in this meaning when the Aramaic-speaking Palestinian
Jewish Christian's narrative with Joseph of Arimathea was translated
into Greek. This suggestion is corroborated by the following two
expressions.

b) The Council / Sanhedrin

Mark 15:43 says Joseph of Arimathea was a respected "member of the
council" (βουλευτής).[132] In the NT this noun is only found here and in
the parallel passage Luke 23:50. It refers back to the Jewish council or
Sanhedrin in Mark 15:1 and 14:55.[133] I suggest that Joseph's being a
member of it also derives from Judaic tradition regarding Num 21:18.

MS "P" of *Frag. Targ.* Num 21:18 states that the well "had been
perfected by the seventy wise men of 'the Sanhedrin' [סנהדרין] of
Israel."[134] MS "V" is slightly different, noting regarding the well: "which
the sages [lit. intelligence] of the world, 'the Sanhedrin,' the seventy wise
men who had been selected, had perfected."[135] The number seventy
derives from Num 11:16, where the Lord instructs Moses to gather that
many elders in order to help him.[136] *Targum Neofiti 1* on Num 21:18 also
mentions the seventy sages, meant as the Sanhedrin.[137] Retrojecting
Second Temple practice back into the time of the wandering in the
wilderness, all four targums speak of "the scribes of Israel" as members

---

[130] Díez Macho 4.199; McNamara 119-20.
[131] Cf. Jastrow 1242-43 with פרשׁ as to distinguish, here the pael pass. participle.
[132] Cf. BAGD 145, as well as Josephus, *Bell.* 2.405.
[133] On the history of the Sanhedrin, also called βουλή and γερουσία , cf. Schürer,
The history 2.199-226. Its references to the nobility and scribes in the council are
important for the previous and the following discussions.
[134] Klein 1.101 and 2.72.
[135] Klein 1.199 and 2.157.
[136] Moses as the seventy-first person would be able to break a tie vote. On this
number, cf. Schürer, *The history* 2.210-11.
[137] Cf. Díez Macho 4.199 and McNamara 119-20.

of this body. For *Pseudo-Jonathan, Neofiti 1*, and the two versions of the *Fragment Targum* these scribes are Moses and Aaron.[138]

Rabbinic comment on the next verse, Num 21:19, substantiates this targumic interpretation. Three different sites mentioned there are interpreted in *Num. Rab.* Ḥuqqath 19/26 as "the Sanhedrin on the Temple Mount," "the Sanhedrin in the Temple Court beside the Altar," and "the Sanhedrin in the Chamber of Hewn Stones."[139]

It thus appears that the "Sanhedrin" imagery still found in the targums on Num 21:18, supplemented by similar rabbinic comment on the next verse, influenced the Aramaic-speaking Palestinian Jewish Christian who composed the Joseph of Arimathea narrative to label him not only a noble, respected person, but also "a member of the council," i.e. the Sanhedrin. In the Gospel of John he is aided in burying Jesus by Nikodemus (19:39-42), who in 3:1 is characterized as "a leader [ἄρχων] of the Jews," in v 10 as "a teacher of Israel," and in 7:50 as "one of them," i.e. the chief priests and Pharisees (v 45; cf. v 48). This certainly means that he was also thought of as a member of the Sanhedrin.

c) Waiting Expectantly for the Kingdom of God

Joseph of Arimathea is described in Mark 15:43 not as a disciple of Jesus, as in the later embellished tradition in Matt 27:57 and John 19:38, but as "waiting expectantly for 'the kingdom of God.'" The latter is the Greek τὴν βασιλείαν τοῦ θεοῦ , also found in Luke 23:51. The Aramaic-speaking Palestinian Jewish Christian who first described Joseph of Arimathea also appears to have modeled "the kingdom of God" here on early Judaic tradition on Num 21:18, the same verse which was the basis for a) and b) above.

The LXX has a major variant reading at this point: "The well, the leaders dug it. The kings of the earth hewed it out of rock 'in their kingdom,' in their being powerful." "In their kingdom" is the Greek ἐν τῇ βασιλείᾳ αὐτῶν . I suggest that this early, definitely pre-Christian Judaic tradition[140] was also known in Palestine in Aramaic and also employed by an Aramaic-speaking Jewish Christian to describe Joseph of Arimathea. The "kingdom" was then expanded very slightly to "of the

[138] The references to the respective passages are the same as those made previously.
[139] Mirkin 10.240; Soncino 6.776-77. On these three courts, cf. *m. Sanh.* 11:2 (Albeck 4.207; Danby 399; Neusner 607-08).
[140] Cf. n. 146 below. Philo allegorizes this verse in *Ebr.* 113; see also *Mos.* 1.256.

Lord,"[141] and later correctly translated into the Greek of the Gospel as τοῦ θεοῦ , the kingdom "of God," as found thirteen other times in the Gospel of Mark.

The cumulative evidence is thus strong that the Jewish Christian who characterized Joseph of Arimathea in Mark 15:43 did so by employing three different terms from Judaic tradition on only one biblical verse, Num 21:18, part of the Song of the Well. It was this well which in Judaic tradition stopped its forty-year wandering through the wilderness on the top of Pisgah, at "Ramatha," precisely on the day when Moses died and at the site where he died and was buried. The composer of the Gospel narrative then transferred this imagery from the scene of the death and burial of Israel's first redeemer, Moses, to the scene of the death and burial of its final redeemer, the Messiah Jesus, describing Joseph of "Arimathea" in terms from the same complex.

B. 4.4   A Tomb Hewn out of the Rock

According to the narrative of Jesus' burial in Mark 15:42-47, Joseph of Arimathea received permission from Pilate to take down Jesus' body from the Cross. He first wrapped it in the linen cloth he had bought for this purpose "and laid it in a tomb that had been hewn out of the rock. He then rolled a stone against the door of the tomb" (v 46). It is not mentioned what he did at this point. It is simply assumed that he departed and, as a pious Jew, kept the Sabbath by resting.

The above phrase "in a tomb that had been hewn out of the rock" is the Greek: ἐν μνημείῳ ὃ ἦν λελατομημένον ἐκ πέτρας . The verb λατομέω means "to hew out of the rock."[142] It is also used with a tomb in LXX Isa 22:16. As noted before, in the NT the verb occurs only here and in the parallel account in Matt 27:60. While the Fourth Evangelist omits a description of what the tomb was made of in 19:41-42, Luke in 23:53 speaks of "a rock-hewn tomb" (μνήματι λαξευτῷ). The latter adjective, λαξευτός , means "hewn out of the rock."[143]

I suggest that the above terminology, both the verbal form and the adjective meaning "hewn out of the rock," derives from the site of the burial of Israel's first redeemer, Moses. As stated above, it was the same site where according to Judaic tradition the well stopped after accompanying the Israelites for forty years in the wilderness.

---

141 Cf. the Aramaic in Karl Georg Kuhn, art. βασιλεύς etc. in *TDNT* 1.571.
142 BAGD 467,1; LSJ 1031: to quarry, hew out.
143 BAGD 466.

The Hebrew of (Mount) "Pisgah" is transliterated in the LXX as Φασγα at Deut 3:17; 34:1; Josh 12:3; and 13:20. Yet it is rendered by τὸ Λελαξευμένον [144] in Num 21:20; 23:14; Deut 3:17 B; and 3:27. This derives from λαξεύω , "to hew in stone,"[145] a synonym of λατομέω employed in Mark 15:46 and Matt 27:60. Here it is conceived of as a toponym: "The Place Hewn Out of Rock." To understand it better, a variant translation should also be considered.

The Hebrew "Pisgah" is also rendered in LXX Deut 4:49 by λαξευτός , "rock-hewn," the same adjective used for Jesus' tomb in Luke 23:53. Aquila also employed it to translate "Pisgah" at Num 21:20; 23:14; Deut 34:1; and Josh 13:20. This shows that λελαξευμένος and λαξευτός are synonyms, as they should also be considered in Mark 15:46 and Luke 23:53, both associated with Joseph of Arimathea.

The above LXX translations of the Hebrew of "Pisgah" are very old. They go back at least to the second, if not to the middle of the third century BCE.[146] I suggest that while they refer to the same site ("Pisgah"), they also recall two events from very early Judaic tradition which "merged" there.

The Hebrew of Deut 34:6 states of the Lord and Moses: "And He buried him in a valley in the land of Moab...." Here God Himself, alone, takes care of Moses' burial, which helps to explain why "no one knows his burial site / grave up to today" (*ibid.*). The LXX, however, already changes this to καὶ ἔθαψαν αὐτὸν ἐν Γαι ἐν γῇ Μωαβ : "And 'they buried' him in Gai in the land of Moab." Here "they buried" refers to the Israelites, and the Hebrew ‎גי , "valley," has probably also become a toponym. The area, however, is definitely thought of as the same as Φασγα or "The Place Hewed Out of Rock" in v 1. The Israelites are thus conceived of here in pre-Christian Judaic tradition as burying Moses in a tomb "hewn out of rock."[147] What was true of Israel's first redeemer, Moses, was then transferred by a Palestinian Jewish Christian to the burial of Israel's final or great redeemer, the Messiah Jesus. Joseph of Arimathea is also represented as burying Jesus in a tomb "that had been hewn out of the rock."

---

[144] Originally, of course, this was in capital letters. The present form of the text is a (correct) choice made by the modern LXX editors.
[145] LSJ 1029.
[146] Cf. Otto Eissfeldt, *The Old Testament. An Introduction* (Oxford: Basil Blackwell, 1966) 604-05.
[147] The alternative translation, "quarry," makes no sense in the context of Moses' burial (in a tomb).

It cannot be overemphasized that both what the LXX rendered as τὸ Λελαξευμένον , "The Place Hewn Out of Rock," and λαξευτός , "hewn out of rock," represent the Hebrew place name "Pisgah," the site of Moses' death and burial. Pisgah, in turn, was rendered by all four extant targums as רמתא / רמתה , "Ramatha," the source of the place name Joseph of "Arimathea," as proposed above. The Palestinian Jewish-Christian author of Jesus' burial narrative thus derived both his images of Joseph of "Arimathea" and "hewn out of rock" from early Judaic tradition known to him in regard to one single word, "Pisgah," the site of both Moses' death and burial.

The second event connected in pre-Septuagintal Judaic tradition to Pisgah was the well's stopping there after accompanying the Israelites in the wilderness for forty years. The LXX at Num 21:18 first states: "The well, the leaders dug it. The kings of the earth hewed it out of rock in their kingdom, in their being powerful." The Greek of "to dig" here is ὀρύσσω , which means both to dig and to bury.[148] The same is true for the Hebrew behind it, חפר,[149] in rabbinic Hebrew.[150] The Greek verb for "hewed it out of rock" here in the LXX is ἐκλατομέω , to hew out of rock / stone.[151] It is a fuller form of the same verb, λατομέω , employed in Mark 15:46 in connection with Jesus' burial. The original Hebrew text has כָּרָה , to dig, also used both of a well and a grave.[152] The two Hebrew verbs employed of the well in Num 21:18 thus made it easy for a Palestinian Jewish Christian with this incident in mind to associate the digging of the well with the act of burying a person. The same was true for a Hellenistic Jewish Christian working with the LXX of the same verse in mind.

According to LXX Num 21:20 the final stop of the well in the wilderness was the top of τὸ Λελαξευμένον , "The Place Hewn Out of Rock" (Hebrew "Pisgah"). Since the top of a mountain always consisted of rock, it was natural for very early Judaic tradition behind the LXX to imagine the shaft of the well at this point as also "hewn out of rock."

Early Judaic tradition thus combined Pisgah, "The Place Hewn Out of Rock," with both the final resting site of the well, which disappeared on

---

[148] LSJ 1257: dig, with IV., bury.

[149] BDB 343,1.a.: dig, with examples of wells.

[150] Cf. Jastrow 493: to dig, hollow out; to dig graves. The noun חֶפֶר also means "grave-digging," and חָפִיר (p. 491) "one for whom a grave is dug."

[151] LSJ 511, I. In reproducing this text, Philo has the simple λατομέω in *Ebr.* 113. A broader description of the well is given in *Mos.* 1.255-56.

[152] BDB 500. The noun בְּרָה is either a cistern or a well (*ibid.*).

the very day of Moses' death, and the site of his death and burial (Deut 34:1 and 6). This is important to note because, as will be shown in the next chapter, the scene of Jesus' Resurrection from the tomb, which was "hewn out of rock," was formulated in terms of another Judaic tradition on what was considered to be the same well, Gen 28:10 and 29:1-14.[153]

Finally, one may ask whether 1 Cor 10:4 is also connected to the above traditions. The Apostle Paul states there that the Israelites in the wilderness "all drank the same spiritual drink. For they drank from the spiritual rock that followed them, and the rock was Christ." Did the Jewish Christians from whom Paul borrowed this haggadah thus also believe that Christ, as the rock / well, continued to give the Israelites water until they reached "The Place Hewn Out of Rock," i.e. Pisgah, which was also the site of the death and burial of Israel's first redeemer, Moses? While the question cannot be answered with certainty, if it was the case, 1 Cor 10:4 would be one more indication that the site of Moses' death and burial in early, pre-Gospel, Jewish Christian tradition was associated with the Messiah (the Christ or Anointed One). He was the "rock," who as the famous well of Judaic lore gave the Israelites very special water up to and including that point, "Pisgah." The latter, both as the final site of the well and of Moses' death and burial, was "hewn out of rock," like the site of Jesus' own burial in Mark 15:46.

After Joseph of Arimathea laid Jesus' body in a tomb that had been hewn out of the rock, he "rolled a stone against the door of the tomb" (v 46). The latter is a prelude to the incident of the "empty tomb" three days later, on Easter Sunday, in Mark 16:1-8. To this I now turn.

---

[153] All of the above points to the Joseph of "Arimathea" incident in Mark 15:42-47, including the specific description of him in v 43, as not being historical. Instead, as stated at the outset, Jesus' body was very probably placed by a servant / slave of the Sanhedrin / Council in one of the burying grounds reserved for criminals. The present narrative removes the terrible offence of a criminal burial for the Messiah by having a "respected" member of the Sanhedrin (which had just strongly advocated Jesus' death!) himself bury him elsewhere at a non-described site. Yet its primary purpose is to prepare in a concrete way for the following scene of the Resurrection, the end of the Passion Narrative and the Gospel's finale: the empty tomb. Mark 15:42-47 is thus a haggadic dramatization. The question of the relationship of haggadah to historicity will be extensively analyzed in chapter IV. below.

III. The Resurrection of Jesus, and the Translation of Moses in Judaic Tradition

A. The Resurrection of Jesus[1]

After Joseph of Arimathea rolled a stone against the door of Jesus' tomb (Mark 15:46), he apparently departed, never to be heard of again. In 16:4 this stone is described as "very large."[2] One sign that the narrative of 16:1-8 is artificially constructed is the strange question asked by Mary Magdalene, Mary the mother of James, and Salome when they are on the way to Jesus' grave: "Who will roll away the stone for us from the entrance to the tomb?" (v 3). Mary Magdalene and Mary the mother of (James the younger and of) Joses had seen where Jesus' body was laid (15:47; cf. v 40 with Salome). They thus could have informed Salome, who accompanied them to the grave on Sunday morning that there was a "very large" stone before its entrance. In addition, they as three women, certainly with at least the equivalent strength of an average man, are represented as incapable of rolling it away: it was simply too large and too heavy.[3] This is a sign that the women's strange question in 16:3 may stem from elsewhere and have been inserted in modified form at this point.

---

[1] For bibliography on Jesus' Resurrection, cf. Craig A. Evans, *Mark 8:27 - 16:20*, 526-29, with 522-26 especially on Mark 16:1-8; Gary Habermas, "Resurrection Research from 1975 to the Present: What Are Critical Scholars Saying?" in *JSHJ* 3 (2005) 135-53; and Casey Elledge, "Contemporary Studies on Resurrection: An Annotated Bibliography," in James Charlesworth et al., *Resurrection: The Origin and Future of a Biblical Doctrine* (Faith and Scholarship Colloquies; New York / London: T & T Clark International, 2006) 233-40.

[2] This could also be translated as "extremely" large. Cf. BAGD 796 on σφόδρα : very (much), extremely, greatly.

[3] The best example of such a large, heavy, round stone before a grave in Jerusalem is "Herod's Family Tomb" behind the King David Hotel. Cf. the description in Küchler, *Jerusalem* 1024-29. He notes that the stone is 1.3 meters high and 31 cm in diameter (p. 1027). See also the next note.

In addition, the archaeologist Amos Kloner has determined that in the first century BCE to 70 CE, some 98% of the stones employed to close a tomb ("blocking stones") in the Jerusalem area were not round, but in the shape of a square.[4] Mark 15:46 does not indicate the size or shape of the stone Joseph of Arimathea "rolled against" the tomb into which he had placed Jesus' body. Only in 16:3 is it considered to be round (and capable of being "rolled away"), and in v 4 it is labeled "very large" and "rolled back." I suggest that this phenomenon of the stone's being characterized as "round," in contrast to overwhelming archaeological evidence for Jerusalem grave stones being square at this time, here points to the use of Judaic tradition in regard to a different "rolling away a large [round] stone" as a major part of the imagery employed by the Palestinian Jewish Christian author of the unit 16:1-8.

The angel inside Jesus' tomb also tells the three women: "Look, there is the place 'they laid' him" (v 6). "They laid" is the Greek ἔθηκαν, third person plural. Yet it was only one person, Joseph of Arimathea, who in 15:46 "laid" (ἔθηκεν, third person singular) Jesus there. The account is thus inconsistent here and points to a new tradition which informed the unit 16:1-8.[5]

---

[4] Cf. his "Did a Rolling Stone Close Jesus' Tomb?" in *BAR* 25/5 (1999) 23-29, 76. See his p. 23: "Of the more than 900 burial caves from the Second Temple period found in and around Jerusalem, only four are known to have used round (disk-shaped) blocking stones." The large rolling stones of "Herod's Family" behind the King David Hotel, and the tomb of Queen Helena of Adiabene (the "Tombs of the Kings") are pictured on pp. 22-23 and 27 respectively. On the latter, see Küchler, *Jerusalem* 990. Kloner incorrectly asserts (p. 29) that the root *galal* can mean not only "to roll," but also "to move." Yet see BDB 164 and Jastrow 249 for only "to roll." In her *Jewish Funerary Customs, Practices and Rites in the Second Temple Period* (JSJSup 94; Leiden / Boston: Brill, 2005), Rachel Hachlili also notes the round rolling-stones of the tombs of Queen Helena of Adiabene and Herod's Family (36-41), yet also notes another near the latter (41), as well as one each on Mt. Scopus, in the Hinnom Valley and the Kidron Valley (64), two more than known to Kloner. It should be noted, however, that at least the first four belong to "monumental graves."

[5] One should avoid the temptation to harmonize the Gospels by thinking of Nikodemus' aiding Joseph of Arimathea in John 19:38-42. In the Synoptics, Joseph of Arimathea acts alone. There is no indication that he "would have had the help of servants or slaves" (Adela Yarbro Collins, *Mark* 795). On Mark 16:1-8 as originally an independent pericope (cf. e.g. the different names of the women in v 1), yet nevertheless part of the Passion Narrative, see Frederick Grant, "The Gospel According to St. Mark," in *IB* (1951) 7.911; Vincent Taylor, *The Gospel According to St. Mark* (London: Macmillan, 1966²) 602; and above all Eduard

The angel also instructs the women: "Go, tell his [Jesus'] disciples and Peter[6] that he is going ahead of you to Galilee; there you will see him, just as he told you" (16:7). This refers back to 14:28, where after the "Lord's Supper" and before the Gethsemane incident, Jesus informs his disciples: "After I am raised up, I will go before you to Galilee." This statement is made directly after Jesus tells the disciples in v 27 that "You will all become deserters," fulfilling Zech 13:7. This then actually takes place in Mark 14:50, where in Gethsemane "All of them deserted him and fled." It should be assumed that the disciples (without Judas Iscariot)[7] now fled for their lives, leaving Jerusalem immediately for their homes in Galilee. As suspected and certainly sought after fellow conspirators of a political "Messiah," they had a one day head start (on Friday) to avoid being arrested before the obligatory Sabbath rest began.[8] In spite of the

---

Schweizer, *Das Evangelium nach Markus* (NTD 1; Göttingen: Vandenhoeck & Ruprecht, 1978[15]) 201.

[6] This infelicitous formulation may derive from the same tradition behind 1 Cor 15:5, where Jesus "appeared to Cephas [Peter], then to the twelve." It presupposes that Judas had already been replaced, as indicated in Acts 1:15-26. It does not mean "but especially Peter" because of his denial in 14:66-72 (against Evans, *Mark 8:27 - 16:20*, 537, agreeing with Vincent Taylor). See especially John 21:15-17, where after Jesus appears to the disciples at the Sea of Tiberias he commissions Peter three times to feed / tend his lambs / sheep. Luke 22:32, after Satan has "sifted" all the disciples like wheat, also has Jesus tell Simon Peter: "and you, when once you have turned back, strengthen your brothers." This probably originally referred to Peter's "conversion" through an appearance of the risen Jesus in Galilee.

[7] On him, cf. my essay "The Name Judas 'Iscariot' and Ahithophel in Judaic Tradition" in *My Name Is "Legion." Palestinian Judaic Traditions in Mark 5:1-20 and Other Gospel Texts*, 155-208.

[8] This would have gotten them at least a third of the way back to Galilee by the straightest route available, passing north through Samaria. It was also the most popular route for Galileans. Cf. Shmuel Safrai, *Die Wallfahrt im Zeitalter des Zweiten Tempels* (Forschungen zum jüdisch-christlichen Dialog 3; Neukirchen: Neukirchener Verlag, 1981) 135-37. The disciples would have taken Jesus' female followers along, such as Mary Magdalene and the others mentioned in Mark 15:40(-41) and 16:1. Women did not travel alone, even in groups, because of banditry and other possible perils of the journey. This means female knowledge of the exact tomb into which Jesus' body was laid is secondary (15:47). Their "looking on from a distance" in 15:40 is also secondary, based on imagery employed of those "standing at a distance to watch" the scapegoat go to its death. See *m. Yoma* 6:5 and the discussion in my *The Wicked Tenants and Gethsemane* 121-22. I agree with Rudolf Bultmann in his *The History of the Synoptic Tradition* (New York: Harper & Row, 1963) 385-86 that Mark 16:7 implies the disciples are

176   *The Resurrection of Jesus, and the Translation of Moses*

statement of 16:7, Jesus' disciples were thus no longer in Jerusalem. Later, in Galilee, Jesus did indeed appear to them, as indicated in 14:28; 16:7; John 21; and Matt 28:16-17. One major emphasis of the narrative of the empty tomb accordingly is to point to the later appearances of Jesus to his disciples (and others) in Galilee.

Finally, 16:5 states that the three women "were astonished / amazed." Therefore the angel in the tomb tells them in v 6: "Do not be astonished / amazed." I suggest that this is the correct translation of the Greek verb ἐκθαμβέομαι here, and not "be alarmed" (NRSV), since the expression derives from Judaic tradition on the reaction to Jacob's "rolling back a large stone" (see below, section B. 1.10).

B.   The Translation of Moses in Judaic Tradition

As pointed out in chapter II. above, Judaic lore on the well which accompanied the Israelites for forty years in the wilderness was intimately connected to the place where Moses died and was buried: Pisgah. Other Judaic traditions on what was considered to be the same well, however, provide the basic framework for the story of the empty tomb and will thus first be analyzed here before I proceed in section 2. to the subject of Moses' "translation" at the end of his life.

B. 1   The Well and the Empty Tomb

In the Mishnah tractate 'Avot 5:6 it is stated that "the mouth of the well" (פִּי הַבְּאֵר - of Num 21:16-18) was one of ten things created on the Eve of the first Sabbath at twilight, i.e. after the six days of creation.[9] It should be noted that "some" maintained that the grave of Moses was also created then,[10] allowing these two objects to be so associated in Judaic tradition.

Ps 105:41-42 states in regard to God's miraculously creating the well for the Israelites in the wilderness: "He opened the rock, and water

---

represented as still in Jerusalem. Because their flight to Galilee was purposely omitted, "it is necessary to have the disciples artificially despatched to Galilee in order to achieve congruity with the old Easter tradition, and this actually happened in the editing of Mk. 16:7 and 14:28." Yet the latter two notes were not creations of Mark, but "from the tradition" (385).

[9] Albeck 4.376; Danby 456; Neusner 686. Cf. Appendix II in Saldarini, *The Fathers According to Rabbi Nathan (B)* 306-10 for numerous other passages with the mouth of the well, or simply the well.

[10] *Ibid.*

gushed out; it flowed through the desert like a river. 42) For He remembered His holy promise, and Abraham, His servant." This mention of Abraham is reflected in the three Palestinian targums on Num 21:18, which are almost identical. *Neofiti 1*, for example, reads regarding the three Patriarchs: "It is the well which the princes of the world, Abraham, Isaac and Jacob, dug from the beginning; the intelligent ones of the people perfected it, the seventy sages who were distinguished; the scribes of Israel, Moses and Aaron, measured it with their rods; and from the wilderness it was given to them as a gift."[11]

The Patriarchs' digging the well "from the beginning" is reflected in Judaic tradition on the ninth of the ten trials of Abraham, when he sent away Hagar and Ishmael in Gen 21:8-21. *Pirq. R. El.* 30 states on this that when Ishmael was about to die of thirst: "The well which was created at twilight was opened for them there, and they went and drank and filled the bottle with water, as it is said: 'Then God opened her eyes and she saw a well of water. She went and filled the skin with water, and gave the boy a drink' (Gen 21:19). And there they left the well."[12] The latter refers to the wilderness of "Beer-sheba" in v 14.

Gen 26:16 refers to the wells Abraham had dug, which Isaac re-dug (v 18). Three other wells were dug by Isaac's servants (vv 19-22) before he went to Beer-sheba (v 23). In *Pirq. R. El.* 35 it is stated in this regard: "Every place where our fathers went, the well [singular] went in front of them, and they dug three times and found it before them. Abraham dug three times and found it before him, as it is said: 'Isaac dug again the wells of water that had been dug in the days of his father Abraham' (26:18). And Isaac dug in the land (of Canaan) four times and found it

---

[11] Díez Macho 4.199; McNamara 119-20. Cf. *Pseudo-Jonathan* in Rieder 2.225, Clarke 248-49; and the *Fragment Targum*, MSS "P" and "V" in Klein 1.101, 199 and 2.72 and 157.

[12] Eshkol 100; Friedlander 218. It should also be noted that *Targ. Ps.-Jon.* Gen 21:19 states that "a well of water was *revealed* to her [Hagar, by the Lord]..." (Rieder 1.29; Maher 76). This is considered the same well as in 16:13-14, where it is called in v 14 "Beer-lahai-roi" (בְּאֵר לַחַי רֹאִי), "the well of the Living One who sees me." The latter phrase is also found in 24:62 and 25:11, dealing with the well at Isaac's dwelling place. Both the usually reticent *Targum Onqelos* as well as the three Palestinian targums emphasize in regard to the last three passages that the Glory of the Lord (or the living angel) was *revealed* to Hagar and Isaac here. Divine revelation thus was thought to take place at the well, which may be related to the message of the angel in Mark 16:5-7. The passage is modeled in part on the scene of Isaac's son Jacob at the well in Gen 29:1-14 (see the following).

before him, as it is said: 'Isaac's servants dug in the valley' (v 19)."[13] At the age of seventy-seven, Jacob then departed "from his father's house, and the well went before him from Beer-sheba[14] to Mount Moriah," where he had a dream at "Bethel." The latter is interpreted here as elsewhere not as a town, but as the "House of God" (*beth-El*), the Temple in Jerusalem. Afterwards Jacob left the well and in the twinkle of an eye came to Haran.[15] It should be noted that in all the above instances, only one specific well is spoken of. It is always considered to be the same well, which later accompanied the Israelites for forty years in the wilderness.[16]

Judaic tradition relates that three famous men met their future mates at the (same) well. *Exod. Rab.* Shemoth 32 on Exod 2:15, "And he [Moses] dwelt in the land of Midian; and he sat down by a well," relates: "He adopted the practice of his ancestors. Three met their marriage-partners at the well - Isaac, Jacob and Moses. Isaac - as it is written: 'And Isaac came from the way of Beer-lahai-roi' (Gen 24:62).[17] And also Rebekah met Eleazar at the well.[18] Jacob - 'and he looked, and behold a well in the field' (29:2). Moses - 'And he sat down by a well.'"[19] This led to Moses' receiving Zipporah as his wife (Exod 2:21). *Tanḥ.* Shemoth 11 on Exod 2:16 states that Laban tells his seven daughters, including Zipporah: "All that you have told me concerning his [Moses'] drawing the water from the well and watering the flock is, indeed, a sign that he is a descendant of those who stood at the well, for the well recognized its master."[20] Regarding Moses' watering the flock of the seven daughters (Exod 2:17), *'Avot R. Nat.* A 20 says: "So long as Moses remained standing at the mouth of the well, the waters [miraculously] continued to flow and rise

---

13 Eshkol 126; Friedlander 263, with notes 2-4.
14 This may either be thought of as the "Well of the Oath" or "Well of the Seven" (ewe lambs). See Gen 21:31.
15 Eshkol 126, 128; Friedlander 263-64, 266-67.
16 In *Gen. Rab.* Vayeṣe 70/8 on "a well in the field" in Gen 29:1, R. Ḥama b. Ḥanina, a second generation Palestinian Amora (*Introduction* 96), interprets this as "the well." The Soncino translator, H. Freedman, remarks in n. 1: "Which supplied Israel with water in the wilderness, v. Num. xxi, 17f." (Theodor and Albeck 805; Soncino 2.641).
17 "Beer-lahai-roi" means "The well at which God appeared to the living": S. Lehrman in Soncino 3.39, n. 5. Cf. also Gen 16:14, 25:11, and n. 12 above.
18 Cf. Gen 24:11 and 20.
19 Mirkin 5.48; Soncino 3.39-40. A parallel is found in *Tanḥ.* Shemoth 10 (Eshkol 216; Berman 328).
20 Eshkol 217; Berman 330.

up toward him. When he stepped back, the waters receded."[21] This motif is borrowed from early Judaic tradition on the well of Num 21:16-20, which accompanied the Israelites in the wilderness for forty years.[22] It shows how all the wells mentioned in Scripture beforehand were also considered to be the same well. Most important for the narrative of the empty tomb in Mark 16:1-8, however, is Jacob's encounter with his future wife Rachel at the well in Genesis 29.[23]

When Isaac blessed his son Jacob and told him not to take a Canaanite wife, he instructed him to go to Paddan-aram and marry a daughter of Laban, his wife Rebekah's brother (Gen 28:1-2). Thus he went to "the land of the people of the east" (29:1). There he saw a "well" in the field, from which the flocks of sheep were watered. "The 'stone' on the well's mouth was 'large' (v 2), and when all the [other] flocks were gathered there, [all] the shepherds would 'roll the stone' from the mouth of the well, and water the sheep, and put 'the stone' back in its place on the mouth of the well" (v 3). Jacob speaks to the (three) shepherds,[24] who are from Haran and inform him that they know Laban. When Jacob suggests that the shepherds in broad daylight should not have simply gathered the animals together at the well, but should instead water and pasture them now, they respond: "We cannot until all the flocks are gathered together, and 'the stone is rolled' from the mouth of the well; then we water the sheep" (v 8).

During Jacob's conversation with the male shepherds, Rachel arrives with her father Laban's sheep. Then "Jacob [alone] went up and 'rolled the stone' from the well's mouth, and watered the flock of his mother's brother, Laban" (v 10). He kisses Rachel, discloses his identity, and ends up after many years of service with two wives, the sisters Leah and Rachel (vv 12-30). I will now indicate how this enchanting narrative, primarily in Judaic tradition, forms a major part of the background of

---

[21] Schechter 72; Goldin 96.

[22] Cf. for example *t. Sukk.* 3:11, "surging and gurgling upward" (Lieberman, *Mo'ed* 268-69; Zuckermandel-Liebermann [sic] 196; Neusner 2.220). In *Tanḥ. Bereshit* 4 on Gen 1:1, R. Ḥanina b. Gamliel II, an older second generation Tanna (*Introduction* 82), states that normally water descends (as rain) from above, but God produced the opposite by "causing water to ascend from below," as in Num 21:17 (Eshkol 2.8-9; Berman 15; before this he mentions the other wilderness gift of manna).

[23] The latter is described extensively, for example, in *Gen. Rab.* Vayeṣe 70/8 on Gen 29:1 (Theodor and Albeck 805-06, with parallels in the notes; Soncino 2.641, with notes 1-4).

[24] One for each of the three flocks.

Mark 16:1-8. First, I indicate five similarities from the biblical narrative itself.

B. 1.1-3   Rolling Away a Large Stone from a Mouth / Opening / Entrance / Door

B. 1.1   Mark 16:3-4 has Mary Magdalene, Mary the mother of James, and Salome at Jesus' tomb ask: "Who will 'roll away' the stone for us from the entrance to the tomb?' 4) When they looked up, they saw that the stone, which was very large, had already 'been rolled back.'" The Greek of "to roll away / back" here is ἀποκυλίω , found only here in the NT along with the two parallel passages in Matt 28:2 and Luke 24:2.[25] It is not found in Philo, and in Josephus only twice in the passive, meaning, however, to tumble down or fall.[26] In the LXX it occurs only four times, once in Judith 13:9 of her "rolling" Holophernes' body off her bed. The other three occasions are precisely in the narrative described above, at Gen 29:3, 8 and 10, the relevance of which the great majority of commentators up to now have missed. The Hebrew text employs גָּלַל here, also "to roll away."[27]

---

[25] BAGD 94. In 15:46 (// Matt 27:60) the verb προσκυλίω is employed of Joseph of Arimathea's "rolling [a stone] up to" the door of the tomb (BAGD 716). The verb is found neither in the LXX, Philo, nor Josephus, and is simply a variant translation of גלל (see below).

[26] Cf. *Ant.* 4.284 and 5.359.

[27] BDB 164. It is used in this chapter twice in the qal, and once in the hiphil. See also Jastrow 249. To my knowledge only Julius Wellhausen in *Das Evangelium Marci* (Berlin: Georg Reimer, 1903) 144-45 correctly thought that Mark 16:3-4 recalls the cover of a well as in Genesis 29, and that the latter narrative influenced the former. He omitted this assertion, however, in the second edition of 1909 (p. 136). Vincent Taylor in *The Gospel According to St. Mark* 605 called attention to LXX Gen 29:3, 8 and 10 (together with Judith 13:9 as examples of "late Greek"). Michael Goulder in "The Empty Tomb" in *Theology* 79 (1976) 206-14 relates the rolling away in Genesis 29 to the Markan narrative (212). Yet he, like Wellhausen and Taylor, is unaware of its development in Judaic tradition. Instead, he considers the rolling away of Joshua 10 to be the main source of the imagery in the empty tomb incident (209, 213). It should also be recalled that the well which accompanied the Israelites for forty years in the wilderness and disappeared at the top of Pisgah / *Ramatha*, the site of Moses' burial, was described in Judaic tradition as shaped like a round stone which "rolled" along (root *galal*; see section II. B.3 above).

B. 1.2   While the size of "the stone" (ὁ λίθος) which is rolled unto or
away from Jesus' tomb in Mark 15:46 and 16:3 is not described, 16:4 notes
that it was "very large," μέγας σφόδρα . I suggest that this motif is
an haggadic embellishment of Gen 29:2, which states that "the stone"
(MT הָאֶבֶן , LXX λίθος) on the mouth of the well, which Jacob later
rolled away, was "large" (MT גְדֹלָה , LXX μέγας).

B. 1.3   Mark 15:46 states that Joseph of Arimathea rolled a stone against
the "door" of the tomb into which he had laid Jesus. In 16:3 the women
ask: "Who will roll away the stone for us from 'the entrance / door' of the
tomb?" Both instances are the Greek ἡ θύρα.[28] I suggest that it is based
on the "mouth" of the well in Genesis 29, emphasized by five-fold
repetition in vv 2, 3 (twice), 8 and 10. The Hebrew for "mouth" here is
פֶה , which the LXX translates literally as τὸ στόμα . A cave can also have
a פֶה in Josh 10:18 ("Roll large stones against 'the mouth' of the cave, and
set men by it to guard them [the five kings hidden there])," 22 ("Open
'the mouth' of the cave"), and 27 ("they set large stones against 'the
mouth' of the cave"). Here a cave becomes the five kings' tomb (v 27).[29] It
thus seems probable that the five-fold "mouth" of Genesis 29 was
modified slightly by the early Palestinian Jewish Christian who
composed the narrative of Mark 16:1-8 to "door / entrance," פֶתַח in
Hebrew, פִתְחָא in Aramaic.[30] The latter Hebrew term is found in 1 Kgs
19:13 of a cave, where Elijah stands "at 'the door / entrance / mouth' of
the cave." A cave could thus be thought of as having either a "mouth" or
a "door," these being synonyms.

The well with its "mouth / entrance" in Gen 29:2, 3, 8 and 10 was
thought of in Judaic tradition (see below) as the same well which
accompanied the Israelites for forty years in the wilderness until it finally
stopped on the top of Pisgah. The latter was labeled "The Place Hewed
Out of Stone" (LXX), the same place where Moses died and was buried.
While hard for a modern person to follow, the above type of association
appears to have encouraged a Palestinian Jewish Christian to speak of

---

[28] BAGD 365,1.b: "of the door-like opening of a cave-tomb *entrance*," with
references. See also LSJ 811, II.

[29] Cf. also the "cave" of Machpelah as the burial site of Sarah (Gen 23:19),
Abraham (25:9), Isaac (35:29), and Rebekah, Jacob and Leah (49:31; 50:13).

[30] Jastrow 1252. Delitzsch employs the Hebrew form of the noun in his Hebrew
New Testament at Mark 15:46 and 16:3 (p. 97). The Hebrew New Testament of
the United Bible Societies, however, first employs פֶה at 15:46, then פֶתַח at 16:3
(p. 140).

the tomb of the final redeemer of Israel, the Messiah Jesus, as having a "mouth / entrance" or "door" just as the well was still thought to have at Pisgah. Moses is at times also represented as being buried in a "cave" (מְעָרָה), certainly thought of as having a "mouth / entrance" or "door."[31]

B. 1.4 *The Inability of Three Persons to Roll Away a Large Stone*

In Mark 15:46 one man, Joseph of Arimathea, is able to roll a stone against the tomb into which he had laid Jesus' body. Two women see where it was laid (v 47). In the following narrative of the empty tomb, there are now three women. This change in number, from two to three, seems strange. In addition, on the way to the tomb the three "had been saying to one another,[32] 'Who will roll away the stone for us from the entrance to the tomb?'" (16:4). This is because the stone was "very large" (v 4). As asked before: Didn't the three women together have at least the strength of one man? The strangeness of this question, however, becomes understandable in light of the narrative of the well in Genesis 29.

When Jacob reached the land of the people of the east, "he saw a well in the field and three flocks of sheep lying there beside it; for out of that well the flocks were watered" (Gen 29:2). Since the stone on the well's mouth was so large, the (three)[33] shepherds of the three flocks present could not roll it away. Only when "all the [other] flocks were [also] gathered there" could the [combined number of] shepherds "roll the stone away from the mouth of the well, water the sheep, and replace the stone on the mouth of the well" (v 3). This is also what the (three) shepherds say to Jacob in v 8: "We cannot [water the sheep] until all the flocks are gathered together, and the stone is rolled from the mouth of the well; then we water the sheep." The Hebrew of "we cannot" is לֹא נוּכַל , for which the LXX has οὐ δυνησόμεθα : "we will not be able to," also emphasizing the three shepherds' present inability.

---

[31] Cf. for example the Tannaitic *Sifre* Ha'azinu 337 on Deut 32:48 (Finkelstein 387; Hammer 346), and 339 on Deut 32:50, where Moses is to have the same manner of death as his brother Aaron, whom he told: "Go into the cave" (Finkelstein 389; Hammer 348).

[32] The imperfect Greek form ἔλεγον implies this.

[33] Judaic tradition reasoned that if there were three flocks, there must have been only three shepherds. Cf. for example *Gen. Rab.* Vayeṣe 70/8 on Gen 29:1, which interprets the three flocks of sheep as Moses, Aaron and Miriam (shepherds of their flock, the Israelites): Theodor and Albeck 805; Soncino 3.641.

I suggest that the number three for the women in Mark 16:1, in contrast to the two of 15:47, is based on the (three) shepherds of three flocks in Gen 29:2. The women's wondering who will roll away the very large stone for them from the entrance / door / mouth of Jesus' tomb is also based on the three shepherds' inability to roll away the stone from the mouth of the well alone. They need to wait for support from the other shepherds who also use the well. The stone is simply too large and heavy for the three of them.

B. 1.5   The Miraculous Strength of Jacob in Genesis

As just indicated, the combined strength of three male shepherds does not suffice to roll away the large stone from the mouth of the well in the narrative of Gen 29:1-14. They need much more outside aid. Yet Jacob alone in v 10 is described as going up, rolling the stone from the well's mouth, and then watering Laban's flock. While not openly stated, his strength is presumed to be phenomenal, even miraculous. As will be seen shortly, Judaic tradition labeled it a "miracle."

I suggest that the "young man, dressed in a white robe, sitting on the right side" of Jesus' tomb in Mark 16:5, is partially described in terms of Jacob here. Although not specifically stated, it is assumed that the young man is the one who rolled away the very large (and heavy) stone from the entrance / door / mouth of the tomb. Judaic tradition on Jacob's tremendous strength at this point underlines this proposal.

*   *   *

The above cluster of five points of similarity, including even an exact equivalent to the rare verb "to roll away" a stone from the entrance / door / mouth of an object (well / grave), makes it probable that the narrative of Jacob's encounter with the shepherds in Gen 29:1-14 provided a major part of the framework for the Palestinian Jewish Christian who first composed the story of the empty tomb in Mark 16:1-8. The following five points of *Judaic tradition* on Jacob's meeting with the three shepherds not only corroborate this proposal, they also add numerous important details to it.

B. 1.6   *The Liturgical Connection of Moses' Death at Pisgah, and Jacob's Encounter at the Well*

In the triennial Palestinian lectionary system, Deut 3:23-29 was read as the Torah lesson on the third or next to the last Sabbath of the month Elul in the third year. It describes Moses' begging the Lord to allow him to enter the Land. Yet the Lord tells him: "Enough from you!" Instead, he should go to the top of Pisgah and view it, appoint Joshua as his successor, (and die there - 31:14, 16; 32:49-50; 34:1). Because of the latter, much comment on Moses' death is already included in Tannaitic interpretation of Deut 3:23-29 in *Sifre* Deut. Va'ethanan 26-29 on these verses,[34] and in *Sifre* Num. Phinehas 134-36 between Num 27:12 and 13.[35]

In the first year of the Palestinian triennial lectionary system, at exactly the same time, the *seder* or Torah lesson was Gen 28:10 (-29:30).[36] This helps to explain how the Palestinian Jewish Christian who composed the framework of the narrative of the empty tomb in Mark 16:1-8 could describe the scene of rolling away the large stone from the tomb in terms of Jacob's rolling away a large stone from the well in Genesis 29. It was already connected liturgically to the death of Israel's first redeemer, Moses, in Deut 3:23-29. Liturgical influence is also visible in the Palestinian targums of the Jacob narrative, as will now be indicated.

B. 1.7   *Five Miracles Done for Jacob*

Because the Torah reading began already at Gen 28:10 (see section B. 1.6 above), all three Palestinian targums relate five miracles performed for and by Jacob in 29:1-10 already at this point.[37] *Targum Neofiti 1* is typical:

---

34 Finkelstein 36-48; Hammer 46-55.
35 Horovitz 180-83; Kuhn 550-60. It includes comment on Deut 34:1-4.
36 Cf. the chart within the art. "Triennial Cycle" by Joseph Jacobs in *JE* (1905/25) 12.254-57; the chart in the similar art. by the editors in *EJ* (1971) 15.1387-88; and the chart on p. 141 of the art. "Triennial Cycle" in *EJ* (2007) 20.140-42. Since in the first year there are five Sabbaths, this is the reading for the fourth out of the five, yet also the next to the last as in the third year. The haftarah or prophetic reading for this Sabbath in the first year was Hos 12:13 (Eng. 12). Gen 28:10(ff.) and Hos 12:13 are the Torah and haftarah readings, for example, in *Aggadat Bereshit* 46 and 47 (Buber 90-96; Teugels 138-45).
37 Maher in *Pseudo-Jonathan* 99, n. 6, and McNamara in *Neofiti 1*, 139, n. 4, also call attention to this. For God's performing "miracles" for the Israelites at the Well,

> Five miracles were performed for our father Jacob the time that he went forth from Beersheba to go to Haran. ... And the fourth miracle: the stone which all the shepherds had come together to roll away from over the mouth of the well and could not, when our father Jacob raised the stone from above the mouth of the well, the well overflowed and came up to its mouth, and was overflowing for twenty years - all the days that he dwelled in Haran. These are the five miracles that were performed with our father Jacob the time he went out from Beersheba to Haran.[38]

It should be noted that Jacob's rolling / raising the stone from the mouth of the well, (as well as the water's then rising to the top and remaining so for twenty years,) is here described as a "miracle" (נִיסָא).[39] In the narrative of the empty tomb in Mark 16:1-8, it is assumed that it was the "young man" (angel) of v 5 who had already rolled back the very large stone from the entrance of Jesus' tomb (vv 4-5). Although not specifically stated, this is also represented as a "miracle."[40]

B. 1.8   Jacob's Tremendous Strength in Judaic Tradition

Jacob's prodigious strength is already described in the biblical account, where in Gen 29:10 he rolls away the stone from the well's mouth by himself, although the (three) shepherds of three flocks (v 2) need the help of other shepherds to do so (v 3). Judaic tradition on v 10 embellishes this motif. The Palestinian targums state that he did so "with one hand,"[41] or "with one of his arms."[42] *Midr. Pss.* 91/7 calls Jacob here

---

and their then singing the Song of the Well (Num 21:17), cf. *Deut. Rab.* ʿEqeb 3/8 on Deut 9:1 (Mirkin 11.61; Soncino 7.76). This is one illustration of "The Rabbis say: Come and see how all the 'miracles' which God performed for Israel He performed only through water." See also II. B. 2, n. 68.

[38] Díez Macho 1.177; I slightly modify McNamara at 139-40. Cf. *Targum Pseudo-Jonathan* in Rieder 1.42 and Maher 99, and the *Fragment Targums*, MSS "P" and "V" in Klein 1.56-57 and 144, 2.19 and 106-07. On the water's rising and overflowing at this point, see also *Pirq. R. El.* 36 (Eshkol 128; Friedlander 268), as well as older sources cited in B. 1.11.5 below.

[39] Cf. Jastrow 915 on נָס , נֵיסָא , נִיסָא .

[40] It also points, of course, to the much greater miracle of God's raising Jesus from the dead. Verse 6 has: "he has been raised" (ἠγέρθη), the divine passive.

[41] Cf. *Neofiti 1* in Díez Macho 1.177, McNamara 139; and the *Fragment Targums* in Klein 1.57 and 144, 2.19 and 107.

"a mighty man" (גִּבּוֹר),[43] for which *Pirq. R. El.* 36 has the variant גִּבּוֹר כֹּחַ , "a strong hero."[44] R. Yoḥanan, a second generation Palestinian Amora,[45] notes on Gen 29:10 that when Jacob rolled the stone from the mouth of the well, this was as easy as "removing the stopper from a bottle."[46] Jacob's wrestling and prevailing over a heavenly being in Gen 32:22-32 is also thought of as displaying his fantastic strength,[47] as well as his erecting a very tall pillar in 31:45.[48] According to *Joseph and*

---

[42] Cf. *Pseudo-Jonathan* in Rieder 1.42; Maher 99. This is repeated at 29:10 (Rieder 1.43; Maher 101). See also v 13 on the "strength" (גבורתיה) of Jacob in this regard.

[43] Cf. Jastrow 205: strong, brave, mighty; hero. The text is found in Buber 400; Braude 2.106.

[44] Eshkol 128; Friedlander 268. Cf. also Laban's hearing of "the power of his might which he had displayed at the well" (Eshkol 129; Friedlander 270).

[45] *Introduction* 94-95.

[46] Cf. *Gen. Rab.* Vayeṣe 70/12 on Gen 29:10 (Theodor and Albeck 811; Soncino 2.645). A parallel is found in *Eccl. Rab.* 9:11 § 1 (Soncino 8.243). The root גלל , "to roll," is found in Gen 29:3, 8 and 10, the latter verse of Jacob's "rolling" the large stone from the well's mouth. The targums for the most part employ the same root, at times from an alternative form, גלגל (Jastrow 244). The same well was thought to "roll" along and accompany the Israelites on their forty year wilderness journey until it disappeared on the very day of Moses' death at the top of Mt. Pisgah / *Ramatha*, where he was buried. The well was described in Judaic tradition as a round stone, which can also be expressed in Aramaic as גַּלְגַּלְתָא (Jastrow 245). A "skull" is גּוּלְגַּלְתָּא and גּוּלְגּוּלְתָא (Jastrow 221), which could also be vocalized as גֻּלְגֻּלְתָּא . Unvocalized, as was usual, "a round stone" and "a skull" could thus have the same form and be easily confused. The site of Joseph of Arimathea's "rolling" a "blocking stone" (called גּוֹלֵל in Hebrew, גּוֹלְלָא in Aramaic - Jastrow 222) against the door of the tomb into which he had laid Jesus' body (Mark 15:46) appears to be represented as not far from where Jesus was crucified, "the place called 'Golgotha'" (v 22; see Str-B 1.1037 on the dropping out of the second lamed for easier pronunciation in Greek), which is then explained as "the place of a 'skull.'" I suggest that the latter may be a secondary, although early pre-Markan explanation of the above Aramaic. It could originally have been borrowed from the site where the first redeemer of Israel, Moses, died and was buried in Judaic tradition. It was the place where the well, a round stone, ceased rolling. This could account for "the place of the 'skull'" as not being attested elsewhere. This topic needs further attention.

[47] Cf. *Gen. Rab.* Vayishlaḥ 78/3 on Gen 32:29 (Theodor and Albeck 920; Soncino 2.717), as well as *Pesiq. R.* 3/4 (Friedmann 12b; Braude 1.80), and *Tanḥ.* Yayeḥi 6 on Gen 48:1 (Eshkol 1.191; Berman 292).

[48] Cf. *Gen. Rab.* Vayeṣe 74/13 on this verse (Theodor and Albeck 870; Soncino 2.685).

Aseneth 22:7, Jacob retained his great physical strength into advanced age.[49] One special source of Jacob's prodigious strength is especially related to the narrative of Jesus' Resurrection. Because of this, I will now describe it more extensively than is done in other sections.

B. 1.9 *The Dew of Resurrection*

Exod. Rab. Bo 15/11 on Exod 12:2, "This month [Nisan, with the Passover] shall mark for you the beginning of months," states that when God "chose Jacob and his sons, He appointed for them a New Moon of 'redemption' (גְּאֻלָּה) in which Israel were redeemed from Egypt and in which they will be redeemed again in the future, as it says: 'As in the days when you came out of the land of Egypt, I will show him marvelous things' (Mic 7:15). In this month Isaac was born, and in this month he was bound [as a sacrifice at the ʿAqedah in Genesis 22]. In this month Jacob also received the 'blessings,' and in this month He hinted to Israel that it would be the beginning of 'salvation' (תְּשׁוּעָה) for them."[50] The Soncino translator of *Exodus Rabbah*, S. Lehrman, correctly explains Jacob's "blessings" here as those "Of the dew of the heavens, and on the first day of Passover we pray for dew."[51]

The date of Jacob's receiving the blessings of dew, here in the month of Nisan, is made more precise in *Targ. Ps.-Jon.* Gen 27:1. Wishing to bless his firstborn son Esau, Isaac called to him "*on the fourteenth of Nisan* and said to him: 'My son, *behold, tonight the heavenly beings praise the Lord of the world* [with the Hallel psalms, 113-18],[52] *and the storehouses of (the) dews are opened.*" Rebekah, however, overheard "through the Holy Spirit" her husband's instructions to Esau to procure him a meal of game from the field. While the latter was gone, she addressed her second son Jacob in v 6 in the following way: "*Behold, tonight the heavenly beings praise the Lord of the world, and the storehouses of (the) dews are opened.*" She therefore commanded him in v 9 to "go to the sheep shed, and bring me from there two *fat* kids, *one for the Passover and one for the festival offerings.*" She will then prepare food from them such as Isaac loves.[53] This is basically also

---

[49] *OTP* 2.238.
[50] Mirkin 5.173-74; Soncino 3.173-74, which I slightly modify.
[51] Soncino 3.174, n. 1. Cf. the similar remark of Friedlander in *Pirke de Rabbi Eliezer* 236, n. 9.
[52] Cf. Mark 14:26, "and when they had sung hymns," not the NRSV: "When they had sung the hymn," as if only one hymn / psalm were meant.
[53] Rieder 1.39; Maher 94-95. The italicized sections are non-biblical.

found in *Pirq. R. El.* 32.[54] *Bereshit Rabbati* on Gen 27:6 also has Rebekah tell Jacob it is the first night of Passover: "On this night the treasuries of dew which cause resurrection / revival are opened; this day is the blessing of the dews."[55] It should be noted that Isaac's blessing his son Jacob then takes place on the 14th of Nisan, just before the beginning of Passover.

The end of *Pirq. R. El.* 32 states regarding the above blessing: "Isaac blessed Jacob with ten blessings concerning the dews of heaven and the grain of the earth, corresponding to the ten words by which the world was created, as it is said: 'May God give you of the dew of heaven' (Gen 27:28), and 'Let peoples serve you...' (v 29). When Jacob went forth from the presence of his father Isaac, he went forth adorned like a bridegroom, and like a bride in her adornment, and 'the quickening dew from heaven' descended upon him, and 'refreshed his bones,' and he became a 'mighty hero.' Therefore it is said: 'By the hands of the mighty Jacob, from there is the shepherd, the stone of Israel' (49:24)."[56]

"The quickening dew from heaven" here is תְּחִיַת טַל מִן הַשָּׁמַיִם , which can also be translated as "the resurrecting dew from heaven."[57] "His bones were refreshed" is the Hebrew נִדְשְׁנוּ עַצְמוֹתָיו . The verb דָּשֵׁן means to be moist, sappy, fat, and the nithpael here: to become sappy, vigorous.[58] This probably alludes to the famous passage on the resurrection, Ezek 37:1-14, where "dry bones" (vv 4 and 11) are filled with new life (vv 5-6, 8). The opening of the graves is referred to in vv 12-13.[59]

The effect of the "quickening dew from heaven" is not only that Jacob's bones become full of sap / vigorous. He also becomes a "mighty hero," literally a "hero of strength and power" (גִּבּוֹר חַיִל וָכֹחַ). Gen 49:24 is then applied to him: אֲבִיר יַעֲקֹב . The latter is not meant here as "the Mighty One [= God] of Jacob," but as "the mighty Jacob."

The above source of Jacob's tremendous strength explains how "like a strong hero he [alone] rolled away the stone from the mouth of the well," comment on Gen 29:10 in *Pirq. R. El.* 36.[60] It is the "quickening dew from

---

[54] Eshkol 111; Friedlander 236-37.

[55] Albeck 114.

[56] Eshkol 112; Friedlander 238.

[57] Cf. Jastrow 1661 on תְּחִיָה : revival, resurrection (of the dead).

[58] Jastrow 326.

[59] On this, cf. *Pirq. R. El.* 33, also with "the quickening dew from heaven" (Eshkol 118-19; Friedlander 249-50).

[60] See above, section B. 1.8.

heaven," the "resurrection dew from heaven," which enables him to do so. This is one major reason the Palestinian Jewish Christian author of the narrative which later became Mark 16:1-8 employed the imagery of Jacob's rolling a stone from the mouth of a well for an angel's doing so in his own narrative. The "young man / angel" is modeled on Judaic tradition on Jacob, upon whom the "quickening / resurrecting dew from heaven" descended. This power of resurrection was then employed in the narrative of the empty tomb, with God's having "raised" or "resurrected" Jesus.

Another factor may have contributed to the latter. In the above haggadic interpretation of Isaac's blessing Jacob, it is pictured as taking place during the daytime of the 14th of Nisan, i.e. just before the feast of Passover began on the 15th, which started at sundown. Accompanied by the well, Jacob journeyed on the 14th from Beer-sheba to Mount Moriah (Jerusalem), which he reached at noon of the second day. There he stayed for the night (Gen 28:11) and had the dream of vv 12-17. Rising early the next morning (v 18), he lifted up his feet, "and in the twinkle of an eye he came to Haran," for which Gen 29:1 is cited. This was one of the five miracles which occurred to him. Then in broad daylight (v 7) he employed his prodigious strength to roll away the very heavy stone from the mouth of the well.[61] Jacob is thus thought of as rolling away the very heavy stone *on the third day* after having been blessed by his father Isaac with the dew of resurrection. This chronological notice of the event's occurring "on the third day" may also have been one factor which encouraged the Palestinian Jewish Christian author of the narrative now found in Mark 16:1-8 to have the women at Jesus' tomb discover the very large stone rolled away from the door of the tomb *on the third day* after Jesus' crucifixion.[62]

While the final form of the sources in which the above haggadic material is found is clearly late, I would contend that the basic material is nevertheless quite early. This is primarily because the scriptural passages

---

[61] Cf. the end of *Pirq. R. El.* 35 (Eshkol 128; Friedlander 267) and the beginning of 36 (Eshkol 128; Friedlander 268). On Jacob's journey from Beersheba to Haran in the twinkling of an eye, or due to the contraction of the earth, as one of the five miracles which now took place, see section B. 1.7 above on all the Palestinian targums to Gen 28:10. See also *Gen. Rab.* Vayeṣe 68/8 on Gen 28:10, where "Our Rabbis said: He reached it [Haran] on that self-same day" (Theodor and Albeck 776; Soncino 2.620), as well as *b. Sanh.* 95b (Soncino 642) and *Ḥull.* 91b (Soncino 512), and *Midr. Pss.* 91/7 (Buber 400; Braude 2.106).

[62] As I will point out below, other factors in regard to the number of three days were even more important, especially Hos 6:2.

already deal with the dew, and because the motif also occurs frequently in other Judaic writings.

Gen 27:28 already has Isaac bless Jacob with the words: "May God give you of the dew of heaven."[63] In addition, a major prophetic text connects dew with the resurrection of the dead in Judaic tradition. Isa 26:19 reads:

> Your [sing.] dead shall live,
> my corpse shall rise.
> O dwellers in the dust,
> awake and cry out for joy!
> For Your [sing.] dew is a radiant dew,
> and the earth will give birth to the shades.

The pre-Christian LXX already interpreted this verse of the final resurrection of the dead:

> The dead shall rise (ἀναστήσονται),
> and those in the tombs shall be raised (ἐγερθήσονται),
> and those in the earth shall rejoice.
> For the dew from You is healing for them.
> But the land of the ungodly will fall / die.

Here God's dew is "healing" (ἴαμα)[64] for the dead at the time of the resurrection. It derives from interpreting the "shades" (רְפָאִים)[65] as from the root רָפָא , to heal, be healed.[66] Although also containing earlier materials, *Second (Syriac) Baruch* appears to have been written originally in Hebrew in Palestine at the beginning of the second century CE.[67] In 29:3 the future revelation of the Anointed One / Messiah is mentioned. At that time "winds will go out in front of Me [the Lord] every morning to bring the fragrance of aromatic fruits, and clouds at the end of the day

---

[63] Esau's abode, in contrast, will be "away from the dew of heaven on high" (v 39). Jacob is also associated with dew in Mic 5:6 (Eng. 7) and Deut 33:28. It should also be noted that *Jubilees* 26:23 already differentiates in Isaac's blessing of Jacob between "the dew of heaven" and "the dew of earth" (*OTP* 2.107; cf. also v 33). Originally in Hebrew, *Jubilees* was written in the middle of the second century BCE in Palestine (2.43-45).

[64] LSJ 815: remedy, medicine.

[65] BDB 952: shades, ghosts.

[66] BDB 950; Jastrow 1489-90.

[67] Cf. A. F. Klijn in *OTP* 1.616-17. Nickelsburg in *Jewish Literature* 283 suggests "towards the end of the first century C.E."

to distill 'the dew of health'" (v 7). Then the treasury of manna will again descend from the heavens (v 8), and the dead will rise (30:1-5). A similar passage is found in 73:1-2.[68] Here the "dew of health / healing," connected to the time of the resurrection, certainly reflects the same interpretation of רפא as healing in Isa 26:19 as in the LXX.[69]

Two Tannaitic passages which associate Isa 26:19, including God's dew, with the resurrection are *b. Sanh.* 90b, with Rabban Gamaliel (II, an older second generation Tanna[70]),[71] and *Sifra* 194, Aḥare Mot, Pereq 13, on Lev 18:4.[72]

In regard to the Israelites' fear that they would die if God spoke directly to them at Mount Sinai, *Mek. R. Ish.* Baḥodesh 9 on Exod 20:18 also relates that R. Judah b. R. Ilai, a third generation Tanna,[73] said: "As the Israelites were scorched [to death] by the heat of the fire from above, the Holy One, blessed he He, said to the clouds of glory: Drop 'the dew of life' (טל חיים) upon My children, as it is said: 'Lord, when You went forth out of Seir, when You marched out of the field of Edom, the earth trembled, the heavens also dropped' (Judg 5:4), and it also says: 'A bounteous rain did You pour down, O God' (Ps 68:10, Eng. 9)."[74] In *Pesiq. R.* 20/4 on Exod 20:2, approximately the same situation is described. "When Israel heard 'I am the Lord your God' (Exod 20:2), their souls at once departed from them. Thereupon the Holy One, blessed be He, 'made the dew descend which at the resurrection will quicken the souls of the righteous, and it revived them,' as it is said: Ps 68:10."[75] The latter verse is also employed as a prooftext in *b. Šabb.* 88b, where God "brought down the dew with which He will resurrect the dead, and He revived them."[76] It also plays an important role in *b. Ḥag.* 12b, which states in regard to the seventh heaven: "'*Araboth* is that in which there are Right and Judgment and Righteousness, the treasures of life and the treasures of peace and the treasures of blessing,

---

[68] *OTP* 1.631. Klijn correctly notes Isa 26:19 in the margin.
[69] For the dew of Isa 26:19 as giving "healing" (רפואות) to the earth, cf. also *Pirq. R. El.* 34 (Eshkol 124; Friedlander 260, with n. 4). The chapter deals with the resurrection of the dead.
[70] *Introduction* 76.
[71] Soncino 604-05.
[72] Weiss 85b; Neusner 3.79.
[73] *Introduction* 84-85.
[74] Lauterbach 2.269-70. A parallel is found in *Midr. Pss.* 68/7 (Buber 317; Braude 1.541-42).
[75] Friedmann 98b; Braude 1.411 with n. 55 for his use here of additional MSS.
[76] Soncino 421.

the souls of the righteous and the spirits and the souls which are yet to be born, and 'dew wherewith the Holy One, blessed be He, will hereafter revive the dead'...(Ps 68:10)."[77] *Targ.* Ps 68:10 also speaks of God's sending "the dew of revival" and "raising the rains of favor" upon His people.[78]

The dew of the resurrection is even once related to the case of a crucified person. *Tanḥ.* B Toledoth 19 on Gen 27:28ff. relates: "'Then the remnant of Jacob shall be [in the midst of many peoples] like dew from the Lord' (Mic 5:6, Eng. 7), for the dew is a sign [סימן] of the resurrection of the dead. So also has Isaiah said: 'Let your dead live! (Let My corpses arise! ... for Your dew is like the dew of lights' - Isa 26:19). Rav Ariste said in the name of R. Berekhyah: Isaiah proclaimed before the Holy One: 'Let your dead live,' (i.e.) those who were dishonored for My sake. One was crucified [נִצְלָב]]. Why? Because he had circumcised his son. Another was burned for observing the Sabbath, and another was killed [by the sword] because he read in the Torah. Thus it says: Isa 26:19."[79]

Although R. Berekhyah was a fifth generation Palestinian Amora,[80] there is no reason to doubt the basic authenticity of this narrative. It certainly refers to the major persecution of Jews by the Roman emperor Hadrian from 132-35 CE. He was well-known for his ban on circumcision.[81] Being "dishonored"[82] through crucifixion for circumcising one's own son here leads to the application of Isa 26:19 to such a person. "Let Your dead live" (with the Lord's "dew") illustrates how dew is "a sign of the resurrection of the dead." The crucifixion death of this Jewish martyr may also imply that it was believed his soul went immediately to God, just as with the Maccabean martyrs who suffered death under the severe persecution of Antiochus Epiphanes in the middle of the second

---

[77] Soncino 71-72. Dew is also found in the seventh firmament in *Apoc. Abraham* 19:4 (*OTP* 1.698; cf. the remarks on p. 685).

[78] Cf. Stec 129-30, who follows other MSS than the one employed by Merino 126. The next verse (11) reads: "You set Your revival in it...."

[79] Buber 138, who mistakenly has נצלוב ; Townsend 165-66. I follow the reading "for My sake" found in *Yalquṭ* on Isa 26:19, as does Paul Billerbeck in Str-B 4.1193.

[80] *Introduction* 105.

[81] Cf. Schürer, *The history* 1.534-39, 555 (with the ban on celebrating the Sabbath and studying the Torah), with n. 190. It refers to *Mek. R. Ish.* Baḥodesh 6 on Exod 20:6, "who love Me and keep My commandments." This is related by R. Nathan, a fourth generation Tanna (*Introduction* 88), showing that R. Berekhiya's source is early. See also chapter II. above, n. 12.

[82] Cf. Jastrow 869 on the nithpael of נבל : to be defaced, degraded, disgraced.

century BCE.[83] Although a century later than the time of the crucifixion of Jesus, this text shows how a Palestinian Jewish Christian could also have had the dew of the resurrection in mind for Jesus' Resurrection. After Jesus' crucifixion by the Roman procurator Pontius Pilate, when he too was terribly "dishonored," the author described him, like other Jewish martyrs, as already having been raised now, and not just at the general resurrection of the dead at the end of time.

Praying for dew within the liturgy of the synagogue and in private is also connected to Passover. Palestine basically has two periods of rain, the "early rain" (יוֹרֶה)[84] and the "latter or spring rain" (מַלְקוֹשׁ).[85] According to *m. Ber.* 5:2, while rain is prayed for in the benediction "The Years," (the ninth benediction of the Eighteen Prayer, spoken daily),[86] one mentions "the Power of Rain" (גְּבוּרוֹת גְּשָׁמִים)[87] in the benediction "the Resurrection of the Dead," (the second in the Eighteen Prayer).[88] In *m. Taʿan.* 1:1, R. Eliezer (b. Hyrcanus, an older second generation Tanna,[89]) states that one mentions the "Power of Rain" "from the first

---

[83] Cf. 2 Maccabees 7, especially v 36: "For our brothers after enduring a brief suffering have drunk of ever-flowing life, under God's covenant." On this issue, see Ulrich Kellermann, *Auferstanden in den Himmel. 2 Makkabäer und die Auferstehung der Märtyrer* (SBS 95; Stuttgart: Katholisches Bibelwerk, 1979), as well as "The Ascension of the Martyrs to Heaven Immediately After Their Death, and Judgment Directly After Death" in my *Samuel, Saul and Jesus. Three Early Palestinian Jewish Christian Gospel Haggadoth*, 178-80.

[84] BDB 435: "from the last of October until the first of December." Cf. also מוֹרֶה , ibid.

[85] BDB 545. Cf. *b. Taʿan.* 6a: "Our Rabbis have taught: Former rain [falls] in Marcheshvan and latter rain in Nisan" (Soncino 20).

[86] For an analysis of the different parts of the "Shemone ʿEsreh," cf. for example Ismar Elbogen, *Der jüdische Gottesdienst in seiner geschichtlichen Entwicklung* (Frankfurt / Main, 1931; Hildesheim: Georg Olms, 1962) 27-60.

[87] Cf. Jastrow 205 on גְּבוּרָה , 2).

[88] Albeck 1.22; Danby 5; Neusner 8 ("the wonder of the rain"). Cf. *b. Taʿan.* 7a (Soncino 24): "As [rain] is equal to the Revival of the Dead, the mention of it has therefore been inserted in the section of the Revival of the Dead." In *Pirq. R. El.* 31 (Eshkol 106; Friedlander 228), Isaac's soul departs when he is about to be slaughtered by Abraham at the ʿAqedah. After God speaks Gen 22:12, his soul returns to his body and he speaks the second benediction, "Blessed are You, O Lord, who revive the dead." *Midr. Leqaḥ Ṭob* Gen 31:42 (Buber, Genesis 161) states that God returned Isaac's soul at this point "by the dew of resurrection." See further the end of section C. 7 below.

[89] *Introduction 77.*

festival day of the feast [of Tabernacles / Sukkoth] ."[90] This was in the fall. In 1:2, R. Judah (b. Ilai, a third generation Tanna,[91]) notes in regard to praying for rain in the synagogue: "On the first festival day of Passover, the first [who passes before the Ark] alone mentions it."[92] This is because the latter or spring rain usually stopped then. In *b. Taʿan.* 4b, this time is specified: "Until the time limit for the slaughtering of the Paschal offering has passed," that is, the afternoon of the 14th of Nisan.[93] Up till then one prayed for rain, thereafter one reckoned with dew. A baraitha in 3a of the same tractate states: "The Sages did not make it obligatory on one to make mention of dew and winds, but if one desires to make mention he may do so." This is "because they are never withheld."[94] Ismar Elbogen notes that the petition for dew (ותן טל לברכה , "And grant dew as a blessing") is found in the ninth benediction of the Eighteen Prayer.[95]

The reference in *b. Taʿan.* 4b above is the reason, for example, that *Aggadath Bereshit* 44C can state: "The dew is mentioned on the first day of Passover."[96] It is also the reason why haggadic tradition related that Jacob received the blessing of the dew (Gen 27:28) on the afternoon of the 14th of Nisan. It was the dew of the resurrection which now gave him prodigious strength, enough to roll away a very heavy stone from the mouth of the well in 29:1-14.

B. 1.10   Astonishment / Amazement at the Removal of a Large / Heavy Stone

In Mark 16:1-8 the three women on the way to Jesus' tomb had been asking themselves: "Who will roll away the stone for us from the

---

[90] Albeck 2.331; Danby 194; Neusner 307.
[91] *Introduction* 84-85.
[92] Cf. n. 90.
[93] Soncino 12, with n. 5.
[94] Soncino 7. In *y. Taʿan.* 1:1, 63d (Neusner 18.141) "the prayer for dew" is mentioned.
[95] Cf. his *Der jüdische Gottesdienst* 49, where he says it applies to the non-winter period. See also *b. Taʿan.* 33a (Soncino 204, n. 5). If Lev 23:9-14 on the ʿ*omer* (first "sheaf" of barley) was at one time the Torah lesson for the second day of Passover, it is interesting that in *Pesiq. Rav Kah.* 8/1, Ps 68:10 is interpreted in this connection as meaning "wave down [dew]," now that the land needs it (Braude and Kapstein 157, with notes 1 and 18). On the ʿ*omer* as "an offering brought to the Temple on the 16th of Nisan," see the art. "Omer" in *EJ* (1971) 12.1382.
[96] Buber 88; Teugels 134.

entrance to the tomb?" (v 3 - NRSV). Then they saw that "the stone, which was very large, had already been rolled back" (v 4). When they entered the tomb, "they saw a young man, dressed in a white robe, sitting on the right side; and 'they were alarmed' (v 5). But he said to them, 'Do not be alarmed....'" (v 6).

The Greek of "they were alarmed" is ἐξεθαμβήθησαν , of "Do not be alarmed" Μὴ ἐκθαμβεῖσθε . The NRSV employs "alarm" here in the sense of "to strike with fear."[97] This is because it translates τρόμος in v 8 as "terror," and ἐφοβοῦντο in the same verse as "they were afraid." Yet I suggest the NRSV translation at least for ἐκθαμβέομαι is inappropriate, in part because of the model or "Vorlage" the Palestinian Jewish Christian employed when he composed this narrative.

The basic meaning of ἐκθαμβέω in the passive is "to be amazed" or "to be astonished." This is also true for ἐκθάμβησις ("amazement"), ἐκθαμβητικός ("astonishing"), and ἐκθαμβός ("amazed, astounded").[98] The NRSV appropriates this meaning in Mark 9:15 : "When the whole crowd saw him [Jesus], they were immediately 'overcome with awe,' and they ran forward to greet him." Thus the basic meaning of "to be amazed / astonished" is also found in Mark. This is a much more positive meaning for ἐκθαμβέομαι than "to be alarmed," with its negative connotation of fear.

I suggest that "to be amazed / astonished" is a more appropriate translation of ἐκθαμβέομαι in Mark 16:5-6 primarily because its Hebrew equivalent is employed in Judaic tradition on the incident of Jacob and the well, which in turn informs 16:1-8. R. Yoḥanan, a second generation Palestinian Amora,[99] in *Midr. Pss.* 91/7 relates Ps 91:11-12 to the angels' taking Jacob from the Well of Sheba (Beer-sheba) to Haran very quickly.[100] He continues: "And the steps of Jacob were not shortened, and his strength was not subdued. And mighty man that he was, he rolled the stone away from the well's mouth, and the well gushed up, the water

---

[97] Cf. *Webster's Ninth Collegiate Dictionary*, 68,3; 1. is "disturb, excite."

[98] LSJ 506; BAGD 240. The latter also recommend "be alarmed" in 16:5-6, and "be distressed" in 14:33. The four occurrences of the verb are only found in Mark. The NRSV, however, translates ἐκθαμβος in Acts 3:11 as "utterly astonished." Adela Yarbro Collins in *Mark* 795-96 cites other reasons for preferring "to be amazed" in Mark 16:5-6. She also notes that the women's silence in v 8 "is a result of their being struck with awe at the extraordinary events" (p. 800).

[99] *Introduction* 94-95.

[100] This is described in the midrash directly before this; it is one of the "five miracles" performed for Jacob at this time: in the twinkling of an eye he was in Haran, leaving one well for another.

brimming over. The herdsmen looked and 'were astonished' that Jacob had rolled the stone away by himself since all of them together could not roll away the stone, for the herdsmen used to say: Gen 29:8, 10b."[101]

As noted before, it is assumed that there are three shepherds / herdsmen here, for there are three flocks of sheep near the well in Gen 29:2. As the shepherds here "see" that Jacob had rolled the (very heavy) stone away by himself, so the three women in Mark 16:4 "look up and see" (ἀναβλέψασαι θεωροῦσιν) "that the stone, which was very large, had already been rolled back." They also now "see" a young man dressed in a white robe, sitting on the right side. Therefore "they were amazed" (v 5).

After "seeing" Jacob's prodigious strength in rolling the (very heavy) stone away "by himself" (לבדו), the shepherds in the above rabbinic text "were astonished" (תָּמְהוּ). The verb תָּמַהּ means "to be astonished, amazed; to wonder."[102] It should be noted that there is no connotation of fear involved here. The three shepherds are not "alarmed." Since this episode in Judaic tradition is clearly the model for the originally Semitic narrative of Mark 16:1-8,[103] there is very good reason to

---

[101] Buber 400; Braude 2.106. A parallel is found in *Pirq. R. El.* 36 (Eshkol 128; Friedlander 268). Cf. Josephus, *Ant.* 1.286, where the shepherds also "wonder" (θαυμάζω), yet as to why Rachel had not arrived yet.

[102] Jastrow 1675. In the Hebrew Bible it means "to be astounded, dumbfounded" (BDB 1069).

[103] Rudolf Pesch in his *Das Markusevangelium. II. Teil* (Herder; Freiburg: Herder, 1984³) 536, n. 35, lists four other indications in the pericope of its having a Semitic "Vorlage." The above Judaic tradition on Jacob at the well excludes the possibility that Daniel in the lions' den in Daniel 6 provided the background to Mark 16:1-8, as proposed by Randel Helms in *Gospel Fictions* (Amherst, NY: Prometheus Books, 1988) 135-37. Nor did Joshua 10 primarily do so, as suggested by Michael Goulder in "The Empty Tomb" in *Theology* 79 (1976) 209 and 213. He here takes up unpublished suggestions made by Austin Farrer (214, n. 1). Adela Yarbro Collins in "Apotheosis and Resurrection" in *The New Testament and Hellenistic Judaism*, ed. Peder Borgen and Søren Giversen (Aarhus: Aarhus University Press, 1995) 88-100 believes "Mark 16.1-8 is best understood as a unified and effective composition by the evangelist..." (90). It is "fiction" (97). Relying heavily on Erwin Rohde's work *Psyche: The Cult of Souls and the Belief in Immortality among the Greeks* (New York: Harcourt Brace Jovanovich, 1925), Yarbro Collins emphasizes the importance of the "translation" or apotheosis of famous Greco-Roman figures here. See also her *Mark* 781, with n. 80, and 791-94, as well as her earlier *The Beginning of the Gospel. Probings of Mark in Context* (Minneapolis: Fortress Press, 1992) 138-43 on "The Ancient Notion of Translation." On the translation / Entrückung of Greco-Roman heroes, including deified Roman emperors, and

translate ἐκθαμβέομαι in vv 5-6 not as "to be alarmed," but rather as "to be amazed / astonished."[104]

* * *

The above ten expressions and motifs *as a cluster* strongly argue for biblical and Judaic tradition on Gen 28:10 and 29:1-14 as the main background for the narrative of the empty tomb in Mark 16:1-8. This argument would be strengthened if it could be shown that the same narrative from the Hebrew Bible also informs another incident in the Gospels in a major way. This is indeed the case, and to this I now turn.

---

figures in the OT and early Judaism, see the art. "Entrückung" by Hans Wissmann and Otto Betz in *TRE* (1982) 9.680-90, with 690 for literature, and the same by Dieter Zeller in *RGG*[4] (1999) 2.1332-33, also with relevant bibliography. Rudolf Pesch in *Das Markusevangelium. II. Teil* 522-25 maintains the genre of Mark 16:1-8 is closest to that of narratives which dramatize the search for, and inability to find, "entrückte" or raised persons (522).

John Dominic Crossan has also recently repeated his conviction regarding the empty tomb narrative: "I think Mark created it." See *The Resurrection of Jesus.* John Dominic Crossan and N. T. Wright in Dialogue, ed. Robert Stewart (Minneapolis: Fortress Press, 2006) 33, as well as 177. He also argued in this direction in "The Resurrection of Jesus in its Jewish Context" in *Neotestamentica* 37 (2003) 30, n. 1. In light of the great influence of Gen 29:1-14, especially in Judaic tradition, on the narrative of the empty tomb, it is also quite surprising for Wolfgang Nauck to maintain that there is no scriptural intertextuality visible here. See his "Die Bedeutung des leeren Grabes für den Glauben an den Auferstandenen" in *ZNW* 47 (1956) 249. The same is true of N. T. Wright, *The Resurrection of the Son of God* (Minneapolis: Fortress Press, 2003) 599-602. Wright repeats this in *The Resurrection of Jesus* 21: "the stories...are remarkably free of scriptural quotation, allusion, and echo...." For a critique of Wright, see James Crossley, "Against the Historical Plausibility of the Empty Tomb Story and the Bodily Resurrection: A Response to N. T. Wright," in *JSHJ* 3 (2005) 153-68. On several of the above authors, see also the discussion in Dale Allison, Jr., *Resurrecting Jesus. The Earliest Christian Tradition and its Interpreters* (New York / London: T & T Clark International, 2005) 301-02 and 320.

[104] While the verb only occurs here, in 9:15 and 14:33 in the NT, it is nevertheless not from Mark at this point, but already in the tradition he appropriated. Against Gerd Luedemann, *The Resurrection of Jesus. History, Experience, Theology* (Minneapolis: Fortress Press, 1994) 113.

B. 1.11   Another Very Early Example in the Gospels of Haggadic Interpretation of Jacob's Well: John 4:1-42

The above sections (B. 1.1 to 1.10) show how an early Palestinian Jewish Christian composed the framework of the narrative of the empty tomb in what is now Mark 16:1-8 in light of Judaic traditions on Jacob's encounter at the well with reference to Gen 28:10 and 29:1-14. Another narrative in the Gospels, that of Jesus' encounter with the Samaritan woman at "Jacob's well" in John 4:1-42, also employs expressions and motifs from the same complex of traditions. Since the Gospel of John is most probably from the end of the first century CE,[105] this means that a number of the Judaic traditions cited in B. 1.1 to 1.10 above, although now found in sources whose final form is quite late (e.g., the targums, *Midrash Psalms, Pirqe de Rabbi Eliezer*), *in their core* go back at least to the first century CE. The following analysis of various aspects of John 4:1-42 demonstrates this.

There are numerous inconcinnities in the episode of Jesus' encounter with the Samaritan woman, pointing to its also being a constructed narrative. The following remarks are indicative of this.

a)   John 4:4 states that Jesus "had to" (ἔδει) go through Samaria on his way from Judea to Galilee. This is not true, for in order to avoid unpleasant encounters with the Samaritans, a number of the Galileans who participated in one or more of the three annual pilgrimage festivals

---

[105] Cf. Raymond Brown, *The Gospel According to John, I-XII,* LXXXVI, for 90-100 CE, as well as Carl Holladay, *A Critical Introduction to the New Testament* (Nashville: Abingdon Press, 2005) 206, yet also 199. Others have also noted the relevance of Judaic traditions on the well to John 4:1-42. Annie Jaubert, "La Symbolique des Puits de Jacob, Jean 4,12," in *L'Homme devant Dieu: Mélanges offerts au Père Henri de Lubac* (Lyons: Aubier, 1963) 1.63-73, and Xavier Léon-Dufour, *Lecture de l'évangile selon Jean* (Paris: du Seuil, 1988) 347-49, have not been available to me. See also Birger Olsson, *Structure and Meaning in the Fourth Gospel: A Text Linguistic Analysis of John 2:1-11 and 4:1-42* (CB, NT ser. 6; Lund: Gleerup, 1974) 162-73, and Jerome Neyrey, "Jacob Traditions and the Interpretation of John 4:10-26" in *CBQ* 41 (1979) 419-37, as well as the Díaz article cited in n. 126. None of the latter, however, relate these traditions to the narrative of the empty tomb, nor is their argumentation the same as mine in regard to John 4:1-42. Commentaries on John which incorporate their studies, after they had been long overlooked, are Francis Moloney, *The Gospel of John* (Sacra Pagina 4; Collegeville, MN: The Liturgical Press, 1998) 120-23, and Hartwig Thyen, *Das Johannesevangelium* (HNT 6; Tübingen: Mohr Siebeck, 2005) 243-44.

to Jerusalem took the route through the Jordan Valley.[106] Jesus could easily have done the same.

b)   Cities / towns /villages were invariably located next to a source of water (river, brook, spring) so that the arduous daily task of carrying water home would be minimized. This is true, for example, for the site עֵין סוֹכֵר , the "Spring of 'Sokher,'" usually thought to lie behind the "Sychar" (Συχάρ) in John 4:5 (the waw can either be read as an "ō," or as a "u" here in the Greek). This site is mentioned in the *Mishnah* and elsewhere as a far-off place from which grain, not available in the vicinity of Jerusalem, was procured for baking the two loaves required as first fruits to the Lord at the festival of Weeks in Lev 23:17. The incident is dated to the Hasmonean period, with Hyrcanus and Aristobulus and a siege of Jerusalem.[107] What is important to note is that Sokher itself has a spring, and thus also a well. There was no reason whatsoever for the Samaritan woman in John 4:28, who "went back to the town," to go off to a different, distant well ("Jacob's Well") and carry heavy water home again. She did not "have to keep coming here to draw water" (v 15, somewhat paraphrastic in the NRSV).

c)   This is the only mention of "Jacob's well," called a "spring" (πηγή) in 4:6 (cf. v 14) and a "well" (φρέαρ) in vv 11-12,[108] in biblical and later Judaic sources. This probably points to its being a constructed designation based primarily on a combination of Genesis 37, where Jacob sends his son Joseph to inquire about the well-being of his other sons and the family flock near Shechem (between Mt. Gerizim and Mt. Ebal in Samaria; cf. John 4:20 for Gerizim), and the well to which Jacob comes in Gen 29:1-14.[109] The catchword "Jacob" led to an association of the two narratives.

d)   According to John 4:7 the Samaritan woman came to draw water from Jacob's well; it was "about noon" (v 6). Drawing water and carrying it home was indeed considered a woman's task at this time in Palestine, yet one did this in the early morning or late afternoon (cf. Gen 24:11) to

---

[106] Cf. Shmuel Safrai, *Die Wallfahrt im Zeitalter des Zweiten Tempels* 134-35 and 137.

[107] Cf. *m. Menaḥ.* 10:2 (Albeck 5.90; Danby 505; Neusner 753); *b. Menaḥ.* 64b (Soncino 381-82); *b. Soṭah* 49b (Soncino 269); *b. B. Qamma* 82b (Soncino 470); and *y. Šeq.* 5:1, 48d (Neusner 15.99) with their respective notes.

[108] The terms often occur together or interchangeably, for the spring fed the well with fresh water. Cf. the references in Rudolf Bultmann, *Das Evangelium des Johannes*, 129, n. 7.

[109] Cf. also Gen 33:19; 48:22; and Josh 24:32 in connection with John 4:5 and 12. Yet a well is mentioned nowhere in the OT accounts.

avoid the noonday heat. The time notice "about noon" is thus very suspicious.

e)   In John 4:7 Jesus tells her: "Give me a drink." She rightly wonders why he asks this of a Samaritan (v 9). Yet more importantly, Jewish men at this time in Palestine did not speak to women unknown to them, especially in public. The disciples are correctly represented as being astonished at this in v 27.

f)   In John 4:8 a parenthetical note states that "His disciples had gone to the city to buy food." They only return in v 27, after Jesus' long conversation with the Samaritan woman. Since it is very improbable that all twelve disciples were needed to carry the groceries, it becomes clear that the absence of *all* of them is necessary dramatically in order to have Jesus first ask for a drink of water, and then speak extensively alone with the Samaritan woman, revealing himself to her as the Messiah (vv 26-27). The result of the whole encounter is that "many Samaritans" from that town believed in him, and also that Jesus is "the Savior of the world" (vv 39-42). The first successes of a later Christian mission to the Samaritans are certainly reflected here.[110] Jesus' eating something from the groceries brought back by the disciples is negated in vv 31-34. Earlier, a different emphasis is placed on him as providing "living water," leading to "eternal life" (vv 10-11, 14).[111]

*   *   *

The above six points make it reasonably clear that the episode now found in John 4:1-42 is an artificially constructed narrative. There is good reason for its absence in the Synoptics. Judaic tradition on Jacob's encounter at the well of Gen 28:10 and 29:1-14 contributes in major ways to a better understanding of this narrative.

B. 1.11.1   "It Was About Noon"

John 4:6 states that Jesus, tired out by his journey, sat down at Jacob's well "about noon." The Greek ὥρα ἦν ὡς ἕκτη literally means: "The hour was about six." Since the day was divided into twelve day and

---

[110] Cf. the "good" Samaritan in Luke 10:25-37; the grateful Samaritan leper in 17:16, who alone returned to thank Jesus for healing him; but primarily Acts 1:8 and 8:1, 4-25.

[111] A number of questions similar to those above are posed in the fine analysis of Hermann Strathmann, *Das Evangelium nach Johannes* 84-86.

twelve night hours, it is in fact around noon.[112] This hour of the day is influenced by the Jacob narrative in Genesis 29.

In Gen 29:7 Jacob tells the shepherds at the well: "Look, it is still 'broad daylight'; it is not time for the animals to be gathered together. Water the sheep, and go, pasture them." "Broad daylight" is the idiomatic Hebrew expression גָּדוֹל הַיּוֹם , literally "the day [is] great," but meant as "the day is high."[113] The LXX translates this literally: ἡμέρα πολλή . While the expression is lacking in the *Fragment Targums*, *Targum Onqelos* also translates literally: יומא סגי .[114] *Targum Pseudo-Jonathan* reads: עדן יומא סגי, literally "time, great day."[115] Michael Maher therefore correctly translates this with "high daytime."[116] *Targum Neofiti 1* has יומא תלי,[117] which Martin McNamara renders as "high day."[118]

The targums, especially *Neofiti 1*, thus agree that in the incident described in Gen 29:7 it was still "high day," thus around noon. The Palestinian Jewish Christian who first composed the framework of the narrative in John 4:1-42[119] most probably borrowed the hour of the day from Gen 29:7 and described it correctly as "about noon." Because of the influence of Gen 29:7, the Samaritan woman does not come to draw water from the well in the cooler morning or late afternoon, as was customary, but rather at noon, a strange time of the day indeed for such strenuous activity.

B. 1.11.2   *Jesus' Speaking in Public with a Woman*

As remarked above, Palestinian Jewish men did not engage women publicly in conversation at this time. Jesus' being at the well first before the Samaritan woman arrives is also based on Jacob's being there before Rachel arrives there with her father's sheep in Gen 29:6, 9-12. Verse 12

---

[112] Cf. Str-B 2.442, who shows that 6 a.m. began the twelve hours of the day. Cf. for example *Gen. Rab.* Vayera 48/8 on "the heat of the day" in Gen 18:1 - "at six hours both the sun and the shade are equally hot" (Theodor and Albeck 484; Soncino 1.410).

[113] BDB 398 on יוֹם .

[114] Sperber 1.45; Grossfeld 105. Cf. Jastrow 954 on סַגִּי : large, great.

[115] Rieder 1.43.

[116] *Genesis* 101.

[117] Díez Macho 1.183. The term תלי can mean "elevated," "high" (Jastrow 1671).

[118] *Genesis* 142.

[119] Or perhaps the Evangelist himself, whom I (together with others) consider to be bilingual.

describes how Jacob, like Jesus, is the first to speak with Rachel at the well, informing her of his true identity: he is a relative, her aunt Rebekah's son.[120] This also recalls Jesus' first speaking to the Samaritan woman at Jacob's well (John 4:7) and his revealing his true identity to her there: he is the Messiah (vv 25-26).

B. 1.11.3   Asking for a Drink

In John 4:7 Jesus tells the Samaritan woman at the well: "Give me a drink" (Δός μοι πεῖν). This motif is repeated in vv 9-10.

In Genesis 29 Jacob does not ask one of the shepherds of Rachel for a drink of water from the well. Yet Josephus, having grown up in Jerusalem, betrays knowledge of such a Judaic tradition. He writes in *Ant.* 1.285 of Jacob: "Here meeting with shepherds in the suburbs, young men and maidens seated beside a well, he joined their company, 'craving for a drink,' and entering into conversation with them, he inquired...." "Craving for a drink" is the Greek χρῄζων ποτοῦ .[121] I suggest that the author of John 4:1-42 expanded this early Judaic motif into Jesus' being tired out by his journey (v 5) and asking for a drink of water at the well in v 7. The long journey and the midday heat encouraged him to do so.

B. 1.11.4   Living Water

In John 4:10 Jesus tells the Samaritan woman at the well: "If you knew the gift of God, and who it is that is saying to you, 'Give me a drink,' you would have asked him, and he would have given you 'living water.'" In v 11 she answers: "Sir, you have no bucket, and the well is deep. Where do you get that 'living water'?" Verses 12-15 then develop this motif.[122]

---

[120] In Josephus, *Ant.* 1.287 and 292, Rachel also speaks with Jacob, as the Samaritan woman speaks to Jesus at Jacob's Well. In *Gen. Rab.* Vayeṣe 70/11 on Gen 29:6, the shepherds tell Jacob at the well that if he desires gossip, "'behold, Rachel is coming with the sheep,' for (much) speech is found in women" (Theodor and Albeck 810; Soncino 2.644). The Samaritan woman may also be represented as "talkative."

[121] Cf. LSJ 2004.2 on χρῄζω : desire, long for, crave.

[122] It should be noted that only two chapters later, in six, the Fourth Evangelist develops the motif of Jesus as the true bread of life, the true manna from heaven. He thus offers in himself both human necessities: water and bread (food). Birger Olsson in *Structure and Meaning in the Fourth Gospel* 165-66 correctly relates the "gift" (δωρέα) of 4:10 to Judaic tradition on the place name "Mattanah" in Num 21:18-19 as a "gift" (מַתָּנָה : BDB 682, Jastrow 863). Many other passages, in

"Living water" here is the Greek ὕδωρ ζῶν and τὸ ὕδωρ τὸ ζῶν. It is equivalent to the Hebrew מַיִם חַיִּים, employed for example in Gen 26:19 of Isaac's servants' digging in a valley and finding there a well of "spring water," and eleven other times in the MT of "flowing," "fresh" or "running water," literally "living water."[123] It stands in contrast to the stale or flat water stored in cisterns.

I suggest that when the narrator of John 4:1-41 describes Jesus as offering people "living water," it is (among other things) reminiscent of the טַל חַיִּים, literally "living dew," condensed moisture / water, but meant as the dew of resurrection leading to eternal life. It was this dew which, as described above, gave Jacob the prodigious strength to roll away the stone from the well of Genesis 29 in Judaic tradition. According to the Fourth Evangelist, Jesus also offers "living water,"[124] which leads to eternal life (4:14). He can even state in 11:25, "I am the resurrection and the life."

B. 1.11.5 *A Spring of Water Gushing Up to Eternal Life*

In John 4:13-14 Jesus responds to the Samaritan woman's question of where he will get the "living water" he offers her in v 10 if he has no bucket with which to draw it from the deep well at which he is sitting. He tells her: "Everyone who drinks of this water will be thirsty again, 14) but those who drink of the water that I will give them will never be thirsty. The water that I will give will become in them a spring of water 'gushing up' to eternal life."

The Greek of "gushing up" in v 14 is from the verb ἅλλομαι. It occurs only two more times in the NT as "leaping" in connection with a person walking: Acts 3:8 and 14:10. This is also the meaning in Josephus, *Bell.* 5.330 and *Ant.* 20.61. It is not found in the LXX or Philo. In connection

---

addition to the targums he cites, could be added, especially in regard to the well and / or the Torah as this gift. See for example *Seder ʿOlam* 10 (Guggenheimer 102) and *Cant. Rab.* 4:5 § 2 (Donsqi 111; Soncino 9.200).

[123] Cf. BDB 312.1.f. on חַי.

[124] At Qumran some "turned and betrayed and departed from 'the well of living waters' (באר מים החיים)" in CD-B 19:34 (*The Dead Sea Scrolls Study Edition* 1.578-79). The latter refers to the Torah as interpreted there, for in regard to the song of the well in Numbers 21 "the well is the Torah" (CD-A 6:4 in 1.558-59). It should also be noted that R. Yohanan interprets the "well of living water" (בְּאֵר מַיִם חַיִּים) of Cant 4:15 in *Cant. Rab.* 4:14 § 1 as the well (of Num 21:17-18) which provided Israelite wives the means to deck themselves and gladden their husbands for forty years in the wilderness (Soncino 9.225).

with water it means "to well up," "to bubble up," a sense only found here.[125] This very rare verb derives from Judaic tradition on the behavior of the water in the well of Genesis 29 after Jacob rolled away the very heavy stone from off its mouth.

As pointed out in section B. 1.7 above, one of the "miracles" done in the incident of Jacob and the well was that "the well 'overflowed' and came up to its mouth, and 'was overflowing' for twenty years - all the days that he dwelt in Haran."[126] The Aramaic verb employed here is טפי , טפא , "to float," "to flood."[127] Michael Klein correctly translates it as "to surge up" in connection with the following verb, סלק , "to rise up."[128] *Midr. Pss.* 91/7 relates that after Jacob rolled the stone away from the well's mouth, "the well 'gushed up,' the water 'brimming' over."[129] The Hebrew verbs employed here are עלה , to ascend, and שפע , to pour out, run, discharge, but also to flow abundantly.[130]

This is a very old motif, deriving from the behavior of the water in the well which accompanied the Israelites in the wilderness for forty years (Num 21:16-20, with "Spring up [עלי], O well!" in v 17). While the Tannaitic *t. Soṭah* 4:2 also employs the verb שפע for the well's "gushing" here,[131] *t. Sukk.* 3:11 notes that the water of the well "bubbled and went upward like a pillar on high."[132] "Went upward" is עלה , while "bubbled" is the verb בעבע , "to cast bubbles."[133] It is precisely this verb from the

---

[125] BAGD 39,2. Cf. LSJ 70, who do not even list this meaning. See also the Norwegian "veller fram" in John 4:14.
[126] This tradition is found in all three Palestinian targums at Gen 28:10. I cite *Neofiti 1* here, as in n. 38. To my knowledge José Ramón Díaz was the first to recognize the relevance of this tradition for John 4:14. See his "Palestinian Targum and New Testament" in *NovT* 6 (1963) 76-77. However, he only quotes *Targum Pseudo-Jonathan* on Gen 28:10 and does not analyze the broader context. He notes that Jesus is represented here as "greater than Jacob," and that "the Haran well has been transferred into Palestine" (p. 77).
[127] Jastrow 546.
[128] Jastrow 997. Cf. Klein, *The Fragment Targums* 2.19 with n. 75, 107; and 1.57 and 144.
[129] Buber 400; Braude 2.106.
[130] Cf. Jastrow 1618 on the latter. The parallel passage in *Pirq. R. El.* 36 has the verb שפך , "to pour out" (Jastrow 1616). See Eshkol 128.
[131] Zuckermandel / Liebermann 298; Neusner 3.160.
[132] Zuckermandel / Liebermann 197; Neusner 2.220. Cf. already the "gushing" (זוב : BDB 264) of the water from the rock, associated in Judaic tradition with the wilderness well, in Ps 78:20; 105:41; and Isa 48:21.
[133] Jastrow 180.

miraculous behavior of the water in the well which provides the background to the very rare verb ἅλλομαι in John 4:14. The water of Jesus' spring / well will "gush up," it will "bubble up" to eternal life.

In this respect it should be noted that such living water was expected in Judaic sources for the time when the Messiah would appear. *Eccl. Rab.* 1:9 § 1 relates for example that R. Isaac (II, a third generation Palestinian Amora,[134]) maintained: "As the former redeemer made a well to rise [Moses in Num 21:17-18], so will the latter Redeemer [גּוֹאֵל] bring up water, as it is stated: 'And a fountain shall come forth from the house of the Lord, and shall water the valley of Shittim' (Joel 4:18)."[135] When Jesus as the Messiah promises to give people "a spring of [living] water gushing up to eternal life" (John 4:14; cf. vv 25-26, 29 and 42), this is in complete accord with Judaic thought.

Zech 14:8 reads: "On that day living waters [מַיִם־חַיִּים ; LXX ὕδωρ ζῶν] shall flow out from Jerusalem." In a chapter dealing with Jacob's blessing in Gen 27:28 ("the dew of heaven") and his leaving his father's house, and just before his encounter at the well of Genesis 29, *Pirq. R. El.* 35 says Zech 14:8 refers to "the well which will arise in Jerusalem in the [messianic] future, and will water all its surroundings. Because they found [the well] seven times, he [Isaac] called it Shib'ah [seven: Beer*sheba*]."[136]

Zech 14:8 also plays an important role in another passage connected to the wilderness well and the messianic future. *Gen. Rab.* Vayera 48/10 deals with Abraham's statement in Gen 18:4, "Let a little water be brought." R. Ḥiyya, a fifth generation Tanna,[137] has God say to Abraham in this regard: "You have said, 'Let a little water be brought.' I swear that I will repay your children (in the wilderness, in inhabited country [the Land of Israel], and in the messianic future).' Thus it is written: 'Then Israel sang this song: Spring up, O well! - Sing to it! (Num 21:17) - that was in the wilderness. Where do we find it in the Land? 'A land of

---

[134] *Introduction* 98.

[135] Vilna 8 or 4b; Soncino 8.33. Here the latter Redeemer is clearly the Messiah, as the citation of Zech 9:9 shows. Interestingly, he is also to cause manna to descend, as Moses did (Exod 16:4). See John 6:22-59.

[136] Eshkol 126; Friedlander 263. Before this an explanation of the number seven is given in regard to the well's always preceding the Patriarchs, Abraham and Isaac (Gen 26:18-19).

[137] *Introduction* 90. I doubt that he is here the third generation Palestinian Amora with the same name (99).

flowing streams' (Deut 8:7). And in the messianic future? Zech 14:8."[138] Palestinian Jewish Christians may very well have thought that because of the Messiah Jesus' Resurrection in Jerusalem, "living waters" had begun to flow out from that city, fulfilling Zech 14:8. Jesus as the Messiah gives these waters, leading to eternal life (John 4:14).

B. 1.11.6   *The Samaritans' Coming from Their Town to Meet Jesus, and His Stay with Them in Their Town*

After the Samaritan woman from Sychar encountered Jesus at Jacob's well outside the town, she returned there (John 4:28) and reported to the inhabitants that she thought he might be the Messiah. Therefore the Samaritans left their town (v 30) and came to Jesus at Jacob's well, where they asked him to stay with them. This he did, for two days (v 40), leading to even more Samaritans believing in him, now "because of his word" (v 41),[139] i.e. because of his teaching. Earlier they had believed in him "because of the woman's testimony" (v 39).

This scene is also based on the narrative of Jacob at the well in Genesis 29. Josephus in *Ant.* 1.285 notes that Jacob proceeded to Mesopotamia (cf. 278) and in time reached Haran. Gen 27:43 had already noted that Rebekah told her son to "flee at once to my brother Laban in Haran."[140] He thus "left Beer-sheba and went towards Haran" (28:10), arriving there after his nocturnal vision of angels on a ladder. Josephus also notes that Jacob met shepherds seated beside a well, which was "in the suburbs" of Haran (1.285). In Gen 29:4 they inform Jacob that they are from Haran. When Rachel arrived with her father's flock, Jacob first rolled the very heavy stone from the well's mouth and watered Laban's flock (v 10). After he revealed his true identity to her, "she ran and told her father" (v 12).

The latter motif is similar to the Samaritan woman's returning from the well to the town (Sychar) after Jesus reveals to her who he really is: the Messiah (4:25-26; cf. 29). She then informs the inhabitants of the city (vv 28-29).

---

[138] Theodor and Albeck 486-87; Soncino 1.411, with the material in parentheses added from the current editions (n. 3). Other passages dealing with living water in the messianic future are found in Str-B 2.436.

[139] Cf. Jacob's telling Laban "all these 'things' (דְּבָרִים)" in Gen 29:13, which can also mean "all these 'words.'"

[140] On Haran, cf. Gen 11:31; it was the city of Nahor (24:10).

After Laban "heard the news about his sister's son Jacob, he ran to meet him ... and brought him to his house [in Haran]" (Gen 29:13). This general movement is similar to that of the Samaritans, who after the woman's description "left the town and were on their way to him" (John 4:30), coming to Jesus in v 40. They then ask him to stay with them (*ibid.*). Gen 29:14 notes that Jacob "stayed with him [Laban] a month." Josephus, probably dependent on Judaic tradition, reduces this in *Ant.* 1.294 to "a few days." John 4:30 has a similar reference to time: "he [Jesus] stayed there two days."

It thus appears that the Palestinian Jewish Christian (or perhaps the Evangelist John) who first composed the narrative of John 4:1-42[141] has modeled the Samaritans' movements out of Sychar to the well, and their returning to their town with Jesus, on Laban's running to meet Jacob and then taking him back (to Haran; cf. "to his house" in v 13) after learning his true identity from Rachel, who in part provides the mediating model for the Samaritan woman. In addition, just as the narrative of Gen 29:1-14 ends by the revelation of the true identity of Jacob, who had come to the well, so the narrative of Jesus and the Samaritan woman also ends by the Samaritans' recognizing that the man whom their female fellow citizen met at Jacob's well is not only the Messiah, but "truly the Savior of the world" (John 4:42).

* * *

The above six similarities in terminology, motifs, and general framework between biblical and Judaic tradition on the narrative of Gen 28:10 and 29:1-14, and John 4:1-42, show that the Palestinian Jewish Christian author of the Johannine pericope (or less probably the Evangelist John) was well-acquainted at the latest in the nineties of the first century CE with such traditions. This in turn supports my proposal that exactly the same complex of Judaic traditions on Gen 28:10 and 29:1-14 also influenced in a major way another passage in the Gospels, the narrative of the empty tomb in Mark 16:1-8, even if the *final* form of some of the sources in which these traditions are now found is admittedly quite late. The large cluster of very exact terminology, motifs, and general framework speaks for itself.

After the above analysis of biblical and Judaic traditions on the well and their relationship to the empty tomb, it will now be helpful to

---

[141] The narrative is full of Johannine terminology and theology, which could either be original or added later to an earlier account.

analyze the influence of Judaic traditions on Moses' "translation" on the narrative of Jesus' Resurrection.

B. 2   *The Translation of Moses Without His First Dying*

The Hebrew text of Deut 34:5 clearly states that "Moses, the servant of the Lord, died there in the land of Moab at the Lord's command." The latter phrase is literally "by the mouth of the Lord," giving rise to the belief that Moses died through a "kiss of God."[142] The following verse, six, then elaborates the contents of five: "He buried him in a valley in the land of Moab, opposite Beth-peor, but no one knows his burial place to this day." The Hebrew of "He buried him" (וַיִּקְבֹּר אֹתוֹ) also clearly states that it was the LORD who did so.[143] Yet some segments of early Judaism maintain, contrary to Scripture, that Moses did not die at all. Instead, he was "translated" or taken up from earth to heaven at the very end of his life. Since this tradition is very important in understanding how the first Christians, all Jews, understood Jesus' Resurrection, I shall now analyze five authors / writings where Moses' translation is either implied or openly stated.

B. 2.1   *Philo of Alexandria*

The LXX was the holy Scripture of the Hellenistic Jew Philo. At Deut 34:6 it reads: "And they buried him" (καὶ ἔθαψαν αὐτόν), i.e. it was not God alone who did so. In his tractate on the life of Moses, the Alexandrian philosopher notes in *Mos.* 2.288 that "the time came when he had to make his pilgrimage from earth to heaven and 'leave this mortal life for immortality' (ἀπαθανατίζεσθαι),[144] summoned thither by the Father, who resolved his twofold nature of soul and body into a single unity, transforming his whole being into mind, pure as the

---

[142] Cf. for example *'Avot R. Nat.* A 12 (Schechter 50; Goldin 65), as well as Michael Fishbane, *The Kiss of God* 17-18.
[143] The NRSV clouds this up: "He was buried." By whom? These two statements about the first redeemer of Israel, about Moses' definitely dying and being buried, can be compared with the statements about the final redeemer of Israel, the Messiah Jesus, in the Apostles' Creed: "he died and was buried." Both emphasize that the death event was not spurious; it actually took place.
[144] Cf. LSJ 174. II., pass.: become immortal.

sunlight."[145] For Philo the conclusion of the holy Scriptures regarding Moses (Deuteronomy 34) is "most wonderful of all" (290):

> when he was already being 'taken up into heaven' (ἀναλαμβανόμενος)[146] and stood at the very barrier, ready at the signal to direct his flight to heaven, the divine spirit fell upon him and he prophesied with discernment while still alive the story of his own death; told before the end how the end came, and how he was buried with none present, surely by no mortal hands but by immortal powers; how he was not laid to rest in the tomb of his forefathers but obtained a special monument which no man has ever seen....[147]

Here Philo relates that Moses actually died. The "immortal powers" (ἀθανάτοις δυνάμεσιν) who buried him are most likely thought by Philo to be angels, the Lord's servants acting on His behalf. Yet Philo also speaks of Moses' "becoming immortal," of his "being taken up into heaven" at this very point. Since God now "resolved his [Moses'] twofold nature of soul and body into a single unity, transforming his whole being into mind, pure as sunlight" (2.288), it must be asked whether the Alexandrian philosopher now thought that Moses' body was now taken up to heaven together with his soul. Other passages in his works suggest this.

In *Sac.* 1-10 Philo comments on God's "adding" in LXX Gen 4:2. The three patriarchs, Abraham, Isaac and Jacob, were all "added" to the divine company when they died (5-7).[148] In 8 he states that God "advanced" (προάγω) others even higher and "'stationed' them beside Himself." The latter Greek verb is ἱδρύω : to make to sit down, seat.[149] Yet Philo clearly means it here in the sense of "standing," for he goes on

---

[145] Cf. *Virt.* 76, which relates that after Moses had ended the hymn of Deuteronomy 32, "he began to pass over from mortal existence to life immortal and gradually became conscious of the disuniting of the elements of which he was composed. The body, the shell-like growth which encased him, was being stripped away and the soul laid bare and yearning for its natural removal hence." This is part of the preparation for Moses' "departure" (ἔξοδος); it is followed by the benedictions of Deuteronomy 33 (77).

[146] Cf. LSJ 110 on ἀναλαμβάνω : take up into heaven. The passive is found of Elijah in 4 Kgdms 2:9-11 and of Jesus in Acts 1:2, 11 and 22. See also the noun ἀνάλημψις of Jesus in Luke 9:51. Here in Philo, F. H. Colson has "being exalted."

[147] *Mos.* 2.291. I slightly modify Colson's translation in the LCL.

[148] Philo employs the verb μετανίστανται of them in 7, which the LCL translator F. H. Colson renders "translated." Cf. LSJ 1115 on μετανίστημι : remove.

[149] LSJ 820. Cf. Josephus, *Ant.* 1.285 and 17.201 for this meaning.

to state: "Such is Moses, to whom He says: 'Stand here with Me' (σὺ δὲ αὐτοῦ στῆθι μετ᾽ ἐμοῦ - Deut 5:31)."[150] In contrast to the three Patriarchs, there was "no room in him for adding or taking away" when Moses died. Rather, "through the Word" (LXX Deut 34:5) of the Supreme Cause Moses is "translated" (μετανίσταται); (it is the same as that) "by which also the whole universe was formed."[151] The "same Word, by which He made the universe, is that by which He 'draws up' (ἀνάγων) the perfect man from earthly things to Himself." In 9 Philo states that God sent Moses "as a loan to the earthly sphere," "appointing him as god" (Exod 7:1). Since god /God is not susceptible of addition or diminution, being fully and unchangeably himself /Himself, we are therefore told (10) that "'no man knows his grave' (Deut 34:6). For who has powers such that he could perceive the passing of a perfect soul to Him that 'IS'?"

Here Philo emphasizes that at Moses' death, God made him stand next to Himself (in heaven). Through God's Word he is "translated," "drawn up," to Him. As "god," his gravesite is unknown. These emphases are also found elsewhere.

Philo employs "Stand here with Me" from Deut 5:31 also in *Post.* 28-30; *Quod Deus* 23; *Gig.* 48-49; *Conf.* 29-31; and *Somn.* 2.227-28. *Post.* 28 is typical when it says of God and Moses: "He makes the worthy man sharer of His own Nature, which is repose." This "standing here with Me" in regard to the first redeemer of Israel, Moses, should be related to the application of Ps 110:1 to the final redeemer of Israel, for Christians the Messiah Jesus: "Sit at My right hand."[152]

Philo was aware of Enoch's being "translated" in Gen 5:24,[153] yet for him Enoch is primarily a model of repentance.[154] In *Quaest. Gen.* 1.86 on Gen 5:24, Philo also mentions Enoch's "translation" (μετάθεσις , μεταβολή).[155] Something very marvelous (θαυμασιώτατον)[156] was that

---

150 Cf. Colson's alternate translation in n. "b" on 8: "Stand with Me Myself." I shall comment on the importance of Deut 5:31 for Philo below.

151 Cf. God's "saying" the words of creation in Genesis 1, as well as John 1:1-5.

152 Cf. for example Mark 12:36; Acts 2:34-35; Rom 8:34; and 1 Cor 15:25. Again, it should be recalled that Philo employs the verb ἱδρύω , to make to sit down, to seat, in this connection in *Sac.* 8, himself changing its meaning to "stand."

153 Cf. *Abr.* 18-19, 24; *Post.* 43; *Mut.* 38; and *Praem.* 16-17.

154 Cf. *Abr.* 17-18; *Praem.* 15-16, 22; and *Quaest. Gen.* 1.83-85 on Gen 5:21-23. See also Sir 44:16.

155 These are suggested by Ralph Marcus in the LCL edition, *Philo, Supplement I*, p. 54, on the basis of the available Greek fragments and Philo's usage elsewhere. The text itself has only survived in Armenian (vii).

Enoch "seemed to be rapt away (ἁρπασθῆναι) and became invisible (ἀόρατος)," moving "from a sensible and visible place to an incorporeal and intelligible form. This gift the proto-prophet [Moses] also obtained, for no one knew his burial place [Deut 34:6]. And still another, Elijah, followed him on high from earth to heaven at the appearance of the divine countenance, or, it would be more proper and correct to say, he 'ascended' (ἀνέβη)." Here Philo refers to Elijah's "ascension" in 2 Kgs (4 Kgdms) 2:11.[157]

For Philo, Moses thus joined the only two figures in the Hebrew and the Greek Bibles who were taken alive during their lifetime into heaven, Enoch and Elijah. Like them he was "translated" by God at the end of his life. The fact that Moses' grave cannot be found seems to imply that he was god-like, being taken up at the end of his life to stand (actually sit) directly next to God. Did he conceive of Moses' tomb (Deut 34:6) as now empty, as in Mark 16:1-8? The question must unfortunately be left open, yet I tend to think he did.

B. 2.2   Josephus

This first-century CE native of Jerusalem, whose mother tongue was Aramaic, relates that when Moses was absent for forty days at Mount Sinai (cf. Exod 32:1), the Hebrews were very worried that he had perished. While some thought "he had fallen a victim to wild beasts," others thought that "he had been taken back to the divinity" (πρὸς τὸ θεῖον ἀνακεχωρηκέναι), since "that he should be 'translated' (μεταστῆναι) by God to Himself by reason of his inherent virtue was likely enough" (*Ant.* 3.96-97). The latter is also emphasized by the Jewish historian in his description of the end of Moses' life.

In *Ant.* 4.315 Moses informs the Israelites that this is the day God had appointed for his "departure" (ἄφιξις).[158] It is the "end" (τελευτή) of his life (320).[159] He then advanced "towards the place where he was about to 'disappear' (ἀφανισθήσεται - 323)," first followed by all, including the elders (324). Arriving at Mount Abarim,[160] Moses then dismissed the elders (325). Josephus continues:

---

[156] Cf. *Mos.* 2.290 for this also of Moses.

[157] The latter certainly became the model for Jesus' ascension in Luke 24:50-51 and Acts 1:2, 9-11.

[158] LSJ 291,2.

[159] LSJ 1771.

[160] Cf. Deut 32:49, "this mountain of the Abarim, Mount Nebo." The latter is named in 34:1 with "the top of Pisgah."

While he bade farewell to Eleazar and Joshua and was yet communing with them, clouds (νέφους) suddenly descended upon him and 'he disappeared' (ἀφανίζεται) in a ravine. But he has written of himself in the sacred books that he died [Deut 34:5], for fear lest they should venture to say that by reason of his surpassing virtue 'he had gone back to the Deity' (πρὸς τὸ θεῖον ἀναχωρῆσαι) (326).[161]

In *Ant.* 5.1 Josephus notes that he has just described how Moses had been "rapt away' (ἀπογεγόντος)[162] from men."

The Jerusalem historian, later writing in Rome, was well aware of God's "taking" Enoch alive to Himself in Gen 5:24, and of Elijah's "ascending into heaven" alive in 2 Kgs 2:11. In *Ant.* 1.85 he writes that Enoch lived 365 years and then "returned to the divinity" (ἀνεχώρησε πρὸς τὸ θεῖον). Since this Greek phrase is the same as that which Josephus employs in *Ant.* 3.96 and 4.326 of Moses,[163] it is fair to assume that Josephus himself thought that Moses was "translated by God to Himself" at the end of his life (3.97, explaining 96).

In *Ant.* 9.28 Josephus writes that Elijah "disappeared" (ἠφανίσθη) from among men, and "no one knows his end to this day." The historian is hesitant about recording Elijah's actual ascension. Nevertheless he continues: "concerning Elijah and Enoch, who lived before the Flood, it is written in the sacred books that they 'became invisible' (γεγόνασιν ἀφανεῖς), and no one knows of their death."

The verb ἀφανίζομαι , "to disappear,"[164] used by Josephus of Elijah's ascending into heaven alive, is the same verb as the Jewish historian employs to describe Moses' "disappearing" at the end of his life in *Ant.* 4.323 and 326. It is thus quite possible that Josephus also meant here that Moses was "translated" bodily into heaven. His noting in 4.326 that

---

161 The Parma MS of the "Departure / Death of Moses" (*Petirat Mosheh*) ends similarly. First all the Israelites follow Moses to Mount Abarim. Yet only the elders then follow him half way up to the top. Moses at this point tells Eleazar to stay with the elders, while Joshua alone ascends with him. At the summit "Moses stole away. Whereupon the clouds of glory came down and snatched him, lifting him upward" (Kushelevsky, *Moses and the Angel of Death* 271-72).

162 Cf. ἀπογίνομαι in LSJ 194, II: to be taken away. The only other occurrence of the verb in Josephus is *Ant.* 19.178 in the sense of "to be rid of." *The Complete Concordance to Flavius Josephus* 1.176 on the perfect in *Ant.* 5.1 has: "to be translated, be departed, be dead."

163 It should be noted that he only uses the phrase in these three cases.

164 LSJ 286, II. Pass., disappear, be missing. Cf. the noun ἀφάνισις II. as "disappearance" (*ibid.*). LSJ point out at ἀφανής that when it is used with γίγνεσθαι , it is equal to ἀφανίζεσθαι (as in *Ant.* 9.28).

Moses wrote of himself in Scripture that he died (Deut 34:5) was lest people "should venture to say that by reason of his surpassing virtue he had gone back to the Deity" (cf. also 3.96). The Jewish historian seems to be intentionally ambiguous here, which points to the probability that some of his earlier Palestinian contemporaries believed Moses had actually died, while others believed he was "translated" to God, he "disappeared," he "went back" to the Deity. Josephus appears to want to do justice to both views, yet his own, the latter, seems to be relatively clear.

Although he later wrote his *Antiquities* in Rome, Josephus does not make use of apotheosis or "divine man" imagery from Greco-Roman sources here.[165] As I will point out in section 2.5 below, Josephus' imagery of a "cloud" and Moses' "disappearing," for example, rather derive from Palestinian Jewish traditions.

B. 2.3   Pseudo-Philo

Written in Palestine in Hebrew in the first century CE, *Pseudo-Philo* quotes Gen 5:24 in 1:16 in regard to Enoch's being taken to heaven by God while still alive.[166] While he nowhere mentions the ascension of Elijah, he describes Phinehas in terms of it in 48:1-2. When Phinehas is about to die, the Lord informs him that he will later "'be lifted up' (*elevaberis*) into the place where those who were before you 'were lifted up,'[167] and you will be there until I remember the world. Then I will make you [pl.] come, and you [pl.] will taste what is death. 2) And Phinehas 'went up' (*ascendit*) and did all that the Lord commanded

---

165 Cf. Dionysius of Halicarnassus, *Ant. Rom.* i. 64.4 on Aeneas, and ii. 56.2 on Romulus, cited by Thackeray in n. "b" on *Ant.* 4.326 in the LCL edition, as well as other sources noted by James Tabor in "'Returning to the Divinity': Josephus's Portrayal of the Disappearance of Enoch, Elijah and Moses" in *JBL* 108 (1989) 225, n. 1, and 230-34. Tabor concludes that Josephus' description of the Moses death scene "is purposely left ambiguous" (238), with which I agree. See also Christopher Begg, "Josephus's Portrayal of the Disappearances of Enoch, Elijah, and Moses: Some Observations" in *JBL* 109 (1990) 691-93. Other Hellenistic sources are cited by Klaus Haacker in "Nachbiblische Traditionen vom Tode Mose" in *Josephus-Studien*, Festschrift Otto Michel, ed. Otto Betz and Martin Hengel (Göttingen: Vandenhoeck & Ruprecht, 1974) 149, n. 8, and 150, n. 10. See also Yarbro Collins in n. 103.

166 *SC* 229.62; *OTP* 2.304. Both texts are by Daniel Harrington.

167 This may be the site under God's Throne of Glory, where Moses, like Enoch and the Patriarchs, is placed after his "translation." See the next section.

him. ... 3) Now in that time when he 'would go up' (*ascenderet*)...."[168]
The latter imagery of "going up" refers to Phinehas' obeying the Lord's
instructions first to dwell in Danaban on the mountain for many years
(1). Yet it may also allude proleptically to his later "ascension" by being
"lifted up." The latter is meant as a divine passive: it is God who will
then "lift up / raise" Phinehas. Yet he will later die, together with others
set in the same place with him beforehand. The strange assertion of
Phinehas' later dying may be directed against those of *Pseudo-Philo's*
contemporaries who laid emphasis on Elijah's (and Moses') never having
died. The latter seems indeed to be the case in the author's description of
Moses' farewell.

Verse seven of chapter 19 reads: "Now I will show you [Moses] the
land before you die, but you will not enter it...."[169] This clearly reflects
Deut 34:1b and 4b. God also tells Moses here: "I will show you the place
where they will serve Me for 740 years. And after this it will be turned
over into the hands of their enemies, and they will destroy it, and
foreigners will encircle it."[170] The Tannaitic midrash *Sifre* Ve'zot ha-
Berakhah 357 on Deut 34:1, "And the Lord showed him all the land, even
Gilead," also explains in regard to Gilead that God "showed him the
Temple established in peace, and then showed to him destroyers
demolishing it," for Gilead means the Temple.[171]

Moses then "*ascended* Mount Abarim as God had commanded him"
(*Pseudo-Philo* 19:8), alluding to Deut 34:1,[172] and in 19:10 God's promise to
show Moses the land is put into effect by *Pseudo-Philo's* quoting sections
of Deut 34:1 and 4.[173] In 19:12 God then tells Moses: "Now I will take you
and glorify you with your fathers, and I will give you rest in your
slumber and bury you in peace. ... But neither angel *nor man* will *know*

---

[168] *SC* 229.320; *OTP* 2.362, which has "went up." The "all" of Harrington's "you all"
in v 1 is not in the Latin, which may point to a smaller group such as I mention in
the previous note. If "all" is nevertheless implied, cf. 23:13, where God tells
Joshua: "I will take your souls and store them in peace until the time allotted the
world be complete" (*OTP* 2.333). *Pseudo-Philo* apparently believes that at death
"the soul is separated from the body" (44:10 in *OTP* 2.359).

[169] *SC* 229.158; *OTP* 2.327.

[170] *SC* 229.158 and 160; *OTP* 2.327. Harrington's note "h" ("Presumably the
Temple") should omit "presumably."

[171] Finkelstein 425; Hammer 378.

[172] Like Josephus, *Pseudo-Philo* avoids the mention of Mount Nebo, the top of
Pisgah, in the biblical verse, which begins by Moses' "ascending."

[173] *SC* 229.160 and 162; *OTP* 2.327.

your *tomb*[174] in which you are to be buried until I visit the world. And 'I will raise up' (*excitabo*) you and your fathers from the land of Egypt in which you sleep, and you will come together and dwell in the immortal dwelling place that is not subject to time." God says that when the time arrives for Him to visit the world, "I will hurry 'to raise up' (*excitare*) you who are sleeping in order that all who can live may dwell in the place of sanctification I showed you" (v 13).[175]

When Moses then heard God's reply to how much time is left for the world, "he was filled with understanding and his appearance became glorious; *and he died* in glory *according to the word of the Lord, and He buried him* [Deut 34:5-6] as He had promised him" (19:16a). After remarks on the heavenly mourning for Moses, *Pseudo-Philo* closes his account in v 16b with another reference to Deut 34:6 : "*And He buried him* with His own hands on a high place and in the light of all the world."[176]

Pseudo-Philo thus interlaces his account of Moses' death with numerous references to Deuteronomy 34, which deals with it. He stresses Moses' later participation in the *general* resurrection of the dead (19:12-13), and that Israel's great leader actually died, for the Lord Himself buried him. In contrast to the biblical account, however, this burial was "in the light of all the world" (v 16), i.e. public. Along with other commentators,[177] I would maintain that *Pseudo-Philo* in this entire chapter is actually trying to combat the belief held by some of his Palestinian contemporaries that Moses never died, for he was

---

[174] An allusion to Deut 34:6.

[175] *SC* 229.162 and 164; *OTP* 2.327.

[176] *SC* 229.164; *OTP* 2.327. It should also be noted that Deut 34:1-3 provides much of the background to the description of Baruch's final hours in 2 Baruch 76:3. Just before this, v 2 states of him: "you will surely depart from this world, nevertheless not to death but to be kept unto (the end) of times." Cf. *OTP* 1.646, and A. Klijn on pp. 616-17 on the writing as originally in Hebrew, Palestinian, and from the beginning of the second century CE, although also incorporating earlier traditions.

[177] Cf. for example Harrington in *OTP* 2.327, n. "u," who calls attention to *Test. Mos.* 1:15. There Moses tells his successor Joshua: "The years of my life have come to an end and, in the presence of the entire community, I am going to sleep with my fathers" (*OTP* 1.927). Josephus, however, should not be cited as support for Moses' burial in public, for there he first signals all the Israelites not to follow him, then dismisses the elders, and is finally alone with Eleazar and Joshua (*Ant.* 4.323-26) when he disappears. See the previous section. Klaus Haacker in "Nachbiblische Traditionen" 156 sees various indications of an "Entrückung" for Moses in *Pseudo-Philo* 19, indicating that the author could not completely excise all signs of Moses' continuing to live.

"translated" to God at the end of his life.[178] *Pseudo-Philo* thus appears to be a negative witness to the latter belief.

B. 2.4   *The Transfiguration of Jesus*

Jesus' Transfiguration is found in Mark 9:2-8, as well as in Matt 17:1-8 and Luke 9:28-36.[179] It is one of the most puzzling pericopes in the Synoptics. In Mark 9:4 it is stated that Elijah "appeared" (ὤφθη) to them (Jesus, Peter, James and John on a high mountain - v 2) "with Moses, and they [Elijah and Moses] were talking with Jesus." In v 5, probably out of respect for the great lawgiver, Peter mentions Moses before Elijah. On the way down the mountain after Jesus' Transfiguration, the three disciples inquire about Elijah's having to come first before the Son of Man's "rising from the dead" (vv 9-11), and Jesus answers their question with other references to Elijah in vv 12-13.

Elijah's role at Jesus' Transfiguration is understandable. He "ascended" alive in a whirlwind into heaven (2 Kgs 2:11; cf. v 1). According to Mal 3:23 (Eng. 4:5), the Lord will send him to the Israelites "before the great and terrible day of the Lord comes." In Sirach 48, originally in Hebrew, from Jerusalem and the early second century BCE,[180] the author first states in v 4: "How glorious you were, Elijah, in your wondrous deeds! Whose glory is equal to yours?" After mentioning his stay at Sinai /Horeb (1 Kgs 19:1-18) in v 7, Sirach notes Elijah's being "taken up" in v 9, and his future return in v 10. The prophet is thus now still alive in heaven (cf. v 11), and first-century scribes or experts in the Scriptures could justly maintain that before the resurrection of the dead "Elijah must come first" (Mark 9:11). Elijah's appearance at Jesus'

---

[178] Another indication of this may be alluded to in the next chapter, where in 20:2 God tells Joshua in reference to Josh 1:1-2 : "Why do you mourn, and why do you hope in vain that Moses *yet lives?* And now you wait to no purpose, because Moses is dead" (*SC* 229.166; *OTP* 2.329). See also 32:9 (*SC* 229.248; Harrington in *OTP* 2.346), where God tells Moses when he is dying: "the heaven that you are [now] to enter." Yet here Moses actually dies, and *celum in quo ingressus es* could also mean "the heaven which you [once before] entered." In addition, in 9:7 it is stated in regard to Moses and his father Amram: "he who will be born from him will serve Me forever..." (*SC* 229.110; *OTP* 2.316).

[179] For recent bibliography on the pericope, cf. Craig Evans, *Mark 8:27 - 16:20*, 30-33 and 39-40, as well as John Donahue and Daniel Harrington, *The Gospel of Mark* (Sacra Pagina 2; Collegeville, MN: The Liturgical Press, 2002) 275-76.

[180] Cf. Nickelsburg, *Jewish Literature* 53, 62-63.

Transfiguration thus creates no difficulties, for the end time is thought of as having arrived.

Moses' appearance there, however, is at first sight very unexpected. Yet it can be explained in part by his being very closely connected to Elijah in Judaic tradition.[181] R. Tanḥum Berabbi, a fifth generation Palestinian Amora known for compiling collections of haggadah,[182] for example, maintained that "Moses and Elijah were alike in every respect." He then made twenty-eight comparisons between them, a number of which are of relevance to the Transfiguration.[183] Many of these comparisons of Moses and Elijah are certainly much older than this well-known compiler and show how the two figures were closely associated in Judaic tradition.

Moses, like Elijah, was also thought of in some sections of first-century CE Hellenistic and Palestinian Judaism as being translated to heaven at his death, without dying (see Philo, Josephus and *Pseudo-Philo* as analyzed above, but especially the next section, B. 2.5, on the rabbinic writings). Thus he is most probably not pictured as coming to the scene of the Transfiguration from his grave (in spite of Deut 34:6), but like Elijah from heaven, to which he had been translated by God.[184]

---

[181] Against the assertion of Paul Billerbeck in Str-B 1.756.

[182] *Introduction* 106.

[183] Cf. *Pesiq. R.* 4/2 in Friedmann 13a-b, and Braude 1.85-88. In *Num. Rab.* Behaʿalothecha 15/13 on Num 10:1 (Mirkin 10.148; Soncino 6.654), it is stated that God gives a share of His own glory to those who fear Him. These are Moses, Elijah, and the Messianic King, whom God "will clothe in His own robes," as Ps 21:6 (Eng. 5) is interpreted.

[184] Cf. *Deut. Rab.* ʿEqeb 3/17 on Deut 10:1 (Mirkin 11.68; Soncino 7.88), where God says to Moses: "I swear to you, as you devoted your life to their [Israel's] service in this world, so too in the time to come when I bring Elijah, the prophet, to them, the two of you shall come together." Elijah's and Moses' appearance at Jesus' Transfiguration is thus one sign that the final time has arrived. To my knowledge Joachim Jeremias in his art. Μωυσῆς in *TDNT* 4.855 was the first to relate the translation / rapture of Moses to the Transfiguration in Mark 9:4-5. He is followed here by Margaret Thrall, "Elijah and Moses in Mark's Account of the Transfiguration" in *NTS* 16 (1970) 305-17, esp. 314. It may also be noted that before the Transfiguration, Matt 16:14 has Jesus' disciples tell him some people say he is John the Baptist, others Elijah, and others Jeremiah or one of the (other) prophets. This presupposes that the latter figures could return (from heaven). On Jeremiah in this regard, see the *Lives of the Prophets* 2:19, which states regarding him: "so that he might become a partner of Moses, and they are together to this day" (*OTP* 2.388, with reference to 2 Macc 15:13-16 in n. "z"; D. Hare considers the writing to be Palestinian and from the first century CE: pp. 380-82).

B. 2.5   Rabbinic Writings

Several passages in rabbinic sources relate, in direct contradiction to Scripture (Deut 34:5), that Moses did not die. One of them is found in the Tannaitic midrash *Sifre* Ve'zot ha-Berakhah 357 on the above verse. In contrast to the majority view, "Others say: Moses never died, and he stands and serves on high (לא מת משה אלא עומד ומשרת למעלה), as is shown by the use of the same adverb 'there' in this verse, ['Then Moses, the servant of the Lord, died *there* in the land of Moab, at the Lord's command,'] and in the verse, 'And he was *there* with the Lord' (Exod 34:28)."[185] The verb שָׁרַת, "to serve," "to minister," is employed here of Moses' present function in heaven ("on high").[186]

In *b. Soṭah* 13b it is similarly related: "It has been taught: R. Eliezer the Elder[187] said: "Over an area of twelve *mil* square, corresponding to that of the camp of Israel, a *bath kol* [heavenly voice] made the proclamation: 'So Moses died there' (Deut 34:5), the great Sage of Israel. Others declare that Moses never died. It is written here, 'So Moses died *there*,' and elsewhere it is written, 'And he was *there* with the Lord' (Exod 34:28). As in the latter passage it means standing and ministering, so also in the former it means standing and ministering."[188] In this talmudic passage the verb employed for "ministering" is שָׁמַשׁ, "to minister," "to officiate."[189] This tradition is also found in *Midr. Tannaim* Deut 34:5,[190] which is the same as *Midrash Haggadol ad loc.*[191] It should also be noted that a Tannaitic tradition cited in *Midrash Haggadol* on God's taking Enoch live into heaven in Gen 5:24 states: "Three ascended 'and served' [וישמשו , meant as 'serve'] on high. And they are: Enoch, Moses and Elijah." The

---

[185] Finkelstein 428; Hammer 381. The same kind of use of "there" in Deut 34:5 and Gen 49:31 just before this makes another point.

[186] Jastrow 1635.

[187] This is Eliezer b. Hyrcanus, an older second generation Tanna (*Introduction* 77).

[188] Soncino 71-72.

[189] Jastrow 1601. While also used of priests, the verb is applied to many non-priests also, as Jastrow's examples show. Against Peter Schäfer in "Nachbiblische Traditionen vom Tod des Mose" 171, with n. 37, as well as Beate Ego, "Der Diener im Palast des himmlischen Königs. Zur Interpretation einer priesterlichen Tradition im rabbinischen Judentum," in *Königsherrschaft Gottes und himmlischer Kult im Judentum, Urchristentum und in der hellenistischen Welt*, ed. Martin Hengel and Anna Maria Schwemer (WUNT 55; Tübingen: Mohr, 1991) 374-75.

[190] Hoffmann 224.

[191] Fisch, *Deuteronomy* 783. It also has the verb שׁרת .

prooftexts given are Gen 5:24 for Enoch, Deut 34:1 (with וַיַּעַל ,
understood as his "ascending") and 6 for Moses, and 2 Kgs 2:11 (with
וַיַּעַל) for Elijah.[192]

Yet how is Moses thought to presently "serve" on high / in heaven?
This depends in part on the expression rendered "the great Sage" of
Israel above: סָפְרָא רבה . While the Aramaic סָפֵר , סָפְרָא , equivalent to
the Hebrew סוֹפֵר , can mean "scholar" or "teacher," its first meaning is
"scribe," "writer of documents," "copyist."[193] This seems more appropriate
here because it means Moses continued in heaven the same activity in
which he was engaged on earth when he wrote the Pentateuch, the "five
books of Moses."[194] *Lev. Rab.* Vayyiqra 1/3 on Lev 1:1 for example states
that one of the ten names of Moses was "Shemaiah." He was called "'the
scribe' [of 1 Chron 24:6] because he was 'the scribe [סוֹפֵר]' of Israel."[195]
Targ. Onq. Deut 33:21 also states regarding Gad: "in his inherited
territory Moses 'the great scribe of Israel' (סַפְרָא רבא דישראל) is
buried."[196] This title is applied to Moses in very many other targumic
passages.[197] *Frag. Targ.* Num 12:7 for example has God say of Moses: "He
is the most trustworthy among all the scribes of My royal court."[198]
Because Moses was so frequently labeled as such on earth, it was
thought that he should continue with this title (and activity) on high / in
heaven.

---

[192] Margulies 132. Addition 2 to *'Avot R. Nat.* A may also be of relevance here:
"like God's angels of service, He hid [Moses] for the life of the world to come, as
it says: 'And no one knows his burial place to this day' (Deut 34:6)" (Schechter
157). Another text which *may* assume that Moses did not die is *b. Tem.* 16a
(Soncino 109). There Rab, a first generation Babylonian Amora who studied with
Rabbi in Palestine (*Introduction* 93), maintains Moses spoke to his successor
Joshua "when he departed [this world] for the Garden of Eden."

[193] Jastrow 1018.

[194] Cf. *b. B. Bath.* 14b-15a (Soncino 71-72). In the Pentateuch see already Exod
17:14; 24:4; 34:27-28; Num 17:17-18 (Eng. 2-3); 33:2; Deut 31:9, 19, 22 and 24.

[195] Mirkin 7.12; Soncino 4.6-7.

[196] Sperber 1.351; Grossfeld 110. The latter points out in n. 57 that the term מְחֹקֵק
(from חקק , to inscribe: BDB 349) here is interpreted of Moses as "the inscriber" =
"scribe," as in *b. B. Bath.* 15a with Job 19:23 and Deut 33:21 (Soncino 73).

[197] Cf. the extensive list in Maher on *Targ. Ps.-Jon.* Gen 27:29 (96, n. 20). It should
also be noted that Moses' teacher in heaven was Zagzagel, "the Master Scribe
[רַב סוֹפֵר] of the children of heaven [= the angels]." See *Deut. Rab.* Ve'zot ha-
Berakhah 11/10 (Mirkin 11.156; Soncino 7.182), as well as *1 Petirat Mosheh*
(Jellinek A) in Jellinek 1.124.

[198] Cf. Klein 1.97 on MS "P," English in 2.67; see also MS "V" in 1.194 and 2.152.

Several passages in the Hebrew Bible speak of God's record book.[199] It is also mentioned for example in *m.* *'Avot* 2:1 and 3:16,[200] and in *b. Roš. Haš.* 16b.[201] The Tannaitic *Sifre* Ha'azinu 312 on Deut 32:4 states that "when one departs from this world," all his deeds confront him in regard to the specific times on which they occurred. When he acknowledges them, they say to him, "Sign!" Job 37:7 is the prooftext for this.[202] The question is, who is meant by "they say" (אוֹמְרִים) here? I suggest not the deeds themselves, but heavenly scribes. These are probably modeled on the earthly Great Sanhedrin, which has "a pair of judges' scribes who stand before these, one at the right and one at the left, and write down the words of those who acquit and the words of those who condemn."[203] An example of two such scribes in heaven is the following.

Mal 3:16 speaks of a "book of remembrance" which was written before the Lord of those who revered Him and thought about His name. *Lev. Rab.* Behar 34/8 relates in the name of R. Levi, a third generation Palestinian Amora:[204] "In times past when a man performed a good deed, the prophet used to record it. But now if a man performs a good deed, who records it? Elijah and the King Messiah, the Holy One, blessed be He, signing beside them, as in Mal 3:16."[205] Elijah is also thought of elsewhere as the heavenly scribe, for example in the Tannaitic *Seder 'Olam,* chapter 17. It states: "now [in heaven] he writes down the deeds of all generations."[206]

---

[199] Cf. BDB 707, 3.g. on סֵפֶר . See also Isa 4:3; Dan 7:10; 12:1; Luke 10:20; Rev 3:5; 13:8; 17:8; 20:12, 15; and 21:27.

[200] Albeck 4.357 and 367; Danby 447 and 452.

[201] Soncino 63. See also *Pesiq. R.* 8/2 (Friedmann 29a; Braude 1.147).

[202] Finkelstein 345; Hammer 312. A parallel is found in *b. Ta'an.* 11a (Soncino 49).

[203] Cf. *m. Sanh.* 4:3 (Albeck 4.181; Danby 387); *Exod. Rab.* Shemoth 5/12 on Exod 4:29 (Mirkin 5.95; Soncino 3.92); and *Lev. Rab.* 'Emor 30/11 on Lev 23:40 (Mirkin 8.126; Soncino 4.392). See also *Gen. Rab.* Vayechi 98/8 on Gen 49:10 (Theodor and Albeck 1259; Soncino 2.956) and *Cant. Rab.* 3:7 § 3 (Donsqi 91; Soncino 9.162) on these two scribes.

[204] *Introduction* 98.

[205] Mirkin 8.166; Soncino 4.435. Cf. the parallel in *Ruth Rab.* 5/6 on Ruth 2:14 (Vilna 19 or 10a; Soncino 8.66 should read the same). For Elijah and the King Messiah together at the eschatological ingathering of the Jews, see *Targ. Ps.-Jon.* Deut 30:4 (Rieder 2.298; Clarke 83).

[206] Guggenheimer 153-54. This activity of Elijah is thus not late or post-talmudic, as claimed by Moses Aberbach in his art. "Elijah, In the Aggadah" in *EJ* (1971) 6.637. Cf. also *b. Qidd.* 70a: "Elijah writes and the Holy One, blessed be He, attests" (Soncino 354). Because both figures were extremely "zealous," Phinehas is often identified with Elijah and is thus viewed as also being in heaven (see the

The same is true for Enoch. Already in the middle of the second century BCE *Jubilees*, originally written in Hebrew in Palestine,[207] noted in 4:23 that Enoch, having been taken up to heaven, "is there writing condemnation and judgment of the world, and all the evils of the children of men."[208] *1 Enoch* 12:1-2 relates that Enoch was hidden, and "his dwelling place and his activities were with the Watchers and the holy ones." Verse 4 labels him "Enoch, scribe of righteousness."[209] This writing is also Palestinian, originally in Aramaic and Hebrew, and this section of it is thought to be pre-Maccabean, i.e. from the early second century BCE.[210] Finally, *Targ. Pseud.-Jon.* Gen 5:24 states that Enoch "was taken away and he ascended to the firmament at the command of the Lord, and he was called Metatron, 'the Great Scribe [ספרא רבא].'"[211] In *b. Ḥag.* 15a, for example, permission is given (by God) to Metatron "to sit and write down the merits of Israel."[212]

The above texts indicate that both Elijah and Enoch, who in biblical and Judaic tradition ascended and / or were taken up live into heaven, were considered to have assumed a scribal activity there. They register

---

passages cited by Aberbach). Yet in contrast to Elijah, his activity is not of a scribal nature. In *b. B. Bath.* 15a (Soncino 72-73), Phinehas is said to have finished writing the book of Joshua after the latter died; yet this was while Phinehas was still on earth, having attained a very advanced age. On his priestly task in heaven, see Ginzberg, *The Legends* 3.389 and the sources in the relevant notes. For Phinehas' ascension or being "lifted up" (*elevaberis*) described in terms of Elijah's ascension already in the first century CE writing *Pseudo-Philo*, see 48:1 (*SC* 229.320; *OTP* 2.362, with n. "a") and section B. 2.3 above.

[207] Cf. O. S. Wintermute in *OTP* 2.43-45.

[208] *OTP* 2.63. In v 25 he offers incense in the evening at the holy place on Mount Qatar, also implying a priestly function.

[209] *OTP* 1.19 and 21. In 15:2 and 16:2 he intercedes on behalf of men.

[210] Cf. E. Isaac in *OTP* 1.6-8. See also Nickelsburg, *Jewish Literature* 46, as well as 50-51, and 354, n. 30, on Ezra the scribe. Are the two angels who "record sins and righteous deeds" in *Test. Abr.* 13:9 (*OTP* 1.890) Elijah and Enoch? Unfortunately, the question cannot be answered.

[211] Rieder 1.8; Maher 37, who remarks in n. 10: "The identification of Enoch with Metatron seems to have taken place sometime after 450 C.E." See the literature he cites there on the Enoch-Metatron traditions, as well as the sources noted by Emil Hirsch in the art. "Enoch" in *JE* (1903/1925) 5.178. In regard to *2 Enoch*, see now Andrei Orlov, *The Enoch-Metatron Tradition* (TSAJ 107; Tübingen: Mohr Siebeck, 2005), although his early dating of the writing in the Second Temple period is very implausible.

[212] Soncino 93. On this scene, cf. also *3 Enoch* 16 and Philip Alexander's notes on it (*OTP* 1.268).

the good and evil deeds of humans on earth in the heavenly book(s) for the final Judgment. I suggest that just as Metatron was later thought to take over this function from Enoch, even to be identified with him, Moses, the "great scribe" of Israel during his lifetime, was also considered to continue this activity in heaven after not having died, i.e. after having been translated there by God.

*   *   *

The above analysis of Moses' not dying, but being "translated" to heaven by God at the end of his life, shows that this is alluded to or "hinted at" by Philo, Josephus and *Pseudo-Philo*; it probably stands behind Moses' appearing in the narrative of Jesus' Transfiguration; and it is openly maintained in several rabbinic writings, at least one of which is Tannaitic (*Sifre* on Deuteronomy). Thus the Resurrection of the final redeemer of Israel, the Messiah Jesus, God's taking him to Himself without Jesus' first dying, could have been based on this alternative model of Israel's first redeemer, Moses. I call this "Model A." Yet both the four Gospels and the early witness of the Apostle Paul (e.g., 1 Cor 15:3-4) emphasize that Jesus definitely died and was buried, as Scripture maintains happened to Moses (Deut 34:5-6). Because early Judaic tradition on the latter also asserted that at his death God took the soul of Moses to Himself in heaven, this second model for God's "raising" Jesus to heaven, which I call "Model B," should now be explored. It assumes that Moses' body remained in its (unknown) grave, just as Jesus' body remained in its (unknown) grave, that common gravesite into which the Jewish Sanhedrin deposited the corpses of executed criminals. It is thus to this second model for Jesus' Resurrection, that of God's taking Moses' soul to heaven at his death, to which I now turn.

B. 3 *The Translation / Raising of Moses' Soul to Heaven at his Death*

Deut 34:5 clearly states that Moses, the servant of the Lord, died "there" (at the top of Pisgah, Mount Nebo - v 1), and v 6 that the Lord Himself buried him at an unknown site. Philo relates this in *Mos.* 2.291, Josephus in *Ant.* 4.327-31, and *Pseudo-Philo* in 19:16.[213] In the Tannaitic *Sifre* Ve'zot ha-Berakhah 357 on Deut 34:5, R. Eliezer (b. Hyrcanus, an older second generation Tanna,[214]) states that then "A heavenly voice

---

[213] *SC* 229.164; *OTP* 2.328.
[214] *Introduction* 77.

went forth from within the camp for twelve miles in every direction proclaiming: 'Moses is dead.'"[215] R. Yoḥanan, a second generation Palestinian Amora,[216] also notes in *Deut. Rab.* Ve'zot ha-Berakhah 11/10 on Deut 31:14, "Your time to die is near," that "Scripture refers ten times to the death of Moses." He then lists these occurrences.[217] The majority opinion in early Judaism was thus that Moses truly died.

B. 3.1 *Moses' Death and the General Resurrection of the Dead*

Resurrection is associated in a number of texts in connection with Moses' death. Yet it refers not to a special resurrection for him directly after his own death, but to the general resurrection of the dead at the end of time. One example is the passage cited above, *Sifre* Ve'zot ha-Berakhah 357 on Deut 34:2. It also relates that when Moses went up to the top of Pisgah, Mount Nebo, just before dying, "the Lord showed him the whole land" (v 1), "as far as the Western Sea" (v 2). "Read not 'as far as the hinder sea (*yam*),' but 'as far as the hinder day (*yom*).' This indicates that He showed him the entire world, from the day of creation to the resurrection of the dead."[218] Another example is *Sifre* Niṣṣabim 305 on Deut 31:14, here dealing with Num 27:18. At Moses' death, Joshua mourns profusely, in part by employing Elisha's words at the ascension of Elijah in 2 Kgs 2:12. God comforts him by saying Moses' death affects Him greatly too. "But he is assured of the world to come, as it is said: 'And the Lord said to Moses, Behold, you are about to sleep with your fathers, but will arise' (Deut 31:16)."[219] The latter phrase is the Hebrew וקם , which in the MT applies to "this people" in the sense of "beginning to do something," as in the NRSV. The Tannaitic *Sifre* purposely changes it to mean Moses' resurrection at the end of days, in "the world to come."[220]

---

[215] Finkelstein 428; Hammer 381, with n. 12 on p. 512. See also *b. Soṭah* 13b in section B. 2.5 above.

[216] *Introduction* 94-95.

[217] Mirkin 11.155; Soncino 7.180. A parallel is found in *Pesiq. Rav Kah.*, Suppl. 1 (Mandelbaum 450; Braude and Kapstein 458-59).

[218] Finkelstein 426; Hammer 379.

[219] Finkelstein 327; Hammer 297.

[220] Cf. *b. Sanh.* 90b (Soncino 604-05) for Deut 31:16 with וקם as a proof from the Torah of God's future resurrecting the dead. In *Petirat Mosheh* A, when there is only half an hour left before he is to die, Moses takes farewell of the Israelites by saying: "'May I see you in peace at the Resurrection.' Then he departed with great weeping" (Jellinek 1.126; Kushelevsky 217).

Pseudo-Philo 19, a first-century CE, Palestinian text on the death of Moses, also has God tell him in v 12: "neither angel 'nor man' will 'know' your 'tomb' [Deut 34:6] in which you are to be buried until I visit the world. And 'I will raise you [sing.] up' and your fathers from the land of Egypt in which you [pl.] sleep, and you [pl.] will come together and will dwell in the immortal dwelling place that is not subject to time." Verse 13 continues by stating of God that "when the time draws near to visit the world," "I will hurry to raise up you [pl.] who are sleeping in order that all who live may dwell in the place of sanctification I showed you."[221] God's "raising up" here is the verb *excito*: to make to rise or stand up, raise up, revive.[222] Moses' being raised up, his resurrection by God, is clearly connected to that of all others, all who now "sleep" (= lie dead), when He visits the world at the end of time.

In *Pesiq. Rav Kah.*, Suppl. 1/20, the tradition noted above of Moses' death as mentioned ten times in Scripture is related. Then God says to Moses: "Moses, 'you exalted' [עלית] Me above all the beings of the world and made Me the only object of love in My world. 'I,' for My part, 'shall exalt' [אני מעלה] you above all the inhabitants of the world that all will know there can be none like you in this world. And in the world to come I shall raise [אני מעלה] you above all the righteous - all of them...."[223] Here the same root is employed for "exalting" and "raising up": עלה.[224] In the world to come God will "raise" Moses above all the other righteous. Yet this too will take place at the general "raising" of the dead.

Other Judaic texts, however, emphasize that at Moses' death and burial, God already "raises" his soul to a special place in heaven.[225] It is these to which I now turn.

---

221 *SC* 229.162 and 164; *OTP* 2.328.
222 Chambers Murray 244, II.
223 Mandelbaum 450-51; Braude and Kapstein 459.
224 Jastrow 1081, with the piel as 1) to elevate, exalt, praise, and the hiphil as 1) to raise, bring up. The qal is to go up, rise, ascend. This is important to note in regard to Jesus' "ascension" in Luke-Acts, part of his Resurrection, and in regard to Jesus' being exalted / raised up as basically the same phenomenon in the Gospel of John.
225 This phenomenon is also found of Abraham in *Test. Abr.* A 20:10-12 (*OTP* 1.895), which may originally be Greek from ca. 100 CE in Egypt (E. P. Sanders, 1.874-75; Nickelsburg, *Jewish Literature* 327), and of Job in *Test. Job* 52:10-11 (*OTP* 1.868), also probably originally in Greek from the first half of the second century CE in Egypt (Nickelsburg 320-21; cf. R. P. Spittler in *OTP* 1.830 and 833 with a broader spectrum for the dating). Yet only God's raising *Moses'* soul to heaven is

B. 3.2 God's Raising Moses' Soul to Heaven at His Death

In *Deut. Rab.* Ve'zot ha-Berakhah 11/10, a heavenly voice declares to Moses: "The end, the time of your death has arrived." When Moses asks that he not be handed over to the Angel of Death, God reassures him that He Himself will attend to him and his burial. Then God descends from the highest heavens "to take the soul" (לִטֹּל נִשְׁמָתוֹ) of Moses, accompanied by three angels of service: Michael, Gabriel, and Zagzagel, who proceed to lay out Moses' bier. When Moses' soul attempts to remain in his pure body, God exclaims: "Soul, go forth, do not delay, 'and I will raise you' [וַאֲנִי מַעֲלֶה אוֹתְךָ] to the highest heavens, and I will place you under the Throne of My Glory next to the Cherubim, Seraphim and troops [of angels]." When Moses' soul again attempts to remain in his uncorrupted body, God kisses Moses, taking away his soul with a kiss of the mouth.[226] The latter refers to the end of Deut 34:5, "by the mouth of the Lord," understood as by a kiss.[227]

The Hebrew of "soul" here is נְשָׁמָה.[228] It is one of five different designations for the "soul."[229] The verb for God's "raising" Moses' soul to

---

relevant here. In contrast to the above Abraham and Job texts, the latter is a Semitic, Palestinian tradition.

[226] Mirkin 11.159-60; Soncino 7.186-87. Cf. also *Petirat Mosheh* B in Jellinek 6.77 and Kushelevsky, *Moses and the Angel of Death* 222. In *Deut. Rab.* Ha'azinu 10/4 on Deut 32:1 (Mirkin 11.145; Soncino 7.169), R. Ḥanina, a first generation Palestinian Amora (*Introduction* 91) says that when Moses was about to die, he didn't know whether his soul would go to heaven or to the earth. God reassures him that it will find rest under the Throne of Glory. On the "soul" and the "body," see Matt 6:25 (// Luke 12:22-23) and 10:28, 4 Ezra 7:78 (*OTP* 1.539), as well as the art. ψυχή , "C. Judaism," by Albert Dihle and Eduard Lohse in *TDNT* 9.632-37. Lohse notes that the Greek idea of the immortality of the soul was already influential in the Tannaitic period, for example in Hillel (9.636). See also Josephus' description of the Pharisees in *Bell.* 2.163 and *Ant.* 18.14, but especially *Bell.* 3.374. Claudia Setzer in *Resurrection of the Body in Early Judaism and Early Christianity: Doctrine, Community, and Self-Definition* (Leiden: Brill, 2004) 20 states: "Streams of belief in resurrection of the body and immortality of the soul as rewards for the righteous ran side by side and often mingled. One did not replace the other over time."

[227] Cf. the passages cited by Kushelevsky in *Moses and the Angel of Death*, n. 105 on pp. 247-48.

[228] Jastrow 941: breath, spirit, soul.

[229] Cf. *Deut. Rab.* Va'ethanan 2/37 on Deut 6:5 (Mirkin 11.52; Soncino 7.65), and *Gen. Rab.* Bereshith 14/9 on Gen 2:7 (Theodor and Albeck 132; Soncino 1.116) with remarks on each term.

the highest heavens, i.e. to where He Himself resides, is again the root עלה , as in the *Pesiqta de Rav Kahana* passage cited above. Moses' soul is now to rest under God's Throne of Glory after having been "raised" there. It should be noted that this is a preliminary "raising" on the part of God. Moses' body still remains in its earthly grave. Only at the general resurrection of the dead will it be reunited with the soul.

A passage in *'Avot R. Nat.* A 12 is a variant of the above. God had commissioned the Angel of Death to bring Him Moses' soul, yet Moses had angrily rebuked him. Finally God told Moses: "Moses, you have had enough of this world. Lo, the world to come awaits you, 'the place prepared for you' [המקום מתוקן לך] already since the six days of Creation. For it is said: 'And the Lord said: Behold, a place together with / beside Me' (מָקוֹם אִתִּי - Exod 33:21).[230] Then the Holy One, blessed be He, took Moses' soul and 'stored / hid it' [גנזה][231] under the Throne of Glory. When He took it, He only did so by a kiss, as it is stated: 'by the mouth of the Lord' (Deut 34:5)."[232]

The preposition אֵת as used of the Lord here in Exod 33:21 can mean either "together with" or "by the side of."[233] Here it attributes special honor to Moses, whom God raises to the place together with Him / beside Him, spelled out as that under His Throne of Glory. *'Avot R. Nat.* A 12 states that this place has been "prepared" (מתוקן) for Moses since the six days of Creation.[234] The piel pass. part. of תקן , "set in order," "prepare,"[235] is employed here, as is the similar Aramaic in *Targum Onqelos*[236] and *Pseudo-Jonathan*[237] on Exod 33:21. *Neofiti 1* has מזמן , also

---

[230] The quotation originally ended here. A scribe, who knew the passage by heart, automatically continued it, not considering that the continuation makes no sense in the context.

[231] Cf. Jastrow 258 on גנז : 1) to save, hoard up, reserve; 2) to remove from sight, hide.

[232] Schechter 50; Goldin 65; Neusner 91. The haggadah continues by stating that the souls of *all* the righteous are hidden / deposited under the Throne of Glory. Although this motif is attested early, it must be a later addition here, for it distracts from Moses' special position. Cf. also *'Avot R. Nat.* B 25 (Schechter 50; Saldarini 150, with n. 18).

[233] BDB 85,1. It "expresses closer association than עִם " (p. 87).

[234] This is similar to the assertion that Moses' tomb was one of the things created at that time. Cf. *m. 'Avot* 5:6 as in notes 9-10.

[235] Jastrow 1691.

[236] Sperber 1.149; Grossfeld 94.

[237] Rieder 1.134; Maher 257.

meaning "prepared."[238] Yet in the Targums and other Judaic tradition this "prepared place" refers to the cave in the rock in which Moses hid himself in order not to die through overexposure to the Lord's passing glory. Here another "place" is meant, that under the Lord's Throne of Glory. This may have been influenced by the early tradition that the Lord is the "place" (מָקוֹם) of the world, for which Exod 33:21 is the prooftext.[239]

Another important text with Moses standing next to God in heaven is Deut 5:31 (28), "But you, stand here by Me." In *b. Šabb.* 87a, a baraitha relates that one of the three things Moses did on the basis of his own understanding, and which was then approved by God, was his decision to separate (sexually abstain) from his wife after God revealed Himself to him. God's approval of this decision is buttressed by the prooftext Deut 5:31.[240] *Targum Pseudo-Jonathan* has God tell Moses here: "But you, remain apart from your wife because in the Sanhedrin that is above, you should stand at My side...."[241]

Philo of Alexandria also relates Deut 5:31 to Moses' "translation" at the end of his life, showing the antiquity of the above baraitha in this regard. In *Sac.* 8 the Alexandrian philosopher, roughly a contemporary of Jesus, speaks of Moses as one of those God stationed beside Himself. To Moses He said: "Stand here with Me" (Deut 5:31). When Moses was about to die, "through the Word of the Supreme Cause he is 'translated' [μετανίσταται - Deut 34:5]...." Philo continues: "that same Word, by which He made the universe, is that by which He 'raises up' [ἀνάγων] the perfect man from things earthly to Himself."[242]

As pointed out in section B. 2.1 above, Philo employs Deut 5:31 five other times for God's telling Moses to stand next to Him. It is important to note here that it is connected to Moses' death, when he is "translated" to heaven by God, when God "raises up" Moses to Himself. The latter is

---

[238] Díez Macho 2.223; McNamara 136. On the pael pass. part. of זמן , see Jastrow 404.

[239] Cf. for example R. Yose b. Ḥalafta, a third generation Tanna (*Introduction* 84), in *Gen. Rab.* Vayeṣe 68/9 on Gen 28:11 (Theodor and Albeck 777-78; Soncino 2.619-20), with a parallel in *Exod. Rab.* Ki Thissa 45/6 on Exod 33:21 (Mirkin 6.173; Soncino 3.524).

[240] Soncino 411-12. Cf. the parallels in *Exod. Rab.* Bo 19/3 on Exod 12:43 (Mirkin 5.222; Soncino 3.231), *b. Yebam.* 62a (Soncino 412), and *'Avot R. Nat.* A 2 (Schechter 10; Goldin 19).

[241] Rieder 2.263; Clarke 24.

[242] I slightly modify the LCL translation of F. H. Colson here. Deut 34:6 is quoted in 10.

thus a kind of preliminary "resurrection" or divine "raising up" of Moses at the time of his death, long before the general resurrection of the dead at the end of time. In part because there was a synagogue of the Alexandrians in Jerusalem,[243] it is probable that "Hellenistic" and Palestinian Judaism influenced each other in regard to the interpretation of Deut 5:31. Just as *'Avot. R. Nat.* A 12 employed Exod 33:21 to mean that at Moses' death God took his soul, gave it "a place with Me," i.e. by placing it under the Throne of Glory, so "Stand here with Me" from Deut 5:31 was also employed of the time of Moses' death, when God "translated" him, "raising" him "up" to heaven. Both *'Avot R. Nat.* A 12 and Philo at this point presuppose Moses' actually dying.[244]

I suggest that because of the frequent comparison in early Judaism of the first redeemer of Israel, Moses, and the last or great redeemer of Israel, the Messiah, early Palestinian and Hellenistic Jewish Christians conceived of their own Messiah, Jesus, as having been raised by God already at his death to have "a place together with / beside Me," to "stand here with Me." This was imagery borrowed from haggadic traditions concerning Moses. It also means that these texts probably played a much more important role in regard to Jesus' Resurrection than has been previously acknowledged, almost all attention up to now having been given to Ps 110:1.[245]

* * *

The above Judaic texts dealing with God's taking Moses' soul to heaven at his death and storing / hiding it there under the Throne of Glory until the general resurrection of the dead, provide what I would like to label "Model B" for Jesus' Resurrection. It too involved his first dying and being buried, but then having his soul raised by God.

Yet the narrative of the empty tomb presupposes that Jesus was raised bodily to heaven by God. That is, not only his soul was taken / raised by God to heaven, his body / corpse also was. It did not remain in the

---

[243] Cf. the sources cited in Str-B 2.663-64.

[244] This is true even though I have argued above that Philo most probably was also aware of Moses' being directly translated to heaven without first dying. He hedges on the issue.

[245] Cf. for example David Hay, *Glory at the Right Hand*: Psalm 110 in Early Christianity (SBLMS 18; Nashville and New York: Abingdon Press, 1973). This is also true for Martin Hengel's extensive essay "'Sit at My Right Hand!' The Enthronement of Christ at the Right Hand of God and Psalm 110:1" in his *Studies in Early Christology* (London: T. & T. Clark, 1995) 119-225, esp. 197-98.

grave. I suggest that the latter is in part dependant on early Judaic belief in Moses' being translated, his ascending to heaven, like Enoch and Elijah, without first having died (my "Model A" above). The fact of Jesus' Crucifixion was undeniable, however, enough to be a "scandal" (1 Cor 1:23; Gal 5:11) to the first Christians, who like all their fellow Jews had indeed expected a victorious, political messianic "king." Jesus' death had to be incorporated into the narrative. It was thus conceived to be also in part like Moses' first dying (although, in stark contrast, he died peacefully) before God immediately took / raised his soul to heaven (my "Model B" above). Together with Judaic haggadic tradition, primarily on the miracle of Jacob's rolling away the large, heavy stone from the opening of the well in Gen 29:1-14 (thanks to prodigious strength gained from the blessing of the dew of resurrection, and leading to great astonishment), this combination of Models A and B employed in regard to the end of Israel's first redeemer, Moses, basically accounts for the origin and development of the haggadic narrative of the empty tomb. Here too Jesus is represented as the new Moses.

The Apostle Paul, our earliest witness to Jesus' Resurrection, shows no knowledge of the narrative of the empty tomb, although he could have made good use of it, for example in 1 Corinthians 15, his famous chapter on Jesus' Resurrection. This is a clear sign of the narrative's later origin. However, it must have been developed by Jewish Christians somewhere in Palestine before having been translated into Greek and becoming available in its core to the Evangelist Mark. In contrast to others, I perceive no major Markan editing in 16:1-8. That is, the unit probably reached its final form in the early sixties CE, then being incorporated by Mark into his Gospel, generally thought to have been written shortly before or after 70 CE.[246] Before its later appropriation by the other three Evangelists, it was only known that Jesus' body was placed by the Sanhedrin in the common gravesite reserved for criminals just outside of Jerusalem. As with the Maccabean and Hadrianic martyrs, and like "Model B" of Moses above, however, Jesus' soul was originally thought to have been immediately "raised" by God to heaven at the time of his actual death. The major factor responsible for the belief in his Resurrection was Jesus' appearing after his Crucifixion to his disciples and others, including the Apostle Paul (Mark 14:28; 16:7; John 21:1-19; 1 Cor 15:5-8). It was these appearances or visions of the Risen Christ which constituted the earliest Easter faith. As personal encounters, they greatly

---

[246] Cf. for example Joel Marcus, *Mark 1-8* (AB 27; New York: Doubleday, 2000) 37-39 (69 to 75 CE), and Craig Evans, *Mark 8:27 - 16:20*, lxiii ("the late sixties").

re-enforced a faith in Jesus which had been drastically damaged at the Crucifixion, or now led to a new faith in him as the Christ, the Son of God, or the Lord on the part of those who had not acknowledged him as such before (for example Paul and Jesus' brother James). The haggadic narrative of the empty tomb put into dramatic form the basis for such personal encounters, Jesus' having been "raised," it clearly pointing to their first taking place in Galilee (16:7).[247]

As shown in 1 Cor 15:4, the belief that Jesus was raised by God "on the third day" arose very early. It too was probably influenced in a major way by Judaic tradition on the death of Moses, and it is this motif to which I now turn.

C. Resurrection on the Third Day

A number of factors may have influenced the very rapid development of belief in Jesus' being raised "on the third day" (τῇ ἡμέρᾳ τῇ τρίτῃ - 1 Cor 15:4), "after three days" (μετὰ τρεῖς ἡμέρας - Mark 8:31; 9:31; 10:34).[248] Since the day began at sunset according to biblical (Gen 1:5) and Jewish thinking, "three" days were possible by counting Jesus' being crucified and buried on a Friday afternoon, followed by the Sabbath as the second day counted from Friday evening to Saturday evening, followed by the third day, beginning on Saturday evening and lasting until Sunday evening. Jesus' being raised / rising before dawn on Sunday (Mark 16:2) was thus thought of as his rising "on the third day." Paul writes in 1 Cor 15:3 that he is relating something to the Corinthian congregation which he himself had "received" from those who were Christians before him. Part of this tradition was the statement that Christ "was raised on the third day in accordance with the Scriptures" (v 4). The plural form of the latter noun is important to note here. The earliest Palestinian Jewish Christians perceived Jesus' Resurrection on the third day as being foretold in more than one passage of their Hebrew Bible. This does not exclude the possibility, however, that one passage was especially important in this regard, attracting other similar ones to it. As I shall point out below, this was indeed the case.

In the following I shall list nine factors, including three specific biblical passages, which contribute to the general picture of, and to the

---

[247] On haggadah and the question of the "historicity" of the empty tomb narrative, see chapter IV. below.

[248] Cf. also "for three days and three nights" in Matt 12:40, dependent on Jonah 2:1 (Eng. 1:17).

specific expression, "on the third day" / "after three days." Then I shall analyze one Tannaitic text regarding the death of Moses which "triggered" the application of "three days" to the death of the new Moses, Jesus.

C. 1   Three Days Travel from Jerusalem to Galilee

As I have emphasized before, the statement in Mark 14:50 that all eleven of Jesus' disciples deserted him and fled at his arrest in Gethsemane should be taken very seriously (cf. v 27). It would be understandable that these men feared for their own lives because of guilt by association and would *not* have remained in Jerusalem, where they could have been recognized and easily betrayed to the authorities.[249] Contrary to what the Gospels, composed some forty and more years later, now relate, the disciples should be thought of as leaving the environs of Jerusalem as soon as possible, i.e. already after the arrest of Jesus in Gethsemane on the Mount of Olives on Thursday evening. Since they were staying overnight outside the city proper (in Bethany - 11:11-12; 14:3), the closing of the city gates at night, even at the Passover festival, would not have impaired them.

If the eleven disciples had traveled back to Galilee as a purely male group, they would have aroused more suspicion and been more easily recognizable as fleeing. It is thus much more probable that they took along those women who had accompanied them to Jerusalem (15:41). In addition, they would not have allowed these women to later travel alone. Being unprotected, these would have been easily subject to banditry and even worse matters.[250] Traveling together may have slowed them all down somewhat, but fleeing for one's life means a much faster pace than a leisurely pilgrimage. Josephus relates in *Vita* 269 (52): "Samaria was now under Roman rule and, for rapid travel, it was essential to take that

---

[249] Galileans were easily recognizable through their accent (cf. the sources cited in Str-B 1.156-57 and Mark 14:70 par.). The disciples were not only present and highly visible at Jesus' "triumphal entry" into Jerusalem (Mark 11:1-10), but also at his "cleansing of the Temple" (vv 15-19), and at his public teaching in the Temple precincts (vv 27-33; chapter 12). The Evangelist John expresses this in 18:19-21. The counter-argument that the disciples could easily have hidden among the multitudes which had come to Jerusalem for the Passover Festival is not valid.

[250] This is another reason I agree with Rudolf Bultmann that the women at the empty tomb are actually only stage properties (*The History of the Synoptic Tradition* 284-85).

route, by which Jerusalem may be reached in three days from Galilee."[251] Even if consideration is made for the disciples' keeping the Sabbath from Friday evening to Saturday evening, assuming a very rapid pace, they still *may* have arrived back in Galilee with their accompanying persons within three days. Jesus *may* have then appeared to them at the end of the third day. Yet this is quite improbable. Because of the women and the Sabbath, a four day journey is much more likely. In addition, John 21 credibly portrays Jesus as appearing to the disciples after at least some of them had taken up their occupation as fishermen again at the Sea of Tiberias in Galilee. Coupled with the lack of a specific number of days for the appearances there (Mark 14:28; 16:7; Matt 28:10, 16), and the mention of individual appearances of the risen Christ some time *after* he was raised on the third day (1 Cor 15:5-8), it seems improbable that Jesus appeared to the remaining eleven disciples already "on the third day" in Galilee. Nevertheless, the well-known fact that it usually took three days to travel from Jerusalem to Galilee by the quickest route through Samaria may have contributed to the *general* motif of three days.

C. 2   *A Three Day Search for Elijah After His Ascension*

The only figures in the Hebrew Bible who were "taken up" or "ascended" to heaven were Enoch in Gen 5:24, and Elijah in 2 Kgs 2:11. The latter "ascended in a whirlwind into heaven." In spite of his successor Elisha's objections, the company of prophets at Jericho sent fifty men to find Elijah. They "searched for three days but did not find him" (v 17) since he had indeed ascended into heaven.

Of the other two Synoptics it is the Evangelist Luke who does not reproduce the notices in Mark 14:28 and 16:7 about the risen Jesus' preceding the disciples to Galilee, where they will "see" him. Rather, he instead has the Resurrection appearances take place on the way to nearby Emmaus[252] and in Jerusalem itself (24:13-49). Directly after this

---

[251] Cf. *m. B. Meṣ.* 2:6 (Albeck 4.70; Danby 349) for three days allowed for returning home from Jerusalem after a festival. In *y. Ber.* 1:1, 2c (Neusner / Zahavy 1.15) the statement occurs: "[We calculate that] an average man can walk forty miles a day." Zahavy on p. 13 explains this distance: "'Mile' refers to 2000 paces, about 1470 meters, which is somewhat less than the modern English mile of about 1609 meters." A man could thus easily walk from Jerusalem to Galilee via the shortest route within three days.

[252] For Emmaus as Moṣa, some 7 km (4.2 English miles) west of the present Jaffa Gate of Jerusalem, cf. my study *The Stilling of the Storm. Studies in Early Palestinian Judaic Traditions*, 223-29.

Jesus "was taken up into heaven" (v 51) at adjacent Bethany (v 50). There is no indication that the latter event did not still take place during the latter part of Easter Sunday, i.e. on the third day after Jesus died.[253] At least here Jesus' having been raised (24:6) and his having been "taken up" are closely connected.

It is probable that Luke (or the Christian community which informed him at this point) modeled Jesus' ascension on that of the prophet Elijah. An intentional contrast may be involved at this point, however. While Elijah ascended into heaven, appearing at that time to no one, and could not be found after a three-day search, after Jesus died he "ascended" / "was taken up" three days later, on Easter Sunday, then appearing to numerous persons.

C. 3   Corpse Identification Only Within Three Days

The Mishnah tractate *Yebamoth* at 16:3 notes that identification of a corpse is only allowed on the basis of "the face together with the nose." Merely seeing someone "crucified" and apparently dead, for example, is not valid proof of his having died. In addition, "evidence [of the identity of a corpse] may be given only during the first three days [after death]."[254]

Because of the frequently very high temperatures in Palestine, a corpse deteriorated then very rapidly, and the above regulation became necessary. When the women are described in Mark 16:2 as coming to Jesus' grave in order to anoint him, it is already the third day after his death according to Jewish reckoning. That is, although they as women were at the time not allowed to give valid legal testimony,[255] they believed Jesus' body had not deteriorated enough since Friday afternoon to have become unrecognizable. According to Jewish law, no one could maintain that they were anointing the wrong, unidentifiable corpse, for the third day had not passed yet. Yet Jesus' body was no longer there. He is represented as having risen some time between Saturday evening and early Sunday morning, that is, "on the third day."

---

[253] Contrast Acts 1:1-11 in Luke's other work, which lists appearances for forty days before Jesus is "lifted up" (v 9). On the ascension as taking place late on Easter day, see for example David Tiede, *Luke* (Augsburg Commentary on the New Testament; Minneapolis: Augsburg Publishing House, 1988) 444.

[254] Albeck 3.71-72; Danby 244; Neusner 376.

[255] Cf. the passages cited in Str-B 3.560, "c."

C. 4   Three Days of Most Intense Mourning

The fifth generation Tanna Bar Qappara[256] states in *Lev. Rab.* Meṣora 18/1 on Lev 15:1-2 that "The full force of mourning lasts for three days." This is because of the reason noted in *m. Yebam.* 16:3 in section 3. above.[257] He also notes that "Until three days [after death] the soul keeps on returning to the grave, thinking that it will go back [into the body]." Even on the third day one should not yet return to work.[258] The normal period of full mourning was for seven days, based on Joseph's mourning for his father Jacob this long in Gen 50:10.[259] It was followed by a period of thirty days of less intense mourning.[260] Yet mourning continued for a full year.[261]

The above passages show that Jesus' rising from the dead "on the third day" meant that this was still during the period when mourning was considered most intense.

C. 5   Revelation of the Lord on the Morning of the Third Day

In Exod 19:11 the Lord tells Moses to have the Israelites "prepare for the third day, because on the third day the Lord will come down upon Mount Sinai in the sight of all the people." Verse 16 notes that "On the morning of the third day there was thunder and lightning, as well as a thick cloud on the mountain, and a blast of a trumpet...," to which v 18 adds fire and smoke.[262]

The usually reticent *Targum Onqelos* states at Exod 19:11 that "on the third day the Lord *will reveal Himself....*" This is also stressed in vv 9, 18

---

[256] *Introduction* 90.

[257] Mirkin 7.203; Soncino 4.226.

[258] Cf. *Gen. Rab.* Vayeḥi 100/7 on Gen 50:10 (Theodor and Albeck 1290; Soncino 2.995). See also *b. Moʿed Qaṭan* 21a (Soncino 134) for not wearing phylacteries for three days.

[259] Cf. *Gen. Rab.*, *ibid.*

[260] *Gen. Rab.*, *ibid.* (Soncino 2.994). Cf. Deut 34:8.

[261] Cf. *b. Kethub.* 103b (Soncino 659). This is expressed metaphorically in *Gen. Rab.*, *ibid.* (Soncino 2.998), where a baraitha states that "during the seven days the sword is outstretched; until thirty days it hovers [quivers], and it does not return to its sheath until twelve months." A later summary of mourning customs is found in *Semaḥoth* in *The Minor Tractates of the Talmud* (Soncino 1.325-400).

[262] God calls these natural phenomena "all My miracles" in *Exod. Rab.* Ki Thissa 42/9 on Exod 32:9 (Mirkin 6.152; Soncino 3.493).

and 20.[263] The same is true with slight variations in *Targum Neofiti 1*,[264] *Pseudo-Jonathan*,[265] and the *Fragment Targums*.[266] The Lord's "revealing Himself on the morning of the third day" at Mount Sinai could thus also be thought of as a part of the total Jewish Christian view that the Lord revealed Himself by raising Jesus on the third day.

C. 6 *Jonah in the Belly of a Large Fish Three Days and Three Nights*

Jonah 2:1 (Eng. 1:17) states: "the Lord provided a large fish to swallow up Jonah; and Jonah was in the belly of the fish three days and three nights."[267] Before this he had identified himself to the sailors of the ship he had boarded for Tarshish, and which was in the midst of a mighty storm, as the / a "servant of the Lord" (1:9 LXX).[268] Jonah encouraged the sailors to throw him into the sea, which would save their lives (1:12), and they did so (v 15).[269]

While in the belly of the huge fish, Jonah prayed to the Lord: "The waters closed in over me unto death" (2:6 in *Targum Jonathan*). The *Targum* continues in v 7: "It is before You to 'raise' my life from destruction, O Lord my God."[270] This "raising" (אסקא),[271] which probably made the Jonah narrative so attractive to Palestinian Jewish Christians, then takes place in 2:11 (Eng. 10), where the fish "spewed Jonah out upon the dry land."[272] *Midr. Pss.* 26/7 on Ps 26:9 states that Jonah was "a completely righteous man," whom God "tried" here. The result was that "Jonah while still alive entered into his glory, into the

---

[263] Sperber 1.121; Grossfeld 52.

[264] Díez Macho 2.123, 125; McNamara 81-82.

[265] Rieder 1.111; Maher 215-16.

[266] Klein 1.82-83 and 174-75; 2.51 and 132-33.

[267] On Jonah, cf. Ginzberg, *The Legends* 4.246-53 and the accompanying notes, as well as the art. "Jonah," "In Rabbinical Literature," by Emil Hirsch in *JE* (1904) 7.226-27.

[268] Here עבדי was read as עבד יי . Cf. Jonah as God's "servant" in 2 Kgs 14:25.

[269] This motif of Jonah's self-sacrifice is emphasized in the (unfortunately undateable) Hellenistic Jewish sermon *De Jona* 54 and 60 (Siegert 17-18).

[270] Sperber 3.437; Levine 43 and 50; Cathcart 107.

[271] Cf. Jastrow 918 on נסק , af.: 1) to cause to rise, to bring up.

[272] In *De Jona* 99 (Siegert 26) this is labeled "a kind of rebirth." In 95 (Siegert 25) Jonah becomes "a sign of rebirth." This may be related to the Gospels' "sign of Jonah."

Garden of Eden."[273] *Tanḥ.* Vayyiqra 8 notes at this point that the sailors saw "all the miracles, signs and wonders" which God did here for Jonah, causing them to renounce idolatry.[274]

While Judaic tradition on Jonah's sleeping soundly in the hold of his ship, caught in a raging storm (Jonah 1), provides the major background to Jesus' stilling a raging storm in Mark 4:35-41 par.,[275] it is the second chapter which informs the Q passage Matt 12:38-41 // Luke 11:29-30, 32 on the sign of Jonah. It is the Jewish Christian Matthew who in 12:40 states: "For just as Jonah was three days and three nights in the belly of the sea monster, so for three days and three nights the Son of Man will be in the heart of the earth." While swallowed up by a huge fish for so long, Jonah did not actually die. His prayer to be "raised" by God was answered. Palestinian Jewish Christians employed the Jonah comparison to maintain that although Jesus actually died and was "in the heart of the earth" just as long, God "raised" him to new life on the third day, Easter Sunday. The comparison with Jonah was made in spite of Jesus' being in the grave for only two nights, not three. The phrase "three days and three nights" was simply taken over literally from Jonah 2:1 (Eng. 1:17). It was close enough to express what was meant: Jesus was raised / rose "on the third day."

C. 7   The "Binding" of Isaac on the Third Day, the 15th of Nisan

Gen 22:1-19 relates the "testing" of Abraham by God's telling him to sacrifice his only son, Isaac (vv 1-2). This involves the "binding" of his son Isaac on top of the wood of an altar (v 9). The incident is therefore labeled the ʿAqedah or "Binding" in Judaic tradition. It was thought of as the last or tenth trial of Abraham.[276] Various aspects of the narrative in

---

[273] Buber 220; Braude 1.363. I doubt whether this is influenced by the Gospels (see Ginzberg, *The Legends* 6.351, n. 38, on this as a possibility).

[274] Eshkol 489. Cf. the parallel in *Pirq. R. El.* 10 (Eshkol 33; Friedlander 72).

[275] Cf. my *The Stilling of the Storm. Studies in Early Palestinian Judaic Traditions*, 1-87.

[276] Cf. Ginzberg, *The Legends* 1.274-86 and the relevant notes, as well as the fine study by Shalom Spiegel, *The Last Trial* (New York: Behrman House, 1967/1979), introduced and translated by one of my teachers, Judah Goldin. *Gen. Rab.* Vayera 56/11 on Gen 22:16 states that "this was the last trial, which was as weighty as all the rest together" (Theodor and Albeck 610; Soncino 1.501). Another of my teachers, Nils Dahl, addressed this theme in "The Atonement - An Adequate Reward for the Akedah?" in *The Crucified Messiah and Other Essays* (Minneapolis: Augsburg Publishing House, 1974) 146-60.

Judaic tradition made it attractive to early Jewish Christians in regard to Jesus' death and Resurrection in Jerusalem, in part because Isaac is called "your son, your only son," in vv 2 and 12.

In Gen 22:2 God tells Abraham to take his son Isaac and go to the land "Moriah" to offer him on "one of the mountains" which He would show him. This is "the mount of the Lord" (v 14). *Jubilees,* written in Palestine originally in Hebrew towards the middle of the second century BCE, already states in 18:13 that this site is "Mount Zion."[277] It is the place of the future Temple in Jerusalem in *Gen. Rab.* Vayera 55/7 on Gen 22:2,[278] and in the Tannaitic midrash *Sifre* Va'ethanan 28 on Deut 3:25, "that goodly mountain, and Lebanon [the Temple]."[279]

A charming haggadah in *Pirqe Rabbi Eliezer* states that the donkey Abraham employed in Gen 22:3 was the same one Moses later used for his wife and sons when they went to Egypt (Exod 4:20 - "*the* donkey"), and the Son of David (the Messiah) will ride on the same animal when he later enters Jerusalem (Zech 9:9).[280]

While Gen 22:5 and 12 label Isaac a "boy" (נַעַר), the standard Jewish chronography, *Seder 'Olam* 1, notes with other sources that he is thirty-seven years old at this point.[281] Verse 4 states that "On the third day Abraham looked up and saw the place [of sacrifice, Jerusalem,] far away." *Jubilees* 17:15 states that "in the first month" (Nisan), "on the twelfth of that month," the last trial of Abraham took place.[282] Abraham in 18:3 "went to the place on the third day."[283] That is, this very early Palestinian writing pictures the 'Aqedah or sacrifice of Isaac as taking place on the 15th of Nisan, the first day of Passover, the same day on which Jesus was crucified. In 18:18 it is related that Abraham made the 'Aqedah into an annual seven-day festival, with rejoicing.[284] The author describes the pilgrimage festival of Booths in 16:20-31, and Shevuot /

---

[277] Cf. O. Wintermute in *OTP* 2.43-45, and 91 for the verse.

[278] Theodor and Albeck 590-91; Soncino 1.487-88.

[279] Finkelstein 44-45; Hammer 52-53. On Lebanon as the Temple, see also 6 (Hammer 32).

[280] Eshkol 104; Friedlander 224-25. Cf. Mark 11:1-10; Matt 21:5 and John 12:15 cite the verse. It is also cited in regard to Gen 22:5 in *Gen. Rab.* Vayera 56/2 (Theodor and Albeck 596; Soncino 1.492).

[281] Guggenheimer 13. Cf. *Gen. Rab.* Vayera 56/8 on Gen 22:9 (Theodor and Albeck 603, apparatus [with the variant 26]; Soncino 1.497, with n. 5).

[282] *OTP* 2.90.

[283] *OTP* 2.91.

[284] *Ibid.*

Weeks, "the feast of the firstfruits of the harvest," in 22:1.[285] This makes the identification of Passover in 18:3 and 18 certain. In *b. Roš. Haš.* 11a it is also stated that Isaac was born on Passover.[286] *Exod. Rab.* Bo 15/11 on Exod 12:2, "This month [Nisan] shall be for you the first of the months," notes that in this month Israel was redeemed from Egypt, and in the same month it will be redeemed in the future. "In this month Isaac was born, and in this month he was bound" (at the ʿAqedah in Gen 22:9).[287] Probably because of the Jewish Christian appropriation of the ʿAqedah motif for Jesus' death, later Jewish sources discontinued the date of the 15th of Nisan.[288]

Gen 22:6 states that "Abraham took the wood of the burnt offering and laid it on his son Isaac, and he himself carried the fire and the knife." Commenting on Isaac's carrying the wood here, *Gen. Rab.* Vayera 56/3 says this is "like one who carries his cross [צְלוּב][289] on his shoulder."[290] *Pesiq. R.* 31/2 notes that "Isaac carried the pieces of wood[291] like a man carrying his cross."[292] This comparison with a cross, which is probably early, also made the ʿAqedah attractive to Christians.

Isaac's willingness to be sacrificed is emphasized in numerous sources. This is expanded into a monologue in the first-century CE *Pseudo-Philo* 32:3. In 40:2 it is also stated: "and the one being offered was ready."[293] *Sifre* Vaʾethanan 32 on Deut 6:5 has R. Meir, a third generation

---

[285] *Ibid.* 2.89 and 97. On the latter, see also 15:1 (2.85) - in the middle of the third month.

[286] Soncino 41.

[287] Mirkin 5.174; Soncino 3.173. The same midrash at 15/12 on Exod 12:5, "Your lamb shall be without blemish, a male of the first year," also relates the ʿAqedah to Passover: "'A lamb,' because 'God will provide Himself the lamb,' etc. (Gen 22:8)" (Mirkin 5.174; Soncino 3.174, with n. 5).

[288] Cf. *b. Meg.* 31a (Soncino 188), where Genesis 22 is read on the second day of New Year (Rosh ha-Shanah) in the triennial lectionary system. This was probably due to the horn (shofar) of a ram blown then, associated with the ram of Gen 22:13.

[289] Jastrow 1282: stake, gallows. Cf. *m. Yebam.* 16:3 (Albeck 3.71; Danby 244; Neusner 376) of this as crucifixion, and the other passages Jastrow cites.

[290] Theodor and Albeck 598; Soncino 1.493.

[291] Cf. Jastrow 1101 for עֵץ as tree, pole, wood, and "the gallows." Here the plural is employed.

[292] Friedmann 143b; Braude 603. *Tanḥ.* B Vayera 46 on Gen 22:6 (Buber 114; Townsend 129) has basically the same, yet with Isaac going out "to be burned."

[293] SC 229.224, 246, and 280; OTP 2.345 and 353. Cf. also 4 Macc 16:20, "he did not cower."

Tanna,[294] comment on "and with all your soul" by noting that Isaac "bound himself upon the altar," as in Gen 22:10.[295] It is thus understandable that *Gen. Rab.* Vayera 56/11 on Gen 22:15-16 has Abraham say God tried not only him, but also Isaac.[296]

Genesis 22 relates that when Abraham was about to kill / slaughter his son (v 10), the angel of the Lord told him not to (v 12). Instead, he offered a nearby "ram, caught in a thicket by its horns" (v 13). Yet several early Judaic sources maintain that Isaac's blood was indeed shed. *Pseudo-Philo* 18:5 states of Abraham: "because he did not refuse, his offering was acceptable before Me, and on account of his [Isaac's] blood I chose them."[297] The *Mekilta de R. Šimeon b. Yoḥai* notes in regard to Isaac that a fourth log of his blood at this point went forth upon the altar.[298] While the present form of *Midrash Haggadol* on Gen 22:8 may be late, it appears to have an early core. Isaac here instructs his father Abraham to do the will of his Father in heaven. It is his wish that a fourth of a log of his own blood "atone for all Israel."[299] The Tannaitic *Mek. R. Ish.* Pisha 7 on Exod 12:13, "when I see the blood," also has God say: "I see the blood of the binding / sacrifice of Isaac."[300]

While the majority opinion follows the biblical account in having Isaac spared, there thus appears to have been at least a minor view that he indeed shed (some of) his blood at the ʿAqedah, for "it is [only] the blood that makes atonement" (Lev 17:11). This minor opinion was probably also suppressed because it could easily be appropriated by Jewish Christians.

Finally, the second benediction of the very early Eighteen Prayer (Shemone ʿEsreh) addresses the Lord as Him "who revives / quickens the dead" (מְחַיֵּה מֵתִים).[301] In *Pirq. R. El.* 31 this is related to Isaac at the ʿAqedah:

---

[294] *Introduction* 84.
[295] Finkelstein 58; Hammer 62.
[296] Theodor and Albeck 608; Soncino 2.501.
[297] *SC* 229.150; *OTP* 2.325, although I disagree with Harrington's n. "g." In *b. Yoma* 5a (Soncino 17-18), which he cites, it is precisely the blood which alone makes atonement (Lev 17:11).
[298] Epstein / Melamed 4. Ginzberg in *The Legends* 5.254, n. 255, agrees here in this regard. A "log" contained the liquid equivalent of six eggs (Danby, *The Mishnah* 798).
[299] Margulies 353.
[300] Lauterbach 1.57, with n. 7.
[301] Cf. Elbogen, *Der jüdische Gottesdienst* 44, and the *Sidur Sefat Emet* (Basel: Victor Goldschmidt Verlag, 1956-64) 41.

When the sword [blade] touched his neck, the soul of Isaac fled and departed. When he heard His voice from between the two Cherubim, saying [to Abraham]: "Do not lay your hand upon the boy" [Gen 22:12], his soul returned to his body, and [Abraham] set him free, and Isaac stood upon his feet. And Isaac knew of the resurrection of the dead from the Torah, that in this manner all the dead in the future will be revived / quickened. He opened [his mouth] and said: "Blessed are You, O Lord, who revive / quicken the dead."[302]

If the core of this haggadic incident is also early, it would mean that Isaac's surviving the ʿAqedah after losing his soul (in another variant, after shedding some of his own blood) is due to the Lord's reviving / quickening him. He was thus the first to be "resurrected," (although he later died a natural death - Gen 35:29). This too would have appealed to early Jewish Christians, who saw in Jesus the first person to be raised / rise from the dead. That the ʿAqedah took place on the 15th of Nisan, the first day of Passover, "on the third day" (Gen 22:4), certainly played a major role here.

C. 8   The Beginning of the Redemption of All the Jews on the Third Day, the 15th of Nisan, in Judaic Traditions on Esther

The biblical book of Esther provides the basis for the annual celebration of the festival of Purim or "lots" (chapter 9). Yet it also provides encouragement and comfort to those Jews under severe persecution. The Persian king Ahasuerus is represented as ruling over 127 provinces from India to Ethiopia (1:1), which would also include the Jewish homeland in Palestine. Judaic tradition interprets this to mean that he ruled over the whole world.[303] After getting rid of his first queen, Vashti, on account of her disobedience,[304] he "tried out" young virgins from his entire kingdom to determine a successor for her. Esther pleased him most and thus became his new queen. She was an orphan brought up by her cousin, the Jew Mordecai (2:7), who was of royal descent, his forebears having been taken from Jerusalem to Babylonia by King

---

[302] Eshkol 106; Friedlander 228. Cf. also n. 88.
[303] Cf. Addition B (13:2), and *Midr. Pss.* 22/26 (Buber 193; Braude 1.320-21) in the name of R. Nehemiah, a third generation Tanna (*Introduction* 85).
[304] The king's banquet in chapter one in Judaic tradition provides a major part of the background to the narratives of the wedding at Cana and Herod Antipas' having John the Baptist beheaded. Cf. my *Water into Wine and the Beheading of John the Baptist. Early Jewish-Christian Interpretation of Esther 1 in John 2:1-11 and Mark 6:17-29.*

Nebuchadnezzar (2:5-6).[305] When two of Ahasuerus' eunuchs conspired to assassinate him, Mordecai learned of the plot, told it to Esther, and she informed the king in his name. This led to the eunuchs' being hanged on the gallows.[306] Although Mordecai's "tip" was duly recorded at the time, he then received no reward from the king (2:2).

When Haman was made the second man in the kingdom, he demanded obeisance also from Mordecai, who as a Jew refused to bow down to him. This led to Haman's plot "to destroy all the Jews, the people of Mordecai, throughout the whole kingdom of Ahasuerus" (3:6; cf. 7:4 and 8:5). To this end he convinced the king to issue such an edict (3:9-15),[307] which was done on the thirteenth of Nisan (3:12; cf. v 7). Having learned of the planned destruction of all the Jews, Mordecai tore his clothes (in mourning) and put on sackcloth and ashes (4:1). He then attempted to get Esther to "go to the king to make supplication to him and entreat him for her people" (v 8). The problem was that "if any man or woman goes to the king inside the inner court without being called, there is but one law - all alike are to be put to death," and Esther had not been there for thirty days (v 11). Nevertheless, Mordecai convinced her to take this risk upon herself (vv 13-14).[308]

Esther's response to Mordecai is found in 4:16, "Go, gather all the Jews to be found in Susa, and hold a fast on my behalf, and neither eat nor drink for three days, night or day. I and my maids will also fast as you do. After that I will go to the king, though it is against the law; and if I perish, I perish." Here Esther is pictured as willing to sacrifice her own life on behalf of her endangered people, the Jews.

---

[305] For Kish as the father of Israel's first king, Saul, see 1 Sam 9:1. Thus both Mordecai and Esther were thought of as "royals." See also Addition A (11:4) on Mordecai as coming from Jerusalem.
[306] On the impact of this incident on the Gospels, cf. "The Release of Barabbas (Mark 15:6-15 par.; John 18:39-40), and Judaic Traditions on the Book of Esther" in my *Barabbas and Esther and Other Studies in the Judaic Illumination of Earliest Christianity*, 1-27.
[307] Its contents are given in Addition B (13:1-7). On the Additions, cf. Carey Moore, *Daniel, Esther and Jeremiah: The Additions* (AB 44; Garden City, NY: Doubleday, 1977), as well as Nickelsburg, *Jewish Literature* 203. Four of the six may originally have been written in Hebrew; all appear to be from the second century BCE, which is also true of LXX Esther.
[308] This is expressed well in *1 Targ. Esth* 4:16, which has Esther say: "so too I perish from the life of this world for the sake of the salvation of the people of the house of Israel" (Grossfeld 21 and 58).

Judaic tradition interpreted these three days as the 13th, 14th and 15th of Nisan, thus ending on the first day of Passover. The standard chronography of early Judaism, *Seder 'Olam*, states in chapter 29 that "On the 13th of Nisan Haman wrote letters 'to destroy, to kill, and to annihilate all Jews...' [Esth 3:13], and on the 15th of Nisan Esther appeared before the king."[309] Rab, a first generation Babylonian Amora who studied under Rabbi in Palestine,[310] comments in *b. Meg.* 15a on Esth 4:17, "And Mordecai 'passed' [וַיַּעֲבֹר]": "This indicates that he made the first day of Passover as a fast day."[311] Since Passover is a joyous festival commemorating the redemption of the Israelites from the Egyptian bondage, normally no fasting was allowed on such a day.[312] *Pirq. R. El.* 50 and *Esth. Rab.* 8/6 comment on Esth 4:16 by saying that these three days were the 13th, 14th and 15th of Nisan. Mordecai at that time asked Esther: "Is not the third day the day of Passover?" She then replied: "You are the head of the Sanhedrin [in Susa] and you say such a thing! If there is no Israel, for whom is the Passover?"[313] In *b. Pesaḥ.* 117a it is also stated that the Hallel (Psalms 113-18) should be recited at every misfortune. R. Yose the Galilean, a second generation Tanna,[314] notes there that "Mordecai and Esther uttered it when the wicked Haman rose against them."[315] It is this Hallel which Jesus and his disciples also recited on the first day of Passover, the 15th of Nisan, at the "Lord's Supper."[316]

Because all Jews, throughout the entire world, were now to be annihilated as the result of Haman's edict, Esther's appearance before King Ahasuerus on the 15th of Nisan was considered to be Judaism's blackest hour. In *Midr. Pss.* 22/5 this situation is described so: "There is no darkness greater than the hour before dawn."[317] This is comment on

---

309 Guggenheimer 250.

310 *Introduction* 93.

311 Soncino 88. Cf. BDB 717, i, on עבר as not only meaning "to pass over," but also "to overstep, transgress."

312 See for example 1 *Targ. Esth* 4:17, which states that Mordecai "transgressed against the joy of the feast of Passover" by fasting and sitting in ashes (Grossfeld 21 and 58).

313 For the first, cf. Eshkol 199; Friedlander's MS has "You are the elder of Israel" (p. 401), which is also found in the *Esther Rabbah* passage (Vilna 27; Soncino 9.107). See also the interpretation of Esth 4:17 given there.

314 *Introduction* 81.

315 Soncino 598-99 and 601.

316 Cf. Mark 14:26, which should be translated: "And when they had sung [the Hallel - i.e., finished singing it], they went out to the Mount of Olives."

317 Buber 182; Braude 1.300.

Ps 22:1 (Eng. superscription), "the hind [female deer] of the dawn," whereby Esther is interpreted as this hind.

Judaic tradition interprets the entire twenty-second psalm as spoken by Esther on the 15th of Nisan just before she implores King Ahasuerus for salvation for her people the Jews, even though she has not been called to him and risks her own life by now approaching him. Palestinian Jewish Christians also appropriated it to describe Jesus' darkest hour (Mark 15:33), his Crucifixion. This was in part due to their reading Ps 22:17b as "they bored my hands and feet" (when fastening[318] these to the Cross). The ὤρυξαν of the LXX here, "they pierced," substantiates such a reading.[319] The following three examples illustrate how Jesus' Crucifixion was described in terms of what were considered to be Esther's words or words applied to her on the occasion noted above.

a)   *Mark 15:24 par.*   "They divided his clothes among them, casting lots to decide what each should take." In the four Gospels, the term κλῆρος , "lot," only occurs in this context. The term and the entire sentence derive from Ps 22:19 (Eng. 18), quoted at this point in John 19:24. Part one of verse 19 is interpreted in *Midr. Pss.* 22/27 of one person's saying: "I will take Esther's purple [royal] robe," and of another person's saying: "I will take her rings and bracelets," and part two of verse 19 also of Esther's "purple robe."[320]

---

[318] The MT has "like a lion" (כָּאֲרִי). Yet cf. BDB 468, II, on כּוּר : "dubious meaning, perhaps *bore* or *dig, hew*." The root כָּרָה is "to dig" (BDB 500). Judaic tradition thought of בָּאַר , pi. "to make repulsive," here (Jastrow 656). See *Midr. Pss.* 22/26 *ad. loc.* (Buber 194; Braude 1.320).

[319] Cf. LSJ 1257 on ὀρύσσω : dig. II. dig through, make a canal through. V. of a wrestler: *dig into, gouge* a tender part. Another factor important for Jewish Christians may have been the mention of "My only one," in the MT יְחִיד (BDB 402), in the LXX μονογενής , "unique" or "only-begotten" (BAGD 527). Heike Omerzu in "Die Rezeption von Psalm 22 im Judentum zur Zeit des Zweiten Tempels" in *Psalm 22 und die Passionsgeschichte der Evangelien*, ed. Dieter Sänger (Biblisch-Theologische Studien 88; Neukirchen-Vluyn: Neukirchener Verlag, 2007) 33-76, only deals with Qumran, Joseph and Asenath and the Wisdom of Solomon. Stephen Ahearne-Kroll in "Challenging the Divine: LXX Psalm 21 in the Passion Narrative of Mark" in *The Trial and Death of Jesus*. Essays on the Passion Narrative in Mark, ed. Geert Van Oyen and Tom Shepherd (CBET 45; Leuven: Peeters, 2006) 119-48 only deals with the Septuagint and does not consider the psalm in Judaic tradition whatsoever.

[320] Buber 194; Braude 1.321 is as very often paraphrastic. Cf. Jastrow 1148 on פּוּרְפּוּרָא : purple, esp. purple cloak, royal garment.

b)   *Mark 15:29-30 par.*   "Those who passed by derided him, shaking their heads and saying, 'Aha! ... 30) save yourself....'" Part of the background to this is Ps 22:8-9 (Eng. 7-8): "All who see me mock me; they make mouths at me, they shake their heads; 9) 'Commit your cause to the Lord, let Him deliver - let Him rescue the one in whom He delights!'" In *Midr. Pss.* 22/22, v 8 is interpreted of Haman's sons (cf. Esth 5:11; 9:10, 13 [ten], 26) who mock the Jews as above. Verse 9a is interpreted by Rab as "Roll it [your burden] upon Me, and I shall bear it." R. Yohanan, a second generation Palestinian Amora,[321] interpreted the same phrase as "Roll the burden of your sins upon Me, and I shall bear them."[322] Verse 9b is then related to Esther, who said: "His desire to rescue me rose up within Him."[323]

c)   *Mark 15:34 par.*   Just before dying at the ninth hour (3 p.m.), Jesus "cried out with a loud voice: 'Eloi, Eloi, lema sabachthani?'" This is a quotation of Ps 22:2a (Eng. 1).[324] *Midr. Pss.* 22/6 on this section of the verse states in regard to the three-day fast of Esther on the 13th, 14th and 15th of Nisan: "On the first day of a fast one says: 'My God'; on the second day one says: 'My God'; only on the third [and most intense] day may one say: 'Why have You forsaken me?' So it was only after Esther cried in a loud voice, 'Why have You forsaken me?' that her cry was heard."[325]

---

[321] *Introduction* 94-95.
[322] I suspect this rendering of *gilgel*, "to roll," may have something to do here with the site of Jesus' Crucifixion, "Golgotha," where he was thought to bear the sins of mankind. At the nearby grave the stone was "rolled away." Cf. Jastrow 244 on גִּלְגֵּל , with an example of rolling a stone. This would mean גּוּלְגּוּלְתָּא , "skull" (Jastrow 221), may be a secondary interpretation, the first being (the place of) "rolling away" (the stone). See n. 46 on this.
[323] Buber 192; Braude 1.317-18.
[324] This appears to be a combination of what is found in the present *Targum* (Merino 92; Spic 57) and the Hebrew, although the Aramaic was certainly fluid at the time. The *Targum* has at v 28 (Eng. 29): "All the ends of the earth shall remember *His miracles*" (Merino 93; Spic 60), emphasizing the miraculous deliverance of the speaker by the Lord.
[325] Buber 183; Braude 1.302. The passage continues with Esther's maintaining the "crying out" of the Israelites in Egypt was not as great an affliction as hers. She then refers to no answer yet from God in spite of the Jews' present fasting and crying out. In *b. Meg.* 15b (Soncino 91), Ps 22:2 is also spoken by Esther at this point. Another motif at Jesus' Crucifixion may also derive from Judaic interpretation of Psalm 22. Mark 15:23 and 36 imply that Jesus was thirsty. This may have been triggered by Ps 22:16, applied to Esther in *Midr. Pss.* 22/25 (Buber 193; Braude 1.320).

The above three examples clearly show the great extent to which Palestinian Jewish Christians viewed the Crucifixion in light of their own haggadic traditions on Judaism's darkest hour. It was also the 15th of Nisan when Esther, later to be called a "redeemer" of Israel,[326] was ready to sacrifice her life to "save" her own people from total annihilation.

The scene of Esther's encounter with the king is highly dramatized in Judaic tradition. Addition C (13:1 - 14:19) contains Mordecai's Prayer and Esther's Prayer at this point. In 14:1 Esther is "seized with deadly anxiety." Addition D (15:1-16) then describes how, "on the third day" (v 1), "her heart was frozen with fear" (v 5). When Esther swooned, the king comforted her by saying she would not die for having come to him without previous permission. That law applied to their subjects (v 10). Esther's recovery at this point is labeled a "miracle" (נס) by R. Judah (bar Ilai, a third generation Tanna,[327]) in *Midr. Pss.* 22/26.[328]

Yet Haman's terrible edict was still valid. To get it removed without arousing his suspicion, Esther invited the king and him to a banquet which she would prepare that day (Esth 5:4). This moment is also called a "miracle" in *Esth. Rab.* 9/2 on the passage.[329] The banquet is assumed to take place on the evening of the same day, which would then be the 16th of Nisan.[330] On this occasion Esther invites the two to another similar banquet the next day (5:8). The *First Targum* at this point notes that this will take place "in the evening,"[331] meaning on the 17th of Nisan.[332]

While King Ahasuerus, Haman and Esther participate in this second banquet, the king repeats his question to Esther. He would grant her up to half of his kingdom if she requested it. In 7:3-4 she asks for her own life and that of her people, the Jews, indicating that Haman is to blame for the terrible situation. The king is infuriated and has Haman hung / crucified on the same gallows / cross he had prepared for Mordecai

---

[326] Cf. for example Josephus, *Ant.* 11.185 for Esther's having "saved" (σῶσαι) the Jewish nation. See also *Esth. Rab.* 6/6 and 7 on Esth 2:7 (Soncino 9.77); 10/13 on Esth 8:15 (Soncino 9.122); and *1 Targ. Esth* 2:5 (Grossfeld 10 and 45).

[327] *Introduction* 84-85.

[328] Buber 194; Braude 1.320. Cf. also *b. Meg.* 15b (Soncino 92).

[329] Vilna 28; Soncino 9.112.

[330] Cf. Friedlander in *Pirke de Rabbi Eliezer* 401, n. 9.

[331] Grossfeld 23 and 60, as well as his n. 22 on pp. 147-48, also dealing with the LXX.

[332] *Pirq. R. El.* 50 (MS Epstein in Friedlander 406) states that Esther had prepared the banquet on the 16th, (it to take place on the evening of the 17th). Cf. also n. 330.

(7:10).[333] The motif of "being crucified" on a "cross" obviously made the Esther narrative attractive to Jewish Christians in order to help describe Jesus' being crucified on a cross.

After rewarding Esther and Mordecai (8:1-2), King Ahasuerus grants Esther's request that he revoke Haman's letters ordering the destruction of all the Jews. His secretaries carry this out on the 23rd of Nisan (8:9), just after what normally would have been the week-long celebration of Passover. Addition E (16:1-24) contains this decree. The narrative then ends in the Hebrew Bible with details of how the festival of Purim should be held (9:20-32), as well as the advancement of Mordecai (10:3).

It is important to note that while Esther (and all the other Jews) fasted from the 13th to the 15th of Nisan, the first day of Passover, and she dared to speak to the king "on the third day" (Esth 5:1), salvation for them came only three days later, at the second banquet she prepared for the king and Haman. This was thought to be on the evening of the second day (7:2), which for Jews was already the beginning of the third day. Jesus was crucified on the afternoon of the first day of Passover (today's "Good Friday"), the second day being a Sabbath and lasting from Friday at sunset until Saturday at sunset. The third day then began, and when the women are pictured as coming to Jesus' tomb very early on Sunday morning, Jesus is represented as having been raised from the dead within the latter period: the third day.

C. 8.1   *God Delivers from Adversity at the Latest on the Third Day*

A widespread Judaic tradition in regard to Esther's going before the king on the 15th of Nisan is helpful for a better understanding of the above. *Esth. Rab.* 9/2 comments on Esth 5:1, "'On the third day' Esther put on her royal robe and stood in the inner court of the king's palace, opposite the king's hall," as follows:

> Israel are never left in dire distress more than three days. For so of Abraham it is written: "On the third day Abraham lifted up his eyes and saw the place afar off" (Gen 22:4). Of Jacob's sons we read: "And he put them all together in prison for three days" (42:17). Of Jonah it says: "And Jonah was in the belly of the fish three days and three nights" (Jonah 2:1; Eng. 1:17). The dead also will come to life only after three days, as it

---

[333] On "crucifying," see σταυρόω in LXX Esth 7:9 and 8:13, and ἀνασταυρόω in Josephus, *Ant.* 11.208, 246, 280 and 289. On the "cross," see σταυρός in 11.261 and 266-67. *Esth. Rab.* 10/5 on Esth 6:11 says Haman had erected a gallows / cross "with ropes and nails" (Vilna 28; Soncino 9.117).

says: "On the third day He will raise us up, that we may live before Him" (Hos 6:2). This miracle [of Mordecai and Esther] was performed after three days of their fasting, as it is written: "On the third day Esther put on her royal robes," and she sent and invited Haman to the banquet on the fifteenth of Nisan.[334]

This narrative is found in an expanded form in "Esther's Psalm," *Midr. Pss.* 22/5 dealing with Esth 4:16, "for three days,"[335] as well as in *Gen. Rab.* Vayera 56/1 on Gen 22:4.[336] In addition, *Gen. Rab.* Miqqeṣ 91/7 comments on Gen 42:17 by saying: "The Holy One, blessed be He, never leaves the righteous in distress more than three days." It continues by commenting on v 18, "On the third day Joseph said to them": "Thus it is written: 'After two days He will revive us, and on the third day He will raise us up, that we may live before Him' (Hos 6:2): on the third day of the tribal ancestors."[337]

"Dire distress" in the *Esth. Rab.* 9/2 passage above is the Hebrew צָרָה : "anguish, trouble, distress, persecution."[338] Judaism's darkest hour, with the probability of total annihilation, is appropriately labeled as such when Esther approaches the king without being summoned, something punishable by death. Jonah's being thrown overboard and being swallowed by a large fish (section C. 6 above) was a similar situation, as was that of the ʿAqedah, when Abraham was about to sacrifice his only son Isaac (section C. 7 above).[339] According to very early Judaic tradition, the latter also took place on the 15th of Nisan, as in the Esther narrative.

[334] Vilna Esther 28; Soncino 9.112.
[335] Buber 183; Braude 1.301-02.
[336] Theodor and Albeck 595; Soncino 1.491.
[337] Theodor and Albeck 1129; Soncino 2.843. In his work *Auferweckt am dritten Tag nach der Schrift* (QD 38; Freiburg: Herder, 1968), Karl Lehmann analyzes especially the *Genesis* and *Esther Rabbah* texts, but he is primarily dependent on the Soncino English translation, the August Wünsche German translation, and Paul Billerbeck (pp. 262-90), as well as on secondary literature. See also Harvey McArthur, "On the Third Day," in *NTS* 18 (1971/72) 81-88 for a number of rabbinic passages in regard to Hos 6:2. Like Lehmann, he notes that God does not allow the righteous or Israel to remain in distress more than three days (84). His citation of *b. Sanh.* 97a and *Roš Haš.* 31a, parallel traditions, is irrelevant to the theme of the resurrection, nor does he note *Sifre* 329, *y. Taʿan.* 1:1, 63c and *Midr. Haggadol* Deut 32:39. Since he nowhere cites the editions with the page numbers he employs, it is very difficult for the non-specialist to check his references.
[338] Jastrow 1300. Cf. especially the last example with Haman given there.
[339] Exod 19:16, analyzed in section C. 5 above, is another key text cited in *Gen. Rab.* Vayera 56/1 on Gen 22:4 (Theodor and Albeck 595; Soncino 1.491, with n. 2).

C. 8.2   A Miracle

King Ahasuerus' not killing Esther for coming to him unsummoned
"on the third day," and the beginning of the salvation of the Jews at this
point, are labeled a "miracle" (נֵס) in the above *Esther Rabbah* narrative.
This agrees with very many occurrences of this term in Judaic tradition
on the episode. One typical statement is found in *Midr. Pss.* 22/10: "As
the dawn ends the night, so all the miracles ended with Esther."[340]
Another is found in *b. Ber.* 57b, where "our Rabbis taught" that "one who
sees the Scroll of Esther [in a dream] will have a miracle wrought for
him."[341] Since Esther's "dire distress" on the 15th of Nisan turned out to be
the miraculous beginning of salvation for the Jews, it is understandable
that Palestinian Jewish Christians, aware of the association of this
tradition with God's "raising" on the third day in Hos 6:2, applied it to
Jesus' Crucifixion on the 15th of Nisan and God's raising him three days
later, early on "Easter Sunday."

C. 8.3   Mordecai as Savior, Redeemer and Righteous

In Judaic tradition it is not only Esther who is labeled a "redeemer" of
Israel. This is also true of Mordecai. It is his revealing the plot of the
king's two eunuchs to kill him (Esth 2:22; 7:9) which leads the king to call
him "our 'savior' [σωτήρ] and benefactor" in Addition E (16:13). Other
texts also label him a "savior" or "redeemer" (גּוֹאֵל).[342] This is one reason
Mordecai is also labeled a "righteous" (צַדִּיק) person.[343]

---

[340] Buber 185; Braude 1.306.
[341] Soncino 355-56. Other examples of miracles in Esther are found in Addition F
(10:9) with "great signs and wonders"; *b. Yebam.* 121b (Soncino 858-59); *Meg.*15b
(Soncino 92); *1 Targ.* Esth 9:26 and 29 (Grossfeld 35-36 and 71-72); and *Midr. Pss.*
22/26 (Buber 194; Braude 1.320).
[342] Cf. Josephus, *Ant.* 11.208, 225-56 and 278 (from the above Addition); *Pirq. R.
El.* 49 (Eshkol 193; Friedlander 389); *1 Targ.* Esth 2:5 (Grossfeld 10 and 45); *Midr.
Pss.* 22/15 (Buber 187; Braude 1.310); and *Esth. Rab.* 10/13 on Esth 8:15 (Vilna 29-
30; Soncino 9.122). This is one factor which contributed to the mocking of Jesus
being modeled on the intended mocking of Mordecai. See the Excursus below.
[343] Cf. *Pirq. R. El.* 50 (Eshkol 197; Friedlander 396); *1 Targ.* Esth 1:5 (Grossfeld 6
and 41) and 7:6 (Grossfeld 28 and 64); and *b. Meg.* 10b and 13b (Soncino 59 and
78). *1 Targ.* Esth 2:5 also calls him "pious" (חסידא - Grossfeld 10 and 45).

C. 8.4   Abasement and Exaltation

In *Tanh.* Toledoth 3 on Gen 41:2, R. Joshua b. Levi, a first generation Palestinian Amora,[344] states:

> Out of adversity comes relief; out of darkness, light; and out of the degradation of the righteous, their exaltation. Thus Scripture says: "If you have done foolishly in lifting yourself up, or if you have planned devices, lay your hand upon your mouth" (Prov 30:32).
>
> Hananiah, Mishael and Azariah were ultimately exalted as a consequence of their humiliation (Dan 3:21), but later they were exalted, as is said: (v 30). Daniel was hurled into the den of lions, and then was exalted: (6:29). It is written concerning Mordecai: "And he put on sackcloth and ashes" (Esth 4:1), but later "Mordecai went forth from the presence of the king in royal apparel" (8:5). About Joseph it is said: (Ps 105:18), but he too was exalted; and Joseph became ruler over the land.[345]

The Hebrew word for "adversity" here is צָרָה , as in *Esth. Rab.* 9/2 on Esth 5:1 and its parallels cited above. "Degradation" is נִבּוּל,[346] and "exaltation" is רוֹמֵמוּת.[347] Mordecai is cited here as an example of such a righteous person (see above). His abasement or degradation is expressed in the clothing he wore: he went from "sackcloth" to "royal apparel." This also illustrates a righteous person's proceeding from "adversity" to "relief." Divine aid is presupposed, just as in the Judaic tradition cited above of God's never allowing an Israelite to remain in "adversity" more than three days.

I suggest that God's causing the position of the righteous savior / redeemer Mordecai to change from "adversity" to "relief," from "abasement" to "exaltation," provided early Palestinian Jewish Christians with a partial background for conceiving Jesus' Resurrection three days after his Crucifixion. Through God's raising him from the dead, the fate of the savior / redeemer Jesus was also changed from adversity to relief;

---

[344] *Introduction* 92.

[345] Eshkol 160; Berman 248. It is significant that a partial parallel appears in the "Esther Psalm" at *Midr. Pss.* 22/7 (Buber 184; Braude 1.304). It applies this to the "righteous" (צַדִּיקִים), such as Mordecai. See also Addition A to Esther (11:11) on how "the lowly were exalted."

[346] Jastrow 902: disfigurement, disgrace, exposure. The parallel in *Midr. Pss.* 22/7 has נְפִילָה , "falling" (Jastrow 924).

[347] Jastrow 1461: elevation, majesty.

his abasement turned into exaltation. The excursus below on "The Mocking of Jesus, and the Mocking of Mordecai," is another concrete indication of how Palestinian Jewish Christians compared the two.

C. 8.5   The Dawn as the Time of Redemption

Ps 22:1 (Eng. superscription) reads: "To the leader: according to 'The Hind of the Dawn' (אַיֶּלֶת הַשַּׁחַר). While the NRSV has "deer" here for אַיָּלָה , that could be either male or female. Yet a female deer, a "doe" or the traditional "hind," is rather meant.[348] The LXX interprets the term as ἀντιλήμψις , hold, support, aid,[349] probably reading the Hebrew as אֱיָלָת , "help."[350] The Targum has here תְּקוֹף , which can mean the same.[351]

Yet "the hind of the dawn" is usually referred in Judaic tradition to Esther and the beginning of salvation for the Jews. *Midr. Pss.* 22/1 states flatly: "This is Esther."[352] In 22/3, Isa 10:17 is cited in this connection: "the light of Israel." "This is Esther, who 'enlightened' [shone upon] Israel like the light of dawn."[353]

R. Yudan, a fourth generation Palestinian Amora,[354] states in *Midr. Pss.* 18/36 on Ps 18:51 that since "deliverance / redemption" (גְּאוּלָה) will be accompanied by great afflictions (צָרוֹת),[355] Israel would not be able to bear its sudden coming. "Hence, deliverance will come little by little, and will be enlarged gradually for Israel. Therefore deliverance is likened to the dawn, as is said: 'Then shall your light break forth as the

---

348 BDB 19.
349 LSJ 158, 2. Cf. the same word in v 20.
350 BDB 33. Cf. the preceding entry there.
351 Jastrow 1690: 1) strength, power; help, protection. For the text, see Merino 92 and Stec 57. This meaning of the word is also found in *Midr. Pss.* 22/7, end (Buber 184; Braude 1.305).
352 Buber 180; Braude 1.297.
353 Buber 181; Braude 1.298. Dawn imagery was also employed by the Teacher of Righteousness to describe his relationship to God in 1QHᵃ12:6, "Like perfect dawn You have revealed Yourself to me with per[fect] light." See Martínez and Tigchelaar, *The Dead Sea Scrolls Study Edition* 1.166-67.
354 *Introduction* 103.
355 Cf. the so-called "messianic woes" in Mark 13:8, and the texts cited in Str-B 1.950.

dawn' (Isa 58:8). Why is deliverance likened to the dawn? Because you know no darkness greater than the hour nearest to dawn."[356]

This thought is mirrored in *Midr. Pss.* 22/13, which comments at this point on Cant 6:10, "Who is this who looks forth like the dawn?" R. Ḥiyya bar Abba and his friend R. Simeon b. Ḥalafta, fifth generation Tannaim,[357] once were walking in the Valley of Arbel near Sepphoris in Galilee.[358] There they saw "'the hind of the dawn,' its light raying out as it rose. R. Ḥiyya remarked: 'The redemption (גְּאוּלָה) of Israel will be like this!'" R. Simeon agreed with him, citing Mic 7:8, to note its gradual spreading. He then noted that "Likewise at the beginning [of redemption]" was Esth 2:21, which was followed by 5:2; 6:11; 7:10; 8:8; 8:15; and finally "The Jews had the light [of redemption] and gladness" (8:16).[359] Here the "hind of the dawn" is also considered a metaphor for the beginning of redemption.

Finally, the dawn is associated with the messianic redemption in *Midr. Pss.* 22/9, which in commenting on "the hind of the dawn" in Ps 22:1 cites Ps 57:9, "Awake, my glory; awake, psaltery and harp; I will awake the dawn." The individual sections of the verse are here interpreted as the four kingdoms. "Awake, my glory" refers to Hananiah, Michael and Azariah, who "were to rise for us in Babylon. 'Awake, psaltery,' means that [the redeemers] Mordecai and Esther were to rise for us in Media. 'Awake,...harp' means that the house of the Hasmoneans was to rise for us in Greece. 'I will awake the dawn' means that the King, the Messiah, will arise for us in Edom [Rome]."[360]

Here the King, the Messiah, is clearly described as redeeming his people, the Jews, from their present oppressors, the Romans, just as the redeemers Mordecai and Esther did for their people at the time of Ahasuerus and Haman. This redemption is associated with the dawn, as in Judaic interpretation of Ps 22:1 in regard to the redeemer Esther.

The above is significant for the narrative of the empty tomb on Easter Sunday morning. Mark 16:2 states that the three women of v 1 went to the tomb "very early on the first day of the week, when the sun 'had

---

[356] Buber 162; Braude 1.269-70. The unit ends with the coming of the King, the Messiah.

[357] *Introduction* 90-91, which states that the latter lived near Sepphoris.

[358] Cf. Jastrow 114 on ארבל .

[359] Buber 187; Braude 1.308-09. A parallel is found in *y. Ber.* 1:1, 2c (Neusner / Zahavy 1.14).

[360] Buber 185; Braude 1.306, who at times incorrectly changes "for them" to "for us." It is clear that the Jews are always meant.

risen.'" The latter verb is the aorist participle of ἀνατέλλω , of the sun's "rising" or "springing up."[361] Here it is meant as "just having begun to rise," as MS "D" interprets it with ἀνατέλλοντος , "[now] rising." The same verb is employed in Addition A 11 to Esther, where in Mordecai's dream "light came, 'and the sun rose,' and the lowly were exalted...."[362] Here it metaphorically refers to the coming deliverance of the Jews in the Esther narrative. The expression "very early" in Mark 16:1 is the Greek λίαν πρωΐ , the latter meaning "early in the morning."[363] "Very" early in the morning, coupled with ἀνατείλαντος τοῦ ἡλίου meant as "just as the sun was rising," implies at the crack of dawn, just as in the incident with R. Ḥiyya bar Abba and R. Simeon b. Ḥalafta in the Vally of Arbel described above. In Judaic tradition, redemption was associated with this time, explicitly through the King, the Messiah (see above). Other sources associate the dawn with the (future) resurrection.[364]

If we were not so well acquainted with the Easter "story," the three women's coming to Jesus' tomb at the crack of dawn would seem quite strange to us. To do so, they would have to have gotten up much earlier, especially if they are thought of as having their pilgrimage quarters with or near the eleven disciples in Bethany, east of Jerusalem.[365] There was, however, no reason for them to rise so early. They could have started later so as not to have to walk in the dark to the site of Jesus' grave, somewhere outside Jerusalem, and to search for it in the shadows. It should finally be acknowledged that the time element here is a haggadic notice. Dawn was a metaphor in early Judaic tradition for salvation, and the first Palestinian Jewish Christians who heard this narrative told to them would have recognized it as such and would have appreciated the allusion to redemption. Unfortunately, such knowledge has been lost for non-Jewish Christians, especially those from a Western culture.

Before a discussion of the great importance of Judaic interpretation of Hos 6:2-3 for Jesus' rising "on the third day," including the major influence of Judaic interpretation of Esth 5:1's "on the third day," the following excursus points to another significant influence of the Esther

---

[361] BAGD 62.

[362] Cf. also Addition F (6), which refers back to this.

[363] BAGD 724.

[364] Cf. *Gen. Rab.* Vayyishlaḥ 78/1 on Gen 32:27 (Eng. 26), "Let me go, for the day is breaking" (Theodor and Albeck 915; Soncino 2.714, with n. 1); *Lam. Rab.* 3:23 § 8 (Soncino 7.201); and *Midr. Pss.* 25/2 on Ps 25:1 (Buber 210; Braude 1.347-48).

[365] Cf. Mark 11:11-12 and 14:3. John 11:18 says it was fifteen stadia (ca. 2 miles or 3 km) away from Jerusalem. K. Clark, art. "Bethany" in *IDB* 1.387-88, believes it was a bit closer to Jerusalem. On it, see now Küchler, *Jerusalem* 920-32.

narrative in Judaic tradition upon the Passion Narrative beyond the use of the "Esther Psalm" (22) at the Crucifixion.

Excursus: The Mocking of Mordecai, and the Mocking of Jesus in Mark 15:16-21a

The Gospels record that Jesus was mocked at his nocturnal "hearing" before the Council or Sanhedrin (Mark 14:65 par.), as well as at the scene of the Crucifixion. In 15:29-30 par. this is described in terms from the "Esther Psalm," 22:8-9 (Eng. 7-8), as indicated above. In Mark 15:31-32 the mocking continues on the part of the chief priests, scribes, and those crucified with Jesus.

Yet the longest mocking scene takes place between the time when Pilate hands Jesus over to be crucified (Mark 15:6-15 par.), and the latter's actually being led out to be crucified at Golgotha (vv 21-24 par.). Mark 15:16-21a is a separate unit, whose omission would provide for a smooth transmission from v 15 to v 20b.[366] It begins in v 16 by stating that the Roman soldiers led Jesus "into the courtyard" (ἔσω τῆς αὐλῆς).[367] The NRSV appropriately translates the latter noun as "the courtyard of the palace."[368] Increasingly, scholars have correctly ceased to identify this with the Roman fortress Antonia in the NW corner of the Jerusalem Temple, and rather to think of it as part of Herod's Upper Palace,[369] which was located at what is today popularly called the Citadel of David, just south of the Jaffa Gate.[370] Philo in *Leg. Gai.* 299 assumes Pilate's residence in Jerusalem was there ἐν τοῖς ... ˊ Ηρῴδου βασιλείοις , "in the royal palace." In *Bell.* 5.176, Josephus labels it "the palace [αὐλή] of the king [Herod]." It "baffled all description; indeed, in extravagance and equipment no building surpassed it," and it could sleep 100 guests (177), making it very appropriate to the procurator and

---

[366] On this pericope, including secondary literature, cf. Brown, *The Death of the Messiah* 1.862-77 and 674-75, as well as Evans, *Mark 8:27 - 16:20*, 486-91.

[367] For ἔσω as "in, into," cf. BAGD 314,1. Matthew improves here by employing εἰς with the accusative in 27:27. He also omits the courtyard.

[368] BAGD 121.4 : "the 'court' of a prince..., then *palace*."

[369] Cf. the discussion in Evans, *Mark 8:27 - 16:20*, 489.

[370] For an extensive history of it, see now Küchler, *Jerusalem* 491-512, esp. 500-02 for the Roman procurators, including Pilate, residing there after the death of Herod the Great in 4 BCE, i.e. when they visited Jerusalem from their main residence in Caesarea on the Mediterranean Sea.

his entourage when they came to visit from Caesarea.[371] To make this expression αὐλή clearer to the reader, Mark 15:16 adds: "that is, 'the governor's headquarters' (πραιτώριον)."[372] The important thing to note about this site is that both the Markan verse and Josephus label it the αὐλή , the "courtyard (of the royal palace)." It is the same Greek term employed of the site of Mordecai's mocking (see below).

In Mark 15:17 some of the soldiers from "the whole cohort" (v 16)[373] "dress"[374] Jesus in "a purple garment." The latter is the Greek πορφύρα , "purple" as a purple garment.[375] In Hebrew and Aramaic it was employed as a loanword: פּוּרְפּוּרָא .[376] The author of this narrative probably thinks here of a Roman soldier's cloak being put around Jesus, which could be called so.[377] Yet the emphasis is on the "royal" character of the garment, as shown in 15:2, where Pilate asks Jesus: "Are you 'the King' of the Jews?" This expression is repeated for emphasis in vv 9, 12 and 26, and v 32 has "the Messiah, the King of Israel." It should also be recalled that the Messiah was usually called in Hebrew "the King, the Messiah" (מֶלֶךְ הַמָּשִׁיחַ), which was also true in Aramaic. The Messiah was expected to be a king, i.e. to rule over his people the Jews, especially to liberate them from their oppressors, at this point the Romans. Jesus'

---

[371] In 182-83 it is twice labeled "the royal palace" (τὰ βασίλεια), and it is described as having circular cloisters with "open courts" (180).

[372] Cf. BAGD 697 with older literature.

[373] Cf. "the *whole* council / Sanhedrin" in 15:1; both instances of "whole" are typically haggadic embellishments. A σπεῖρα (BAGD 761) had ca. 600 men.

[374] Cf. BAGD 263 on ἐνδιδύσκω ; it only occurs here and in Luke 16:19 in the NT, both times connected to a purple garment. It should be noted that as the soldiers remove the purple cloak from Jesus and put his own clothes back on him (Mark 15:20a), so Mordecai after his "mocking" similarly removed the king's purple robe and again put on his sackcloth and ashes (Esth 4:1 and Judaic tradition on 6:12 such as the *First Targum* in Grossfeld 27 and 63). The difference, of course, is that Mordecai does this himself.

[375] BAGD 694; LSJ 1451 point out that it is equivalent to πορφυρίς , "purple garment."

[376] Jastrow 1148: purple, esp. purple cloak, purple garment. Cf. also Krauss, *Lehnwörter* 2.435-36.

[377] Cf. Caesar's military cloak as designated so in Appian, *Bell. Civ.* 2.150. In 2.90 the same garment is called χλαμύς , more reddish in color (BAGD 882). Matthew intentionally substitutes this term for "purple garment" in 27:28 and 31, adding "red / scarlet" (κόκκινος - BAGD 440). It is used of the mocking scene of Carabas in Philo, *Flacc.* 37, and was also a designation of the "military cloak" of foot-soldiers (LSJ 1993, 2).

opponents would certainly have informed Pilate of this clear implication of the title "Messiah."

Mark 15:17b par. states that after the Roman soldiers had twisted some thorns into a "crown," they put it on Jesus. The Greek word for "crown" here is στέφανος, which can mean both "wreath" and "crown."[378] It is used, for example, of King Herod the Great at his death in 4 BCE in Josephus, *Ant.* 17.197. There it is a "golden wreath / crown" on top of a diadem; it is mentioned in connection with his purple robes.[379] A king's wreath / crown would normally be of gold. Since this was obviously not available to the soldiers, they are pictured in the Gospel narrative as gathering twigs of thorns and plaiting them into what somehow resembled a wreath / crown. Its primary intention, however, was not to cause Jesus physical pain at this point. Instead, the soldiers now mock him by using words similar to those employed by Roman soldiers for their emperor: "Hail, King of the Jews!"[380]

In Mark 15:19 the soldiers are pictured as striking Jesus' head with a "reed," representing the scepter a king would normally also have.[381] In v 36 a similar "reed" is thought to be long enough to reach Jesus (up) on the Cross. Matthew rewrites the Markan account at this point to have the soldiers mock Jesus as a king by putting "a reed in his right hand" (27:29).[382] Again, the description of the soldiers' "striking"[383] Jesus' head with a reed was not primarily meant to hurt him, but to mock him. In addition, it seems strange that the Markan account has the soldiers strike Jesus' "head" (κεφαλή) with a reed. It should be emphasized that there is no similar usage with a royal scepter except in the Esther narrative, which I analyze below. Uncomfortable with this strange usage, Matthew modified it in a major way. It is entirely absent in John 19:2-5.

The soldiers' "spitting"[384] on Jesus in Mark 15:19 par. probably is an attempt to represent Jesus as the Suffering Servant of Isaiah, who states

---

[378] BAGD 767.

[379] In addition, another word for purple (ἁλουργής - LSJ 73) is employed here for the covering on his golden bier. On the διάδημα , see LSJ 393 and 1 Macc 13:32.

[380] Cf. Brown, *The Death of the Messiah* 868: "Mark's salutation makes likely that he intends the scene as a burlesque of the 'Ave Caesar' acclamation of the emperor."

[381] Cf. BAGD 398, 2 on κάλαμος : "stalk, staff."

[382] Cf. Josephus, *Ant.* 17.197, where dead King Herod's "sceptre" (σκῆπτρον - LSJ 1609, 2) lay beside his right hand.

[383] BAGD 830 on τύπτω .

[384] BAGD 257 on ἐμπτύω . For previous spitting, cf. Mark 14:65, as well as the third passion prediction in 10:34.

in 50:6, "I did not hide my face from insult and 'spitting.'"[385] The soldiers' final act of mocking is their "kneeling down in homage" to Jesus in Mark 15:19. This is the Greek expression τιθέντες τὰ γόνατα προσεκύνουν , lit. "bending the knees,[386] they prostrated themselves" before him. This was a typically Persian custom "in the presence of their deified king,"[387] and the "wise men from the East [Persia]" are represented as doing so to the baby Jesus in Matt 2:2 and 11 (also with "kneeling down").

The six acts above are characterized together in Mark 15:20 par. as the soldiers' "mocking" Jesus. This is the Greek verb ἐμπαίζω : to ridicule, make fun of, mock someone.[388] After doing these acts to Jesus, the soldiers removed his "purple garment" (πορφύρα) and put his own garments back on him.[389] Then they led Jesus out to crucify him.

Scholars have suggested various sources for the above mocking scene. Raymond Brown describes them under the headings "Historical Incidents," "Games of Mockery," "Theatrical Mimes," and "Carnival Festivals."[390] T. E. Schmidt thinks here of the description of a Roman emperor at his triumph.[391] Rudolf Bultmann had already proposed that the mocking of Mark 15:16-20a came from "pagan Hellenism," including "some traditional military custom...."[392]

Yet the mocking of Jesus in Mark 15:16-20a is not of Greco-Roman, but rather Palestinian Jewish origin. It deals with a specific aspect of the Esther-Mordecai narrative described above, the intended mocking of Mordecai by Haman, as it developed in Judaic tradition. Josephus, a native of Jerusalem whose mother tongue was Aramaic, is the earliest

---

[385] "Striking" also occurs here, but of the Servant's back.

[386] BAGD 165 on γόνυ : as a sign of respect for superiors.

[387] BAGD 716-17 on προσκυνέω : (fall down and) worship, do obeisance to, prostrate oneself before, do reverence to.

[388] BAGD 255, 1.

[389] That is, the soldier who loaned out his purple / red cloak now got it back. Nothing is now said of the wreath / crown of thorns and the reed. If the purple / red garment was removed, however, these too should probably also be thought of as having been discarded. Art works showing Jesus on the Cross still wearing his wreath / crown of thorns thus may not correspond to the Markan portrayal.

[390] Cf. his *The Death of the Messiah* 1.874-77 and bibliography on pp. 674-75. He falsely states on p. 874: "There is little likelihood that the scene took its inspiration from Israelite tradition...." Adela Yarbro Collins believes "there may have been a mime that could be called 'the mocked king'" which "served as a model for this scene" (*Mark* 723).

[391] Cf. his "Mark 15.16-32: The Crucifixion Narrative and the Roman Triumphal Procession" in *NTS* 41 (1995) 1-18.

[392] Cf. his *The History of the Synoptic Tradition* 304-05 and 272, with n. 3.

witness to it (first century CE), and rabbinic sources fill out the picture. The following eight concrete expressions, all from the Esther / Mordecai / Haman controversy, speak in favor of this new proposal.

1. Bowing Down and Doing Obeisance

Haman, the second man (Esth 3:1) in the world-wide kingdom of King Ahasuerus (LXX Artaxerxes),[393] became infuriated at the Jew Mordecai (3:4) because he did not "bow down and do obeisance" to him, as the king had commanded all his servants to do (vv 2 and 5; cf. 5:9). This led to his having a royal decree made that not just Mordecai, but *all* the Jews should be killed. The Hebrew verbs here are "to bow down" (כָּרַע)[394] and "to bow down, prostrate oneself, before a monarch or superior, in homage" (the hithpalel of שָׁחָה).[395] The LXX has προσκυνέω for both of them.[396] I suggest that the longer expression in Mark 15:19, τιθέντες τὰ γόνατα προσεκύνουν , including the same Greek verb as in the LXX, is an attempt to render the combination of the two Hebrew verbs noted above. It is important to note that this is a controversy between Haman and Mordecai, who play the main roles in all the other points now to be noted.

2. Crucifixion

Because Mordecai refused to bow down and to do obeisance to Haman, the latter "plotted to destroy all the Jews, the people of Mordecai, throughout the whole kingdom of Ahasuerus" (Esth 3:7). He succeeded not only in persuading the king to issue such a decree (vv 9-15), he also had a "gallows" made on which Mordecai should be "hanged" (5:14; cf. 6:4). Later he himself was hanged on it (7:10). The LXX and especially Josephus in his retelling of this narrative employ the verb "to crucify" (σταυρόω and ἀνασταυρόω) together with the noun "a

---

[393] Cf. *b. Meg.* 11a (Soncino 64), where "Our Rabbis taught" that Ahasuerus was one of the three humans who "ruled over the whole globe." See also LXX Addition B (13:2) for Ahasuerus as "master of the whole world."

[394] BDB 502, 1, end.

[395] BDB 1005, 1. The *First Targum* has Aramaic equivalents at this point (Grossfeld 14 and 16, 49 and 52). On this motif, see also LXX Addition C (13:12-14).

[396] Josephus also employs this Greek verb in regard to Mordecai and Haman in *Ant.* 11.209-10 and 230. Adela Yarbro Collins, in contrast, thinks "to kneel" in Mark 15:19 "is probably a Latinism (*genua ponere*)" and "to show reverence" is "typically Greek" (*Mark* 728).

cross" (σταυρός) here.[397] Another indication of a crucifixion is found in the expression "ropes and 'nails,'" which Haman employs of his gallows in *Esth. Rab.* 10/5 on Esth 6:10-11.[398] In *Pirq. R. El.* 50 the crossbeam, taken from Haman's house, is even said to have originated in the Holy of Holies of the Jerusalem Temple.[399]

It is important to note that the intended "mocking" of Mordecai takes place directly before he is supposed to be "crucified" on a "cross," just as the mocking of Jesus was done at this point.

3. *The Courtyard of the Palace, and the Praetorium*

As noted in the introductory remarks, the NRSV translates the αὐλή of Mark 15:16 as "the courtyard of the palace." It then puts into explanatory parentheses: "that is, the governor's headquarters." The latter is the Greek πραιτώριον , the Latin *praetorium*, the "official residence"[400] of the procurator Pilate when visiting Jerusalem from Caesarea on the Mediterranean Sea.

Jesus is represented as being led by Roman soldiers into the αὐλή . This is not simply a "courtyard," but "the 'court' of a prince," a "palace."[401] Here it is the "royal palace" extravagantly built by Herod the Great as described in the introductory remarks. I suggest that both of these terms in Mark 15:16, αὐλή and πραιτώριον , derive from Judaic interpretation of the Esther narrative, concerned at this point with Mordecai.

Mordecai is described ten times as sitting at "the king's gate" (Esth 2:19, 21; 3:2, 3; 4:2, 6 - the open square of the city Susa was before it; 5:9, 13; 6:10, 12). The LXX has αὐλή for this gate seven times (2:19; 3:2-3; 5:9, 13; 6:10 and 12).[402] In connection with "praetorium," I propose that it forms the background of the αὐλή in Mark 15:16.

---

[397] Cf. the references given in n. 333.

[398] Cf. Vilna 28; Soncino 9.117. Nails were not employed of a hanging.

[399] Eshkol 203; Friedlander 407, quoting Ezra 6:11. The "Lebanon" of 1 Kgs 7:2, as so often, is considered to be the Temple. On this crossbeam, see also 1 *Targ.* Esth 7:9 (Grossfeld 29 and 65), as well as "The Deed of Sale of Haman" at 3:2 (Grossfeld 51).

[400] Cf. n. 372.

[401] Cf. n. 368.

[402] Including the Additions, the noun occurs twenty-one times in LXX Esther. Josephus employs it seven times in his retelling of the Esther narrative: *Ant.* 11.222, 244, 246 (twice), 251, 252 and 256. This is out of a total of fifty occurrences in his works.

This is confirmed by the *First Targum* to Esther. It explains "the king's gate" eight times by תרע פלטירין דמלכא , "gate of the פלטירין of the king" (3:2, 3; 4:2 [twice], 6; 5:13; 6:10 and 12).[403] The loanword פְּלֵטְרִין with its variants derives from the Greek πραιτώριον , Latin *praetorium*. In rabbinic Hebrew (and Aramaic here) it can mean both "headquarters" and "palace, residence."[404] Here the above phrase clearly means "the gate of the king's 'palace,'" Ahasuerus' royal residence in the capital of Susa. This is where Mordecai is considered to have spent his time. Yet the term פלטירין also means "headquarters," and this is the meaning it has in Mark 15:16. The NRSV thus correctly translates it as "the governor's 'headquarters.'"

The Palestinian Jewish Christian who first composed the narrative of Jesus' being mocked by Roman soldiers knew of Judaic tradition on the intended mocking of Mordecai (see below), who had his location "in the פלטירין of the king." When the narrative was translated by Hellenistic Jewish Christians into Greek, the "gate" (Hebrew שַׁעַר , Aramaic תרע) was rendered by αὐλή as so often in the LXX of Esther. Then the Aramaic פלטירין was translated not by a Greek word for "palace" such as τὸ βασίλειον / τὰ βασίλεια ,[405] but by πραιτώριον , from which it actually derived. Just as the addition of פלטירין to "the gate of the king" clarified that gate, so in Mark 15:16 the πραιτώριον explains the αὐλή .

The most convincing evidence for the above proposal is found in the *First Targum* on Esth 6:10 and 12. When King Ahasuerus discovered that Mordecai had received no reward for saving his life after two of the king's eunuchs conspired to assassinate him (vv 2-3), he asked Haman's advice on how he should honor such a person (v 6). Thinking that only he himself could be the person meant, Haman suggested in vv 8-9: "let royal robes be brought, which the king has worn, and a horse that the king has ridden, with a royal crown 'on its / his head.'[406] 9) Let the robes and the horse be handed over to one of the king's most noble officials. Let them robe the man whom the king wishes to honor, and let them conduct the man on horseback throughout the open square of the city,

---

[403] Cf. the convenient table in Grossfeld, *The First Targum* 113. It shows that the *Second Targum* also employs the expression at 4:2. Only once (4:2a) is פלטירא used in the *First Targum* instead of פלטירין . See also n. 5 on p. 112.

[404] Jastrow 1180. Cf. also Krauss, *Lehnwörter* 2.455-56 on פלטור , etc.: "Feldherren-zelt, Regierungspalast."

[405] LSJ 309. Josephus has it, for example, in *Ant.* 11.203, 204, 208 and 221.

[406] The Hebrew בְּרֹאשׁוֹ can mean both. Cf. section 6. below with n. 425.

proclaiming before him: 'Thus shall it be done for the man whom the king wishes to honor.'"

The king takes up Haman's advice, and to the latter's great chagrin the king tells him to carry out the above things quickly in respect to "the Jew Mordecai who sits at the king's gate" (6:10). This Haman then does in v 11. The *First Targum* at v 10 has the king tell Haman he should do these things "to the one for whom Esther established the Sanhedrin at 'the gate / entrance of the royal palace.'" The latter phrase, as indicated above, is the Aramaic תרע פלטירין דמלכא,[407] which also can be rendered as "the gate / entrance of the praetorium / headquarters of the king." This is important to note because Judaic tradition on the "mocking" of Mordecai comments on the next verse (11). Before examining it, however, it will be helpful to explain Mordecai's position at this point in the Jewish community of Susa.

In *b. Menaḥ.* 65a Mordecai is represented as being a member of the Sanhedrin.[408] This is also noted in the *First Targum* at 1:10; 2:21; 5:9, 13; 6:10 and 12. It was also thought of as the center for studying the Torah. The *First Targum* notes at 5:9 that Mordecai and "children" (טפל יא)[409] were occupied "with the precepts of the Law in the Sanhedrin which Esther had made for them."[410] In v 13 Haman sees "Mordecai the Jew sitting with 'the young men' (עולמיא)[411] in the Sanhedrin at the palace gate of the king."[412] They too are assumed to be studying the Torah. *Esth. Rab.* 9/4 comments on Esth 5:14 by saying that after he made the gallows for Mordecai, Haman went to him and found him "in the house of study with the [school] children sitting before him...." There were 22,000 of them who called Mordecai "our teacher."[413]

Most important for the scene of Mordecai's intended "mocking," however, is the tradition found in *Esth. Rab.* 10/4 on Esth 6:10-11 and its parallels. Haman "went to find Mordecai, who when told that he was

---

[407] Grossfeld 26 and 62.
[408] Soncino 383. As such he knew seventy languages, enabling him to interpret the eunuchs' plan in the Tarsean language to kill the king. On this, see *b. Meg.* 13b (Soncino 78), where Mordecai is described as "one of those who had seats in the Chamber of Hewn Stone," the place where the Sanhedrin met in Jerusalem. See also Grossfeld, *The First Targum* 106 (which has 15b by mistake), as well as *b. Meg.* 16b (Soncino 100).
[409] Jastrow 548.
[410] Grossfeld 24 and 60.
[411] Jastrow 1051, 2.
[412] Cf. n. 410.
[413] Vilna 28; Soncino 9.113.

coming was greatly frightened. He was sitting with 'his disciples' before him and said to them: 'Run away from here so that you do not come to harm through me, for the wicked Haman is coming to kill me.' They said to him: 'If you are killed, we will die with you.'" They then said a prayer and afterwards "discussed the laws of the precept of the ʿ*Omer*, that day being the sixteenth of Nisan on which the ʿ*Omer* used to be brought when the [First] Temple was standing."[414] The latter refers to Lev 23:10.

Like Jesus, Mordecai has "disciples" (תַּלְמִידִים) here.[415] It is also the second day of the festival of Passover, the 16ᵗʰ of Nisan. In contrast to loud-mouth Peter in Mark 14:29 ("Even though all [the other disciples] become deserters, I will not"), and Jesus' arrest in Gethsemane, when all of the disciples abandoned him (v 50), Mordecai's disciples do not desert him here when they think he will be arrested and killed / crucified. The parallel in *Lev. Rab.* ʾ*Emor* 28/6 expresses this well. His disciples tell Mordecai: "Whether to be killed or to remain alive, we are with you, and will not desert you!" And they do not.

All of the above sets the stage for the intended "mocking" of Mordecai.

4. *Mocking*

After Haman suggests to King Ahasuerus what should be done to the man he wishes to honor (Esth 6:7-9), the king instructs him to carry this out (v 10), which he does (v 11).

Josephus in *Ant.* 11.256 has Haman convey three things to Mordecai, whom he finds before the palace (αὐλή) clothed in sackcloth. In 257 Mordecai, not recognizing the true state of things, thought he was "being mocked" and said: "O basest of all men, do you thus 'laugh at' our misfortune?" By the latter he means the impending annihilation of all the Jews in the kingdom. The first Greek verb here is χλευάζω : to jest, scoff, jeer at, treat scornfully. Cognate nouns mean "mockery" and "mocker."[416]

---

[414] Vilna 28; Soncino 9.116.

[415] This term is also found in *Esth. Rab.* 10/5 (Vilna 28; Soncino 9.117), as well as in the parallel traditions in *Lev. Rab.* ʾ*Emor* 28/6 (Mirkin 8.105; Soncino 4.365 - "His disciples were sitting and learning in his presence"); *Pesiq. Rav Kah.* 8/4 on Lev 23:10 (Mandelbaum 1.143; Braude and Kapstein 162); and *Pesiq. R.* 18/6 on the same verse (Friedmann 93a; Braude 1.389-90). In *b. Meg.*16a on Esth 6:11 (Soncino 94), Haman "went and found [Mordecai with] the Rabbis sitting before him while he showed them the rules of the 'handful.'"

[416] LSJ 1994. Cf. χλευασία , χλεύασμα , χλευασμός , and χλευαστής .

The second verb is ἐπεγγελάω : to laugh at, exult over.[417] From the first century CE, Josephus is a witness to Mordecai's believing he is being mocked as a very old motif.

The rabbinic parallels cited in section 3. above have Mordecai ask Haman twice: "Would you 'show contempt' for royalty?" By this Mordecai probably means two things. First, it is improper to appear before the king unbathed and without a haircut. Haman therefore ends up bathing Mordecai and trimming his hair, showing Haman's abasement and Mordecai's exaltation. Secondly, the hearer / reader knows that Mordecai will later become the king of the Jews (see below). Thus Mordecai can, with irony, be indicating to Haman that he would be showing contempt for him, Mordecai, soon to become a king, by not bathing him and giving him a haircut before he dons the royal accoutrements Haman has brought him.

The Hebrew verb for "to show contempt" in the rabbinic passages is בָּזָה : to despise, spurn, degrade, piel to show contempt for, sneer at, insult. The Aramaic is the same.[418]

The above Judaic tradition of Mordecai's believing he is being "mocked" by Haman in connection with the event of Esth 6:8-11 appears to provide the major background to the soldiers' "mocking" (ἐμπαίζω) of Jesus in Mark 15:16-20a. Four individual items in the Mordecai incident will now be examined in regard to their specific relevance to the Gospel account.

5. A Purple Robe

Haman suggests to King Ahasuerus that for the man he wishes to honor, "let 'a royal robe' be brought, which the king has worn" (Esth 6:8).[419] The *First Targum* calls it "'the purple robe' with which they dressed the king on the day he ascended [the throne of] his kingdom...." The Aramaic of "the purple robe" is לבוש ארגוונא , which also occurs in

---

[417] LSJ 612.
[418] Jastrow 152-53. The term is found in *Esth. Rab.* 10/4 on Esth 6:10-11 (Vilna 28; Soncino 9.116-17); *Lev. Rab.* 'Emor 28/6 (Mirkin 8.106; Soncino 4.366); *Pesiq. R.* 18/4 (Friedmann 93a; Braude 1.390); and *Pesiq. Rav Kah.* 8/4 (Mandelbaum 1.144; Braude and Kapstein 163).
[419] The noun לְבוּשׁ , garment, clothing, raiment (BDB 528), is thought of as singular here; the plural "robes" of the NRSV is misleading. The LXX also has the sing. στολή .

vv 9-11.[420] Here, at what in Judaic tradition is considered Mordecai's intended "mocking" by Haman, Haman "dressed" him in "a purple robe." In *Ant.* 11.255 Josephus labels this a "robe" (στολή), and in 256 twice simply calls it τὴν πορφύραν, "the purple [robe]."

I suggest this "purple robe" is the background for the Roman soldiers' "clothing [Jesus] in 'a purple cloak'" - πορφύραν (Mark 15:17). In Esth 6:9 Ahasuerus tells Haman: "'let them robe' the man whom the king wishes to honor."[421] The expression "let them clothe / robe" here is the Hebrew הִלְבִּישׁוּ , the hiphil of לבֹשׁ : to clothe, array with.[422] The Palestinian Jewish Christian who first composed the narrative of Jesus' being mocked simply transferred this "them" to the Roman soldiers of Mark 15:16. It is they who "dress" (ἐνδιδύσκουσιν)[423] Jesus in "a purple robe" (v 17).[424]

6. *Weaving a Wreath / Crown*

In Esth 6:8 Haman recommends in regard to the man whom King Ahasuerus wishes to honor: "Let a royal robe be brought, which the king has worn, and a horse that the king has ridden, with 'a royal crown' on its / his head." The latter expression, as pointed out above, is the Hebrew בְּרֹאשׁוֹ , whereby the waw can mean either "its" (the horse's, as in the NRSV), or "his" (the man's).[425]

"A royal crown" here is the Hebrew כֶּתֶר מַלְכוּת . The noun כֶּתֶר is found only here in the MT of the king's crown, and in 1:11 and 2:17 of the

---

[420] Cf. Grossfeld 26 and 62-63, with notes 8-9 regarding purple on p. 156. See Jastrow 115 on אַרְגְּוָן : purple (garment), as well as אַרְגָּמָן in BDB 71: purple, red-purple, and Jastrow 115 on this: purple dye, purple garment. There may be influence here from Esth 8:15. The Abraham Epstein MS of *Pirq. R. El.* 50 also has Haman tell Mordecai: "Arise, and put on the purple of the king" (Friedlander 404; it is not in the Eshkol edition at p. 201).

[421] The *First Targum* also has the third person plural in 6:8-9 (Grossfeld 26 and 62).

[422] BDB 527-28.

[423] Cf. n. 374.

[424] On God's later giving His own (royal, purple) robe to the Messiah, cf. *Num. Rab.* Naso 14/3 on Num 7:48 (Mirkin 10.94; Soncino 6.573-74).

[425] Only a fine linen robe and a horse are mentioned by the LXX in this verse. The *First Targum* appears to refer the "royal crown" to the horse (Grossfeld 26 and 62). For the head decoration of Persian horses, see Carey Moore, *Esther* (AB 7B; Garden City, NY: Doubleday, 1971) 65, and Hans Bardtke, *Das Buch Esther* (KAT 17.5; Gütersloh: Mohn, 1963) 348 with n. 12.

queen's crown. Probably due to the influence of Mordecai's receiving "a great golden 'crown' (עֲטָרָה)"[426] in Esth 8:15, Judaic tradition also interprets the crown of 6:8 as Mordecai's, not the horse's.

Esth. Rab. 10/4 on Esth 6:10-11 has Haman tell Mordecai, now clothed in sackcloth and ashes (4:1):[427] "Take this crown and put it on." Mordecai responds by speaking of "a royal crown."[428] In 10/5 on the same text, Haman says: "Yesterday I was busy erecting a gallows for him, and God is preparing for him 'a crown.'"[429] Here the noun employed is כְּלִילָא : wreath, crown.[430]

Pirq. R. El. 50 interprets Esth 6:8 to mean Haman spoke to the king of "the crown which was put upon the head of the king on the day of his coronation."[431] Here כֶּתֶר is used. In his retelling of the Esther narrative, Josephus in *Ant.* 11.254 and 256 instead speaks of "a necklace of gold" (περιαυχένιον χρυσοῦν).[432] Yet the native of Jerusalem, whose mother tongue was Aramaic, employs a different term in 255 for the same object: τὸν στρεπτόν. Ralph Marcus in the LCL edition of Josephus misleadingly translates this as "the chain." The adjective στρεπτός , however, means: easily twisted, pliant. As a substitute, ὁ στρεπτός is a "collar [necklace] of twisted or linked metal," which derives from the verb στρέφω , "to twist, plait."[433] That is, by purposely employing the term ὁ στρεπτός as a synonym for "a necklace of gold," Josephus most probably betrays knowledge here of an early Judaic tradition that the wreath / crown of Esth 6:8 was "plaited" or "twisted." This is also true of Mordecai's

---

[426] BDB 742: crown, wreath. Of its twenty-one occurrences in the MT, this is the only one in Esther. Cf. Josephus on this in n. 434 below, with Mordecai's golden wreath / crown as "twisted / linked."

[427] Cf. also Josephus, *Ant.* 11.256.

[428] Cf. the fact that Mordecai's later fame (Esth 9:4) was that of one of four persons "whose coinage became current in the world" according to *Gen. Rab.* Lech Lecha 39/11 on Gen 12:2 (Theodor and Albeck 375; Soncino 1.320). The coinage showed "sackcloth and ashes on one side, and 'a golden crown' on the other."

[429] Vilna 28; Soncino 9.117. The same noun is found in the parallel texts.

[430] Jastrow 642.

[431] Eshkol 200-01; Friedlander 403 with n. 6.

[432] In 257 it occurs without "gold." Cf. LSJ 1369, II: necklace, collar. The adjective περιαυχένιος means "put round the neck." It does not occur in the LXX. See also Philo, *Ios.* 150 (twice) of the golden neck chain Pharaoh gave Joseph in Gen 41:42.

[433] Cf. LSJ 1653, II, for the adjective, and 1654, IV, for the verb.

"twisted / linked necklace" (τὸν στρεπτόν) for the Hebrew "royal wreath / crown" in Esth 8:15, as Josephus labels it in *Ant*. 11.284.[434]

I suggest that Judaic tradition, primarily on Esth 6:8, is the background of the phrase in Mark 15:17b, πλέξαντες ἀκάνθινον στέφανον , the soldiers' "having plaited / woven a wreath / crown of thorns." The Greek verb here is πλέκω : "weave, plait," found only here, in Matt 27:29, and John 19:2 in the NT.[435] The Palestinian Jewish Christian who composed this narrative could very well have employed the verb אֲרַג here: "to plait, braid, weave."[436]

Jesus is mocked by the Roman soldiers' making him not a wreath / crown of gold, but one plaited of (twigs of) thorns.[437] R. Eliezer (b. Hyrcanus, a second generation Tanna,)[438] states in *Exod. Rab*. Shemoth 2/5 on Exod 3:2 that "the 'thorn bush' [סְנֶה][439] is the lowliest of all trees in the world."[440] There R. Joshua b. Qorḥa, a third generation Tanna,[441] also notes that God chose a thorn bush from which to speak to Moses "to teach you that no place is devoid of God's presence, not even a thorn bush."[442] Jesus' wreath / crown of thorns is thus a sign of his present lowliness, his abasement. As "King of the Jews" he should rather have received a wreath / crown of exactly the opposite material, gold.[443]

---

[434] Cf. also *Ant*. 10.235 for a necklace of "linked / plaited" gold, in connection with purple dress, as well as 240 (both of Belshazzar and Daniel; see Dan 5:16). Addition C of Esther (14:2 or 4:17k) may refer to her "plaited" hair.

[435] BAGD 667. Examples are given of weaving / plaiting a wreath.

[436] Jastrow 114. He points out a wordplay of this verb with *argaman* (purple) in two *Numbers Rabbah* passages. In the MT the verb is employed of Delilah's "weaving" the seven locks of Samson's hair in Judg 16:13, and in Isa 59:5 of "weaving" a spider's web (BDB 70).

[437] On various theories as to which plant / bush is thought to be involved, cf. Brown, *The Death* 1.866-67. Michael Zohary, professor of botany at the Hebrew University in Jerusalem, favors *sarcopoterium spinosum*, very widespread in Jerusalem. It grows to some 50 cm. See his *Pflanzen der Bibel* (Stuttgart: Calwer Verlag, 1983) 156. The English version, *Plants of the Bible*, is not available to me.

[438] *Introduction* 77.

[439] BDB 702; Jastrow 1005.

[440] Mirkin 5.62; Soncino 3.53. On the relative worthlessness of thorns, see also Jesus' saying in Matt 7:16 // Luke 6:44.

[441] *Introduction* 85.

[442] Mirkin 5.61, with parallels in n. 6; Soncino 3.53.

[443] For God's setting His own crown (of gold) on the head of the King Messiah, cf. again *Midr. Pss*. 21/2 on Ps 21:4 (Eng. 3) (Buber 178; Braude 1.294). See also *Exod. Rab*. Va᾿era 8/1 on Exod 7:1 (Mirkin 5.117-18; Soncino 3.115).

Haman's wife and friends encourage him to have a gallows (lit. "tree" - עֵץ) made upon which Mordecai should be hanged the next day (Esth 5:14; cf. 6:4; 7:9-10). It is fifty cubits high (ca. 24 meters or 75 feet),[444] a fantastic assertion leading to much speculation about its nature and origin. In *Esth. Rab.* 9/2 on Esth 5:14 the question is asked: "Of what kind of tree was that gallows made? Our Sages said: When he [Haman] came to make it ready, God called all the trees of creation and said: 'Which will offer itself for this man [Haman] to be hanged on?'" Then thirteen very useful trees, all connected positively to Israel, volunteer. The "thorn" (קוֹץ)[445] thereupon says: "'Sovereign of the Universe, I who have no claim to make offer myself because my name is thorn, and he [Haman] is a pricking thorn, and it is fitting that a thorn be hanged on a thorn.' So they found one of these and they made the gallows."[446]

If this haggadic interpretation of Haman's gallows / tree is basically early and was well-known in Palestine ("Our Sages said") because of the very popular Purim festival, the earliest Palestinian Jewish Christian hearers / readers of the mockery narrative in Mark 15:16-20a may have made the following association: Mordecai, the redeemer of Israel, thinks he will first be mocked on the day Haman had planned to have him hanged / crucified on the gallows / cross he had made from the "thorn" tree.[447] On the day the true redeemer of Israel, the Messiah Jesus, is actually put to death on a tree / cross, he is in fact mocked, in part by receiving a wreath / crown plaited from "thorns." It showed his true abasement, for the thorn was considered the lowliest tree.

7. Hailing the King of the Jews

Mark 15:18 states that the Roman soldiers in the royal palace / praetorium began "to acclaim" Jesus by saying: "Hail, King of the Jews!" "To acclaim" here is from the Greek root ἀσπάζομαι . When used of doing homage to a king, it means "hail, acclaim."[448] "Hail" (Χαῖρε) is the

---

[444] Josephus in *Ant.* 11.246 and 266 even has sixty cubits.

[445] BDB 881; Jastrow 1339-40.

[446] Vilna 27; Soncino 9.110-12. Cf. the parable of the trees in Judg 9:8-15, where other trees seek to anoint the bramble or buck-thorn (אָטָד in BDB 31) as their king. See also Ginzberg, *The Legends* 6.479, n. 184, for parallels to the rabbinic narrative. In *b. Meg.* 10b (Soncino 58) Haman is the thorn of Isa 55:13.

[447] Cf. R. Eliezer's terminology above. Botanically, it was a bush and of course never grew fifty cubits high.

[448] BAGD 116-17: 1.a, end. They call attention to Josephus, *Ant.* 10.211, where King Nebuchadnezzar fell on his face in the manner of worshiping God, and

singular imperative of χαίρω . When used as a form of address, it means "hail (to you)."[449] It also occurs as a loanword in Hebrew (and Aramaic): כֵּירִי , "hail!"[450] Vocalized slightly differently as כִּירִי , it means "captive."[451] The vocative form of κύριος , "lord," is also very similar: קִירִי .[452] If either of the latter two was heard as a possible additional meaning of כֵּירִי in the originally Semitic form of Jesus' mocking by the soldiers, irony would have been involved: "the King of the Jews" is also addressed either as a captive, which he was, or as lord / Lord.

The commentators correctly call attention here to Roman soldiers' saluting the emperor as: *Ave, Caesar, victor, imperator*.[453] If "Hail, emperor, they who are about to die salute you!"[454] was regularly spoken by soldiers about to wage battle, at least some of the readers of Mark's Gospel may have been acquainted with this usage. In that case, Jesus' being acclaimed with "Hail, King of the Jews" by Roman soldiers reversed the usual circumstances. Here it is ironically not the soldiers who are now about to risk losing their life; the one hailed, however, will definitely now lose his.

The mocking of Jesus also ultimately goes back to the scene of Mordecai's intended mocking. Esth 6:9 has Haman suggest to King Ahasuerus in regard to the man he wishes to honor: "let them conduct the man on horseback through the open square of the city, 'proclaiming' before him: 'Thus shall it be done for the man whom the king wishes to honor.'" Haman then carries this out in v 11, also with the same verb for "proclaiming." It is the Hebrew קָרָא , "to call, proclaim."[455] The *First Targum* employs the verb קלס here: to praise.[456] Grossfeld correctly translates it as "proclaim praises."[457] In his retelling of the incident, Josephus in *Ant.* 11.254-55 and 258 employs the Greek κηρύσσω , to

---

"hailed" Daniel; and to Philo, *Flacc.* 38, where people pretend to "salute" the lunatic Carabas in Alexandria, otherwise also dressed up to represent a king (in 39 the verb ἀποκαλέω is used of their "hailing" him as "lord").
449 BAGD 874.
450 Jastrow 636; Krauss, *Lehnwörter* 2.287, III.
451 Jastrow 636; Krauss, *Lehnwörter* 2.287, I: χέιριος - "Sklave."
452 Jastrow 1369; Krauss, *Lehnwörter* 2.539, I.
453 Cf. n. 380 as well as Evans, *Mark 8:27 - 16:20*, 490, and Donahue and Harrington, *The Gospel of Mark* 435.
454 Cf. Suetonius, "Claudius" 21 (reference from Evans, 490).
455 BDB 894-96.
456 Jastrow 1379, II: to call out; to praise, as here.
457 Cf. *The First Targum* 26 and 62, as well as 27 and 63.

"announce, make known by a herald," "proclaim aloud."[458] He also reveals knowledge of the haggadic development of this episode by noting that the proclaiming took place "throughout the whole city" (11.254 and 259), and not just in the public square as in the Hebrew Bible. In *b. Meg.* 16a Haman also leads Mordecai, mounted on the king's horse, "through the street where Haman lived...,"[459] which is also reflected in *1 Targ.* Esth 6:11.[460] Finally, *Esth. Rab.* 10/7 on Esth 6:12 states that Haman had performed four (menial) tasks in regard to Mordecai, one of which was as "a herald" or "public crier" (כָּרוֹז).[461] Haman walked before Mordecai, mounted on the king's horse, and publicly "proclaimed" him as the king's friend, the man whom the latter wished to honor.

Because of the joyful annual celebration of the very popular Purim festival, with the book of Esther read in the synagogue and sermons given on it there, and relevant lectures in the house of study, early Palestinian Jewish Christians knew the final outcome of this intended "mocking" of Mordecai incident almost by heart. Mordecai, who thought Haman was coming on the second day of Passover, the 16th of Nisan, to hang / crucify him, changed sackcloth and ashes for a purple robe and a golden wreath / crown. He became "King of the Jews." The following helps to understand the latter, important for Jesus' being hailed as "king."

King Ahasuerus had promoted Haman to be second in his kingdom (Esth 3:1). In Addition D (5:11) Haman tells his friends and his wife how

---

[458] BAGD 431.

[459] Soncino 95.

[460] Grossfeld 27 and 63.

[461] Vilna 29; Soncino 9.118. The text has כּוֹרֵז , for which Jastrow in 625 refers to כָּרוֹז on p. 664: public crier. The verb כרז means to call out, announce (665). It should be noted that one of the other three tasks mentioned here was to help Mordecai, weakened by his three-day fasting, to mount the king's horse. Since this was the task of a common Roman soldier or "orderly" in respect to the cavalryman he served, the midrash labels Haman here a גוליֵיר or גַלְיֵיר . See also Haman as such in 7/2 on Esth 3:1 (Vilna 21; Soncino 9.80). Jastrow at 221 derives this noun from *galearius,* "soldier's boy, common soldier." See also Krauss, *Lehnwörter* 2.168: "Knappe, Trossknecht." If this was an early tradition, Haman's performing the services of a Roman soldier at the intended mocking of Mordecai may have encouraged the Palestinian Jewish Christian who composed the incident of Mark 15:16-20a to have Roman soldiers mock Jesus. Haman's cutting Mordecai's hair as a "barber," one of the other two menial tasks he performed, is part of a Tannaitic tradition mentioned in *b. Meg.* 16a (Soncino 95). The remaining task was that of a bath attendant.

the king "had advanced him to be the first in the kingdom."[462] In Addition E (16:11) the king recalls how Haman had been called "our father."[463] Yet after his hanging / crucifixion, "King Ahasuerus gave to Queen Esther the house of Haman" (Esth 8:1). Then he removed his signet ring, "which he had taken from Haman, and gave it to Mordecai.[464] So Esther set Mordecai over the house of Haman" (v 2). The LXX clarifies the latter by saying "over everything which had been Haman's." It should also be noted that the book of Esther does not end with remarks about her, but about "the high honor of Mordecai, to which the king advanced him" (10:2). He was not only "next in rank to King Ahasuerus,"[465] but also "powerful among the Jews and popular with his many kindred..." (v 3).

It is Esth 8:15, however, which best expresses Mordecai's rise from adversity to exaltation. In *Esth. Rab.* 10/12 on this verse R. Phinehas (bar Ḥama, a fifth generation Palestinian Amora),[466] says: "Mordecai was 'king of the Jews.'[467] A king wears purple [פורפרין], and Mordecai wore purple. A king has a crown [עטרה] encircling his head, and Mordecai was arrayed 'with a great crown of gold.' The fear of the king is over all the land, and so the fear of Mordecai was upon them (9:3). A king's coinage is current throughout the land, and Mordecai's coinage was current. What was the coinage of Mordecai? It had Mordecai on one side and Esther on the other."[468] As remarked before in n. 428, the variant tradition in *Gen. Rab.* 39/11 has for the latter: "Sackcloth and ashes on one side, and a golden crown on the other."

---

[462] Cf. also Addition B (13:13), which states that Haman "had attained the second place in the kingdom."

[463] Cf. also Addition B (13:6), where Haman "is in charge of affairs and is our second father."

[464] A comparison of Joseph and Mordecai's rise from adversity to greatness is made in *Gen. Rab.* Vayesheb 87/6 on Gen 39:10 (Theodor and Albeck 1069-70; Soncino 2.810-11). Joseph receives Pharaoh's signet ring (Gen 41:42), and Mordecai the king's ring as here; Joseph is clothed in fine linen, as is Mordecai, etc. See also *Tanḥ.* Miqqeṣ 3 on Gen 41:2 for Mordecai (Esth 4:1 and 8:5) and Joseph as examples of the rise from humiliation to exaltation (Eshkol 160; Berman 248).

[465] Cf. Josephus, *Ant.* 11.295, where "Mordecai shared the power / rule" with the king. Earlier Josephus had stated that he was "one of the chief men of the Jews" (11.198).

[466] *Introduction* 105.

[467] Lit., Mordecai "reigned over the Jews."

[468] Vilna 29; Soncino 9.121.

The above biblical and post-biblical materials point to how Mordecai, now endowed with a purple robe, a crown, and the king's ring, was now thought of not only as "powerful among the Jews," but also as "the King of the Jews," as reigning over them. When Mordecai was led around on the king's horse by Haman, with a purple robe and a crown, Haman hailing him as the king's friend, the above was already anticipated. Mordecai was depicted in advance as the King of the Jews. Hailing him as such is part of the background of Mark 15:18, where the Roman soldiers salute / acclaim Jesus with the words: "Hail, King of the Jews!"

8. A Reed as Scepter

Mark 15:19a states that the soldiers struck Jesus' "head" (κεφαλή) with a "reed." The latter noun is the Greek κάλαμος , which can mean both "reed" and "stalk, staff."[469] The term is also employed in v 36 for the "stick" upon which a sponge filled with sour wine is put and given to Jesus on the Cross to drink. This "stick" is thus thought of as long enough to reach Jesus' mouth (up) on the Cross. The reed / staff with which the soldiers strike Jesus' head, upon which is now a wreath / crown of thorns, should also be thought of as having some length. The term was a loanword in rabbinic Hebrew and Aramaic, so it could even have been employed in the original Semitic version of the mocking narrative.[470] Yet the soldiers' striking Jesus' "head" with a reed / staff seems somewhat strange unless one thinks they intentionally want to inflict pain on him, to torture him, which is improbable. The similar incident of the mocking of the lunatic Carabas as a king in Alexandria, in part by giving him a piece of papyrus to hold as his scepter (Philo, *Flacc.* 37), would also speak against this. A king's scepter was in his right hand, as shown by the manner in which Herod the Great was laid out for his funeral in 4 BCE.[471] Matthew also revises Mark by having the soldiers "put a reed in his [Jesus'] right hand" (27:29). Here too I propose that the Esther narrative in Judaic tradition provides the background for the scepter motif at Jesus' mocking.

Esth 4:11 relates: "All the king's servants and the people of the king's provinces know that if any man or woman goes to the king inside the

---

[469] BAGD 398, 1. and 2.
[470] Cf. Jastrow 1328 on קוֹלְמוֹס and קוּלְמוֹסָא , with the Latin *calamus* (Greek κάλαμος). He points out that the latter Aramaic occurs at 2 *Targ.* Esth 3:9. See also קְלָמוֹס on p. 1378, and Krauss, *Lehnwörter* 2.506.
[471] Cf. Josephus, *Bell.* 1.671 and *Ant.* 17.197, as well as n. 382 here.

inner court without being called, there is but one law - all alike are to be put to death. Only if the king holds out 'the golden scepter' to someone, may that person live." The golden "scepter" here is the Hebrew שַׁרְבִיט .[472] The *First Targum* has at this point הוּטְרָא , "staff,"[473] and the LXX ῥάβδος , rod, wand, "staff" of office.[474] The latter already shows early interpretation of this verse by rendering "are to be put to death" as "he has no salvation [σωτηρία]." For "may that person live" the LXX reads: "that person shall be saved [σωθήσεται]."[475]

Josephus makes the throne incident in Esther even more gruesome by noting a Judaic tradition that "round his throne stood men with axes to punish any who approached the throne without being summoned" (*Ant.* 11.205). The *First Targum* states that the above law of being put to death if one approached the king unsummoned derived from wicked Haman.[476]

Ahasuerus' golden "scepter" thus easily lent itself to haggadic comment. This is especially true of the turning point in the entire Esther narrative. Because of Haman's having convinced the king to issue an edict for the total annihilation of all the Jews in the entire kingdom, from India to Ethiopia, Esther fasted for three days and "on the third day," the 15th of Nisan, the first day of Passover, she approached the king unsummoned, knowing that she might perish thereby (Esth 4:11b - 5:1 in Judaic tradition). *Esth. Rab.* 9/1 on Esth 5:1 states that when the king now saw Esther, "he was furiously angry because she had broken his law and come before him without being called." In fact, "his eyes were flashing like fire with the wrath which was in his heart." Nevertheless, when he noted her reactions to this, he ran to her and stated that the law did not apply to her as his queen.[477] Josephus notes at this point that Esther had fainted, causing the king to leap from his throne, raise her (from the floor) in his arms, and bring her back to consciousness. He then explained that the law did not apply to her. "So saying, he placed his scepter in her hand and held out his staff over her neck in accordance

[472] BDB 987 notes that it is only found in Esth 4:11; 5:2; and 8:4.
[473] Grossfeld 21 and 57. Cf. Jastrow 1646.
[474] LSJ 1562.
[475] Cf. Josephus, *Ant.* 11.226, where the king can extend his golden staff to someone who comes unsummoned to him, thus "saving" (σώζειν) him. "For only one to whom the king did so, on his coming in to him without being summoned, obtained pardon and was 'saved' [σώζεται] from death."
[476] Grossfeld 21 and 57.
[477] Vilna 27; Soncino 9.109.

with the law, and thus freed her from anxiety" (*Ant.* 11.238). She then revived (240).

Josephus strangely has two staffs here, first a "scepter" (σκῆπτρον), then a "staff" (ῥάβδος). He had also called the latter a λύγος in 205.[478] Like others acquainted with court ceremony, the Jewish historian thought that at this point Esther fell at Ahasuerus' feet, as in Esth 8:3. Then "the king held out the golden scepter to Esther, and Esther rose and stood before the king" (8:4-5). Therefore Josephus can say in regard to Esth 5:2 that Ahasuerus "held out his staff over her neck," which Ralph Marcus in the LCL correctly interprets as "over her bowed head." The LXX at this point also states that the king placed the golden staff "upon her neck."

It should be noted, however, that the Hebrew of Esth 5:2 says Ahasuerus "held out to her the golden scepter that was in his hand. Then Esther approached and touched the 'top' of the scepter." The "top" here is literally the "head" (ראש), which also occurs in the *First Targum* at this point.[479] When Ahasuerus is represented as holding out the "head" (tip) of his scepter over prostrate Esther's "neck," the "head" (tip) is just above her neck and probably thought to touch, not to strike her head. This could very well be the broader background of the Roman soldiers' striking Jesus on the "head" with a reed / scepter. It should be recalled that the scene with Esther, considered a "redeemer" of Israel, took place on the first day of Passover, the same day as Jesus' mocking.

Popular concern with Ahasuerus' scepter at precisely this point may undergird the above. R. Yohanan, a second generation Palestinian Amora,[480] states in *b. Meg.* 15b in regard to Esth 5:2, "Three ministering angels were appointed to help her at that moment: one to make her head [lit., neck] erect, a second to endow her with charm, and a third to stretch the golden scepter." R. Jeremiah, a fourth generation Palestinian Amora,[481] said: "It was two cubits long, and he made it twelve cubits. Some say, sixteen, and some again, twenty-four. In a Baraitha it was stated, sixty."[482] R. Eleazar (b. Pedat) maintains that his teacher, R. Yohanan, said two hundred.[483] The above baraitha (a Tannaitic

[478] LSJ 1063: twig, withe (branch). See the cross-reference to ἄγνος on p. 12: chaste-tree.
[479] Grossfeld 22 and 59.
[480] *Introduction* 94.
[481] *Ibid.*, 102.
[482] Soncino 91.
[483] Soncino 92. See *Introduction* 98 on this third generation Palestinian Amora.

tradition not found in the Mishnah) shows that this playful speculation already took place at least in the Tannaitic period.

Midr. Pss. 22/27 on Ps 22:20 also comments on Esth 5:2. "R. Tahalifa[484] said: 'We have a tradition that Ahasuerus' scepter was lengthened in that instance by thirty-two cubits. And the second miracle was even greater than the first, for as Esther drew nearer, the scepter shrank back to its former length.'"[485] Here one "miracle" (□]) is thought to follow another. R. Isaac (II, a student of R. Yohanan and a third generation Palestinian Amora,)[486] states after the above: "If the scepter of a mere mortal brings life to an entire people [the Jews threatened with total annihilation], how much more life does the scepter of the Holy One, blessed be He, bring (Mic 7:4)."[487] Here the incident of Esther's being rescued "on the third day" by having the head (tip) of Ahasuerus' scepter touch her neck / head is considered a "miracle," bringing salvation / deliverance to an entire people, the Jews.

Finally, another rabbinic passage speaks of the staff God will give the King Messiah in the future. *Num. Rab.* Korach 18/23 on Num 17:21, "the staff of Aaron," states: "That same staff was held in the hand of every king until the [first] Temple was destroyed, and then it was [divinely] hidden away. That same staff is also destined to be held in the hand of the King Messiah (may it be speedily in our days!); as it says: 'The staff of your strength the Lord will send out of Zion. Rule in the midst of your enemies' (Ps 110:2)."[488] Ps 110:1, "The LORD says to my lord, 'Sit at My right hand until I make your enemies your footstool,'" was applied by the first Jewish Christians to their Lord, Jesus, in part because he himself cited the passage (Mark 12:35-37 par.). The application of the "staff" of v 2 to the King Messiah is thus consistent. At this point at the latest, Jesus as the Messiah is thought of as having a real staff / scepter, although that employed of the King of the Jews at Jesus' mocking was merely a reed.

* * *

The above eight expressions and motifs can be questioned individually. Together, however, they provide a very strong argument for the narrative of Jesus' mocking in Mark 15:16-20a as being for the

---

[484] Cf. Str-B 5/6.243 for him as a Palestinian, ca. 270?
[485] Buber 194-95; Braude 1.321.
[486] *Introduction* 98.
[487] Buber 195; Braude 1.321.
[488] Mirkin 10.215; Soncino 6.743-44.

most part dependent on Palestinian Judaic traditions on the intended mocking of Mordecai in Esth 6:7-11, as well as on those regarding the scepter incident close by in the Esther narrative (5:2), thought to take place on the 15th of Nisan. The latter was the first day of Passover, the day on which Jesus was also first represented as being mocked, and then crucified. The basic difference, however, should not be overlooked. Despite the perceived intention to mock him, Mordecai survives, in contrast to Jesus. Mordecai is not crucified by Haman, who planned to do so, as Jesus is by the Roman soldiers. Yet both "redeemers" of Israel proceed from mockery / affliction / abasement to exaltation. Mordecai becomes the King of the Jews, and Jesus, first mocked as the King of the Jews, is exalted by God three days later, at his Resurrection.

Craig Evans thinks "it is hard to believe that the evangelist, or a Christian tradent before him, would invent a story in which Jesus is so shamefully abused and mocked." He cites others who also claim the mocking incident is historical.[489] Yet even a scholar such as Raymond Brown, who usually represents a cautiously balanced position, can ask: "Under orders to crucify Jesus and with a certain press of time to have the execution finished by evening (in order not to rile the Jewish populace so sensitive about the oncoming Sabbath), would the Romans have held up the execution to play games victimizing Jesus?"[490] No, they would not have, and they didn't. The earliest Passion Narrative, as Bultmann proposed, proceeded directly and smoothly from Mark 15:15b ("And after flogging Jesus, [Pilate] handed him over to be crucified") to 20b ("Then they led him out to be crucified"). The incident of Jesus' mocking is a later, yet pre-Markan haggadic development. A Palestinian Jewish Christian considered it appropriate to transfer expressions and motifs from the intended mocking of another redeemer of Israel, Mordecai, "King of the Jews," when Haman sought to hang / crucify him on a gallows / cross, at the time of Passover in Judaic tradition on Esther 5-7, to his own "King of the Jews," the King, the Messiah Jesus, on the first day of Passover. His first Jewish and Jewish Christian hearers / readers would have greatly appreciated the clear allusions to the intended mocking of Mordecai in Judaic tradition, just as they also

---

[489] Cf. his *Mark 8:27 - 16:20*, quotation p. 489; 487 lists the others. Joel Marcus in "Crucifixion as Parodic Exaltation" in *JBL* 125 (2006) 84, n. 46, also believes that "this pattern and exegesis go back to events in the life of the historical Jesus." He is not aware of the abasement / exaltation motif in Judaic tradition on Mordecai.
[490] *The Death* 1.871. Cf. 867: "if one thinks the basic story is historical...." "There is no way of knowing whether this happened historically..." (p. 874).

appreciated the application of various parts of the "Esther Psalm" (22) to Jesus on the Cross. Such haggadic additions were typical of the way they themselves dealt with Scripture, and no one would have thought of raising the question whether such additions or embellishments were historical or not. That is instead a modern question, which I shall address more extensively in the next chapter on "Haggadah and the Questions of Historicity and Truth in the Gospels."

C. 9 Hos 6:2 and Resurrection on the Third Day

Hos 6:1-3 reads in the NRSV:

1) Come, let us return to the Lord;
   for it is He who has torn,
   and He will heal us;
   He has struck down,
   and He will bind us up.
2) After two days He will revive us;
   on the third day He will raise us up,
   that we may live before Him.
3) Let us know, let us press on to know the Lord;
   His appearing is as sure as the dawn;
   He will come to us like the showers,
   like the spring rains that water the earth.

The above verses, especially verse two, were especially important to the first Palestinian Jewish Christians in regard to Jesus' being raised by God from the dead "on the third day."[491] I shall begin my analysis with the third verse.

---

[491] Cf. the art. ἡμέρα by Gerhard Delling in *TDNT* 2.949, where he thinks Jesus himself, "being certain of the resurrection in accordance with an inner necessity, found the relative day of His resurrection in the OT, namely, in the בַּיּוֹם הַשְּׁלִישִׁי of Hos 6:2." As will become clear below, I believe "on the third day" was only *later* applied to the time after Jesus' death. Hans Walter Wolff in his *Dodekapropheten 1, Hosea* (BKAT XIV/1; Neukirchen-Vluyn: Neukirchener Verlag, 1976) deals with Hos 6:1-2 on pp. 148-51. He asserts that originally v 2 had nothing to do with resurrection. Yet if the earliest Palestinian Jewish Christian community wanted a scriptural prooftext for "on the third day," "dann kann kaum an eine andere Stelle gedacht sein als an Hos 6,2..." (p. 150). Francis Andersen and David Noel Freedman in *Hosea* (AB 24; Garden City, NY: Doubleday & Company, 1985) deal with Hos 6:1-3 on pp. 417-25. In regard to v 2

Literally, Hos 6:3 says of the LORD: "His going forth is as sure as the dawn." The first Palestinian Jewish Christians interpreted "the LORD" (יהוה) here as their own Lord, the Messiah Jesus.[492] "His going forth" (מוֹצָאוֹ) was for them his going forth from the grave / tomb "on the third day" (v 2). The catchword "dawn" (שַׁחַר), employed here in connection with the Lord's "going out," was one source for the similar imagery in Mark 16:2. There the three women go to Jesus' tomb "very early" on the first day of the week, "just as the sun had risen / was rising." It is therefore dawn. There they discover that Jesus had already "gone forth." The catchword "dawn" also connects Hos 6:1-3 to the "Esther Psalm" (22), where she is interpreted as "the hind of the *dawn*." Salvation was thought to begin at that point when she dared to approach King Ahasuerus "on the third day," the 15th of Nisan or the first day of Passover, in regard to saving her people, the Jews (see above). Finally, the "spring rains" in Hos 6:3 refer to those of March / April,[493] the time when Jesus was crucified. As noted before, the life-giving, restorative effect of rain was compared to the resurrection of the dead in numerous Judaic sources. Therefore it was also mentioned in the second blessing of the Eighteen Prayer, "The Resurrection of the Dead."[494]

It is Hos 6:2, however, which played the central role in the earliest Palestinian Jewish Christian interpretation of God's having raised Jesus "on the third day." Verse 2a reads of the Lord: "After two days He will 'revive' us." The Hebrew of "revive" is the piel of חיה : restore to life.[495] Hebrew parallelism means that one should interpret "after two days" to be the same unit as in 2b, "'on the third day' He will raise us up."[496] The Hebrew verb for "raise up" here is the hiphil of קום : to cause to arise, raise.[497] *Targum Jonathan* interprets similarly, placing v 2b in parallelism

---

they in contrast say: "Explicit hope for resurrection of the body can hardly be denied in this passage, but commentators have been reluctant to admit it" (420).

[492] Cf. the interpretation of "The LORD is our righteousness" in Jer 23:6 as the King Messiah in the passages cited by Str-B 1.66, "k." See also 1 Cor 16:22's *Marana tha*, "Our Lord, come!" and Rev 22:20.

[493] Cf. BDB 545 on מַלְקוֹשׁ .

[494] Cf. *y. Ber.* 5:2 (Neusner / Zahavy 1.201-02); *Ta'an.* 1:1, 63c (Neusner 18.139); and *Deut. Rab.* Ki Thabo 7/6 on Deut 28:12 (Mirkin 11.114; Soncino 7.137).

[495] BDB 310-11, pi. 3: "quicken, revive, refresh. a. *restore to life*, the dead: 1 Sam 2:6; Deut 32:39; Hos 6:2." Cf. the expression תְּחִיַּית הַמֵּתִים , the "'resurrection' of the dead" (Jastrow 1661).

[496] Cf. Andersen and Freedman, *Hosea* 422: "The day *after* two days coincides with the third day, the day of the resurrection."

[497] BDB 878, 1.a.

with 2a, and referring the Lord's "raising" to "the day of the resurrection of the dead": "He will give us life in the days of consolations that will come; on the day of the resurrection of the dead He will raise us up, and we shall live before Him."[498]

The Lord's "raising" the dead "on the third day" in Hos 6:2 was then applied by Palestinian Jewish Christians to God's "raising" Jesus on the third day (which began on Saturday evening). The young man / angel can thus tell the women inside Jesus' tomb at the crack of dawn on Easter Sunday (Mark 16:6): "'He has been raised'; he is not here." The former verb is the divine passive, ἠγέρθη . It is God who has "raised" Jesus already now, and not only in the future, at the general resurrection of the dead,[499] as meant in *Targ. Jon.* Hos 6:2.

Judaic interpretation of Hos 6:2 as referring to the resurrection of the dead, in addition to the *Targum*, aided in Palestinian Jewish Christians' applying it to Jesus' Resurrection "on the third day." According to the Tannaitic midrash *Sifre Ha'azinu* 329 on Deut 32:39, "I kill, and I make alive," the phrase "After two days He will revive us" (Hos 6:2) is "one of the four assurances given to Israel which hint at the resurrection of the dead."[500] In addition, Hos 6:2 is cited in regard to the resurrection of the dead in *y. Sanh.* 11:6, 30c,[501] which is also true of *Pirq. R. El.* 51.[502]

Most important for 1 Cor 15:4 ("he was raised 'on the third day' in accordance with the Scriptures" - plural) and the narrative of the empty tomb, however, is the tradition found in *Esth. Rab.* 9/2 on Esth 5:1, "Now it came to pass 'on the third day' that Esther put on...," and parallels. As noted above, it states: "Israel are never left in dire distress more than three days." The Hebrew noun for "dire distress" here is צָרָה : anguish,

---

[498] Sperber 3.395; Cathcart 41.

[499] Cf. the Apostle Paul, who describes Christ as "the first fruits" of those who have died in 1 Cor 15:20 and 23.

[500] Finkelstein 379; Hammer 340. Hos 6:2 is cited as one of the ten passages which hint at the resurrection of the dead in *Midr. Haggadol* Deut 32:39 (Fisch 730; see also *Midrasch Tannaim zum Deuteronomium*, Hoffmann 202).

[501] Neusner 31.388.

[502] Eshkol 204; Friedlander 411. In *Eliyyahu Rabbah* (5)6 the author designates the three days of Hos 6:2 as "life in this world," "life in the time of the Messiah," and "life in the world to come" (Friedmann, ER 29; Braude and Kapstein 107). This, however, is against all early tradition, which sees "after two days" and "on the third day" in parallelism with one another.

trouble, distress, persecution.[503] Examples are then given which are relevant to God's delivering Jesus from the "anguish" of death by raising him within three days: a) "On the third day" in Gen 22:4 applies to the ʿAqedah, at which Isaac was to be killed by Abraham, but was miraculously delivered from death (see section C. 7 above). b) Jonah's being in the belly of the fish "three days and three nights" (Jonah 2:1, Eng. 1:17) also presumes he would normally have died because of this. Yet he too was miraculously delivered by God through His causing the fish to spew him out upon the dry land (2:11, Eng. 10 - see section C. 6 above). c) "The dead also will come to life only after three days, as it says: Hos 6:2." d) Finally, the "miracle" (נֵס) of Esther's not being killed because she went unsummoned to King Ahasuerus (Esth 4:11, 16), but which rather initiates the process of redemption for all the Jews of the kingdom, occurs after three days of their fasting. "Now it came to pass 'on the third day' that Esther put on her royal apparel..." (5:1).[504]

It is important to note that this takes place on the 15th of Nisan or the first day of Passover.[505] As redemption for the Jews was thought to *begin* then, Palestinian Jewish Christians could also maintain that Jesus' Crucifixion on the same day was actually the *beginning* of redemption for them. This act was then considered to have been completed three days later, on Easter Sunday, when God "raised" Jesus from the dead, fulfilling Hos 6:2.

The Apostle Paul "hands on" to the Christian community in Corinth a tradition he in turn had received from those who had become Christians before him. It is that Christ "was raised 'on the third day' in accordance with the Scriptures," the latter in the plural. This alludes to, or echoes,

---

[503] Jastrow 1300. Cf. also BDB 865: straits, distress, travail. It occurs for example in Ps 22:11 (Eng. 12); Jonah 2:3 (Eng. 2); and Dan 12:1, with resurrection described in v 2.

[504] Vilna 28; Soncino 9.112. Cf. the parallels in the "Esther Psalm," *Midr. Pss.* 22/5 (Buber 182-83; Braude 1.301-02), and *Gen. Rab.* Vayyera 56/1 on Gen 22:4 (Theodor and Albeck 595; Soncino 1.491; it cites Hos 6:2 for "the third day, of the resurrection of the dead"). While the latter lacks the explicit assertion that God "never leaves the righteous in distress more than three days," this is found in *Gen. Rab.* Miqqiṣ 91/7 on Gen 42:17 of Joseph; it also cites Hos 6:2 (Theodor and Albeck 1129; Soncino 2.843). In regard to the empty tomb, it should also be recalled that in Judaic tradition Jacob rolls away the very heavy stone from the mouth of the well on the third day after having been blessed by his father Isaac with the dew of resurrection. See section B. 1.9 above.

[505] As pointed out above, this was also the time the ʿAqedah took place according to very early Judaic tradition.

not only Hos 6:2,[506] but most probably also to at least three passages intimately associated with it in Judaic tradition: Gen 22:4; Esth 5:1; and Jonah 2:1 (Eng. 1:17), with the latter's delivery / redemption in 2:11 (Eng. 10). Early Jewish Christians definitely applied the Jonah Scripture to Jesus' Resurrection, as shown in Matt 12:40.

In light of the numerous quotations of, and allusions to, the "Esther Psalm" (22) in the Crucifixion scene, and the major influence of Judaic traditions regarding Esth 6:8-11 on the mocking of Jesus just before it (see the above Excursus), it is probable that the phrase "on the third day" in Esth 5:1, after Hos 6:2, exerted most influence on the formation of the belief that God raised Jesus from his situation of dire distress, from the affliction of death, "on the third day."[507] Because of the tradition now found in *Esth. Rab.* 9/2 and parallels, which appears to be very early, it would have been hard for Palestinian Jewish Christians *not* to describe him in such terms.

It was another Judaic source, however, one dealing with Moses, which "triggered" the entire motif of Jesus' having been raised after three days / on the third day. In conclusion, it is this to which I now turn.

C. 10 *Mourning for Moses for Three Days*

Deuteronomy 34 states that after Moses died and was buried, "The Israelites wept for Moses in the plains of Moab thirty days; then the days of the weeping of the mourning for Moses were ended" (v 8).[508] Here the total period of mourning for Moses is clearly thirty days - after his death and burial.

The Tannaitic midrash *Sifre* Ve'zot ha-Berakhah 357 on the above verse, however, interprets the period of mourning very differently. It states: "'And the Israelites wept for Moses' - behold, one [day]. 'And the days were ended' - behold, two [days]. 'The weeping of the mourning for

---

[506] The motif of Jesus' being killed and rising / being raised after three days is also found in all three Passion predictions (Mark 8:31 par.; 9:31 par.; and 10:34 par.). They too reflect Hos 6:2.
[507] This may also add support to the proposal I made earlier that the "Paschal Pardon," with the release of Barabbas (Mark 15:6-15a par.), is based on Judaic tradition in regard to the "amnesty" granted by King Ahasuerus in Esth 2:18. See "The Release of Barabbas (Mark 15:6-15 par.; John 18:39-40), and Judaic Traditions on the Book of Esther" in my *Barabbas and Esther and Other Studies in the Judaic Illumination of Earliest Christianity*, 1-27.
[508] Cf. Num 20:29, where "all the house of Israel mourned for [Moses' brother] Aaron thirty days."

Moses' - behold, three [days]. These are [a total of] three days. What is their peculiarity? It teaches that they wept for him before his death for thirty days."[509]

Here the Israelites are represented as weeping for Moses thirty days in advance of his death. Then at his actual death they mourned for a total of three days.[510] I suggest that this definitely Tannaitic tradition was known to the first Palestinian Jewish Christians. They reasoned: As our predecessors the Israelites mourned for Israel's first redeemer, Moses, for three days after his death and burial, so the (eleven) disciples and his other followers mourned for Israel's final or great redeemer, the Messiah Jesus, for three days after his death and burial. This notice of time (three days) then triggered a reference to the very popular passage Hos 6:2. It was interpreted by the earliest Christians, as in general Judaic tradition, of God's "raising on the third day." This in turn was then reinterpreted by them not of the general resurrection of the dead at the end of time, but of Jesus' Resurrection already now, "on the third day" after his Crucifixion, i.e. on Easter Sunday. Jesus was the beginning or "first fruits" of the general resurrection of the dead, expected quite soon.

As pointed out earlier, Palestinian Jewish Christians knew of two different traditions in regard to Moses' end. The first (my "Model A") openly contradicted Scripture and maintained that Moses did not die at all, but was "translated" by God to heaven. The second (my "Model B") was that he actually died and was buried, yet his soul was immediately taken up ("raised") by God and placed by Him under His Throne of Glory. The earliest Palestinian Jewish Christians, for whom the Messiah Jesus was a second Moses, described Jesus as dying and being buried, but they added that God "raised" him (bodily, like Moses) from the dead "on the third day." In addition to Judaic tradition on Deut 34:8 and Hos 6:2, other Scriptural passages such as Esth 5:1, Gen 22:4, and Jonah 2:1 (Eng. 1:17), also as understood in Judaic tradition, aided them in making this assertion in regard to "the third day."

---

[509] Finkelstein 430; Hammer 382. A parallel is found in *Midr. Haggadol* Deut 34:8 (Fisch 789), which is the same as *Midrasch Tannaim* on the same verse (Hoffmann 227). See also *Yalquṭ* 965 *ad loc.* ("Deuteronomy," ed. Kook 714). "Days," "weeping" and "mourning" in Deut 34:8 are also considered to be three days in *b. Moʿed Qaṭan* 21a (Soncino 134, with n. 5).

[510] This may have been in part influenced by Josh 1:11, where Joshua tells the people: "in three days [lit., the day after tomorrow] you are to cross over the Jordan." See also 3:2, which may indicate that the narrative of Rahab and the spies (2:1-24) is a later insertion at this point.

The above also helps to explain how the Apostle Paul knew of a "tradition" from earlier Jewish Christians already ca. 54 CE[511] when he wrote 1 Cor 15:4, "that [Christ] was raised 'on the third day' in accordance with the Scriptures." Only some twenty-five years after Jesus' death, his being raised "on the third day" is thus attested as a received tradition, showing that it most probably arose even much earlier. Since Paul could have employed the narrative of the "empty tomb" very well to buttress his case, but does not do so,[512] this also shows that the haggadic narrative of the "empty tomb" arose later, in its final form probably first in the sixties CE. On the basis of "Model B" regarding Moses, whereby Moses died, it added "Model A" also regarding him, whereby Jesus like Moses was "translated" bodily to heaven by God. Thus the account of the "empty tomb" came about. Pre-Markan, this narrative was then translated from Aramaic (or less probably Hebrew) into Greek by Hellenistic Jewish Christians and so became available to the Evangelist. As noted before, most scholars consider the Gospel of Mark to have been written just before or after 70 CE. Matthew and Luke appropriated the narrative of the empty tomb from him, and the Evangelist John in 20:1-10 probably employed and modified a similar pre-Markan source.

The "trigger" to all of this, however, was early Judaic tradition on the Israelites' weeping for Moses *for three days* after his death and burial. As one wept / mourned three days for the first redeemer of Israel, Moses, so there should be three days of weeping / mourning for the final redeemer of Israel, the Messiah Jesus. And as the burial site of the first redeemer of Israel, Moses, was never found, in well-attested early tradition because he was "translated" bodily to heaven by God, so the burial site of the final redeemer of Israel, the Messiah Jesus, was never found,[513] in part because he was "raised" bodily to heaven by God.[514] The Palestinian

---

[511] Cf. chapter II., n. 52.

[512] Against Christian Wolff, *Der erste Brief des Paulus an die Korinther*, Zweiter Teil, 161.

[513] That is, until it was "discovered" by Constantine at the beginning of the fourth century CE.

[514] While terror / amazement / fear on the part of the women in Mark 16:8 could reflect the Evangelist's own emphasis on such a reaction to miracles and the revelation of Jesus' identity (cf. e.g. 4:41; 5:15, 33, 42; and 9:6) and his own interest in the "Messianic secret," it nevertheless remains a strange way to end a Gospel, the "good news" (1:1). This explains why so many alternative explanations have been suggested, including the relating of a Resurrection appearance in Galilee after v 8. Yet if the story of Jesus' earthly life culminated in 16:1-8, this could be

Jewish Christian haggadic narrative of the empty tomb in a very creative way expresses the latter "religious truth": God raised His Son Jesus as the first of the dead, and he would very soon appear to his followers, beginning in Galilee, as a confirmation of his Resurrection.[515]

---

thought of as reflecting in part the end of Moses' earthly life in Deuteronomy 34, (his "biography" having begun in Exodus 1). Deut 34:11 speaks of "signs and wonders" connected with Moses, and the very last verse, twelve, not only of "mighty deeds," but also of "terrifying displays of power." The latter is the Hebrew הַמּוֹרָא הַגָּדוֹל , literally "the great fear / terror" (BDB 432 on מוֹרָא). The usually reticent *Targum Onqelos* interestingly translates here with "great vision" (Drazin 318-19, with n. 12; Grossfeld 114: "great manifestations"); *Neofiti 1* with "great manifestations" (Díez Macho 5.297; McNamara 175, with n. 18, referring to 4:34 on p. 40, with the longer n. 39); and *Fragment Targum* "N" with "the great visions" which Moses brought about (Klein 1.236; 2.193). This is due to the term מוֹרָא as considered to be not from the root ירא , to fear, but from ראה , to see (for LXX examples with these two verbs, see the *Greek-English Lexicon of the Septuagint*, p. 650; a rabbinical example of reading "seeing" in a biblical text as "fearing" is found in *Cant. Rab.* 4:5 § 2 [Donsqi 111, with n. 13; Soncino 9.200]). The Aramaic is similar for all of these (see Jastrow 442 on חיזוונא). Can these "visions / manifestations" be related somehow to the "appearances" of Jesus after his death?

While Deuteronomy 34 merely mentions Moses' death and burial, many first-century Jews also believed that Moses did not die, but was then translated bodily to heaven, as described above in this chapter. Thus the earthly lives of the first and the last redeemers of Israel, Moses and the Messiah Jesus, may have purposely been represented as ending similarly, with "great fear / terror," and /or with "great visions / manifestations," the latter alluded to but not spelled out. This topic should be given more study.

[515] It is these appearances to which the Apostle Paul refers in 1 Cor 15:5.

IV. Haggadah and the Questions of Historicity and Truth in the Gospels

1. Definition

The terms הַגָּדָה or הֲגָדָה , "haggadah," and אַגָּדָה or אֲגָדָה , "aggadah," are synonyms.[1] They derive from the hiphil verb form הִגִּיד (root נגד): to declare, make known, expound.[2] Haggadah "is usually defined in a negative manner, i.e., that portion of rabbinic teaching which is not *halakhah*, i.e., which is not concerned with religious laws and regulations."[3] Halakhah deals for example with officially permitting or prohibiting something, declaring something / someone fit or dis-qualifying it / the person, ruling something / someone clean or unclean, and acquitting or condemning someone.[4] Louis Ginzberg maintained that haggadah, in contrast, is "a name that can be explained by a

---

[1] Cf. Jastrow 330 and 11 on the two nouns.

[2] Jastrow 871 and BDB 616, 2. On this topic, cf. Wilhelm Bacher, "Der Ursprung des Wortes Haggada (Agada)" in *Die Agada der Tannaiten 1* (Straßburg: Karl Trübner, 1903) 451-75; art. "Haggadah" by Joseph Jacobs in *JE* (1904 / 1916 / 1925) 6.141; art. "Midrash Haggadah" by J. Theodor in *JE* (1904 / 1916 / 1925) 8.550-69; Louis Ginzberg, *The Legends* 1. VIII-XV; Paul Billerbeck in Str-B 1.561; Emil Schürer, *The history* 2.346-55; Herman Strack and Günter Stemberger, *Introduction* 58-60; Judah Goldin, *The Song at the Sea* (Philadelphia / New York: The Jewish Publication Society, 1990; original 1971) 27-30; art. "Aggadah (or Haggadah...)" by Ed., Moshe David Herr, and the *Encyclopaedia Hebraica* in *EJ* (1971) 2.354-66; Jacob Neusner, *The Halakhah and the Aggadah* (Studies in Ancient Judaism; Lanham, MD: University Press of America, 2001); and the art. "Aggadah or Haggadah" in *EJ* (2007) 1.454-64, with bibliography on pp. 463-64, from the *Encyclopaedia Hebraica*, and by Dvora Weisberg, Judith Baskin, Carol Bakhos and Stephen Wald.

[3] Cf. the art. "Aggadah..." in *EJ* (1971) 2.354.

[4] Cf. the discussion in *Num. Rab.* Beha῾alothekha 15/22 (Mirkin 10.157; Soncino 6.668). This is definitely not the purpose of the aggadist, as stated in *y. Hor.* 3:5, 48c (Neusner 34.126).

circumlocution, but cannot be translated."[5] Sometimes the two categories are characterized as "law" and "lore."[6]

Haggadah can contain various things: the creative rewriting of biblical history,[7] miracle stories, parables, proverbs, speeches, lists of similar things, and much more. Its purposes were manifold. Sometimes it intended to exhort, at other times to inspire, to teach, or to comfort. And sometimes its main intention was simply to delight. *Eccl. Rab.* 2:8 § 1 on "and delights" says, for example: "these are the *haggadoth*, which are the delightful parts of Scriptural exposition."[8] One can even speak of "the obvious pleasure taken by the aggadists in the actual telling of a story."[9]

2. The Use and Attractiveness of Haggadah

Haggadah was employed extensively by the rabbis in their sermons given in the synagogue worship services, both on normal Sabbaths and on the festivals, just as modern-day rabbis, pastors and priests embellish their sermons with relevant illustrations. These remained in the people's minds much better than any flatly expressed "theological truths." The same applied to expositions of Scripture in the study house (beth ha-midrash). This made haggadic midrash, the homiletical exposition of Scripture, so influential. It appealed to the popular mind, kept the listeners' attention, and significantly aided in conveying the homilest's / lecturer's point. The following passages illustrate the great attractiveness of haggadah.

Sifre 'Eqeb 49 on Deut 11:22, "and cling to Him," relates: "Expounders of *haggadoth* say: 'If you wish to come to know Him who spoke, and the world came into being, study haggadah, for thereby you will come to know Him and to cling to His ways."[10] R. Eleazar of Modi'im, a second generation Tanna,[11] notes in *Mek. R. Ish.* Vayassa 6 on Exod 16:31 that

---

[5] Cf. *The Legends* 1. IX.
[6] Cf. Jacob Neusner, *The Halakhah and the Aggadah* 28.
[7] Cf. already 1-2 Chronicles as a rewriting of 1-2 Samuel and 1-2 Kings.
[8] Vilna 14; Soncino 8.59. Cf. Jastrow 1072 on עֲנוּג .
[9] Cf. the art. "Aggadah (or Haggadah...)" in *EJ* 2.361. The relatively long length of the narrative concerning the death of John the Baptist in Mark 6:14-29 is a good example of this. On this, see "Herod Antipas' Birthday Banquet in Mark 6:17-29, and Ahasuerus' Birthday Banquet in Judaic Traditions on Esther 1" in my *Water into Wine and the Beheading of John the Baptist,* 39-74.
[10] Finkelstein 115; Hammer 106. I derive some of the following references from Bacher.
[11] *Introduction* 78.

"the word of haggadah...attracts the heart of man."[12] *Sifre* Ha'azinu 317 on Deut 32:12 maintains that "haggadoth attract the heart of man like wine."[13] *Cant. Rab.* 2:5 § 1 states that haggadoth "have a fragrance and taste like apples," i.e. they are "refreshing," as in the biblical verse.[14] Finally, in 8:2 § 1 it is related that haggadoth "are tasty like a pomegranate."[15]

The foregoing passages demonstrate what great attractiveness haggadah had within popular piety.

3. The Limits of Haggadah, and the Questions of Historicity and Truth

3.1   *The Limits of Haggadah*

It was generally recognized in Judaic thought that a biblical verse could have several meanings, all of them considered to be valid. In *m.* '*Avot* 5:22 Ben Bag-Bag, perhaps a disciple of Hillel, states of the Torah: "Turn it and turn it again, for everything is in it."[16] In regard to a particular verse, *b. Sanh.* 34a notes that "In R. Ishmael's School it was taught: 'And like a hammer which breaks the rock in pieces' (Jer 23:29): i.e., just as [the rock] is split into many splinters, so also may one biblical verse convey many meanings."[17] *Cant. Rab.* 1:1 § 11 says similarly: "There is no verse without two or three senses."[18] That is, even when commenting on a specific scriptural word or verse, one haggadic interpretation was never regarded as excluding others.

The authors of haggadah also felt free to apply material from one section of Scripture to another, even though centuries may have

---

[12] Lauterbach 2.123. Cf. Vayassa 1 on Exod 15:26 (Lauterbach 2.95), where haggadoth are characterized as valuable and "to be listened to by all men."

[13] Finkelstein 359; Hammer 324. Cf. *b. Šabb.* 87a (Soncino 413), where "Moses told words which draw one's heart like an aggadah." In *b. Ḥag.* 14a (Soncino 85) the masters of aggadah "draw the heart of man like water by means of the aggadah." The arduous task of fetching fresh water at that time in often dry Palestine stands in the background here.

[14] Vilna 29; Soncino 9.104.

[15] Vilna 77; Soncino 9.303.

[16] Albeck 4.381; Danby 458, with n. 11; Neusner 689.

[17] Soncino 214, with n. 9.

[18] Vilna 6; Soncino 9.18 has "reflections," which can be misleading.

separated the sections.[19] The Tannaitic midrash *Mek. R. Ish.* Shirata 7 on Exod 15:9 states seven times, for example: "no strict order as to 'earlier' and 'later' is observed in the Torah."[20] Since this principle was generally recognized, no one felt it strange when, for example, material from a very early context was employed as part of a description in a very late context.[21]

Often two or more haggadic interpretations are left standing right next to each other. At times the expression "and some say" is also employed. A good example of this is found in *b. Meg.* 15b on the length of Ahasuerus' scepter as noted in the previous chapter: 2, 12, 16, 24 or 60 cubits.[22] Even though the last figure is cited as Tannaitic, the integrity of the other opinions is not questioned. I. Epstein states of midrash that "it keeps its gates open. It never closes a debate...."[23] This is true of haggadic midrash and of haggadah in general. No single interpretation claims by the exclusion of others to be the only correct one.

Haggadic narratives also possessed no binding quality. Even if cited as part of the oral Torah given to Moses at Sinai, they could not be employed in a discussion of halakhah.[24] In *Gen. Rab.* Vayera 56/6 on Gen 22:10, for example, R. Hiyya the Elder, a fifth generation Tanna,[25] asked Rab if Rabbi, (Judah the Prince, also a fifth generation Tanna,)[26] had told him something as a haggadah. If so, he might retract it.[27] H. Freedman, the Soncino translator, notes appropriately: "Deductions made in the spirit of *haggadah* are not binding laws."[28]

---

[19] On this, cf. Isaiah Gafni, "Rabbinic Historiography and Representations of the Past" in *The Cambridge Companion to the Talmud and Rabbinic Literature*, ed. Charlotte Fonrobert and Martin Jaffee, 295-312. Contrast the modern historical-critical method.

[20] Lauterbach 2.54-55. Cf. *Eccl. Rab.* 1:12 § 1 (Vilna 9; Soncino 8.37-38).

[21] I will call attention to the relevance of this in remarks below on the application of Jacob traditions to the narrative of the empty tomb.

[22] Soncino 91.

[23] Cf. *Genesis Rabbah* in Soncino 1. xxi. See also the remark of Philip Alexander in "Midrash and the Gospels" in *Synoptic Studies. The Ampleworth Conferences of 1982 and 1983*, ed. Christopher Tuckett, 6 in regard to the additional Torah thought to have been given to Moses at Sinai: "In its oral form Torah is open-minded, undefined, continually evolving: it is responsive to life."

[24] Cf. *y. Pe'ah* 2:6, 13a in Neusner / Brooks 2.128-29, contradicting the previous opinion of R. Joshua b. Levi.

[25] *Introduction* 90.

[26] *Ibid.*, 89.

[27] Theodor and Albeck 602.

[28] Soncino 1.496, n. 3.

Finally, in regard to the limits of haggadah, Malcolm Doubles writes: "The haggadist was allowed to give free rein to his imagination as long as he remained within the bounds of Judaism."[29] And those boundaries were very broad. Moshe David Herr writes, for example: "No surprise was felt by a person familiar with [haggadah's] methods at the strangest and the most unexpected interpretations...."[30] In addition to other reasons cited previously, this helps to explain how Palestinian Jewish Christians could apply Judaic traditions about Moses to Jesus, who lived centuries later, something which appears very strange to modern NT interpreters unacquainted with the workings of haggadah.

3.2   The Questions of Historicity and Truth

3.2.1   The Question of Historicity

As remarked above, one of the earliest examples of haggadah is found in the Chronicler's rewriting of the books of Samuel and Kings in the Hebrew Bible: names, large numbers, speeches and prayers were added, gaps were filled in, and certain things were completely omitted, while others were given a much greater emphasis.

Did the Chronicler "forge" or "fake" history as represented in the four biblical books he rewrote? Malcolm Doubles states in this regard: "The idea that this was a falsification of history presumably never occurred to him."[31] Nor did it occur to his readers. They readily accepted this rewriting and embellishment as a part of their (oral and) literary culture. Other later examples of this creative retelling / rewriting of biblical history are *Jubilees*, the *Genesis Apocryphon* at Qumran, *Pseudo-Philo*, and Josephus' *Jewish Antiquities*. The latter two clearly demonstrate how this still prevailed in Palestine in the first century CE.[32] The three extant Palestinian targums (*Pseudo-Jonathan*, *Neofiti 1*, and the *Fragment*

---

[29] Cf. Schürer, *The history* 2.353. On p. x he is cited as having translated and revised this section of the work.

[30] Cf. the art. "Aggadah (or Haggadah...)" in *EJ* (1971) 2.354, with examples of such strange interpretations.

[31] Cf. Schürer, *The history* 2.347.

[32] While he later wrote the *Antiquities* in Rome, Josephus' mother tongue was Aramaic, and he grew up in Jerusalem with primarily Palestinian traditions. The amount of haggadah present in his retelling of the Esther narrative, for example, is very great, as pointed out in chapter III. above. Of course, he was also well acquainted with and made use of the LXX and the "Additions" to Esther, yet only two of the six (B and F) were probably originally in Greek.

Targums) by numerous embellishments also "reshaped" the narratives found in the Pentateuch, although they were originally oral, recited from memory, and only written down centuries later. When such translation embellishments were recited within a synagogue worship service, no one considered them strange or inappropriate. The opposite was the case: it was thought that they helped the meaning of Scripture to come alive, which was their intention.

In conclusion, one can only agree with Philip Alexander when he states that rabbinic (haggadic) anecdotes appear to have "little interest in history for its own sake," and "in general the Rabbis were not concerned with historiography...."[33] This was also true for the predecessors of the rabbis such as those responsible for the early works cited above. No one posed the question of the historicity of an anecdote or a narrative, nor was there any interest in such a question. That is and has been a modern issue, especially since the Enlightenment and the rise of the historical-critical method in biblical scholarship. One should not retroactively apply it to Palestinian Judaic and Jewish Christian sources of the first century CE.

3.2.2   The Question of Truth

Biblical fundamentalists and some very conservative Evangelicals tend today to employ black and white thinking in regard to sayings or narratives in the Gospels. For them these can only be "true" or "false." "Historicity" and "facticity" are opposed to "theological tales," which are "fiction." The Evangelists do not intend to "deceive" their readers, especially with haggadah, which is "fable" and "Jewish myth."[34]

---

[33] Cf. his "Rabbinic Biography and the Biography of Jesus: A Survey of the Evidence" in *Synoptic Studies. The Ampleworth Conferences of 1982 and 1983*, ed. Christopher Tuckett, 19-50, quotations pp. 43 and 39. It is strange that Samuel Byrskog in *Story as History - History as Story. The Gospel Tradition in the Context of Ancient Oral History* (WUNT 123; Tübingen: Mohr Siebeck, 2000) has sections on "Historical Truth" (179-84) and "Factual Truth and Interpreted Truth" (184-86), yet only notes Greek historians. See also his extensive bibliography of them on pp. 309-14.

[34] Cf. the use of these terms in Charles Quarles, *Midrash Criticism*. Introduction and Appraisal (Lanham, MD: University Press of America, 1998), *passim*. He is concerned with "biblical inerrancy" (xiii), for example in regard to the Matthean and Lukan birth narratives. He feels threatened by what he considers "The Erosion of the Historical Foundations of the Christian Faith" (93). While such a fine scholar as Dale Allison, Jr., can correctly note: "Just as the Romans crucified

In John 18:38 Pilate is represented as asking Jesus: "What is truth?" The answer, of course, depends on how one defines the term. *Webster's Ninth New Collegiate Dictionary* offers several options. One is "the state of being the case: FACT."[35] This is the definition preferred by those who take the Scriptures literally. What a particular verse says is "the case," it is a "fact." Yet there is another valid definition of "truth": "a transcendent fundamental or spiritual reality."[36] It is in the latter sense in which I (and many other biblical scholars)[37] employ the term "truth." For Jews, Christians and Muslims, for example, Moses was and is a great prophet who revealed part of God's will for us humans in the Hebrew Bible. This is for the three monotheistic religions a "transcendent spiritual reality" or a "religious truth," a truth which is part of their own inherited religious traditions. Yet it is not "true," it is not a "truth" for a Hindu or a Buddhist; the adherents of these religions have their own religious truths.

The above discussion applies especially to the nature of haggadah. A good example is the statement found in *Pseudo-Philo* 9:13,[38] b. *Soṭah* 12a

---

Jesus and Christian haggadah embroidered the fact...," and can speak of "Matthew's haggadic infancy narrative" (*Resurrecting Jesus*, 332 and 355), he unfortunately also employs terms such as "deceit" and "self-deception" (215), "quaint," "bizarre," "nonsense" (220-21), "conscious deceit" (296), "haggadic fiction" (302), "sheer fiction" (311), and "unadulterated legend" (312). These are less than helpful and miss the mark as to what haggadah wishes to express. The same is true for Alfred Loisy, who in *L'Évangile selon Marc* (Paris: Émile Nourry, 1912) 485 labels the discovery of the empty tomb "an apologetic fiction" (see also Mark's "fiction" on p. 483).

[35] Cf. p. 1268.

[36] *Ibid.*

[37] Cf. the use of the term "religious truth" by Gerd Luedemann in his *The Resurrection of Jesus* 249, n. 679, regarding the appearances of the resurrected Christ Paul mentions in 1 Cor 15:5-8: "A vision is a primary experience and bears the religious truth completely in itself." (This, however, does not mean that I share Luedemann's interpretation of Jesus' Resurrection.) Maurice Casey's fine volume on the Fourth Gospel is entitled *Is John's Gospel True?* (London / New York: Routledge, 1996). Casey correctly castigates John's anti-Jewish character, which greatly furthered anti-Semitism, and its breaking the bounds of Jewish monotheism. He also includes a section on "Historicity and Truth" (218-23), and can speak of the "theological truth" in the Gospel (223). Yet because he omits a discussion of the nature of Jewish haggadah, he unfortunately employs phrases like "untrue from beginning to end" and "a presentation of falsehood" (198). However, what Michael Goulder says of midrash also applies to haggadah: It "is not apologetic lying, it is the [quest for the - R.D.A.] discovery of the truth." See his "The Empty Tomb" in *Theology* 79 (1976) 210.

[38] *SC* 229.112; *OTP* 2.316.

on Exod 2:2,[39] and *Exod. Rab.* Shemoth 1/20 on the same verse,[40] that Moses was born circumcised. According to my wife, a pediatrician, this (apparent) phenomenon can indeed happen, but only extremely rarely (*hypospadias* in an advanced form). The first Jewish hearers of this haggadah, however, did not ask whether Moses' being born circumcised was factually, biologically true. Rather, they understood its original intention to glorify Moses, the future redeemer of Israel, at the time of his birth. He was already then someone very special.[41] For them this was a religious "truth." It is such truths which haggadah is capable of expressing very well.[42]

It is Moshe David Herr who in his discussion of haggadah is very helpful in clarifying what kind of "truth" is found there. He notes that haggadoth / aggadoth

> are for the most part...moral and ethical teachings dealing with the problems of faith and the art of living. The *aggadah* is therefore didactic. From this point of view, it certainly cannot be said that the *aggadah* is not truth. On the contrary, the *aggadah* does contain truth which is greater than that of historical and philological reality, and more important than that of the natural sciences. From the point of its aim, the truth of the *aggadah* is that of the moral and ethical principles of the art of living, while from the point of view of its form, its truth is that of artistic poetic work. The fact that in this topic there is no place for rational and unambiguous decisions does not diminish its importance.[43]

---

[39] Soncino 61.

[40] Mirkin 5.34, with other parallels in n. 3; Soncino 3.27.

[41] Cf. my *Matthew 1-2 and the Virginal Conception in Light of Palestinian and Hellenistic Judaic Traditions on the Birth of Israel's First Redeemer, Moses* 83, n. 178.

[42] Another example of such a truth is found in *b. Sanh.* 92b (Soncino 618-19) in regard to the dry bones of the dead whom Ezekiel resurrected in Ezekiel 37. For R. Judah (b. Ilai, a third generation Tanna: *Introduction* 84-85), this preliminary resurrection was "truth; it was a parable." That is, for him its religious truth consisted in its metaphorically (parabolically) pointing to the general resurrection of the dead at the end of time. Cf. also Carl Holladay's definition of a parable as "a narrative or saying of varying length, designed to illustrate a truth especially through a comparison or simile" (*A Critical Introduction to the New Testament* 62). In his *Das Evangelium nach Johannes* 85 regarding Jesus' encounter with the Samaritan woman at Jacob's well, Hermann Strathmann generalizes regarding the Fourth Evangelist by saying that "he treats scenes, figures and dialogues quite freely as the means to present religious truths."

[43] Cf. the art. "Aggadah (or Haggadah...)" in *EJ* (1971) 2.355. See also the important remark on p. 359: "The *aggadah* knows of no conflict between literal and figurative explanations."

The modern fundamentalist who can only interpret the Bible, especially the Gospels, literally will have a major problem with the above explanation of "truth" in regard to haggadah. Such a person is only interested in "facts," measurable as in the natural sciences, and in "history" as it is pursued today at the university level. This is extremely regrettable, for by not being willing to deal extensively with haggadaic texts and their peculiarities, such a person cannot appreciate the great richness of the traditions they contain, including their "religious truths." It is one of the tragedies of the Christian church that the number of its Palestinian Jewish members dwindled so rapidly after the very successful missionizing of Gentiles. The latter soon made the former into small sects such as the Palestinian Ebionites. Early Palestinian and later even Hellenistic Jewish Christians, however, could have conveyed to Gentile Christians the nature of Jewish haggadah, and the centuries-old Gentile Christian debate about the "historicity" or "facticity" of haggadic sayings or narratives would have been basically unnecessary.

4. Examples in the Gospels of Jesus and Judaic Haggadah

By now citing seven examples of Judaic haggadah found in the Gospel narratives, I hope to contribute to the scholarly discussion of the questions of "historicity" and "truth" in regard to such haggadic accounts.

4.1 *The Twelve-year-old Jesus in the Temple in Luke 2:41-52*

In Luke 2:41-52 Jesus is portrayed in terms of the boy Samuel, who in Judaic tradition also made an annual pilgrimage to the Temple (then Shiloh, not yet Jerusalem) with his parents. When he was two years old, Samuel is represented as a child prodigy who gives instructions in the Temple as to the proper ritual slaughtering there. Josephus, the earliest Judaic chronography in *Seder 'Olam* 13, and other texts have Samuel as twelve in the Temple when he was called and began to prophesy there,[44] the same age as Jesus.

The Evangelist received this narrative from a Hellenistic Jewish Christian community, which in turn got it from Palestinian Jewish

---

[44] Cf. the discussion of *b. Ber.* 31b and other relevant texts in "The Child Jesus in the Temple (Luke 2:41-51a), and Judaic Traditions on the Child Samuel in the Temple (1 Samuel 1-3)" in my *Samuel, Saul and Jesus. Three Early Palestinian Jewish Christian Gospel Haggadoth*, 1-64, especially 30 and 22-24.

Christians in the original Aramaic or possibly Hebrew.[45] It typically applies Judaic traditions on one of Israel's great heroes, Samuel, to its own hero, the Messiah Jesus, who is also represented as a twelve-year-old child prodigy, amazing the teachers with his understanding, questions and answers (Luke 2:46-47). Did the first Palestinian Jewish Christian hearers of the incident consider this a "falsification of history"? No. On the contrary, since they were accustomed in Judaic tradition to the glorification of early Israelite heroes, they appreciated how well this was also done in the present instance. For them, Jesus, who later excelled in wisdom, certainly also did so much earlier, like Samuel. For them, that was an haggadic "truth."

4.2   The Stilling of the Storm in Mark 4:35-41

The Palestinian Jewish Christian who first composed the narrative of Mark 4:35-41 applied here sixteen different Judaic traditions in regard to the popular prophet Jonah, primarily concerning Jonah One, to Jesus. Among other things, he transferred the setting from the Mediterranean Sea to the Sea of Galilee, where a ferocious storm also came up, which Jesus "stilled."

Although this haggadic narrative is not historical, it expresses several "religious truths": Jesus as the Son of God is also lord of the sea; Jesus is more than Jonah; Jesus is also superior to Julius Caesar, the deified Roman emperor, who unsuccessfully attempted to cross the Adriatic Sea in a severe windstorm; and Jesus strengthens present-day disciples' faith, weakened through persecution and other distress.[46]

4.3   The Healing of the Gerasene Demoniac in Mark 5:1-20

The Palestinian Jewish Christian author of this narrative employed biblical and Judaic traditions on the very popular Israelite strongman Samson in Judges 13-16 in order to describe the fantastically strong madman or demoniac at Kursi on the east side of the Sea of Galilee.

While the narrative of Jesus' healing this demoniac is not historical, among other things it expresses the "religious truths" that Jesus is lord of the unclean spirits / demons, and as the Son of the Most High God he is

---

[45] Cf. the discussion in *ibid.*, 48-53.
[46] Cf. "The Stilling of the Storm: Jesus, Jonah and Julius Caesar in Mark 4:35-41" in my *The Stilling of the Storm. Studies in Early Palestinian Judaic Traditions*, 1-87.

stronger than the strongest human known to Jews - Samson, or a madman described in terms of him.[47]

4.4 *The Mocking of Jesus in Mark 15:16-20a*

As noted in the Excursus in chapter III., a Palestinian Jewish Christian described the mocking of Jesus in Mark 15:16-20a in terms of Haman's intended mocking of another redeemer of Israel, Mordecai. This is based on the biblical passage Esth 6:7-11 as developed in Judaic tradition. Just at this point, at the beginning of Passover, Haman had intended to hang / crucify Mordecai on a gallows / cross, making the Judaic traditions all the more attractive to the Jewish Christian author of the incident because of Jesus' imminent Crucifixion, also at Passover.

Again, the incident is not historical. Yet it expresses among other things the "religious truth" that even when he had been flogged and was about to be crucified, Jesus was the true "King of the Jews," as the inscription on the Cross also mockingly indicated (15:26). Considered by his followers to be the Messiah, as such Jesus was automatically also thought of as "the *King*, the Messiah" (מלך המשיח). A purple cloak, a wreath / crown of thorns, public acclamation with "Hail, King of the Jews," a reed as a scepter, and kneeling down in homage before him all also mockingly characterize Jesus as a king, who stands in contrast to the ostensibly all-powerful Roman emperor. For the earliest (and later) Christians, this severe degradation of Jesus pointed forward to the "religious truth" that three days later his exaltation also would take place, just as the redeemer Mordecai, who thought he was going to be mocked by Haman, also was later exalted as King of the Jews. By God's raising him as the first of the dead, Jesus' identity as the *King*, the Messiah, was confirmed. He, and not a deified Roman emperor, also was and is the true Son of God.

4.5 *Jesus' Concern for His Mother When He Is About to Die (John 19:25-27)*

In John 19:25-27 Jesus, about to die on the Cross (v 30), shows his concern for his mother Mary by committing her to the care of "the disciple whom he loved." This then takes place in v 27b.

---

[47] Cf. "My Name Is 'Legion': Palestinian Judaic Samson Traditions in Mark 5:1-20" in *My Name Is "Legion." Palestinian Judaic Traditions in Mark 5:1-20 and Other Gospel Texts*, 1-99.

Either a Palestinian Jewish Christian, employed as a source by the bilingual Evangelist John, or the Gospel writer himself, composed this very short but moving anecdote on the basis of Judaic tradition on Moses' concern for his very aged mother Yochebed just as he himself was about to die. There Moses is represented as appointing his main disciple, Joshua, to take care of her, which he then did (see chapter I., section 8. above).

The incident in John is thus not historical, yet it basically expresses two "religious truths." First, while Moses was the first redeemer of Israel, Jesus as the "new Moses" is the final redeemer of Israel, the Messiah. Secondly, as Moses' concern for his very aged (and widowed) mother Yochebed at the time of his death showed his great compassion and care, so Jesus as the second Moses just before his own death showed his great compassion and care for his (presumably widowed) mother Mary. It is the final example of Jesus' compassion and concern for people such as children, the poor, the persecuted, the sick and the outcasts of society in the Gospels.

4.6   Darkness at the Crucifixion (Mark 15:33), and the Tearing of the Temple Curtain (v 38)

Mark 15:25 states that it was the third hour, i.e. 9 a.m., when Jesus was crucified. At the sixth hour, i.e. 12 p.m., there was a darkness over the whole land until the ninth hour, i.e. 3 p.m. (v 33). At this time Jesus "gave a loud cry and breathed his last" (v 37). "And the curtain of the Temple was torn in two, from top to bottom" (v 38).

While solar eclipses were related as having taken place at the death of famous non-Jews, as well as of famous Jews, this is always represented as occurring directly at their death, and not beforehand. In addition, if a three-hour eclipse had taken place at Jesus' death, i.e. as of 3 p.m., it would have made Jesus' burial before the beginning of the Sabbath (v 42) extremely difficult. Nor has a total eclipse of the sun ever lasted more than seven minutes, a partial darkening at the most two hours. Astronomy thus speaks against the historicity of the Gospel account.

The background of the very extensive eclipse before Jesus' death, however, is found elsewhere, primarily in Scripture. Amos 8:9 has the Lord God say: "On that day I will make the sun go down at noon, and darken the earth / land in broad daylight." In v 10 He adds: "I will make it like the mourning for an only son." In addition, at the death of R.

Samuel b. R. Isaac, a third generation Palestinian Amora,[48] fire from heaven, peals of thunder, and flashes of lightning "for three hours" are related.[49] This length of time thus may have been traditional.

The fulfillment of Scripture was so important for the Palestinian Jewish Christian author of this prodigium that he intentionally changed the beginning of God's mourning via a solar eclipse from the moment of Jesus' death to three hours beforehand. The "noon" of Amos 8:9 is exactly the sixth hour, as in Mark 15:33. The "religious truth" of this non-historical phenomenon is that it signifies God's mourning for His only Son, also fulfilling Amos 8:10. Here, then, the first Palestinian Jewish Christians who heard the narrative related in a worship service recognized the description of Jesus' dying accompanied by a solar eclipse beginning at noon as pointing to him as God's only Son.[50]

Mark 15:38 states that directly after Jesus' death, "the curtain of the Temple was torn in two, from top to bottom." It was already a biblical custom to tear or rend one's garments at the death of a relative or friend (beginning with Gen 37:29 and 34 on the ostensible death of Joseph). For one's parents (and presumably also children) one tore or rent one's garment to the heart / chest, and it was not sewn up again. The two curtains of the Second Temple in Jerusalem were made of purple. God, the King of Kings, is represented as mourning not only by rending His royal purple garment / robe in heaven, but also the purple curtain of the Herodian Temple, His earthly dwelling, thought of as directly below. This would be the outer curtain, for that before the Holy of Holies inside was only seen by a very limited number of Temple personnel (priests) and would not be a public sign of God's mourning.

The "religious truth" of the Temple curtain's "being torn" (the divine passive), while the incident is not historical, is that God, the King of Kings, tore not only His royal purple garment / robe in deep mourning at the death of His only Son in heaven, but also the purple curtain of His

---

[48] *Introduction* 99.
[49] Cf. *y. ʿAbod. Zar.* 3:1, 42c (Neusner 33.113) and the parallel in *y. Peʾah* 1:1, 15d (Neusner 2.58). On the three hours, see Peter Kuhn, *Gottes Trauer und Klage in der rabbinischen Überlieferung (Talmud und Midrasch)* 339, n. 7.
[50] The centurion at the Cross who saw that Jesus breathed his last "in this way," in contrast, only exclaimed "Truly this man was God's Son!" (Mark 15:39) after the curtain of the Temple was also torn. On the above, cf. my "The Prodigia at Jesus' Crucifixion," "B. The Sun's Eclipse," in *Samuel, Saul and Jesus*, 134-47.

earthly dwelling in Jerusalem. "From top to bottom" expresses the great intensity of this mourning.[51]

4.7   Jesus' Resurrection Appearance on the Road to, and in, Emmaus in Luke 24:13-35

The first Resurrection appearances of Jesus definitely took place in Galilee (Mark 14:28 and 16:7; cf. Matt 28:16 and John 21). Yet just as John 20:11-29 relates other appearances in Jerusalem, so Luke omits the relevant Markan references to Galilee and first extensively describes an appearance of the risen Lord on Easter Sunday on the road to, and in, Emmaus (24:13-35). This settlement should be equated with Moṣa, a site ca. 7 km or 4.2 miles west of Jerusalem.[52] This appearance takes place in Judea because Luke's source at this point, "Special Luke," derived from Judean (possibly even Jerusalemite) Jewish Christians who understandably desired another local Resurrection appearance, in addition to that in Jerusalem described in Luke 24:36-49, before Jesus "ascended" to heaven from nearby Bethany (vv 50-53). The latter episode clearly recalls Elijah's ascension to heaven without dying in 2 Kgs 2:1-12. The narrative just before the prophet's ascension, and the figure of Elijah in general in Judaic tradition, also greatly influenced the account in Luke 24:13-35.

The expression "two of them" in Luke 24:13 derives from "the two of them" (Elijah and his disciple Elisha) in 2 Kgs 2:6-7 and 11. Cleopas and his companion's "talking and discussing" with each other on the road (24:14-15, 17, 32) goes back to 2 Kgs 2:2, 4, 6 and 9-10, but especially to Elijah and Elisha's "continued walking and talking" in v 11. In Luke 24:25-26 Jesus chides his followers whom he has joined on the road to Emmaus and then "interprets" or "explains" the Scriptures to them in v 27 (cf. also v 32 with his "opening" the Scripture to them). This type of behavior was typical of the ascended Elijah, who when doing so was thought to suddenly appear and disappear, as Jesus does here. A number of other motifs and expressions point to 2 Kings 2 and Elijah in Judaic tradition as the major background to this haggadic narrative of Jesus' Resurrection appearance on the road to, and in, Emmaus.[53]

---

[51] Cf. the complete discussion in my *Samuel, Saul and Jesus* 147-57, including how the Evangelist Mark may have understood this prodigium.

[52] On its location, cf. "The Road to Emmaus (Luke 24:13-35)" in my *The Stilling of the Storm*, 217-29.

[53] See the full analysis in *The Stilling of the Storm* 137-216. James Dunn, in contrast, suggests that "Luke came across the Emmaus story in his search for eyewitness testimony (Luke 1.2)" (*Jesus Remembered* 848-49).

Joachim Jeremias once remarked that "No biblical figure so exercised the religious thinking of post-biblical Judaism as that of the prophet Elijah...."[54] When a Palestinian, probably Judean or even Jerusalemite Jewish Christian represented the resurrected Jesus as appearing to two of his disciples (not members of the eleven) and as interpreting the Scripture to them on the road to Emmaus shortly before he, like Elijah, ascended to heaven, then his first hearers would not have asked whether this haggadic narrative was historical or not. Instead, they would have greatly appreciated Jesus' being described in terminology strongly reminiscent of the most popular figure in the Hebrew Bible, Elijah. He too was closely associated with the final redemption, which he himself was thought to usher in (Mal 3:23-24, Eng. 4:5-6), and a number of his activities were considered messianic.[55]

The Resurrection appearance of Jesus to two of his followers on the road to, and in, Emmaus is a good example of what my former teacher Judah Goldin in his discussion of haggadic interpretation labels "imaginative dramatization."[56] The Palestinian Jewish Christian who composed it created a dramatic scene, just as hundreds of his fellow Jews had done before him and continued to do after him. When he represented Jesus as the Resurrected One, opening the Scriptures to his followers in order for them to better understand the necessity of the Crucifixion, neither he himself nor his listeners conceived of this as "falsifying" history, of "deluding" others with a "tall tale." On the contrary, the listeners were very grateful to him for the great artistic skill he employed in his narrative. They were used to this type of hero glorification, and as Judeans, they now even had their own Resurrection account at and near Jerusalem.

* * *

The above seven examples of the application of haggadic Judaic traditions to Jesus in the Gospels show that asking the question of their historicity is inappropriate today. It was simply not asked by the first Palestinian Jewish Christian hearers of the incidents before they entered

---

[54] Cf. his art. Ἡλ(ε)ίας in *TDNT* 2.928.

[55] Cf. *The Stilling of the Storm* 179-81 and 172-77.

[56] Cf. his *The Song at the Sea* 27, where this is one of "the familiar devices of haggadic midrash." Luke 24:13-49 is not properly a midrash, even though it develops various motifs and expressions from 2 Kings 2. A true midrash would openly cite and comment on various verses. Nevertheless, Goldin's remarks also apply here to haggadah in general.

the Gospels. Instead, they greatly appreciated the respective narrator's creative abilities in reshaping traditions already known to them in order to express a religious truth (or truths) about Jesus, their Lord, the Messiah of Israel. This especially applies to the incident of the empty tomb, to which I now turn in conclusion.

5. The Empty Tomb Narrative in Mark 16:1-8

I am not aware of any Christian who questions the basic "historicity" or "truth" of the appearances of the risen Christ as the Apostle Paul lists them in 1 Cor 15:5-8. This applies even though it is difficult for us today, for example, to imagine who the "500 brothers and sisters" were in v 6, to whom Jesus appeared at one time, and how Jesus' appearance to Paul in v 8 is exactly related to the various accounts of the "Damascus Road" experience (Acts 9:1-19; 22:6-16; 26:12-18).

Nor do I know of any Christian who doubts whether the appearances of the risen Lord in Galilee, announced in Mark 14:28 and 16:7, actually took place there. These appearances are also referred to in Matt 28:16 and in John 21, where seven of the eleven disciples are mentioned in v 2 as being gathered at the Sea of Tiberias / Galilee.

The historicity of the empty tomb narrative in Mark 16:1-8, however, is a very controversial issue in modern biblical scholarship. In the previous section (4.) I pointed out how in haggadic Gospel narratives Jesus is frequently described in terms of biblical and early Judaic traditions on Israel's great heroes: Samuel in 4.1.; Jonah in 4.2.; Mordecai in 4.4.; Moses in 4.5.; and Elijah in 4.7., also a Resurrection narrative. The first Palestinian Jewish Christian hearers of these narratives greatly appreciated their own hero, the Messiah Jesus, the Son of God, being described in terms of these very popular heroes from the Hebrew Bible. As indicated before, they by no means considered this a falsification of history, just as they by no means considered Chronicles to be a falsification of Samuel and Kings. The opposite was the case: they cherished such new haggadic narratives because they were well acquainted with them from the synagogue worship service (sermons) and from the school house (lectures in the beth ha-midrash), and because the new narratives led them to new insights, to new "religious truths," in regard to the person and work of their Messiah and Lord, Jesus, the Son of God.

The same holds true for the haggadic narrative of the empty tomb in Mark 16:1-8. Jacob, as the third of the three Patriarchs and the father of the twelve tribes of Israel, was a very popular and important hero in

Jewish lore. As I pointed out in chapter III., sections B. 1. 1-10 above, Gen 28:10 and 29:1-14 in Judaic tradition describe Jacob's tremendous strength after his father Isaac blessed him on the 14th of Nisan, just before Passover, with the dew of resurrection. He thus could "roll away" the large stone from the well's mouth three days later with only one hand, a "miracle," something the (three) shepherds were incapable of doing together. It caused "astonishment / amazement." This well was thought to be the same one which later followed the Israelites for forty years in the wilderness. Like a round stone, it rolled after them and finally ceased rolling at the top of Mount Pisgah / *Ramatha*, where Moses was buried. The site of Moses' burial and the site of Jesus' burial were thus described in similar terms. The Palestinian Jewish Christian who first composed the haggadic narrative of the empty tomb employed motifs and even exact terminology (e.g. "rolling away" a "large stone" from the "mouth / entrance / door") from the above narrative of Jacob at the well in order to describe another "miracle," God's raising Jesus from the dead so that the tomb was now empty. The three women, like the (three) shepherds of the three flocks, are now "astonished / amazed" (Mark 16:5). The author of the empty tomb episode then has the angel instruct the women to "tell [Jesus'] disciples and Peter that he is going ahead of you to Galilee; there you will see him, just as he told you" (v 7). The first Palestinian Jewish Christian hearers of this narrative would have caught and deeply appreciated the above "echoes" of the Judaic interpretation of Gen 28:10 and 29:1-14.

Regardless of how Mark 16:8 is to be interpreted, it is clear from v 7 that the angel's instructions, after the statement that Jesus has been raised (by God, the divine passive - v 6), are the second major point in the account. Jesus' Resurrection here is thus a haggadic narrative which basically expresses two "religious truths": God raised His Son Jesus on the third day as the first of the dead, and the promise of appearances of the resurrected Jesus in Galilee is made by one of God's own representatives, an angel. The haggadic narrative of the empty tomb, while not historical and originally not intended to be considered so,[57]

---

[57] James Dunn asks: "can it be seriously argued that such a story would be contrived in the cities and / or village communities of first-century Palestine, a story which would have to stand up before public incredulity and prejudice?" (*Jesus Remembered* 833). His terms "contrived" and "public incredulity and prejudice" show that he has not grasped the haggadic nature of the narrative. Cf. also p. 841 for the tradition of Mark 16:1-8 par., which "seems to have begun as the expression of eyewitness testimony"; it was "probably being told in Jerusalem shortly after the event" (p. 836). Richard Bauckham in his *Jesus and the*

thus also points to the "reality" of the first appearances of the resurrected Christ to Cephas (Peter) and the (reconstituted) twelve, as related in 1 Cor 15:5. And no Christian today would deny that the latter were "historical" and "true," especially for those who received them, later including Jesus' own brother James and the Apostle Paul, even though such appearances cannot be measured by modern scholarly methods of the natural and social sciences.

The time has come to cease asking the wrong questions of "historical" or "non-historical," and "true" or "false," in regard to the haggadic narrative of the empty tomb.[58] The Palestinian Jewish Christian who created it was not concerned with such questions, nor were his first hearers. Such thought categories were foreign to them. In addition to a well-told narrative, the hearers (and later readers) were interested in its religious truths. That God had raised His Son from the dead, and that his disciples would soon see / encounter their beloved Master again in Galilee, was a message of tremendous hope and encouragement to them. Even if all his disciples had abandoned Jesus in Gethsemane and fled (home to Galilee), he thus did not abandon them. The resurrected Jesus appeared to them and filled them with such new strength and hope that in the following period they could even found a community of those who (had retained or) now regained their belief in him: the church. One important task for the Christian church today is to rediscover, and to learn to properly appreciate, the tremendous riches contained in Jewish and Jewish Christian haggadah, especially in regard to the narrative of the empty tomb.

Eyewitnesses. The Gospels as Eyewitness Testimony (Grand Rapids, MI / Cambridge, U.K.: Eerdmans, 2006) thinks that "in imagining how the traditions reached the Gospel writers, not oral tradition but eyewitness testimony should be our principal model" (8). He too does not recognize the great role Jewish Christian haggadah played in the formation of the Gospel narratives. Mark Waterman in *The Empty Tomb Tradition of Mark: Text, History, and Theological Struggles* (Theology, History, and Biblical Studies Series 1; Los Angeles: Agathos, 2006. At $150.00 for 225 pages unavailable to me) is the latest to argue for the historicity of the empty tomb, which he considers firmer than the appearance traditions (198). See the review by Michael Licona in the *2007 Review of Biblical Literature* 374-78.

[58] Cf. the statement by Alan Segal in *The Resurrection of Jesus*. John Dominic Crossan and N. T. Wright in Dialogue, 135: "I believe that the whole enterprise of trying to prove that the resurrection is a historical fact is a category mistake."

Summary

A widespread Judaic saying was "As the first redeemer of Israel, so the last redeemer of Israel": as Moses, so the Messiah. This was a major reason why the death, burial and translation of Moses in primarily Palestinian Judaic tradition greatly influenced the descriptions of the death, burial and Resurrection of Jesus in the Gospels.

Chapter I. first points to seven aspects of Gospel materials which lead up to Jesus' death, all of them influenced by Judaic traditions on the imminent death of Moses. Examples are Jesus' rebuke of Peter in Mark 8:31-33 for rejecting the necessity of his death, and Moses' rebuke of the Angel of Death / Sammael just before his own death; the scene of Jesus' washing his disciples' feet, especially those of his main disciple Peter, in John 13:1-20 during the "Lord's Supper," and Moses' washing his main disciple Joshua's hands (and feet) just before he dies; and Jesus' struggle with death and his arrest in Gethsemane, and Moses' final struggle with death. In addition, Jesus' concern on the Cross for the welfare of his mother after his death in John 19:25-27 is shown to reflect Moses' concern in Judaic tradition for the welfare of his mother after his own imminent death.

Chapter II. deals with similarities between the burial of Jesus and the burial of Moses in Judaic tradition. The well of Num 21:16-20 was thought to be the same one which accompanied the Israelites for forty years in the wilderness. Rolling along like a round stone, it finally ceased rolling and disappeared at the top of Mt. Pisgah (v 20), precisely on the day of Moses' death and at the site where he died and was buried (Deut 34:1 and 6). All four extant targums have *ramatha(h)* for "Pisgah," which a Palestinian Jewish Christian employed as the basis for the name Joseph of "Arimathea." This is made more probable by the derivation of the terms "respected," "council / Sanhedrin," and "kingdom" to describe Joseph of Arimathea in Mark 15:43 from Judaic tradition on the well in Num 21:18, with Pisgah in v 20. In addition, Pisgah is frequently rendered in the Septuagint by "The Place Hewn Out of Rock," the same Greek term employed in Mark 15:46 for Joseph of Arimathea's placing Jesus' body in a tomb "that had been hewn out of the rock."

Chapter III. compares the Resurrection of Jesus and the translation of Moses in Judaic tradition. Before this, the well mentioned above is described as also being considered the same one which Jacob visited in Gen 29:1-14. Because his father Isaac had blessed him beforehand (28:3), in Judaic tradition with the "dew of resurrection," he was able to "roll away" the "large stone" from the well's mouth / opening with only one hand. This was considered a "miracle," for the (three) shepherds of three flocks were "unable" to roll it away. Thus they were "astonished / amazed," like the three women at the empty tomb when the large stone was rolled away, something they "could not do." This incident with Jacob was represented as having taken place only a few days after Passover. Judaic tradition on Gen 28:10 and 29:1-14 thus provided the basic framework and several exact terms for the narrative of the empty tomb in Mark 16:1-8. Another early and independent example of the use of the same incident of Jacob at the well of Genesis 29 is found in John 4:1-42, Jesus' encounter with the Samaritan woman at "Jacob's well" (v 6).

Several early Jewish sources imply that Moses was translated to heaven by God without first dying: Philo of Alexandria, Josephus, *Pseudo-Philo*, and the Gospel account of Jesus' Transfiguration (Mark 9:2-8). This is openly stated in an early (Tannaitic) rabbinic source ("Model A"). Other Judaic sources note that Moses indeed died as in the biblical account, yet God then "raised" his soul to heaven to be beside Him or under His Throne ("Model B"). A Palestinian Jewish Christian combined these two models in the narrative of the empty tomb. Since Jesus' Crucifixion emphasized his death as a fact, as was true of Moses in "Model B," he then borrowed the motif of God's translating Jesus bodily to heaven from the other model of Judaic tradition on Moses ("Model A"). This bodily translation or resurrection (raising up) is represented as occurring on the third day after Jesus' death. It is primarily due to the Judaic motif of God's rescuing a person in great distress on the third day, in some sources also associated with the 15th of Nisan, i.e. Passover. Hos 6:2 in Judaic tradition is most important as a scriptural text in this regard. The "trigger" to this entire motif, however, also derives from Judaic tradition on the death of Moses. The Israelites are described in an early (Tannaitic) source as mourning for him for three days.

Chapter IV. defines the characteristics and limits of Judaic "haggadah." First-century CE Palestinian Jews in this regard were interested first of all in a well-told story, and not in the (modern) issue of historicity, i.e. whether something is "true" or "false." Secondly, they attached great importance to what today can be called the "religious truth(s)" of an anecdote. Seven examples of the latter are given in regard to narratives connected with Jesus in the Gospels. This culminates in final remarks on the incident of the empty tomb in Mark 16:1-8.

The above studies show the great extent to which Gospel accounts of the events leading up to, and including, Jesus' death, burial and Resurrection were influenced by Judaic traditions on Moses. Motifs and sometimes exact terminology pertaining to the first redeemer of Israel were applied by the first Palestinian Christians, all of whom were Jews, to him whom they considered to be the final redeemer of Israel, their Messiah Jesus. By seeking to understand how and why they did so, contemporary Christians can better appreciate the very creative oral (and later literary) artistry of the earliest Jewish Christians, and they can better recognize how and why certain narratives about Jesus came about as they did. Contemporary Jews can also better appreciate the great extent to which Judaic interpretations of Moses influenced Palestinian Jewish Christian interpretations of the Jew Jesus.

Sources and Reference Works

I. The Bible

Kittel, *Biblia Hebraica*, ed. Rudolf Kittel et al. (Stuttgart: Privilegierte Württembergische Bibelanstalt, 1951[7]).

Rahlfs, *Septuaginta*, ed. Alfred Rahlfs (Stuttgart: Württembergische Bibelanstalt, 1962[7]).

Wevers, *Numeri*, ed. John Wevers (Septuaginta III,1; Göttingen: Vandenhoeck & Ruprecht, 1982).

Dorival, *La Bible d'Alexandrie. Les Nombres*, ed. Gilles Dorival et al. (Paris: du Cerf, 1994).

Wevers, *Deuteronomium*, ed. John Wevers (Septuaginta III,2; Göttingen: Vandenhoeck & Ruprecht, 1977).

Dogniez and Harl, *La Bible d'Alexandrie. Le Deutéronome*, ed. Cécile Dogniez and Marguerite Harl (Paris: du Cerf, 1992).

Hatch and Redpath, *A Concordance to the Septuagint*, ed. Edwin Hatch and Henry Redpath (Oxford: Clarendon, 1897; corrected reprint Grand Rapids, MI: Baker Book House, 1983).

Nestle / Aland, *Novum Testamentum Graece*, ed. Erwin Nestle, Kurt Aland et al. (Stuttgart: Deutsche Bibelgesellschaft, 1990[26]).

Aland, *The Greek New Testament*, ed. Barbara Aland et al. (Stuttgart: Deutsche Bibelgesellschaft, United Bible Societies, 2001[4]).

Hebrew New Testament, by Franz Delitzsch (Berlin: Trowitzsch and Son, 1885).

Hebrew New Testament (Jerusalem: The United Bible Societies, 1979).

II. The Targums

Sperber, *The Bible in Aramaic*, ed. Alexander Sperber (Leiden: Brill, 1959), 4 volumes.

Rieder, *Targum Jonathan ben Uziel on the Pentateuch*, ed. with a Hebrew translation by David Rieder (Jerusalem, 1984), 2 volumes.

Díez Macho, *Neophyti 1*, ed. Alejandro Díez Macho (Madrid - Barcelona: Consejo Superior de Investigaciones Científicas, 1968-78), 5 volumes.

Klein, *The Fragment-Targums of the Pentateuch*, ed. and trans. Michael Klein (AnBib 76; Rome: Biblical Institute, 1980), 2 volumes.

Grossfeld, *The Targum Onqelos to Genesis*, trans. Bernard Grossfeld (The Aramaic Bible 6; Edinburgh: T & T Clark, 1988).

Maher, *Targum Pseudo-Jonathan: Genesis*, trans. Michael Maher (The Aramaic Bible 1B; Edinburgh: T & T Clark, 1992).

McNamara, *Targum Neofiti 1: Genesis*, trans. Martin McNamara (The Aramaic Bible 1A; Edinburgh: T & T Clark, 1992).

Grossfeld, *The Targum Onqelos to Exodus*, trans. Bernard Grossfeld (The Aramaic Bible 7; Edinburgh: T & T Clark, 1988).

Drazin, *Targum Onkelos to Exodus*, ed. and trans. Israel Drazin (New York: Ktav; Denver: Center for Judaic Studies, University of Denver, 1990).

Maher, *Targum Pseudo-Jonathan: Exodus*, trans. Michael Maher (The Aramaic Bible 2; Edinburgh: T & T Clark, 1994).

McNamara, *Targum Neofiti 1: Exodus*, trans. Martin McNamara (The Aramaic Bible 2; Edinburgh: T & T Clark, 1994).

Grossfeld, *The Targum Onqelos to Leviticus*, trans. Bernard Grossfeld (The Aramaic Bible 8; Edinburgh: T & T Clark, 1988).

Maher, *Targum Pseudo-Jonathan: Leviticus*, trans. Michael Maher (The Aramaic Bible 3; Edinburgh: T & T Clark, 1994).

McNamara, *Targum Neofiti 1: Leviticus*, trans. Martin McNamara (The Aramaic Bible 3; Edinburgh: T & T Clark, 1994).

Grossfeld, *The Targum Onqelos to Numbers*, trans. Bernard Grossfeld (The Aramaic Bible 8; Edinburgh: T & T Clark, 1988).

Clarke, *Targum Pseudo-Jonathan: Numbers*, trans. Ernest Clarke (The Aramaic Bible 4; Edinburgh: T & T Clark, 1995).

McNamara, *Targum Neofiti 1: Numbers*, trans. Martin McNamara (The Aramaic Bible 4; Edinburgh: T & T Clark, 1995).

Drazin, *Targum Onkelos to Deuteronomy*, ed. and trans. Israel Drazin (Hoboken, NJ: Ktav Publishing House, 1982).

Grossfeld, *The Targum Onqelos to Deuteronomy*, trans. Bernard Grossfeld (The Aramaic Bible 9; Edinburgh: T & T Clark, 1988).

Clarke, *Targum Pseudo-Jonathan: Deuteronomy*, trans. Ernest Clarke (The Aramaic Bible 5B; Edinburgh: T & T Clark, 1998).

McNamara, *Targum Neofiti 1: Deuteronomy*, trans. Martin McNamara (The Aramaic Bible 5A; Edinburgh: T & T Clark, 1997).

Harrington and Saldarini, *Targum Jonathan of the Former Prophets*, trans. Daniel Harrington and Anthony Saldarini (The Aramaic Bible 10; Edinburgh: T & T Clark, 1987).

Stenning, *The Targum of Isaiah*, ed. and trans. J. Stenning (Oxford: Clarendon, 1949).

Hayward, *The Targum of Jeremiah*, trans. Robert Hayward (The Aramaic Bible 12; Edinburgh: T & T Clark, 1987).

Cathcart and Gordon, *The Targum of the Minor Prophets*, trans. Kevin Cathcart and Robert Gordon (The Aramaic Bible 14; Edinburgh: T & T Clark, 1989).

Levine, *The Aramaic Version of Jonah*, ed. and trans. Étan Levine (New York: Sepher-Hermon Press, 1981).

Merino, *Targum de Salmos*, ed. with a Latin translation by Luis Diez Merino (Madrid: Consejo Superior de Investigaciones Científicas, 1982).

Stec, *The Targum of Psalms*, trans. David Stec (The Aramaic Bible 16; Collegeville, MN: Liturgical Press, 2004).

Alexander, *The Targum of Canticles*, trans. Philip Alexander (The Aramaic Bible 17A; Collegeville, MN: Liturgical Press, 2003).

Grossfeld, *The First Targum to Esther*, ed. and trans. Bernard Grossfeld (New York: Sepher-Hermon Press, 1983).

Grossfeld, *The Two Targums of Esther*, trans. Bernard Grossfeld (The Aramaic Bible 18; Edinburgh: T & T Clark, 1991).

III. The Mishnah and Tosefta

Albeck, *Shisha Sidre Mishnah*, ed. Chanoch Albeck (Jerusalem and Tel Aviv: Bialik Institute and Dvir, 1975), 6 volumes.

Danby, *The Mishnah*, trans. Herbert Danby (London: Oxford University Press, 1933).

Neusner, *The Mishnah*, trans. Jacob Neusner (New Haven: Yale University Press, 1988).

Zuckermandel, *Tosephta*, ed. Mosheh Zuckermandel, with a supplement by Saul Liebermann (Jerusalem: Wahrmann Books, 1970).

Lieberman, *The Tosefta*, ed. Saul Lieberman [sic] (New York: The Jewish Theological Seminary of America, 1955-92), 10 volumes.

Neusner, *The Tosefta*, trans. Jacob Neusner et al. (Hoboken, NJ: KTAV, 1977-86), 6 volumes.

IV. The Talmuds

Soncino, *The Babylonian Talmud*, ed. Isidore Epstein, various translators (London: Soncino, 1952), 18 volumes and index.

Soncino, *The Minor Tractates of the Talmud,* ed. Abraham Cohen, various translators (London: Soncino, 1965), 2 volumes.
Goldschmidt, *Der Babylonische Talmud,* ed. with a German translation by Lazarus Goldschmidt (Haag: Nijoff, 1933), 9 volumes.
Krotoshin, *Talmud Yerushalmi,* Krotoshin edition (Jerusalem: Shilah, 1969).
Neusner, *The Talmud of the Land of Israel,* trans. Jacob Neusner et al. (Chicago: University of Chicago Press, 1982-95), 34 volumes.

V. Halakhic Midrashim

Lauterbach, *Mekilta de-Rabbi Ishmael,* ed. and trans. Jacob Lauterbach (Philadelphia: The Jewish Publication Society of America, 1976), 3 volumes.
Epstein and Melamed, *Mekhilta d'Rabbi Šim'on b. Jochai,* ed. Jacob Epstein and Ezra Melamed (Jerusalem: Hillel Press, 1955; reprint 1979).
Weiss, *Sifra.* Commentar zu Leviticus, ed. Isaac Weiss (Vienna: Jacob Schlossberg, 1862).
Neusner, *Sifra.* An Analytical Translation, trans. Jacob Neusner (BJS 138-40; Atlanta: Scholars Press, 1988), 3 volumes.
Winter, *Sifra.* Halachischer Midrasch zu Leviticus, German by Jakob Winter (Breslau: Stefan Münz, 1938).
Horovitz, *Siphre ad Numeros adjecto Siphre zutta,* ed. Haim Horovitz (Jerusalem: Wahrmann Books, 1976).
Neusner, *Sifré to Numbers,* trans. Jacob Neusner (BJS 118-19; Atlanta: Scholars Press, 1986), 2 volumes.
Kuhn, *Der tannaitische Midrasch Sifre zu Numeri,* German by Karl Kuhn (Stuttgart: Kohlhammer, 1959).
Börner-Klein, *Der Midrasch Sifre zu Numeri,* German by Dagmar Börner-Klein (Stuttgart: Kohlhammer, 1997).
Börner-Klein, *Der Midrasch Sifre Zuta,* German on Numbers by Dagmar Börner-Klein (Stuttgart: Kohlhammer, 2002).
Finkelstein, *Sifre on Deuteronomy,* ed. Louis Finkelstein (New York: The Jewish Theological Seminary of America, 1969).
Hammer, *Sifre.* A Tannaitic Commentary on the Book of Deuteronomy, trans. Reuven Hammer (YJS 24; New Haven: Yale University Press, 1986).
Neusner, *Sifre to Deuteronomy.* An Analytical Translation, trans. Jacob Neusner (BJS 98 and 101; Atlanta: Scholars Press, 1987), 2 volumes.

VI. Haggadic Midrashim and Midrashic Collections

Midrash Rabbah, with the five Megilloth at the end of volume 2 (Vilna: Romm, 1887), 2 volumes.

Mirkin, *Midrash Rabbah,* Pentateuch. Ed. and vocalized by Mosheh Mirkin (Tel Aviv: Yavneh, 1981), 11 volumes.

Soncino, *Midrash Rabbah,* ed. H. Freedman and Maurice Simon, various translators (London: Soncino, 1939), 9 volumes and index.

Theodor and Albeck, *Midrash Bereshit Rabba,* ed. Judah Theodor and Chanoch Albeck (Jerusalem: Wahrmann Books, 1965), 3 volumes.

Margulies, *Leviticus Rabbah:* Midrash Wayyikra Rabbah, ed. Mordecai Margulies (Jerusalem: Ministry of Education and Culture of Israel, American Academy for Jewish Research, 1953-60), 5 volumes.

Neusner, *Judaism and Scripture.* The Evidence of Leviticus Rabbah, trans. Jacob Neusner (Chicago Studies in the History of Judaism; Chicago: University of Chicago Press, 1986).

Liebermann, *Midrash Debarim Rabbah,* ed. Saul Liebermann (Jerusalem: Wahrmann Books, 1964[2]).

Donsqi, *Midrash Rabbah. Shir ha-Shirim,* ed. Shim'on Donsqi (Jerusalem: Dvir, 1980).

Midrash Tanḥuma, Eshkol edition (Jerusalem: Eshkol, no date).

Berman, *Midrash Tanhuma-Yelammedenu.* An English translation of Genesis and Exodus ... by Samuel Berman (Hoboken, NJ: KTAV Publishing House, 1996).

Buber, *Midrasch Tanḥuma:* Ein agadischer Commentar zum Pentateuch, ed. Salomon Buber (Vilna: Romm, 1885).

Townsend, *Midrash Tanḥuma (S. Buber Recension),* Vol. I, Genesis, trans. John Townsend (Hoboken, NJ: KTAV Publishing House, 1989). Vol. II, Exodus and Leviticus, 1997.

Bietenhard, *Midrasch Tanḥuma B,* German by Hans Bietenhard (Judaica et Christiana 5-6; Bern: Peter Lang, 1980-82), 2 volumes.

Schechter, *Aboth de Rabbi Nathan* (A and B), ed. Solomon Schechter (Vienna, 1887; reprinted New York: Feldheim, 1945).

Goldin, *The Fathers According to Rabbi Nathan (A),* trans. Judah Goldin (YJS 10; New Haven: Yale University Press, 1955).

Neusner, *The Fathers According to Rabbi Nathan.* An Analytical Translation and Explanation, trans. Jacob Neusner (BJS 114; Atlanta: Scholars Press, 1986).

Saldarini, *The Fathers According to Rabbi Nathan (B),* trans. Anthony Saldarini (SJLA 11; Leiden: Brill, 1975).

Friedmann, *Pesikta Rabbati*, ed. Meir Friedmann (Vienna, 1880; reprint Tel Aviv, 1962-63).

Braude, *Pesikta Rabbati*, trans. William Braude (YJS 18; New Haven: Yale University Press, 1968), 2 volumes.

Mandelbaum, *Pesikta de Rav Kahana*, ed. Bernard Mandelbaum (New York: The Jewish Theological Seminary of America, 1962), 2 volumes.

Braude and Kapstein, *Pesikta de-Rab Kahana*, trans. William Braude and Israel Kapstein (Philadelphia: The Jewish Publication Society of America, 1975).

Neusner, *Pesiqta de Rab Kahana*. An Analytical Translation, trans. Jacob Neusner (BJS 122-23; Atlanta: Scholars Press, 1987), 2 volumes.

Friedmann, *Seder Eliahu rabba und Seder Eliahu zuta*, ed. Meir Friedmann (Vienna, 1902-04; reprint Jerusalem, 1969).

Braude and Kapstein, *Tanna debe Eliyyahu*, trans. William Braude and Israel Kapstein (Philadelphia: The Jewish Publication Society of America, 1981).

Buber, *Midrasch Tehillim*, ed. Salomon Buber (Vilna: Romm, 1891).

Braude, *The Midrash on Psalms*, trans. William Braude (YJS 13,1-2; New Haven: Yale University Press, 1959), 2 volumes.

Visotzky, *Midrash Mishle*, ed. Burton Visotzky (New York: The Jewish Theological Seminary of America, 1990).

Visotzky, *The Midrash on Proverbs*, trans. Burton Visotzky (YJS 27; New Haven: Yale University Press, 1992).

Wünsche, "Der Midrasch Sprüche," German by August Wünsche in *Bibliotheca Rabbinica* (Leipzig: Schulze, 1885) 4.1-77.

Eshkol, *Pirqe Rabbi Eliezer*, Eshkol edition (Jerusalem: Eshkol, 1973).

Friedlander, *Pirke de Rabbi Eliezer*, trans. Gerald Friedlander (London, 1916; reprint New York: Hermon Press, 1970).

Buber, *Aggadat Bereshit*, ed. Salomon Buber (Cracow: Fischer, 1903; reprint New York, 1959).

Teugels, *Aggadat Bereshit*, trans. Lieve Teugels (Jewish and Christian Perspectives Series 4; Leiden: Brill, 2001).

Albeck, *Midraš Berešit Rabbati*, ed. Chanoch Albeck (Jerusalem: Mekize Nirdamim, 1940).

Midrash Haggadol on the Pentateuch (Jerusalem: Kook, 1975-76). Genesis, ed. Mordecai Margulies; Exodus, ed. Margulies; Leviticus, ed. ʿAdin Steinsalz; Numbers, ed. Zvi Rabinowitz; Deuteronomy, ed. Solomon Fisch.

Hoffmann, *Midrasch Tannaim zum Deuteronomium*, ed. David Hoffmann (Berlin: Itzkowski, 1908-09; reprint Jerusalem, 1984).

Buber, *Lekach tob (Pesikta sutarta)*, ein agadischer Commentar zum ersten und zweiten Buche Mosis von T. Tobia ben Elieser, ed. Salomon Buber (Vilna, 1884).

Kook, *Yalquṭ Shemʿoni* (Jerusalem: Kook, 1973-91), 9 volumes from Genesis to Deuteronomy.

Guggenheimer, *Seder Olam. The Rabbinic View of Biblical Chronology*, ed. and trans. Heinrich Guggenheimer (Northvale, NJ, and Jerusalem: Jason Aronson, 1998).

Milikowsky, *Seder Olam. A Rabbinic Chronography*, ed. and trans. Chaim Milikowsky (1981 Yale University Ph.D. dissertation).

Ratner, *Seder Olam Rabbah: Die grosse Weltchronik*, ed. Ber Ratner (Vilna, 1897).

Jellinek, *Bet ha-Midrasch*. Sammlung kleiner Midraschim und vermischter Abhandlungen aus der ältern [sic] jüdischen Literatur, ed. Adolph Jellinek (Jerusalem: Wahrmann Books, 1967³), 6 volumes in 2.

Wünsche, *Aus Israels Lehrhallen*. German by August Wünsche (Leipzig: Pfeiffer: 1907-09; reprint Hildesheim: Olms, 1967), 5 volumes.

Eisenstein, *Ozar Midrashim. A Library of Two Hundred Midrashim*, ed. Jehuda David Eisenstein (New York: E. Grossman's Hebrew Book Store, 1956).

Wertheimer, *Batei Midrashot.* Twenty-five Midrashim..., ed. Shlemo Wertheimer, 2nd edition A. Wertheimer (Jerusalem: Kook, 1954), 2 volumes.

* * *

Siegert, *Drei hellenistische Predigten*, trans. from Armenian into German by Folker Siegert (WUNT 20; Tübingen: Mohr, 1980).

VII. Apocrypha, Pseudepigrapha, Philo, Josephus, and the Dead Sea Scrolls

Apocrypha: see Rahlfs, *Septuaginta*.

OTP. *The Old Testament Pseudepigrapha*, ed. James Charlesworth (Garden City, NY: Doubleday, 1983-85), 2 volumes.

Delamarter, *A Scripture Index to Charlesworth's The Old Testament Pseudepigrapha*, by Steve Delamarter (Sheffield: Sheffield Academic Press, 2002).

APOT. *The Apocrypha and Pseudepigrapha of the Old Testament*, II. *Pseudepigrapha*, ed. Robert Henry Charles (Oxford: Clarendon, 1913).

Harrington, *Les Antiquités Bibliques*, ed. Daniel Harrington, French by Jacques Cazeaux (*SC* 229-230; Paris: du Cerf, 1976), 2 volumes.

Tromp, *The Assumption of Moses: A Critical Edition with Commentary*, ed. and trans. Johannes Tromp (SVTP 10; Leiden: Brill, 1993).

LCL, *Philo*, Greek and English translation by F. H. Colson, G. H. Whitaker and Ralph Marcus (Loeb Classical Library; Cambridge, MA: Harvard University Press, 1971), 10 volumes with 2 Supplements: *Questions and Answers on Genesis*, and *Questions and Answers on Exodus*.

The Philo Index, ed. Peder Borgen, Kåre Fuglseth, and Roald Skarsten (Grand Rapids, MI: Eerdmans, 2000).

LCL, *Josephus*, Greek and English translation by H. St. John Thackeray, Ralph Marcus and Allen Wikgren (Loeb Classical Library; Cambridge, MA: Harvard University Press, 1969), 9 volumes.

The Complete Concordance to Flavius Josephus, Study Edition, ed. Karl Rengstorf (Leiden: Brill, 2002), 2 volumes, including the *Namenwörterbuch zu Flavius Josephus* by Abraham Schalit.

Martínez and Tigchelaar, *The Dead Sea Scrolls Study Edition*, ed. and trans. Florentino García Martínez and Eibert Tigchelaar (Leiden: Brill, 2000), 2 volumes.

Fitzmyer, *The Genesis Apocryphon of Qumran Cave 1: A Commentary*, trans. Joseph Fitzmyer (Rome: Pontifical Biblical Press, 1971²).

Charlesworth, *Graphic Concordance to the Dead Sea Scrolls*, ed. James Charlesworth et al. (Tübingen: Mohr; Louisville: Westminster / John Knox, 1991).

Washburn, *A Catalog of Biblical Passages in the Dead Sea Scrolls*, by David Washburn (Text-Critical Studies 2; Atlanta: Society of Biblical Literature, 2002).

VIII. The Early Church

Jaubert, *Origène, Homélies sur Josué*, ed. Annie Jaubert (*SC* 71; Paris: du Cerf, 1960).

Stählin, *Clemens Alexandrinus*, II. Stromata Buch I-VI, ed. Otto Stählin, Ludwig Früchtel and Ursula Treu (GSC 52; Berlin: Akademie-Verlag, 1985).

IX. Dictionaries and Reference Works

BDB, *A Hebrew and English Lexicon of the Old Testament*, by Francis Brown, S. R. Driver and Charles Briggs (Oxford: Clarendon: 1962).

Jastrow, *A Dictionary of the Targumim, the Talmud Babli and Yerushalmi, and the Midrashic Literature*, by Marcus Jastrow (Peabody, MA: Hendrickson Publishers, 2005; original 1903).

Levy, *Neuhebräisches und chaldäisches Wörterbuch über die Talmudim und Midraschim*, by Jacob Levy (Berlin and Vienna, 1924²), 4 volumes.

Alcalay, *The Complete Hebrew-English Dictionary*, ed. Reuben Alcalay (Tel Aviv and Jerusalem: Massadah, 1965).

Krauss, *Griechische und Lateinische Lehnwörter in Talmud, Midrasch und Targum*, by Samuel Krauss (Berlin: Calvary, 1898-99), 2 volumes.

Hyman, *Torah Hakethubah Vehamessurah*. A Reference Book of the Scriptural Passages Quoted in Talmudic, Midrashic and Early Rabbinic Literature, by Aaron Hyman, second edition by Arthur Hyman (Tel Aviv: Dvir, 1979), 3 volumes.

IDB. The Interpreter's Dictionary of the Bible, ed. George Buttrick et al. (New York and Nashville: Abingdon Press, 1962), 4 volumes. *Supplementary Volume*, ed. Keith Crim, 1976.

Schürer, *The history of the Jewish people in the age of Jesus Christ (175 B.C. - A.D. 135)*, by Emil Schürer, ed. Geza Vermes, Fergus Millar and Matthew Black (Edinburgh: T. and T. Clark, 1973-86), 3 volumes and index.

Strack and Stemberger, *Introduction to the Talmud and Midrash*, by Hermann Strack and Günter Stemberger (Minneapolis: Fortress, 1992).

Ginzberg, *The Legends of the Jews*, by Louis Ginzberg (Philadelphia: The Jewish Publication Society of America, 1968), 6 volumes and index.

Str-B, *Kommentar zum Neuen Testament aus Talmud und Midrasch*, by (Hermann Strack and) Paul Billerbeck (Munich: Beck, 1924-61), 6 volumes.

Krauss, *Talmudische Archäologie*, by Samuel Krauss (Leipzig: Gustav Fock, 1910-12), 3 volumes.

Nickelsburg, *Jewish Literature Between the Bible and the Mishnah*, by George Nickelsburg (Minneapolis: Fortress Press, 2005²).

JE. The Jewish Encyclopedia (New York: Funk and Wagnalls, 1905), 12 volumes.

EJ. Encyclopaedia Judaica (Jerusalem: Keter, 1971), 16 volumes. New edition 2007².

TWAT. Theologisches Wörterbuch zum Alten Testament, ed. G. Johannes Botterweck and Helmer Ringgren (Stuttgart: Kohlhammer, 1973-2000), 10 volumes. English translation as *TDOT, Theological Dictionary of the Old Testament* (Grand Rapids, MI: Eerdmans).

LSJ. *A Greek-English Lexicon*, by Henry Liddell, Robert Scott and Henry Jones (Oxford: Clarendon, 1966⁹).

Greek-English Lexicon of the Septuagint, Revised edition, ed. Johan Lust, Erik Eynikel and Katrin Hauspie (Stuttgart: Deutsche Bibelgesellschaft, 2003).

BAGD. *A Greek-English Lexicon of the New Testament and Other Early Christian Literature*, by Walter Bauer, William Arndt, F. Wilbur Gingrich and Frederick Danker (Chicago: University of Chicago Press, 1979²).

TDNT. Theological Dictionary of the New Testament, ed. Gerhard Kittel and Gerhard Friedrich (Grand Rapids, MI: Eerdmans, 1964-76), 9 volumes and index.

Chambers Murray, *latin-english Dictionary*, ed. William Smith and John Lockwood (Edinburgh: Chambers; London: Murray, 1986).

Author Index

About the Author

Roger David Aus, b. 1940, studied English and German at St. Olaf College, and theology at Harvard Divinity School, Luther Seminary, and Yale University, from which he received the Ph.D. degree in New Testament studies in 1971. He is an ordained clergyman of the Evangelical Lutheran Church in America, and pastor emeritus of the German-speaking Luther-Kirchengemeinde Alt-Reinickendorf in Berlin-Reinickendorf, Germany. His study of New Testament topics always reflects his great interest in, and deep appreciation of, the Jewish roots of the Christian faith.

Other Volumes by Roger David Aus

Imagery of Triumph and Rebellion in 2 Corinthians 2:14-17 and Elsewhere in the Epistle. An Example of the Combination of Greco-Roman and Judaic Traditions in the Apostle Paul (Studies in Judaism; Lanham, MD: University Press of America, 2005).

Matthew 1-2 and the Virginal Conception in Light of Palestinian and Hellenistic Judaic Traditions on the Birth of Israel's First Redeemer, Moses (Studies in Judaism; Lanham, MD: University Press of America, 2004).

My Name Is "Legion." Palestinian Judaic Traditions in Mark 5:1-20 and Other Gospel Texts (Studies in Judaism; Lanham, MD: University Press of America, 2003). Essays on Mark 5:1-20; Luke 4:16-30; The Name "Iscariot" and Ahithophel in Judaic Tradition; Luke 19:41-44; John 8:56-58; Matt 24:28 // Luke 17:37b; and Luke 13:34b // Matt 23:37b.

The Stilling of the Storm. Studies in Early Palestinian Judaic Traditions (International Studies in Formative Christianity and Judaism; Binghamton, NY: Global Publications, Binghamton University, 2000). Essays on Mark 4:35-41; 1:16-20; and Luke 24:13-35.

"Caught in the Act," Walking on the Sea, and the Release of Barabbas Revisited (South Florida Studies in the History of Judaism, 157; Atlanta: Scholars Press, 1998). Essays on John 7:53 - 8:11; Mark 6:45-52 par.; and 15:6-15 par.

The Wicked Tenants and Gethsemane (International Studies in Formative Christianity and Judaism, University of South Florida, 4; Atlanta: Scholars Press, 1996). Essays on Mark 12:1-9 par.; 14:32-42 par.; 2 Cor 12:1-10; and Judas' handing Jesus over to certain death through a kiss.

Samuel, Saul and Jesus. Three Early Palestinian Jewish Christian Gospel Haggadoth (South Florida Studies in the History of Judaism, 105; Atlanta: Scholars Press, 1994). Essays on Luke 2:41-51a; Mark 6:1-6a par.; and the prodigia at Jesus' Crucifixion.

Barabbas and Esther and Other Studies in the Judaic Illumination of Earliest Christianity (South Florida Studies in the History of Judaism, 54; Atlanta: Scholars Press, 1992). Essays on Mark 15:6-15 par.; John 11:45-54; Luke 15:11-32; Matt 2:1-12; Gal 2:9; Isa 66:7, Revelation 12 and 2 Thessalonians 1; 2 Thess 2:6-7; Rom 11:25; and 2 Thess 1:3.

Weihnachtsgeschichte, Barmherziger Samariter, Verlorener Sohn. Studien zu ihrem jüdischen Hintergrund (ANTZ 2; Berlin: Institut Kirche und Judentum, 1988). Essays on Luke 2:1-20; 10:30-37; and 15:11-32.

Water into Wine and the Beheading of John the Baptist. Early Jewish-Christian Interpretation of Esther 1 in John 2:1-11 and Mark 6:17-29 (Brown Judaic Studies, 150; Atlanta: Scholars Press, 1988).

STUDIES IN JUDAISM
TITLES IN THE SERIES
PUBLISHED BY UNIVERSITY PRESS OF AMERICA

Judith Z. Abrams
The Babylonian Talmud: A Topical Guide, 2002.

Roger David Aus
The Death, Burial, and Resurrection of Jesus, and the Death, Burial, and Translation of Moses in Judaic Tradition, 2008.

Matthew 1-2 and the Virginal Conception: In Light of Palestinian and Hellenistic Judaic Traditions on the Birth of Israel's First Redeemer, Moses, 2004.

My Name Is "Legion": Palestinian Judaic Traditions in Mark 5:1-20 and Other Gospel Texts, 2003.

Alan L. Berger, Harry James Cargas, and Susan E. Nowak
The Continuing Agony: From the Carmelite Convent to the Crosses at Auschwitz, 2004.

S. Daniel Breslauer
Creating a Judaism without Religion: A Postmodern Jewish Possibility, 2001.

Bruce Chilton
Targumic Approaches to the Gospels: Essays in the Mutual Definition of Judaism and Christianity, 1986.

David Ellenson
Tradition in Transition: Orthodoxy, Halakhah, and the Boundaries of Modern Jewish Identity, 1989.

Roberta Rosenberg Farber and Simcha Fishbane
Jewish Studies in Violence: A Collection of Essays, 2007.

Paul V. M. Flesher
New Perspectives on Ancient Judaism, Volume 5: Society and Literature in Analysis, 1990.

Marvin Fox
Collected Essays on Philosophy and on Judaism, Volume One: Greek Philosophy, Maimonides, 2003.

Collected Essays on Philosophy and on Judaism, Volume Two: Some Philosophers, 2003.

Collected Essays on Philosophy and on Judaism, Volume Three: Ethics, Reflections, 2003.

Zev Garber

Methodology in the Academic Teaching of Judaism, 1986.

Zev Garber, Alan L. Berger, and Richard Libowitz

Methodology in the Academic Teaching of the Holocaust, 1988.

Abraham Gross

Spirituality and Law: Courting Martyrdom in Christianity and Judaism, 2005.

Harold S. Himmelfarb and Sergio DellaPergola

Jewish Education Worldwide: Cross-Cultural Perspectives, 1989.

Raphael Jospe

Jewish Philosophy: Foundations and Extensions (Volume One: General Questions and Considerations), 2008.

Jewish Philosophy: Foundations and Extensions (Volume Two: On Philosophers and Their Thought), 2008.

William Kluback

The Idea of Humanity: Hermann Cohen's Legacy to Philosophy and Theology, 1987.

Samuel Morell

Studies in the Judicial Methodology of Rabbi David ibn Abi Zimra, 2004.

Jacob Neusner

Amos in Talmud and Midrash, 2006.

Ancient Israel, Judaism, and Christianity in Contemporary Perspective, 2006.

The Aggadic Role in Halakhic Discourses: Volume I, 2001.

The Aggadic Role in Halakhic Discourses: Volume II, 2001.

The Aggadic Role in Halakhic Discourses: Volume III, 2001.

Analysis and Argumentation in Rabbinic Judaism, 2003.

Analytical Templates of the Bavli, 2006.

Ancient Judaism and Modern Category-Formation: "Judaism," "Midrash," "Messianism," and Canon in the Past Quarter Century, 1986.

Bologna Addresses and Other Recent Papers, 2007.

Building Blocks of Rabbinic Tradition: The Documentary Approach to the Study of Formative Judaism, 2007.

Canon and Connection: Intertextuality in Judaism, 1987.

Chapters in the Formative History of Judaism, 2006.

Dual Discourse, Single Judaism, 2001.

The Emergence of Judaism: Jewish Religion in Response to the Critical Issues of the First Six Centuries, 2000.
Ezekiel in Talmud and Midrash, 2007.

First Principles of Systemic Analysis: The Case of Judaism within the History of Religion, 1988.

Habakkuk, Jonah, Nahum, and Obadiah in Talmud and Midrash: A Source Book, 2007.

The Halakhah and the Aggadah, 2001.

Halakhic Hermeneutics, 2003.

Halakhic Theology: A Sourcebook, 2006.

The Hermeneutics of Rabbinic Category Formations, 2001.

Hosea in Talmud and Midrash, 2006.

How Important Was the Destruction of the Second Temple in the Formation of Rabbinic Judaism? 2006.

How Not to Study Judaism, Examples and Counter-Examples, Volume One: Parables, Rabbinic Narratives, Rabbis' Biographies, Rabbis' Disputes, 2004.

How Not to Study Judaism, Examples and Counter-Examples, Volume Two: Ethnicity and Identity Versus Culture and Religion, How Not to Write a Book on Judaism, Point and Counterpoint, 2004.

How the Halakhah Unfolds: Moed Qatan in the Mishnah, Tosefta, Yerushalmi, and Bavli, 2006.

How the Halakhah Unfolds, Volume II, Part A: Nazir in the Mishnah, Tosefta, Yerushalmi, and Bavli, 2007.

How the Halakhah Unfolds, Volume II, Part B: Nazir in the Mishnah, Tosefta, Yerushalmi, and Bavli, 2007.

How the Halakhah Unfolds, Volume III, Part A: Abodah Zarah in the Mishnah, Tosefta, Yerushalmi, and Bavli, 2007.

How the Halakhah Unfolds, Volume III, Part B: Abodah Zarah in the Mishnah, Tosefta, Yerushalmi, and Bavli, 2007.

The Implicit Norms of Rabbinic Judaism, 2006.

Intellectual Templates of the Law of Judaism, 2006.

Isaiah in Talmud and Midrash: A Source Book, Part A, 2007.

Isaiah in Talmud and Midrash: A Source Book, Part B, 2007.

Is Scripture the Origin of the Halakhah? 2005

Israel and Iran in Talmudic Times: A Political History, 1986.

Israel's Politics in Sasanian Iran: Self-Government in Talmudic Times, 1986.

Jeremiah in Talmud and Midrash: A Source Book, 2006.

Judaism in Monologue and Dialogue, 2005.

Major Trends in Formative Judaism, Fourth Series, 2002.

Major Trends in Formative Judaism, Fifth Series, 2002.

Messiah in Context: Israel's History and Destiny in Formative Judaism, 1988.

Micah and Joel in Talmud and Midrash, 2006.

The Native Category – Formations of the Aggadah: The Later Midrash-Compilations – Volume I, 2000.

The Native Category – Formations of the Aggadah: The Earlier Midrash-Compilations – Volume II, 2000.

Paradigms in Passage: Patterns of Change in the Contemporary Study of Judaism, 1988.

Parsing the Torah, 2005.

Praxis and Parable: The Divergent Discourses of Rabbinic Judaism, 2006.

Rabbi Jeremiah, 2006.

Rabbinic Theology and Israelite Prophecy: Primacy of the Torah, Narrative of the World to Come, Doctrine of Repentance and Atonement, and the Systematization of Theology in the Rabbis' Reading of the Prophets, 2007.

The Rabbinic Utopia, 2007.

The Rabbis, the Law, and the Prophets. 2007.

Reading Scripture with the Rabbis: The Five Books of Moses, 2006.

The Religious Study of Judaism: Description, Analysis, Interpretation, Volume 1, 1986.

The Religious Study of Judaism: Description, Analysis, Interpretation, Volume 2, 1986.
The Religious Study of Judaism: Context, Text, Circumstance, Volume 3, 1987.

The Religious Study of Judaism: Description, Analysis, Interpretation, Volume 4, 1988.

Struggle for the Jewish Mind: Debates and Disputes on Judaism Then and Now, 1988.

The Talmud Law, Theology, Narrative: A Sourcebook, 2005.

Talmud Torah: Ways to God's Presence through Learning: An Exercise in Practical Theology, 2002.

Texts Without Boundaries: Protocols of Non-Documentary Writing in the Rabbinic Canon: Volume I: The Mishnah, Tractate Abot, and the Tosefta, 2002.

Texts Without Boundaries: Protocols of Non-Documentary Writing in the Rabbinic Canon: Volume II: Sifra and Sifre to Numbers, 2002.

Texts Without Boundaries: Protocols of Non-Documentary Writing in the Rabbinic Canon: Volume III: Sifre to Deuteronomy and Mekhilta Attributed to Rabbi Ishmael, 2002.

Texts Without Boundaries: Protocols of Non-Documentary Writing in the Rabbinic Canon: Volume IV: Leviticus Rabbah, 2002.

A Theological Commentary to the Midrash – Volume I: Pesiqta deRab Kahana, 2001.

A Theological Commentary to the Midrash – Volume II: Genesis Raba, 2001.

A Theological Commentary to the Midrash – Volume III: Song of Songs Rabbah, 2001.

A Theological Commentary to the Midrash – Volume IV: Leviticus Rabbah, 2001.

A Theological Commentary to the Midrash – Volume V: Lamentations Rabbati, 2001.

A Theological Commentary to the Midrash – Volume VI: Ruth Rabbah and Esther Rabbah, 2001.

A Theological Commentary to the Midrash – Volume VII: Sifra, 2001.

A Theological Commentary to the Midrash – Volume VIII: Sifre to Numbers and Sifre to Deuteronomy, 2001.

A Theological Commentary to the Midrash – Volume IX: Mekhilta Attributed to Rabbi Ishmael, 2001.

Theological Dictionary of Rabbinic Judaism: Part One: Principal Theological Categories, 2005.

Theological Dictionary of Rabbinic Judaism: Part Two: Making Connections and Building Constructions, 2005.

Theological Dictionary of Rabbinic Judaism: Part Three: Models of Analysis, Explanation, and Anticipation, 2005.

The Theological Foundations of Rabbinic Midrash, 2006.

Theology of Normative Judaism: A Source Book, 2005.

Theology in Action: How the Rabbis of the Talmud Present Theology (Aggadah) in the Medium of the Law (Halakhah). An Anthology, 2006.

The Torah and the Halakhah: The Four Relationships, 2003.

The Treasury of Judaism: A New Collection and Translation of Essential Texts (Volume One: The Calendar), 2008.

The Treasury of Judaism: A New Collection and Translation of Essential Texts (Volume Two: The Life Cycle), 2008.

The Treasury of Judaism: A New Collection and Translation of Essential Texts (Volume Three: Theology), 2008.

The Unity of Rabbinic Discourse: Volume I: Aggadah in the Halakhah, 2001.

The Unity of Rabbinic Discourse: Volume II: Halakhah in the Aggadah, 2001.

The Unity of Rabbinic Discourse: Volume III: Halakhah and Aggadah in Concert, 2001.

The Vitality of Rabbinic Imagination: The Mishnah Against the Bible and Qumran, 2005.

Who, Where and What is "Israel?": Zionist Perspectives on Israeli and American Judaism, 1989.

The Wonder-Working Lawyers of Talmudic Babylonia: The Theory and Practice of Judaism in its Formative Age, 1987.

Zephaniah, Haggai, Zechariah, and Malachi in Talmud and Midrash: A Source Book, 2007.

Jacob Neusner and Renest S. Frerichs
New Perspectives on Ancient Judaism, Volume 2: Judaic and Christian Interpretation of Texts: Contents and Contexts, 1987.

New Perspectives on Ancient Judaism, Volume 3: Judaic and Christian Interpretation of Texts: Contents and Contexts, 1987

Jacob Neusner and James F. Strange
Religious Texts and Material Contexts, 2001.

Theology in Action: How the Rabbis of the Talmud Present Theology (Aggadah) in the Medium of the Law (Halakhah). An Anthology, 2006.

The Torah and the Halakhah: The Four Relationships, 2003.

The Treasury of Judaism: A New Collection and Translation of Essential Texts (Volume One: The Calendar), 2008.

The Treasury of Judaism: A New Collection and Translation of Essential Texts (Volume Two: The Life Cycle), 2008.

The Treasury of Judaism: A New Collection and Translation of Essential Texts (Volume Three: Theology), 2008.

The Unity of Rabbinic Discourse: Volume I: Aggadah in the Halakhah, 2001.

The Unity of Rabbinic Discourse: Volume II: Halakhah in the Aggadah, 2001.

The Unity of Rabbinic Discourse: Volume III: Halakhah and Aggadah in Concert, 2001.

The Vitality of Rabbinic Imagination: The Mishnah Against the Bible and Qumran, 2005.

Who, Where and What is "Israel?": Zionist Perspectives on Israeli and American Judaism, 1989.

The Wonder-Working Lawyers of Talmudic Babylonia: The Theory and Practice of Judaism in its Formative Age, 1987.

Zephaniah, Haggai, Zechariah, and Malachi in Talmud and Midrash: A Source Book, 2007.

Jacob Neusner and Renest S. Frerichs
New Perspectives on Ancient Judaism, Volume 2: Judaic and Christian Interpretation of Texts: Contents and Contexts, 1987.

New Perspectives on Ancient Judaism, Volume 3: Judaic and Christian Interpretation of Texts: Contents and Contexts, 1987

Jacob Neusner and James F. Strange
Religious Texts and Material Contexts, 2001.

Leslie S. Wilson

The Serpent Symbol in the Ancient Near East: Nahash and Asherah: Death, Life, and Healing, 2001.